The formula behind every company that changed the world

CRACKING THE GROWTH CODE

How Leaders Build Trust, Inspire People, And Remove Excuses For Growth

Jim Bramlett

For permissions, licensing, or inquiries, contact:
JEB Enterprises, LLC
19448 W. 102nd St.
Lenexa, KS 66220
Jimbramlett.com

TABLE OF CONTENTS

FOREWORD

Growth is the single greatest responsibility of every business leader—and the greatest source of stress. You can delegate sales, marketing, operations, even partnerships. But you cannot delegate growth. The vision, the strategy, and the relentless pursuit of customers ultimately rest on your shoulders. That weight never goes away.

I've lived this reality both as an entrepreneur and as a coach to CEOs and business owners. This is my third book on growth, and with each one I've learned the same lesson: leaders don't need more theory. They need clarity, tools, and a framework they can put into practice today. My goal is simple: to give you something you can use immediately.

The truth is, leadership is hard. It can be isolating, frustrating, and overwhelming—if you let it be. But it doesn't have to be. Growth can happen the hard way, or it can happen the smarter way. The smarter way is to learn from the companies that have already cracked the code—companies that placed their customers at the center and refused to make excuses.

At the heart of this book is a belief I've tested over decades: when you understand the psychology of the buyer, you unlock the path to growth. This has never been about you. It has always been about your customers—what they want, what they value, and how they decide.

So let me ask you: think back to your last few purchases. A cup of coffee. A plane ticket. A car. Why did you choose the one you did? What made you confident? And just as important, why didn't you choose one of the alternatives? What excuse did you give yourself for saying no?

Most buying decisions boil down to four timeless reasons:

- **Convenience** – It saved you time, effort, and energy.
- **Price** – It was competitive and transparent.
- **User Experience** – It made you feel better than before.
- **Trust** – You believed the promise would be kept.

These Four Pillars drive every purchase. They're why an online marketplace overtook the world's largest retailer. Why a small DVD-by-mail company dethroned a giant of home entertainment. Why a simple app reshaped transportation in every major city.

These companies grew because they delivered on all four pillars at once. And while it isn't easy, it's possible.

Will this book make you the next household name? I can't promise that. But I can promise this: if you commit to understanding your buyers, leading with clarity, and applying the principles in these pages, you will outgrow your competitors.

The Growth Code isn't theory. It's a formula. And now it's in your hands.

If you read this book with an open mind, reflect honestly, and act with discipline, you will not only crack the Growth Code—you will eliminate excuses, inspire your people, and build a business that grows with clarity and confidence.

INTRODUCTION

The Relentless Obsession

In the mid-1990s, a young entrepreneur left behind the comfort of a Wall Street career to chase an idea few believed in. At a time when most businesses thought about customers only in terms of transactions and quarterly revenue, he envisioned something radical: a company where the customer wasn't just part of the equation but the center of the universe. He believed growth would be the natural byproduct of obsessive customer focus.

The idea was daring. Shopping online was nearly unheard of. Most people doubted that consumers would ever trust their credit card numbers to a computer screen, let alone make it their preferred way to buy. Industry leaders dismissed the model outright. Analysts rolled their eyes. Friends told him it was reckless to walk away from a stable career to pursue something so risky.

From day one, the company faced an uphill battle. Logistics were messy. Warehouses had to be built and systems invented that simply didn't exist. Every dollar seemed to go right back into infrastructure, and profits were nowhere in sight. Quarter after quarter, Wall Street analysts mocked the business. The headlines were merciless: "This company is burning cash," they declared. "It refuses to pivot. It will collapse under its own weight."

But while critics obsessed over losses, the founder obsessed over customers. He believed that if everything was engineered around the customer—every decision, every system, every innovation—growth would come. His leadership team adopted a mantra: obsess over the customer, not the competition.

The first obsession was **convenience**. Ordering a product had to be simpler than driving to a store. The team worked on methods to reduce friction, such as implementing one-click ordering, improving search functionality, and speeding up delivery processes. Even when skeptics said the logistics were impossible, he insisted it had to be done. If customers could save time and effort, loyalty would follow.

The second pillar was **pricing**. He believed customers had to trust that they were always getting a fair deal. Margins could wait; loyalty couldn't. When competitors tried to lure customers with flashy promotions, his approach was to make low prices an expectation, not a surprise.

Third was the **user experience**. Shopping wasn't just about a transaction; it had to feel intuitive, simple, even enjoyable. Competitors often added complexity—cluttered interfaces, confusing checkout processes. He demanded simplicity, clarity, and a sense of ease. Every design choice was judged by a single question: does this make the customer's life easier?

Finally, there was **trust**. Customers needed to believe that this new digital marketplace was safe, reliable, and consistent. He invested in secure payments, transparent policies, reliable shipping, and customer service that solved problems quickly. He knew that trust was the foundation of loyalty. If people could count on the company once, they would return again and again.

The road wasn't easy. Each quarter, analysts scolded him for losses. Investors questioned his sanity. Competitors scoffed. But through every storm, he returned to the same belief: put the customer at the center, and growth will follow.

Over time, the critics grew quieter. The company that was once mocked as a cautionary tale became a juggernaut. It didn't just succeed; it redefined the way business is done around the world. By engineering convenience, pricing, user experience, and trust into every decision, it cracked the code for growth.

Only then does the name become obvious. The founder was Jeff Bezos. The company was Amazon.

But this wasn't the only industry transformed by putting the customer at the center. Around the same time, families across America gathering for movie night were about to experience a similar shift...

The Movie Night Revolution

At the turn of the century, a familiar ritual played out in living rooms across America. Families would choose a movie for the evening, drive to the local rental store, and hope their first choice was still available. More often than not, the shelves were missing the most popular titles. Customers settled for second or third choices, walking back to their cars frustrated, but resigned. This was the way it had always been.

The transaction didn't end when the movie was taken home. Hanging over every rental was the looming deadline to return it. Miss the due date, even by a few hours, and the cost of the evening doubled or tripled. Families who thought they had paid a few dollars for entertainment often ended up facing late fees larger than the rental itself. It was a system designed not for customer satisfaction but for company profit. Customers grumbled, but they had no alternative.

Then, a small company emerged with a radical idea. Instead of forcing customers to rearrange their schedules to fit a store's hours, they brought the experience directly to the customer's doorstep. A website allowed people to select the movies they wanted, and within a day or two, DVDs appeared in the mailbox. For the first time, customers controlled the process. Convenience shifted entirely—no lines, no wasted trips, no negotiating with other shoppers over the last copy.

They went further. They removed one of the most frustrating parts of the old model: late fees. Instead of penalizing customers for forgetting to return a DVD, they introduced a flat subscription price. For a small monthly fee, people could keep movies as long as they wanted. Watch one in a night or keep it for a month—it didn't matter. The rules were simple, transparent, and fair. Customers immediately felt the difference. Pricing was no longer a punishment; it was a promise.

The user experience itself improved as well. Customers no longer had to wander aisles hoping for inspiration. They could build queues of movies online, receive personalized suggestions, and anticipate the arrival of their next selection. Choice expanded. Control shifted to the customer. What had once been a frustrating errand became something to look forward to. Later, as broadband internet grew, this company leapt again—streaming films directly into homes. No waiting, no mail delays. Movie night became instantaneous, intuitive, and limitless.

Throughout these changes, one principle held constant: trust. Customers needed to believe the DVDs would arrive on time. They needed to trust that billing would be accurate and fair. They needed assurance that when technology evolved, the company would invest in making the user experience better rather than more complicated. Over and over, the company delivered. Where its competitor profited from customer missteps, this new player built loyalty by keeping promises.

The industry leader barely noticed this at first. Flush with revenue from thousands of stores across the country, it saw little reason to worry about a mail-order service. The profits from late fees alone accounted for a substantial portion of its income. Analysts praised its dominance and assumed its model would continue indefinitely. Meanwhile, the smaller company steadily grew.

As streaming emerged, the skepticism grew louder. Executives scoffed. "People won't watch movies on a computer," they argued. Others claimed internet speeds were too slow, the libraries too thin, the technology too clumsy. The incumbent doubled down on its physical locations, confident that its size guaranteed survival. Customers, however, quietly shifted. Each family that tried the new service discovered it was easier, cheaper, more enjoyable, and more reliable. Word spread. Growth accelerated. The gap between what customers wanted and what the industry giant provided widened every year.

In the end, the conclusion became inevitable. The rental giant that once defined an industry collapsed under the weight of its own outdated model. The challenger, once dismissed as insignificant, became a household name and a force in global entertainment. By prioritizing convenience, fairness in pricing, a superior user experience, and unshakable trust, it rewrote the rules of the industry.

Only then does the story reveal itself. The company that fell was Blockbuster. The company that rose was Netflix.

And just as this company reshaped entertainment, another was about to reinvent something even more basic: how we move from one place to another…

Reinventing the Ride

For decades, hailing a ride in most cities followed the same frustrating pattern. Commuters stood on sidewalks, waving at passing taxis, never knowing if one would stop. If it did, questions loomed: Would the car be clean? Would the driver be courteous? Would the meter spin faster than expected, leaving a fare that felt unpredictable and unfair?

Travelers arriving at airports late at night often found themselves in long taxi lines, waiting as dispatchers slowly cycled cars forward. Others called central dispatch numbers that sometimes ranged endlessly or resulted in uncertain promises that a cab was "on the way." For customers, transportation was a gamble. Convenience was limited, and choice was almost nonexistent.

Into this environment came a new idea; an idea that would seem almost too obvious once people experienced it. What if, instead of hoping a taxi appeared, you could press a button on your phone and a car would come directly to you? No standing in the rain. No guessing. No uncertainty. With a simple tap, a ride would appear.

From the start, this company engineered everything for **convenience**. A mobile app let riders see available cars nearby, request one instantly, and track its arrival in real time. Instead of helplessly waiting at a curb, customers could relax indoors, confident that their ride was on its way. The shift in control was immediate and profound. For the first time, riders—not drivers or dispatchers—controlled the experience.

Next, the company tackled **pricing**. The old model was opaque: a spinning meter and a final fare revealed only at the end. This fresh approach offered upfront estimates. Customers could see what their trip would cost before they ever stepped into the car. Payment was automatic through the app. No cash exchanges. No awkward haggling. Though prices sometimes surged at peak times, the transparency itself felt refreshing compared to the mystery of the taxi meter.

The **user experience** of riding fundamentally improved. Drivers were rated by passengers, and passengers by drivers. This mutual accountability elevated behavior on both sides. Cars were typically cleaner, drivers friendlier, and routes optimized by GPS navigation. What had once felt like a stressful chore became easier, smoother, and in many cases, enjoyable. Riders shared stories of their positive experiences, turning ordinary trips into word-of-mouth marketing.

Underlying it all was **trust**. Profiles of drivers included photos, license plate numbers, and ratings. Riders could share their trip details with friends or family in real time, a safety feature unheard of in the traditional model. Digital receipts documented every detail, eliminating disputes. The company made reliability and accountability central to its brand. For a customer base long accustomed to uncertainty, this new level of trust was transformative.

The established taxi industry didn't see the threat at first. Protected by decades of regulation, permits, and city contracts, it believed no upstart could challenge its dominance. Critics brushed off the new service as a novelty or niche offering. Industry leaders scoffed: "People will never trust strangers with their personal cars. Regulators will shut it down."

But while skeptics laughed, customers kept pressing the button. Each successful ride reinforced the appeal. Every moment saved, every hassle avoided, every seamless transaction deepened loyalty. The service spread city by city, fueled not by traditional advertising but by delighted customers telling their friends. Soon, what began as an experiment in one city became a global phenomenon.

The taxi industry, once considered untouchable, eroded. Long waits, unpredictable fares, and outdated systems could no longer compete with a model that placed the customer at the center. Customers had experienced something better, and there was no going back.

In time, the company's name became synonymous with modern transportation. The simple act of pressing a button to summon a car reshaped how people thought about mobility itself. The company was Uber.

These three stories reveal a timeless truth: when companies deliver on convenience, fair pricing, remarkable user experiences, and trust, they don't just grow—they transform industries. That is the Growth Code. And while the scale of Amazon, Netflix, and Uber may be unique, the formula they used is not. It is available to every business leader willing to rethink how they define value and put the customer at the center.

In the chapters ahead, we'll unpack these four pillars, explore the leadership disciplines that sustain them, and provide a roadmap for applying them in your own organization.

Growth isn't about luck or timing. It's about understanding what every buyer is seeking and delivering upon it. This works for every business and every offering.

CHAPTER 1

CRACKING THE GROWTH CODE, THE FORMULA BEHIND MARKET LEADERS

Growth isn't random. Market leaders don't stumble into dominance. They follow a formula—sometimes consciously, sometimes instinctively—that aligns perfectly with what buyers value most.

Every purchase decision, whether it's a cup of coffee or a multimillion-dollar contract, comes down to four criteria: **convenience, price, user experience, and trust.** These are the pillars of the Growth Code. Ignore them, and your business will struggle. Deliver on them, and growth follows.

Why the Four Pillars Matter

Think back to the stories from the Introduction. An online bookstore, ridiculed for burning cash, engineered convenience, competitive pricing, intuitive experiences, and trust into everything it did—and became the world's largest retailer. A DVD-by-mail startup stripped away late fees, created a simple subscription model, and built loyalty through convenience and trust, eventually reshaping global entertainment. A ride-hailing app solved the headaches of taxis by putting convenience, price clarity, user experience, and trust into the palm of a customer's hand, changing transportation forever.

Amazon, Netflix, and Uber didn't just innovate. They tapped into the same four criteria that guide every buying decision. Their success went beyond luck by tapping into an alignment with the buyer's mind.

It's Always About the Buyer

One of the biggest mistakes entrepreneurs make is building a business around themselves. *"I love to cook, so I'll open a restaurant."* Or, *"I enjoy fashion, so I'll start a clothing brand."* Passion is important, but it doesn't guarantee growth.

The truth is simple: customers don't care about *your* passion. They care about *their* needs.

A restaurant succeeds when it delivers convenience (quick service or easy access), competitive and transparent pricing, a great dining experience, and food people trust. A software company grows when it makes users' lives easier, offers fair pricing, creates a seamless user experience, and earns trust through reliability.

Whether you're running a startup or a Fortune 500 company, the formula doesn't change.

The Four Pillars and Their Sub-components

Convenience

Buyers crave anything that saves them **time, effort, or complexity.** Convenience isn't just about the product or service itself; it's also about the buying process. Amazon wins not only because packages arrive quickly but also because the purchase is one click away. If it's hard to buy from you, or hard to use what you sell, buyers will find someone else.

Price

Customers always consider price, but not always in the way sellers think. The cheapest option isn't always the winner, but the **most**

competitive and transparent one usually is. Hidden fees, fine print, surcharges, and gimmicks destroy confidence. Buyers want to know exactly what they will pay before they commit, with no surprises later.

User Experience

User experience is broad, but it boils down to how the customer feels during and after the interaction. It includes **feeling valued, being treated like the only customer, and being supported at every step.** It's shaped by responsiveness, proactive communication, and delivering on promises. For businesses with physical locations, it also means **clean, well-lit, well-stocked facilities, enough staff to serve promptly, and a sense of order.** User experience is the criterion most under your control as a seller—and often the most neglected.

Trust

Trust is the foundation of all long-term business. It's about more than liking someone; it's about believing they will deliver what they promise. When buyers are selecting what they are choosing, they form a perception of what they are going to get in exchange for their money. Thus, they want protection and seek **recourse**: easy returns, guarantees, warranties, testimonials, references. Trust gives buyers confidence that if something goes wrong, they won't be left stranded. Without trust, even convenience, price, and user experience fall short.

The Hard Truth

It's extremely difficult to excel in all four pillars at once. Few companies ever do. But the most successful companies commit to them all, and they work relentlessly to strengthen the weakest areas. You don't need perfection. You need progress. The key is to never be vulnerable with any single pillar and to constantly improve across all four.

The Buyer's Value System

Every customer has a value system that prioritizes these pillars differently. Some care most about price. Others care most about user experience. Some are driven by convenience above all. Still others won't move forward until they trust the seller completely.

Market leaders understand this. They don't try to be everything to everyone, but they consistently deliver across all four pillars while excelling in one or two. That's how they win. When companies cannot deliver on all four, they have to target a market segment of customer whose value system exactly matches what they offer. Companies that can match all have an advantage as they are attractive to a larger segment of the buying population.

Reflection for Leaders

So, your challenge is to look at your business honestly, and these questions help do this effectively:

- How convenient is it for customers to buy from you?
- How transparent and competitive is your pricing?
- How consistent and memorable is the user experience you deliver?
- How much do your customers really trust you?

Your answers to these questions determine your growth trajectory.

What's Ahead

In the chapters ahead, we'll take each of these four pillars and examine them in depth. You'll see how leaders across industries have built growth on these foundations, and how you can apply the same principles to your own business.

Sustainable growth isn't about chasing the next trend or hoping for luck. It's about aligning your company with what buyers truly value. And once you do that, you've cracked the Growth Code.

KEY TAKEAWAYS

- Every buying decision comes down to four pillars: **convenience, price, user experience, and trust.**
- These pillars apply both to the **buying process** and to the **product or service itself.**
- Each pillar has critical sub-components:
    - **Convenience** = saving time, reducing effort, keeping it simple.
    - **Price** = competitive and, above all, **transparent** (no surprises).
    - **User Experience** = feeling valued, responsiveness, proactive communication, and for physical spaces: clean, well-lit, and well-staffed environments.
    - **Trust** = recourse through guarantees, warranties, testimonials, and consistently delivering on promises.
- It's rare for a company to excel at all four pillars simultaneously, but the most successful continually strengthen each and avoid being weak on any.
- Market leaders dominate because they align with what buyers value most—not by luck, but by applying this formula consistently.

The Growth Code: Four Pillars and Their Sub-Components

Convenience

- Save time
- Reduce effort
- Keep it simple
- Make life easier

Price

- Competitive
- Transparent (no surprises)
- Fair value

User Experience

- Feeling better than before
- Responsiveness
- Proactive communication
- Clean & well-lit spaces
- Well-stocked & well-staffed

Trust

- Guarantees
- Warranties
- Easy returns
- Testimonials
- References

CHAPTER 2

BUYERS SEEK CONVENIENCE

If there's one truth about buyers today, it's that people choose the path of least resistance. They gravitate toward the option that saves them time, reduces effort, makes life simpler, and eases friction. In short, they seek convenience.

Convenience isn't a luxury. It's a primary driver of choice. Every company, no matter the industry, is competing on convenience, whether they acknowledge it or not.

Amazon and the Power of Frictionless Buying

Few companies have rewritten the rules of convenience like Amazon. What started as a website selling books is now the default destination for millions of buyers; not because it always has the lowest prices, but because it's the easiest place to shop.

- **One-click ordering** removed friction at checkout.
- **Ordering from anywhere** with nothing but a connection to the internet
- **Fast and reliable delivery** set new expectations for speed.
- **Search, filters, and recommendations** made finding products simpler than walking a store aisle.

Amazon understood something competitors missed: if the buying process is harder than it needs to be, customers will leave. By making purchasing nearly effortless, Amazon transformed convenience into loyalty.

The Buying Process vs. the Product Itself

Convenience applies in two dimensions:

1. **The buying process** – How much time and effort are required to make the purchase, and how simple and easy is it to make the purchase?
2. **The product or service itself** – Does the offering save time and effort, and how easy is it to use once purchased?

Consider Home Depot. For years, customers grumbled about confusing store layouts, hard-to-find products, and long checkout lines. Then Home Depot began investing in better signage, improved online ordering with in-store pickup, and self-checkout options. They made the *process of buying* more convenient.

But they didn't stop there. Their product offering—DIY supplies and tools—also needed to be easier for customers to understand and use. By offering how-to guides, online tutorials, and in-store workshops, they made the *product itself* more accessible. Convenience was engineered on both sides of the transaction. They even installed lockers up front where you could order and pay online and then quickly recover your items and leave.

Sub-components of Convenience

To better understand convenience, let's break it down into four sub-components:

1. **Saving time:** Time is the one resource no one can replenish. Customers choose what's faster. That's why TSA PreCheck

allows travelers to bypass long security lines. It's not about luxury; it's about giving back time.

2. **Reducing effort:** Sometimes, effort matters more than speed. Ordering groceries through Instacart might not always be faster than driving to the store, but it saves the effort of parking, walking aisles, and waiting at checkout.
3. **Keeping it simple:** Simplicity means clarity. Disney mastered this with its parks. Maps, apps, and mobile food ordering make navigating a complex environment straightforward. Even though a day at Disney involves thousands of moving parts, the user experience feels manageable because it's designed to be simple.
4. **Making life easier:** Convenience ultimately comes down to ease. Chick-fil-A's drive-thru isn't just fast; it's designed to be stress-free. Clear lanes, friendly staff, and accurate orders create a sense that everything is handled. Customers leave not only with food but with relief.

Saving time and reducing effort often overlap. Simplicity and ease often feel the same. But each has its own weight. Something can be simple without being easy—running a marathon is conceptually simple but physically hard. The most successful companies pay attention to all four, knowing each shapes the customer's perception of convenience.

Everyday Examples Customers Recognize

Think about the small choices we make:

- Escalators exist right next to stairs, yet nearly everyone chooses the escalator.
- Self-checkout lines grow longer even when staffed registers are open.

- People use Uber more than a traditional taxi because it's cheaper, and because pressing a button is easier than hailing a cab. People can see how much time it is going to take for the car to show up and when it should arrive. Riders save time when arriving by simply leaving the car and not having to exchange cash or credit cards with the driver. That is much more convenient.

Each choice underscores the same point: customers prefer what saves them time, reduces effort, keeps it simple, and makes life easier.

The Leader's Lens: Evaluating Convenience

As a CEO or business owner, your most critical question is: *Is it harder to do business with us than it should be?*

Convenience isn't just about adding more services. It's about identifying and removing friction at every stage. Sometimes the smallest improvements—clearer signage, faster checkout, cleaner restrooms, simpler forms—make the biggest difference in loyalty.

Leaders must evaluate convenience in both dimensions:

- **The buying process.** How easy is it for a customer to pay you, order from you, or access your services? Are there bottlenecks, delays, or unnecessary steps?
- **The product or service itself.** Once customers have it, how easy is it to use, learn, maintain, or enjoy? Does it simplify their life or add complexity?

Market leaders never stop asking these questions. They know that if a competitor makes life easier, customers will switch.

Reflection Checklist

Ask yourself and your leadership team:

1. How much time does it take for a customer to buy from us compared to our competitors?
2. How much effort do customers expend to get what they need?
3. How simple is our buying process—are there unnecessary forms, steps, or approvals?
4. Does our product or service make life easier for the customer, or does it add complexity?
5. What recurring complaints or frustrations do customers express about working with us?
6. Where can we remove friction immediately?

KEY TAKEAWAYS

- Buyers don't just prefer convenience—they expect it.
- Convenience applies both to the **buying process** and to the **product/service itself.**
- The four sub-components of convenience are: **saving time, reducing effort, keeping it simple, and making life easier.**
- Market leaders continually remove friction in both buying and using their products.
- CEOs must evaluate their business through the lens of convenience and act relentlessly to simplify, speed up, and ease the customer's path.
- Some think time is our most precious commodity and treat it accordingly.

Use this checklist with your leadership team to evaluate how convenient it is for customers to buy from you and to use your products or services. Identify areas of friction, then take action to remove them.

Convenience Reflection Checklist

☐ How much time does it take for a customer to buy from us compared to competitors?

☐ How much effort do customers expend to get what they need?

☐ How simple is our buying process—are there unnecessary forms, steps, or approvals?

☐ Does our product or service make life easier for the customer, or does it add complexity?

☐ What recurring complaints or frustrations do customers express about working with us?

☐ Where can we remove friction immediately?

CHAPTER 3

MORE THAN PRICE POINTS

When buyers make decisions, price always matters. But it rarely matters in the way many companies think. Leaders often assume that being the cheapest is the only way to win, but research and daily experience prove otherwise. Price is only one of four pillars, and when it dominates at the expense of convenience, user experience, or trust, growth is hard to sustain.

What matters more than being the lowest is being **competitive** and being **transparent.** Customers don't necessarily demand the cheapest option, but they do expect fairness and clarity.

The Problem with Hidden Fees

Few industries illustrate pricing frustration better than airlines. For years, the base ticket price looked competitive, but the real cost ballooned with add-ons: baggage fees, seat selection charges, food and beverage costs, and change fees. The lack of transparency left customers feeling tricked.

Contrast that with Southwest Airlines. Their "bags fly free" policy was simple, clear, and trustworthy. Customers didn't have to guess the real cost of flying—it was right there, upfront. Southwest wasn't always the cheapest, but it won loyalty by being transparent.

The same story plays out in hotels with "resort fees," car rentals with insurance add-ons, or telecom providers with activation and termination charges. Buyers don't mind paying; what they hate is being surprised. In fact, car rental and cell phone companies transitioned away from complicated pricing that could not be predicted to monthly subscription plans that were more all-inclusive. Rather than rent a car by the day and per mile, they changed to a flat rate per day with all miles included. Phone companies changed from per-minute and per-megabyte pricing to all-inclusive flat rates per month, based on various plans. Buyers like the predictability.

Competitive, But Not Always the Lowest

Competitive pricing matters. If you're wildly out of range, customers won't even consider you. But lowest pricing is not always the winning strategy.

If it were, Motel 6 would dominate the hotel industry, and Nordstrom would have gone out of business years ago. Instead, both survive by playing different games. Motel 6 wins customers who prioritize price above everything else. Nordstrom thrives by offering superior user experience and trust, even though its prices are higher.

Marriott doesn't compete with Motel 6 on price, just as Four Seasons doesn't compete with Holiday Inn. Customers understand the trade-off: higher price for better convenience, better user experience, and stronger trust.

This is the reality of **trade-off companies**. Some businesses—like Aldi, Dollar General, or Allegiant Airlines—lead with low price, but sacrifice convenience, user experience, or trust to make it work. Others—like Four Seasons or Nordstrom—charge more but deliver superior performance on the other three pillars.

Trade-offs may win customers in the short term, but they also give buyers a reason to leave. When convenience is lacking, customers have an excuse to go somewhere easier. When pricing is murky, they have an excuse to choose transparency. When the user experience disappoints, they have an excuse to try the competitor.

Dominant companies avoid giving customers excuses. They may not be perfect, but they strive to deliver across all four pillars—convenience, price, user experience, and trust—so buyers feel no need to look elsewhere. That is the Growth Code in action.

When a company cannot be the low-price provider, it's important that they overextend on the other three pillars of being convenient, providing an exceptional user experience, and being more trustworthy.

Complexity Kills Confidence

In some industries, pricing is so complex that it alienates buyers altogether. Consider less-than-truckload (LTL) freight shipping. Rates depend on distance, weight, freight class, density, fuel surcharges, and countless other variables. So complex, in fact, that specialized software is often required to calculate the true cost.

For customers, this kind of opacity creates mistrust. If they can't easily understand what they're paying for, they assume they're being taken advantage of. Complexity erodes trust; and without trust, price loses its power to persuade. Companies that resist the temptation to profit from hidden fees and complex pricing schemes are better viewed by buyers.

The Leader's Lens on Price

Leaders must see price through the customer's eyes. Competitive doesn't mean cheapest; it means fair compared to alternatives. Transparent doesn't mean listing every microscopic detail, but it does mean no surprises.

When your price is higher, you must deliver more in convenience, user experience, or trust to justify it. Customers will gladly pay more for a Marriott than a Motel 6 if the user experience, reliability, and trust are worth it. They'll pay more for Chick-fil-A than for a generic drive-thru because the user experience and consistency are better.

The danger comes when leaders hide behind low prices or, worse, use hidden fees to appear competitive. Both are short-term tactics that undermine long-term growth.

Reflection Checklist

Ask yourself and your leadership team:

1. Do our customers know the full cost upfront, without surprises?
2. Are we competitive within our segment, even if not the lowest?
3. Do our pricing practices (fees, fine print, surcharges) create frustration or resentment?
4. If our prices are higher, do we deliver enough in convenience, user experience, or trust to justify them?
5. Is our pricing system clear and simple, or is it so complex customers struggle to understand it?
6. Do we give customers excuses to look elsewhere because of how we handle price?

KEY TAKEAWAYS

- **Competitive pricing** matters, but you don't have to be the cheapest to win.
- **Transparency** is critical. Hidden fees, fine print, and "gotcha" tactics erode trust.
- Trade-offs give buyers excuses to leave; dominant companies eliminate excuses by delivering across all four pillars.
- Customers will pay more when price is supported by convenience, user experience, and trust.
- Complexity kills confidence. Simple, upfront pricing wins loyalty.

CHAPTER 4

THE BUYING AND PRODUCT EXPERIENCE IS CRITICAL

A memorable scene in the movie *Pretty Woman* captures the power of user experience. Julia Roberts, playing Vivian, walks into a high-end boutique on Rodeo Drive. She's dressed inappropriately for the store's image, and the sales associates dismiss her, refusing to help. Later, after buying expensive clothes elsewhere, she walks back in carrying bags from other boutiques and delivers the unforgettable line: *"Big mistake. Huge."*

That scene resonates because it illustrates something every buyer feels: the sting of being treated poorly. The sales associates didn't lose a sale; they lost a customer. And they lost her for good.

User experience matters because buyers exchange their hard-earned money for a product or service, and in return, they want more than the item itself. They want to feel respected. They want to feel appreciated. Above all, they want to feel like their choice was the right one.

Few things drive growth—or kill it faster—than customer experience.

Why Customer Experience Matters

Of all the four pillars of the Growth Code, **user experience is the one most under your control.** You may not be able to beat every competitor's price. You may not always be the most convenient. But you can always control how customers feel when they buy from you and when they use your product or service.

User experience is broad. It stretches across every touchpoint of a customer's interaction with your company, from the moment they consider buying to the lasting impression after the purchase. It has two distinct dimensions:

1. **The Buying Experience** – what it feels like to become your customer.
2. **The Product/Service Experience** – what it feels like to use what you sell.

The Buying Experience

The buying experience is the most controllable of all. Leaders decide how their people interact, how facilities are maintained, how digital platforms are designed, and how responsive communication will be.

- **Physical businesses.** Think about the details: Is the parking lot clean and well-lit? Are the restrooms maintained? Is the store well-stocked, orderly, and staffed with people ready to help? Customers notice these things. A dirty restroom in a restaurant or gas station may seem minor, but it can drive customers away forever.
- **Restaurants.** Contrast Chick-fil-A and McDonald's. At Chick-fil-A, orders are accurate, staff are friendly, and the phrase "my pleasure" has become a signature. At McDonald's, customers often encounter long waits, indifferent service, or missing items. Price points may be similar, but the buying experience sets them apart.

- **Online businesses.** A confusing website is equivalent to a messy store. Buyers expect intuitive design, easy navigation, minimal clicks, and mobile functionality. Amazon's dominance is due not just to what it sells, but how seamless it makes buying. Compare that to sites with broken links, slow load times, or endless required fields—customers abandon carts in frustration.
- **Service businesses.** For service providers, proactive communication is everything. Customers want rapid responses, clear expectations, and follow-through on commitments. Silence, delays, or excuses destroy confidence. A consulting firm that calls back within hours earns trust; one that takes a week loses credibility.

Service Recovery: Turning Mistakes into Loyalty

No company gets it right every time, and mistakes happen: wrong orders, delayed shipments, missed appointments. What separates average companies from market leaders is how they handle those mistakes.

This is the art of **service recovery.**

- Airlines that cancel flights but offer clear rebooking options, vouchers, and sincere apologies salvage relationships.
- Restaurants that replace a wrong dish quickly—and often without charge—turn frustration into delight.
- Retailers with hassle-free returns build loyalty, even if the product fails.

Research shows that customers who experience a well-handled recovery are often more loyal than those who never had a problem in the first place. Why? Because the company demonstrated care, accountability, and urgency when it mattered most. Service recovery is not just about fixing problems; it's about proving your company can be trusted.

With the growth and use of social media, an unhappy customer is much more likely to spread their dissatisfaction, than a happy one. However, when a delighted customer spreads the word about their great experience, you will receive the best marketing there is.

The Product/Service Experience

Once the purchase is made, the user experience continues with the product or service itself. This is where companies either reinforce confidence or create regret.

- **Technology.** Apple built its reputation not only on sleek hardware but also on intuitive usability. From unboxing an iPhone to setting it up in minutes, the product experience reinforces simplicity and delight.
- **Automotive.** Tesla transformed the driving experience by providing over-the-air software updates, meaning cars improve long after purchase. The product evolves with the customer, creating loyalty that extends far beyond the showroom.
- **Restaurants.** The dining experience isn't just about taste, but about temperature, presentation, and service. A hot meal served quickly reassures customers that their choice was right. A cold or delayed dish leaves them questioning whether to return.
- **Hospitality.** Disney is legendary for creating immersive experiences. Every detail, from the cleanliness of the parks to the friendliness of staff, reinforces the brand promise. Visitors pay premium prices, but they feel it's worth it because the product experience matches the expectation.

When Apple launched the iPod and later the iPhone, the technology wasn't new. MP3 players existed; smartphones existed. What Apple did differently was obsess over the *experience*. They made it simple with "1,000 songs in your pocket." They made it elegant with minimal buttons and a sleek design. And they made it seamless through the ecosystem of connected devices, music, and services. Customers didn't just buy a product; they bought an experience that made them feel better, smarter, and more capable.

Treating Customers as Special

Across industries, one truth holds: buyers want to be treated as special. This doesn't mean extravagant gestures. It means respect, recognition, and appreciation.

- A handwritten thank-you note.
- A personalized follow-up email.
- Staff greeting customers by name.
- Proactive updates that anticipate questions before they're asked.

These details tell customers: *You matter.* And when customers feel special, they return.

The Leader's Lens

As a leader, you control more of the user experience than you might realize. The choice is yours: to settle for mediocre interactions that drive customers away, or to create consistent experiences that fuel growth.

The question is not whether you can afford to invest in user experience. The real question is: *Can you afford not to?*

Reflection Checklist

Ask yourself and your leadership team:

1. What is the first impression customers have when they interact with us: physically, online, or by phone?

2. Are our facilities clean, well-lit, well-stocked, and welcoming?
3. Is our website intuitive, fast, and easy to navigate?
4. Do we respond quickly and proactively to customer inquiries and issues?
5. How do we handle mistakes? Do we turn problems into opportunities for loyalty through **service recovery**?
6. Does our product or service deliver consistently on the promises we make?
7. Do customers feel appreciated and treated as special after doing business with us?

KEY TAKEAWAYS

- **User experience** is the most controllable pillar of the Growth Code.
- It has two dimensions: the **buying experience** and the **product/service experience.**
- The buying experience includes everything from cleanliness and friendliness to online usability and proactive communication.
- The product/service experience is about usability, reliability, and ongoing fulfillment of promises.
- Service recovery is critical; how you handle mistakes can create more loyalty than perfection.
- Regardless of industry, buyers want to feel appreciated and treated as special.

The Growth Code: Experience Framework
Buying Experience vs. Product/Service Experience

Buying Experience

- Clean, well-lit, well-stocked facilities
- Ample parking and easy access
- Friendly, attentive staff
- Intuitive websites and mobile apps
- Minimal clicks and fast navigation
- Proactive communication
- Rapid response to questions/issues
- Accurate orders and efficient checkout
- Effective service recovery when mistakes happen

Product/Service Experience

- Product reliability and quality
- Ease of use and intuitive design
- Consistent delivery on promises
- Proactive updates or improvements
- Presentation, taste, and timeliness (restaurants)
- Immersive, detail-oriented environments (Disney)
- Ongoing support and responsiveness
- Customers feel appreciated and special

CHAPTER 5

BUYERS NEED TO TRUST SELLERS

When Kia Motors entered the U.S. market in the 1990s, few believed the company would survive. As a South Korean brand, it faced a wall of skepticism. American buyers had already embraced Honda, Toyota, and Nissan, but Kia was virtually unknown. Its cars were cheaper, but they carried no track record, no reputation, and no trust.

For many buyers, the math didn't work. Why spend thousands of dollars on a vehicle from a company they had never heard of, with no assurance it would last? Cars are among the most important purchases families make. They aren't impulse buys; they are investments. And with major investments, trust is paramount.

Kia understood this. They knew that competing on price alone wouldn't be enough. Low cost might bring attention, but without trust, it wouldn't bring sales. To win in a market dominated by long-established Japanese and American brands, Kia had to give buyers more than affordability. They had to remove doubt.

So, they launched one of the boldest warranty programs the industry had ever seen: a **10-year, 100,000-mile powertrain warranty** and a **5-year, 60,000-mile bumper-to-bumper warranty.** This wasn't a gimmick; it was a signal. Kia was telling buyers, "We stand behind our cars. If something goes wrong, we'll fix it. You can trust us."

That warranty became the foundation of Kia's U.S. growth story. Buyers who might have dismissed the brand took a second look. The warranty reduced the risk of trying something new, and in doing so, it built trust where none had existed. Over time, Kia's product quality improved, its designs became more competitive, and its market share grew. But it all began with the intentional building of trust, engineered into the customer experience from day one.

Costco built one of the most trusted retail models in the world. Their no-questions-asked return policy signals confidence: *"We trust our customers, and you can trust us."* The company even limits markups on products (no more than 14–15%) so customers know they're getting fair value. That transparency and guarantee-driven culture create trust so strong that Costco members pay for the privilege of shopping there, with a renew rate above 90%.

The Foundation of Trust

Every purchase is an exchange. Buyers trade their money for something they expect in return. That expectation may come from advertising, reputation, or simple logic. A brand's promise amplifies that expectation.

Sometimes the promise is explicit: *Federal Express* promised overnight delivery. *24/7 Plumbing* promises service at any hour. *Discount Liquors* signals lower prices. When companies fail to meet those promises, they don't just disappoint customers; they break trust.

Trust is fragile. It takes time to build but can be lost in a single interaction. For new customers especially, trust is the deciding factor. When buyers encounter a company for the first time, they want assurance that what is advertised is what will be delivered. Without that assurance, they hesitate—or walk away.

Brand Promises

A brand promise is more than a slogan. It's a commitment. Customers may forgive higher prices or slower service, but they rarely forgive a broken promise.

- **Federal Express.** Its name alone implied reliability and speed. "Absolutely, positively overnight" grew into more than just a tagline, but a promise millions trusted daily.
- **Jiffy Lube.** The brand promise is right there in the name: quick, dependable service. A slow oil change violates the very essence of the brand.
- **24/7 Plumbing.** If the phone rings at midnight and no one answers, trust is shattered instantly.
- **Quick Delivery.** When an order is late, customers lose patience and confidence.

Every company makes promises, whether intentional or implied. The test of trust is whether those promises are consistently kept.

Trust-building Mechanisms

So how do companies build trust, especially with first-time buyers? There are proven mechanisms:

- **Social Proof.** Referrals from peers, testimonials from customers, reviews from strangers. Buyers trust other buyers more than they trust marketing copy. Word of mouth remains the most powerful trust-builder.
- **Risk Reduction.** Guarantees, warranties, and hassle-free return policies tell buyers, "If something goes wrong, you won't be stuck." Zappos built its brand on free returns. Costco's return policy is legendary. Kia's warranty changed the game.

- **Longevity and Recognition.** Years in business, awards, and industry certifications all signal credibility. When a business has endured and been recognized, customers assume it is trustworthy.
- **Transparency and Recourse.** Clear communication, visible policies, and easy access to support reassure buyers. Amazon's return process is simple and visible. QuikTrip guarantees its gasoline quality. LL Bean once promised a lifetime guarantee. These are powerful signals of trust.

When Trust Breaks

Nothing destroys trust faster than deception. Scam artists know this well. A fake Facebook ad offering luxury shoes at a fraction of the price. A Craigslist rental that looks too good to be true. A phishing email promising quick riches.

Most people don't like to admit when they've been scammed. There's embarrassment in being fooled. But the emotional damage lingers: betrayal, anger, suspicion. Once trust is broken, it's almost impossible to win back.

That's why legitimate companies must avoid even the appearance of dishonesty. Hidden fees, fine print, bait-and-switch tactics are "scam-like" behaviors that drive buyers away. You don't need to commit fraud to lose trust; all it takes is creating the impression that your company is taking advantage of customers.

Positive Examples of Trust-building Brands

The strongest companies don't wait for trust to form by accident, but engineer it deliberately.

- **Amazon.** Its hassle-free return process reassures buyers before they even make a purchase. They know if it doesn't work out, they won't be stuck.

- **Zappos.** Its culture of customer service is legendary. Stories of representatives going above and beyond are proof of trustworthiness.
- **QuikTrip.** It backs its gasoline with a guarantee, signaling to customers that quality is never in question.
- **Kia.** Its warranties reassured skeptical buyers and changed its reputation.
- **Costco.** Its return policy is simple: bring it back, no questions asked. That's trust.

These companies prove that a trust-building strategy improves your chances of success.

The Leader's Lens

Trust is the foundation of repeat business. It's slow to build and fast to lose. First-time buyers need reassurance before they buy. Repeat customers need consistency to keep buying. Leaders must ask: Are we engineering trust into every touchpoint, or are we leaving it to chance?

Every interaction is a test of trust. Deliver on your promises, make recourse easy, and eliminate behaviors that resemble deception. That is how companies win.

Reflection Checklist

Ask yourself and your leadership team:

1. Do we deliver consistently on the promises we make—both explicit and implied?
2. Do our customers know exactly what to expect before they buy?
3. Do we provide clear assurances via warranties, guarantees, or easy returns?

4. Are we actively gathering and publishing testimonials, reviews, and references?
5. Is it easy for customers to get recourse if something goes wrong?
6. Do our policies or practices ever resemble scams (hidden fees, bait-and-switch, fine print)?
7. Do we proactively communicate when something goes wrong to preserve trust?

KEY TAKEAWAYS

- Trust is the foundation of growth. Without it, price, convenience, and user experience cannot sustain loyalty.
- Every buyer has expectations in exchange for their money. Trust is the bridge between promise and delivery.
- Brand promises amplify expectations, and breaking them destroys trust instantly.
- Trust is built through mechanisms like social proof, risk reduction, transparency, and recourse.
- Scams highlight the opposite: the betrayal that makes customers cautious forever.
- Market leaders deliberately engineer trust into every interaction.

The Growth Code: Trust-Building Framework

Social Proof

- Referrals from peers
- Testimonials and reviews
- Case studies
- Ratings and word-of-mouth

Risk Reduction

- Guarantees
- Warranties
- Hassle-free returns
- Free trials

Longevity & Recognition

- Years in business
- Awards and certifications
- Industry affiliations
- Reputation for consistency

Transparency & Recourse

- Clear communication
- Visible policies
- Easy access to support
- Proactive problem resolution

CHAPTER 6

BEAT YOUR COMPETITION AND GROW

On Sunday afternoons in the fall, NFL stadiums across America come alive. Players take the field, fans cheer, and games unfold that look spontaneous. But behind every play is a week of preparation. No coach shows up on game day wondering who the opponent is or what they like to do. They know.

They've watched film. They've studied strengths and weaknesses. They know if the other team prefers to run or pass, whether the quarterback struggles under pressure, whether the defense favors zone or man coverage. They craft game plans to exploit weaknesses and minimize strengths. That's how winning teams operate. Those hall of fame coaches you know were the best at exploiting the opposition's weaknesses and leveraging their own strengths.

Contrast that with how many businesses behave. Too often, CEOs show up to the "game" without knowing who their competitors are, what they do well, or where they're vulnerable. They assume their existing strengths will carry them. They hope customers will stay loyal. But hope is not a strategy.

If coaches prepared like many companies do, they'd be out of a job by Monday morning. You win by beating the competition. You grow by being better than your competitors with what matters most for buyers: convenience, price, user experience and trust, our four pillars covered earlier.

The Reality of Competition

An old African proverb says: *"Every morning in Africa, a gazelle wakes up. It knows it must run faster than the fastest lion or it will be killed. Every morning, a lion wakes up. It knows it must outrun the slowest gazelle or it will starve. It doesn't matter whether you are a lion or a gazelle—when the sun comes up, you'd better be running."*

That proverb captures the truth of business. It doesn't matter if you're the biggest competitor in your market (the lion) or the smaller one trying to grow (the gazelle). Every day you wake up, the race is on. Competitors are coming for your customers, and if you don't keep moving, improving, and strengthening your position, you'll get caught. It's exactly why competitors appear. They see a weakness and plan to exploit it.

The Castle with One Wall

Some companies cling to a single competitive advantage. They're cheaper. Or more convenient. Or have a strong reputation. They believe one edge will protect them forever.

But think of it like a castle. A fortress with one wall is easily defeated. Enemies eventually discover the unprotected sides and attack there. The same is true in business. If price is your only advantage, competitors can undercut you. If convenience is your only strength, customers will defect if the price feels unfair or if trust is shaky. If trust is all you have, but your experience is poor, buyers eventually drift elsewhere.

Winning companies build strong defenses on all sides. They don't rely on one pillar. They strengthen convenience, sharpen pricing and transparency, invest in better experiences, and engineer trust into every interaction. That makes them harder to beat.

Lessons from Market Leaders

The pattern is clear when you study companies that reshaped industries.

- **Uber vs. Taxis.** Taxis relied on street hails, opaque pricing, and inconsistent experiences. Uber studied those weaknesses. It offered app-based convenience, transparent fares, cleaner cars, and driver accountability through ratings. Uber didn't just win on one pillar—it improved all four.
- **Amazon vs. Retailers.** Bookstores thought selection and location were enough. Amazon made shopping more convenient with one-click ordering and delivery, more transparent with upfront pricing, more enjoyable with a seamless online experience, and more trustworthy with easy returns and reviews. Layer upon layer, it removed reasons to buy elsewhere.
- **Netflix vs. Blockbuster.** Blockbuster frustrated customers with late fees, limited selection, and trips to the store. Netflix eliminated late fees, simplified the process, made access more convenient, and built trust with reliable service. Blockbuster's single advantage—physical presence—wasn't enough. Netflix outflanked them on every pillar.

Market leaders don't just innovate. They study competitors' weaknesses, strengthen their own defenses, and deliver across all four pillars so customers have no excuse to leave.

The Danger of Single-advantage Thinking

History is full of companies that leaned too heavily on one edge.

- Price-only players were undercut.
- Convenience-only providers lost when pricing was unfair.
- Trust-heavy brands eroded when their products disappointed.

In every case, the failure wasn't a lack of talent or even demand, but a reliance on a single wall of the castle. Competitors eventually exploit whatever you're neglecting.

That's why the companies that dominate invest in all four pillars. They continually improve convenience, sharpen transparency in pricing, elevate user experiences, and reinforce trust. They give buyers no excuses to go anywhere else.

Why Most Companies Don't Do This

If the path is so clear, why don't more businesses act this way?

- **Leaders underestimate competitors.** They assume rivals aren't improving.
- **They skip the hard work.** Studying competitors takes time and discipline.
- **They settle for "good enough."** Being above average feels safe—until a competitor raises the bar.

In the NFL, failing to study film is career suicide. In business, failing to study competitors is a slow death.

The Call to Arms

If you want growth, you can't rely on hope, assumptions, or outdated advantages. You must study your competitors the way coaches study game film. Know their plays. Understand their strengths. Identify their weaknesses. Build your plan to exploit those weaknesses while reinforcing your own vulnerabilities.

The companies that last aren't just good. They're better than their competition in the areas that matter most to buyers: convenience, pricing transparency, user experience, and trust.

When you're stronger across all four, competitors hesitate to challenge you, customers have no reason to leave, and growth becomes sustainable.

So, study your competition. Strengthen your castle. Build walls on every side. And play to win.

Reflection Checklist

Ask yourself and your leadership team:

1. Do we know our top three competitors and how they perform across the four pillars?
2. Where are we stronger, and are we reinforcing those strengths?
3. Where are we weaker, and how might a competitor exploit that?
4. Are we relying too heavily on one competitive advantage?
5. What would happen if a new competitor entered our market tomorrow? Could they beat us easily?
6. Are we systematically improving across all four pillars to remove buyer excuses?

KEY TAKEAWAYS

- No winning coach goes into a game blind, and neither should a CEO.
- Competition is constant: lions and gazelles must both keep running.
- A single competitive advantage is too easy to exploit.
- Sustainable growth comes from being stronger across all four pillars.
- Studying competitors and acting on insights is a discipline, not an option.
- Growth favors leaders who prepare, plan, and play to win.

CHAPTER 7

STRATEGIC PLANNING

In June 1944, Allied forces launched one of the most ambitious military operations in history: the invasion of Normandy. D-Day was massive in scale: thousands of ships, planes, and soldiers converged on the beaches of France to begin the liberation of Europe. It involved multiple countries and was meticulously planned, down to the tides and timing.

But as Dwight D. Eisenhower later reminded us, Normandy wasn't the plan; it was one initiative. The actual plan was to win the war.

That's the difference between operational planning and strategic planning. The operation was D-Day. The strategy was total victory in Europe.

Too often, businesses confuse the two. They pour energy into annual goals, campaigns, or projects without stepping back to ask, "What's our true long-term direction? Where are we trying to go over the next 2–5 years?" Without that clarity, they may fight battles, but they risk losing the war.

Starbucks and the Return to Strategic Clarity

In the mid-2000s, Starbucks was on top of the world with thousands of stores, rapid expansion, and a brand that symbolized more than coffee. But behind the growth, something was breaking. Stores had become cluttered with merchandise, baristas were rushing transactions instead of connecting with customers, and the smell of fresh coffee was often replaced with reheated breakfast sandwiches.

Starbucks had lost its way.

When Howard Schultz returned as CEO in 2008, instead of tactics, he started with a strategic reset. He shut down every store in America for one afternoon of retraining, a bold and costly move. He reminded employees of what Starbucks was supposed to be: a "third place" between home and work, where people felt a sense of connection.

From there, the company redefined its strategic priorities:

- **Reinvest in the core experience** by making coffee the hero again.
- **Streamline operations** by cutting the distractions that didn't add value.
- **Align around culture** by empowering baristas to connect, not just serve.

The turnaround was remarkable. Starbucks regained customer loyalty, stabilized financially, and then launched into its next wave of growth with digital ordering and loyalty programs.

The lesson is clear: growth without strategy is dangerous. Starbucks was expanding but drifting. Strategic planning restored alignment, clarity, and energy.

What Strategic Planning Is (and Isn't)

Strategic planning is not about predicting the future. It's about creating ***alignment*** around a vision and the broad initiatives that will carry the company forward over several years.

- **Strategic planning** sets the direction for two to five years, articulating vision, goals, and top initiatives.
- **Operational planning** defines the tactics and projects for the next 12 months or fewer.

Confusing the two is like mistaking a playbook for a season-long strategy. Plays matter, but without a vision for the season, the team drifts.

Why Strategic Planning Matters

Eisenhower once said, "In preparing for battle I have always found that plans are useless, but planning is indispensable."

The point wasn't that plans don't matter. It is the process of planning that creates clarity, surfaces assumptions, forces alignment, and prepares leaders to adapt when reality changes.

That's just as true in business as in war. Without a plan, companies drift. With one, they row in the same direction. Strategic planning gives people clarity about:

- Where we are going.
- How we intend to get there.
- The resources we'll need.
- Who is responsible for what.

The Strategic Planning Process: Step by Step

1. **Vision and Goals.** The CEO sets the vision—what the company aspires to become—and broad goals for growth.
2. **Leadership Alignment.** The leadership team weighs in, refines, and ensures shared ownership.
3. **Strategic Initiatives.** Focus on the top three initiatives, in order, that will drive growth over the next two to five years.

4. **Objectives and Timeframes.** Translate initiatives into annual objectives and quarterly priorities. Near-term goals are clearer; longer-term goals are directional.
5. **Accountability.** Assign ownership. A quarterback or integrator organizes meetings, monitors progress, and provides updates. This is not just the CEO's plan; it's the company's plan.
6. **Communication.** Share the plan across the company. Every employee should know where the organization is headed and how their role connects.

Frameworks That Support Planning

Review several established frameworks that support effective planning:

- **SWOT Analysis** (Strengths, Weaknesses, Opportunities, Threats) helps leaders understand where they stand internally and externally.
- **OKRs** (Objectives and Key Results) break initiatives into measurable outcomes. Google and many others use this system to create clarity.
- **Balanced Scorecard** ensures leaders measure progress not only in financial terms, but also across customer, process, and people metrics.

The Growth Code's four pillars—convenience, price, user experience, and trust—should be woven into any framework. They reflect what buyers value and therefore what strategies must support.

Adaptability and Adjustments

Strategic plans are living frameworks that must adapt to changing circumstances.

- The pandemic of 2020 shifted entire industries overnight, forcing most to change initiatives and priorities.
- Tariffs and supply chain disruptions forced rapid adjustments.
- Technology breakthroughs, such as AI, continuously reshape thinking and priorities.

That's why the best companies review their strategic plans quarterly. They don't rewrite the vision every time conditions change, but they adjust initiatives, reallocate resources, and adapt.

It's like football: the strategic plan is to win the Super Bowl. The initiatives are to build a strong run game, a dominant passing attack, and a top-five defense. But from week to week, the game plan adjusts. Opponents change, injuries happen, conditions shift. You adapt the plays, but you don't change the goal.

The CEO and the Quarterback

The CEO's role in strategic planning is to initiate vision and direction. But the plan should never be seen as the CEO's plan. It must belong to the company.

That's why the role of a "quarterback" or integrator is essential. This leader coordinates the planning process, ensures follow-ups, tracks progress, and keeps the plan alive. Without this role, plans too often gather dust on a shelf.

The CEO provides vision. The quarterback ensures execution. Together, they make the plan the company's plan.

Examples of Strategic Planning in Action

- **Starbucks.** In 2008, Starbucks faced declining performance. Instead of chasing short-term fixes, leadership shut down stores to retrain baristas and refocus on coffee quality as the strategic foundation. It was painful in the moment but vital for long-term growth.
- **Apple.** Apple's strategy wasn't about selling one product. It was about building an ecosystem of devices and services that worked seamlessly together. That long-term vision guided decisions for decades.
- **Southwest Airlines.** While other airlines shifted strategies constantly, Southwest stayed focused on being the low-cost, simple, no-frills carrier. That clarity became a competitive fortress.

Each of these companies succeeded because their plans weren't static documents. They were living frameworks, revisited and adapted regularly and communicated throughout their organizations.

Reflection Checklist

Ask yourself and your leadership team:

1. Do we have a written strategic plan that defines our vision and top initiatives?
2. Have we narrowed to the top three priorities that will drive growth in the next two to five years?
3. Do we review and adjust our plan quarterly to reflect changing realities?
4. Have we assigned clear accountability with who owns which initiatives?
5. Is our plan communicated broadly so every employee knows where we're going?

6. Do we confuse operational plans (short-term projects) with strategic plans (long-term direction)?

KEY TAKEAWAYS

- Strategic planning is about creating alignment, not predicting the future.
- The plan itself may change, but the process builds clarity and unity.
- Strong plans balance vision, initiatives, objectives, and accountability.
- Strategic frameworks like SWOT, OKRs, and Balanced Scorecards reinforce clarity.
- Plans must adapt, and quarterly reviews keep them alive.
- CEOs provide vision, but integrators keep the plan active.
- Growth requires direction. Without a plan, companies drift. With one, they thrive.

Strategic Planning Framework: From Vision to Execution

Vision & Goals

- CEO sets vision and growth goals
- Defines what success looks like

Leadership Alignment

- Engage leadership team
- Refine and share ownership of vision

Strategic Initiatives

- Identify top 3 priorities for 2-5 years
- Focus on what drives growth

Objectives & Timeframes

- Break initiatives into annual objectives
- Define quarterly priorities for clarity

Accountability

- Assign ownership for each initiative
- Quarterback/integrator drives process

Communication

- Share plan across the company
- Ensure every employee knows direction

CHAPTER 8

LEADERSHIP: MANAGERS, MENTORS, AND COACHES

In January 2024, the Kansas City Chiefs hoisted yet another Lombardi Trophy, cementing their place as one of the NFL's modern dynasties. On the field, much of the credit went to Patrick Mahomes' brilliance, Andy Reid's steady hand, and a roster filled with talent. But ask the players on the defensive side of the ball, and you'll hear another name whispered with reverence: *Steve Spagnuolo.*

"Spags," as his players call him, has built a reputation as one of the NFL's greatest defensive coordinators. He never played in the NFL. He wasn't a Hall of Fame linebacker or a Pro Bowl safety. He came from a small school, Springfield College, where he played wide receiver on the *offensive* side of the ball. Yet year after year, he inspires millionaire athletes to give him everything they have.

In 2007, his New York Giants defense stunned the undefeated New England Patriots in Super Bowl XLII, holding Tom Brady's record-setting offense to just 14 points. Years later, with the Chiefs, he orchestrated defenses that contained some of the most explosive quarterbacks of the modern era. His schemes were creative, yes, but his players would tell you his true genius wasn't X's and O's. It was how he led them.

He coached them in a way that made them believe in themselves—and in him. He asked questions. He listened. He challenged their thinking. He made them feel part of the plan. His players were so inspired they created shirts that read, *"In Spags We Trust."*

I once asked a group of CEOs, "How many of your employees have ever created a t-shirt that says 'In (Your Name) We Trust'?" That question usually gets nervous laughter. But it lands on the point: leadership is not about authority or expertise. It's about inspiration. And the very best leaders, like Steve Spagnuolo, lead as coaches.

Leadership Has Three Flavors

In business, as in sports, leadership is the cornerstone of performance. The top leader, be it Owner, CEO, President, or other title, is responsible for the growth of the organization. While certain functions, like sales or marketing, can be assigned, the buck stops with the leader when it comes to growth performance. But leadership comes in different flavors. I believe there are three non-exclusive flavors of leadership: **Managers, Mentors, and Coaches.**

All three matter. Leaders will often move between them depending on the situation. But the most enduring, impactful leaders lean heavily on the third: coaching.

Flavor 1: Managers

Managers are task focused. They assign work, monitor performance, set goals, and ensure deadlines are met. Their focus is activity, tasks, and compliance.

Managers tend to speak 80–90% of the time, leaving little space for questions or discovery. Vulnerability, in their view, is weakness. Their strength lies in control: knowing, directing, and correcting.

Simon Sinek, in his essay "5 Things Managers Do That Leaders Never Would," describes the difference this way:

- Managers see numbers; leaders see people.
- Managers assign tasks; leaders inspire action.
- Managers demand performance; leaders create the environment for performance.

Good managers are necessary. But when leaders only manage, they stifle initiative, suppress creativity, and disengage their teams.

Flavor 2: Mentors

Mentors are teachers. They guide by sharing knowledge, offering advice, and transferring wisdom. A mentor might say, "Here's how I did it; let me show you the way."

Mentorship matters. It helps people develop skills, avoid mistakes, and learn faster. Employees often value having a mentor who invests in their development.

But mentorship has limits. It assumes the mentor has the answers. It is less about self-discovery and more about passing down lessons. Mentorship builds capability, but it doesn't always inspire ownership.

Flavor 3: Coaches

Coaches are different. Coaches don't just assign tasks or dispense wisdom, but inspire people to perform at their best.

Coaches ask more than they say. They speak 20–30% of the time, leaving 70–80% for questions, listening, and reflection. They are nonjudgmental, not rushing to judgment but instead seeking to understand. They probe with open-ended questions to uncover values and beliefs. They help people confront self-limiting assumptions.

Coaches know that leadership is not about forcing improvement. You cannot demand motivation. You cannot order engagement. Instead, coaches inspire by connecting to what people value and believe, helping them see a bigger purpose.

This is why coaching is especially powerful across generations. Baby Boomers, Millennials, Gen X, and Gen Z all bring different values and motivators. But great coaches don't stereotype; instead, they engage each person as an individual, discovering what drives them and adjusting accordingly.

A Mini Playbook: The 5 Coaching Steps

Coaching is not just a philosophy. It is a skill, one that can be practiced with discipline. Here are five steps I share with leaders:

1. **Don't Rush to Judgment / Get Their Story.**

   Create space for people to tell their story fully. Don't cut them off or assume you know where they're going.

2. **Dig Under Their Story.**

   Ask questions that go deeper. What's really happening? What's being left unsaid? What's driving the surface issue?

3. **Uncover Their Beliefs.**

   People act based on values and beliefs. Good coaches dig until those underlying beliefs are on the table. How do they feel? What do they believe?

4. **Encapsulate Emotions.**

   Acknowledge and reflect back what you're hearing. People don't move until they feel heard.

5. **Challenge Self-limiting Beliefs.**

   Often, people are stuck because of assumptions: "I'm not ready." "We've tried this before." "That's not possible." A coach gently but firmly challenges those beliefs, helping the person see they might be limiting themselves.

When leaders follow these steps, people expand their thinking. They see new possibilities. They inspire themselves into action. That's the power of coaching. Often, it's through no fault of the leader as they often learn how to manage based on how they were managed. Other than the military academies, many schools don't adequately teach and train their students in true and meaningful leadership skills.

Managers Direct, Mentors Teach, Coaches Inspire

When leaders only manage, they create compliance. When leaders mentor, they create learning. But when leaders coach, they create inspiration.

This is why Steve Spagnuolo has won the trust of every locker room he's led. He doesn't just draw up plays. He inspires belief. He doesn't demand just effort. He unlocks discretionary effort; the kind that comes from within. His players wear shirts that say, "In Spags We Trust." That is the measure of a coach.

In business, the stakes are no different. The companies that thrive are those where leaders inspire trust, loyalty, and effort—not through authority, but through coaching.

Reflection Checklist

Ask yourself:

1. Do I spend more time talking or listening?
2. Am I asking open-ended questions to uncover beliefs, or am I rushing to judgment?
3. Do I inspire people to find their own answers, or do I always provide them?
4. Am I seen more as a boss, a mentor, or a coach?
5. Do I influence others through authority, or through inspiration?

KEY TAKEAWAYS

- Leadership has three flavors: Manager, Mentor, and Coach.
- Managers direct tasks, Mentors teach skills, Coaches inspire performance.
- The best leaders move between all three, but coaching has the greatest impact.
- Coaching is about listening, asking questions, uncovering beliefs, and challenging limitations.
- Leadership is about influencing without authority: winning hearts and minds.
- Steve Spagnuolo proves that great leaders don't need to be the most credentialed or experienced—they need to inspire.

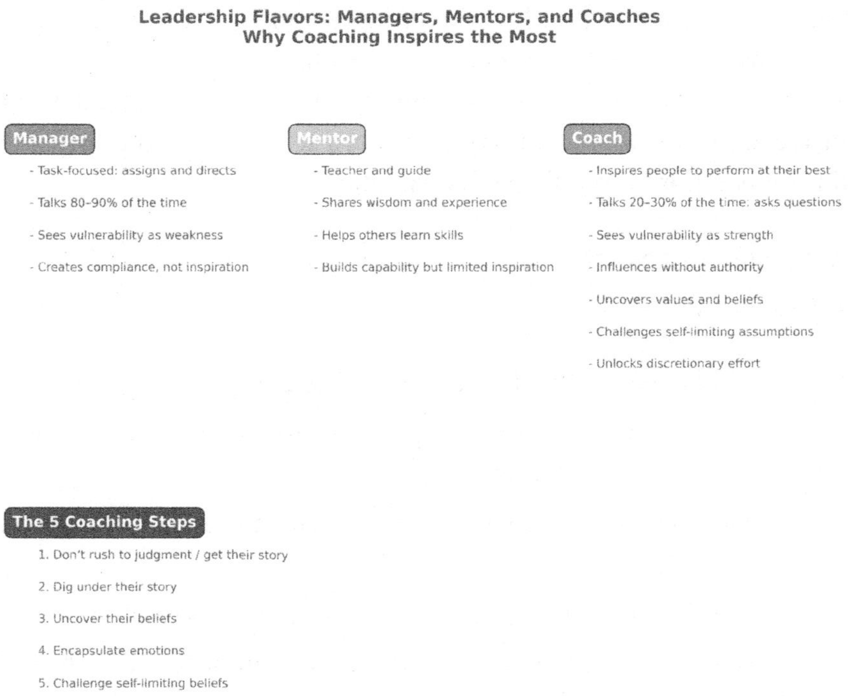

CHAPTER 9

CULTURE THAT WORKS

At the Four Seasons, service isn't left to chance. One of their cultural "fundamentals" is simple yet powerful: if a guest asks for directions, employees never point. Instead, they personally escort the guest to the location. Whether it's the restaurant, the pool, or the restroom, the behavior is consistent. Every employee knows it. Every guest experiences it. That consistency builds confidence and loyalty.

Southwest Airlines demonstrates the same principle in a different way. From the earliest days, Southwest built a culture of humor, warmth, and putting people first. Flight attendants crack jokes in safety briefings. Gate agents go out of their way to make travel less stressful. Pilots hand out peanuts. These aren't accidents or individual quirks; they're part of a culture that encourages employees to bring personality and care into every interaction.

And then there's Chick-fil-A, with the single phrase "my pleasure" becoming a cultural signature. Employees don't just say "you're welcome." They deliver a consistent behavior that reinforces the company's promise of care, courtesy, and hospitality. Customers notice. They come back.

These examples illustrate an important truth: culture isn't a poster on the wall. It's the behaviors people consistently demonstrate.

Defining Culture

Culture is the set of shared values, beliefs, and, most importantly, behaviors that define how people act and interact in an organization. David J. Friedman, in his excellent book *Culture By Design*, explains that culture is not accidental. Left undefined, culture forms on its own, usually shaped by the loudest or strongest personalities. But when culture is intentional, defined by the leader, and reinforced with discipline, it becomes one of the most powerful drivers of growth.

According to Friedman's CultureWise framework, culture is built on **fundamentals**: specific, teachable behaviors that everyone in the organization is expected to practice. Unlike vague values (integrity, teamwork, excellence), fundamentals are actionable. They tell people exactly how to behave.

For example, here are a few drawn from CultureWise's library of fundamentals:

- **Honor Commitments.** Do what you say you're going to do.
- **Be a Fanatic About Response Time.** Respond quickly to questions and concerns.
- **Practice Blameless Problem-solving.** Focus on solutions, not finger-pointing.
- **Deliver Legendary Service.** Create user experiences that people will tell others about.
- **Do What's Best for the Customer.** Put long-term relationships ahead of short-term gain.
- **Take Ownership.** Don't pass the buck—see things through to completion.

These kinds of fundamentals go far beyond slogans. They establish clear expectations for behavior. They remove ambiguity. They tell every employee: "This is how we act here."

Why Disciplined Culture Matters

If culture isn't defined, it will still form, but often not in ways leaders want. When behavior is left unchecked, the strongest personalities set the tone. That can lead to inconsistency, favoritism, or even toxic work environments. Customers notice. Vendors notice. Employees disengage.

When culture is intentional and disciplined, magic happens. Everyone behaves the same way. Customers know what to expect. Employees feel aligned and secure. Vendors trust the consistency.

Research consistently shows that companies with strong cultures outperform their peers in engagement, productivity, and growth. The reason is simple: when people know exactly how to behave and see those behaviors modeled every day, energy isn't wasted on confusion or conflict. It's channeled into performance.

But discipline is non-negotiable. If exceptions are made because someone is related to the owner, or has been around a long time, then those exceptions redefine the culture. Culture is what you tolerate, not just what you preach.

The Role of Fundamentals and Rituals

CultureWise emphasizes two keys to building culture:

1. **Defining the fundamentals.** Leaders determine the specific behaviors they want their people to demonstrate. Input can be gathered, but ultimately the leader decides.
2. **Creating rituals.** Fundamentals must be practiced consistently. This often means focusing on one fundamental each week, reinforcing it through meetings, stories, and recognition.

The best leaders spend the first hour or two of a new employee's onboarding reviewing the fundamentals, ensuring they understand how central culture is to the organization's success. And rituals don't stop at onboarding, they're ongoing. Repetition drives habits. Habits become culture.

Culture Types: What The Discipline of Market Leaders Teaches Us

In their book *The Discipline of Market Leaders*, Michael Treacy and Fred Wiersema outlined three types of companies that consistently dominate their industries: product leaders, operationally excellent (efficiency-centric) companies, and customer intimate (customer-centric) companies.

These aren't just business strategies, but reflections of culture.

- **Product-centric Cultures.** Companies driven by innovation, like Apple or Dyson, create cultures where behaviors center around curiosity, creativity, and a constant search for improvement. Employees are encouraged to experiment, challenge assumptions, and push boundaries. The culture rewards new ideas and tolerates failure in the pursuit of innovation.
- **Efficiency-centric Cultures.** Companies like UPS or Walmart thrive on efficiency. Their cultures promote behaviors that seek to streamline, cut waste, and maximize productivity. Employees are trained to look for process improvements, minimize errors, and measure everything against cost and speed.
- **Customer-centric Cultures.** Companies like Amazon and Zappos engineer cultures where every behavior ties back to serving the customer better. Employees are empowered to go the extra mile, to solve problems creatively, and to ensure the customer feels valued and cared for.

And then there's a fourth category: **no clear cultural type.** These companies simply exist. They have no defining behaviors, no intentional alignment, and no cultural discipline. In these organizations, the culture defaults to the loudest personalities or whatever habits emerge by accident. These companies rarely grow because employees don't know what's expected or valued.

What Treacy and Wiersema showed us is that the most successful companies don't just pick a strategy, but build cultures that support it. Strategy and culture are inseparable. The leader's job is to decide which cultural type aligns with their vision and then reinforce it through fundamentals and rituals.

Culture as a Marketing Advantage

Most companies treat culture as an internal matter. But in some industries, culture itself can become a differentiator in the marketplace.

Consider a company that provides safety professionals to construction sites. On the surface, it might seem hard to differentiate; safety staff are safety staff. But imagine that company hands a prospect a pocket-sized card listing their fundamentals: *Honor Commitments. Be a Fanatic About Response Time. Practice Blameless Problem-solving. Take Ownership.*

Now imagine the company saying, "This is how our people behave. This is what you can expect when you engage us."

That's powerful. It sets expectations, builds confidence, and positions the company as more reliable than competitors. In a world where most providers talk about services, this company talks about behavior. That's memorable. That's differentiating. And that's culture as a growth driver.

Reflection Checklist

Ask yourself and your leadership team:

1. Have we defined our culture in terms of specific behaviors (fundamentals) rather than vague values?
2. Do we have rituals to reinforce those fundamentals consistently?

3. Are exceptions tolerated, or do we hold everyone accountable to the same standards?
4. Do new employees learn our culture on day one?
5. Could we use our culture as a marketing differentiator by sharing our fundamentals externally?
6. Do our employees, customers, and vendors experience our culture consistently?
7. Does our cultural orientation align with our long-term strategy (product, efficiency, or customer)?

KEY TAKEAWAYS

- Culture isn't accidental; it's intentional, defined, and reinforced.
- Fundamentals are specific, actionable behaviors that remove ambiguity.
- Rituals keep fundamentals alive and consistent over time.
- Discipline matters: exceptions undermine the culture.
- Successful companies often align their culture type (product, efficiency, or customer) with their strategy.
- Strong, intentional cultures drive engagement, productivity, and growth.
- In some industries, culture itself can become a powerful marketing advantage.
- For deeper study, David J. Friedman's *Culture By Design* and his CultureWise framework offer outstanding tools and practices.

CHAPTER 10

COMMUNICATION THAT INSPIRES

In one company, the CEO made it a personal discipline to send a monthly newsletter to every employee. It wasn't ghostwritten. It wasn't a corporate memo filled with jargon. It was a letter: direct, personal, and authentic.

Each month, he highlighted accomplishments, celebrated anniversaries, and recognized individuals who had gone above and beyond. He reminded everyone of the company's goals and priorities, updated progress, and pointed out where focus was needed next. He even shared book and podcast recommendations. Employees came to look forward to that letter. It was more than words; it was leadership in action.

Internal communication like this builds alignment. It tells employees, "You matter, and here's where we're going together."

External communication matters just as much. I once drove past a lake in the Midwest and noticed a boat covered in a bright red tarp. On the tarp was a sign that read: "Uncover a clean boat in 60 seconds or less."

That simple phrase told buyers everything they needed to know: convenience (60 seconds), less effort (no scrubbing), and better experience (more time on the lake). Compare that to the typical sign: "Boat covers on sale" or "Most popular boat cover." Those focus on features. The red tarp focused on value.

These two stories—one internal, one external—illustrate a truth leaders cannot ignore: **communication is the bridge between vision and execution**. Done poorly, it disengages employees and confuses customers. Done well, it inspires people to act, aligns energy, and drives growth.

The State and Cost of Employee Engagement

Employee engagement is one of the most significant challenges leaders face. Optimistic research shows that:

- Roughly 30% of employees are engaged.
- About 50% are not engaged.
- Around 20% are actively disengaged.

Engaged employees buy into the mission, purpose, and success of the enterprise. They volunteer for projects, embrace training, and go the extra mile.

Non-engaged employees are "clock punchers." They show up, do their jobs, and go home. They don't disrupt, but they don't drive growth either.

Actively disengaged employees are toxic. They complain, criticize, and recruit others to their negativity. They wait for things to fail so they can say "I told you so," even though they didn't contribute ideas in the first place.

The financial cost of disengagement is staggering:

- **Gallup** estimates actively disengaged employees cost the world **$8.8 trillion annually** in lost productivity, 9% of global GDP.
- In the U.S. alone, disengagement costs **$450–$550 billion per year.**

- Disengaged employees are **37% more absent**, cause **60% more errors and defects**, and **49% more accidents.**
- Turnover driven by disengagement is costly, with replacing an employee costing **30%–150% of their salary** depending on the role.

On the flip side, companies with engaged employees:

- Outperform competitors by up to **202%.**
- See **20% higher productivity.**
- Report **10% higher customer ratings** and **20% higher sales.**

The conclusion is inescapable: disengagement is not a soft issue. It is a billion-dollar drain. And poor communication is often the root cause. Gallup has found that **over 50% of employees who quit voluntarily leave because of their supervisor.** They don't quit the company; they quit their boss.

Internal Communication that Inspires

Great leaders recognize that employees want to feel valued, informed, and connected. They want answers to four simple questions:

1. Where are we going?
2. How are we getting there?
3. Who is involved?
4. When do things have to happen?

Best practices to address these questions include:

- **Monthly CEO newsletters** recognize people, update goals, share insights.
- **Company yearbooks** can include photos, roles, and event highlights to build community.

- **Town halls** create transparency by letting employees ask questions and hear directly from leaders.
- **Ritual recognition** celebrate anniversaries, project completions, and personal milestones.

A real example comes from **Campbell Soup under CEO Doug Conant.** Facing declining performance and morale, Conant made employee engagement a priority. He sent over 30,000 handwritten thank-you notes during his tenure, recognizing individual contributions. He held leaders accountable for engagement scores. Over time, Campbell Soup's engagement levels soared, and the company rebounded.

The lesson is that internal communication isn't "extra." It's the foundation of engagement and performance.

External Communication that Inspires

If internal communication aligns employees, external communication attracts customers. Nearly every prospect will check a company's website before making contact. That first impression must resonate.

Yet too many companies confuse **features** with **value propositions.**

- Feature-driven: *"Fastest processor, 12-gig memory, aluminum body."*
- Value-driven: *"Work faster. Store more. Carry less."*

Buyers don't value features. They value convenience, fair and transparent pricing, great user experiences, and trust. Your communication must connect to those pillars.

Some classic examples:

- **FedEx:** "When it absolutely, positively has to be there overnight."

- **Geico:** "15 minutes could save you 15% or more on car insurance."
- **Dollar Shave Club:** "Shave time. Shave money."

These value propositions are simple, memorable, and buyer-focused.

The boat cover story proves you don't need a global brand to communicate well. A small company can inspire just as much by speaking to what buyers truly want.

StoryBrand and the Power of Framing

Donald Miller's StoryBrand framework offers a practical guide:

- The customer is the hero.
- The company is the guide.
- The customer has a problem.
- The guide offers a plan.
- The customer avoids failure and finds success.

When companies position themselves as the guide, not the hero, the message resonates. Customers don't want to hear, "We're the best." They want to hear, "We understand your challenge, here's how we'll help, and here's the success you'll experience."

That's why StoryBrand works. It aligns communication with the buyer's story, not the company's ego.

Sales Messaging and Elevator Pitches

External communication isn't limited to websites. Sales teams, proposals, and elevator pitches all carry the brand. Too often, pitches focus on the vendor: "We've been in business 25 years. We have X locations. We serve Y clients."

But customers are thinking: "How will you solve my problem? How will you make my life easier, cheaper, better, or safer?"

A powerful elevator pitch sounds like this: "We help business leaders align their teams, grow organically, and eliminate buyer excuses, so they can achieve growth without stress and chaos."

Notice the difference: it's about the customer's benefit, not the vendor's résumé.

Reflection Checklist

Ask yourself and your leadership team:

1. Do our employees know where the company is going and their role in getting there?
2. Do we regularly communicate progress, recognition, and direction?
3. Do we have a strategy for engaging non-engaged employees before they drift away?
4. Does our website clearly communicate a value proposition in five seconds or fewer?
5. Is our messaging framed around what buyers value: convenience, pricing, user experience, and trust?
6. Do our sales pitches and elevator pitches put the customer first, or us?
7. Are we consistently acting as the guide in the customer's story?

KEY TAKEAWAYS

- Internal communication drives engagement—and disengagement is a multi-billion-dollar problem.
- Gallup estimates disengagement costs the U.S. **$450–$550 billion annually.**

- Engaged employees drive **20% higher productivity** and **20% higher sales.**
- Simple practices like newsletters, recognition, and town halls inspire alignment.
- External communication must focus on value, not features.
- Great brands, big and small, win with clear, buyer-focused propositions.
- StoryBrand provides a powerful framework: the customer is the hero, the company is the guide.
- Sales messaging and elevator pitches must focus on benefits, not bragging rights.
- Communication that inspires aligns employees, attracts customers, and fuels growth.

CHAPTER 11

STAYING AHEAD

If you walk onto a car lot today, you'll see more than just one model on display. Automakers like Ford, Toyota, and Tesla know better than to offer a one-size-fits-all product. Instead, they provide a spectrum of choices: economy cars for buyers who prioritize price, hybrids and electrics for those who value efficiency, luxury trims for customers seeking status and experience, and rugged SUVs or trucks for buyers who trust performance and durability.

This goes beyond marketing and into diversification, designed to meet the different value systems that drive customer decisions. Some people lead with price, others with convenience, others with the user experience of the product, and still others with trust in safety, reliability, or reputation. By offering multiple options, automakers capture more customers and make it harder for competitors to lure them away.

Amazon takes this idea to another level. Known as "the everything store," Amazon has built its empire by ensuring that no matter what a customer values (lowest price, fastest delivery, highest quality, or niche selection), there's always an option available. The sheer breadth of its offerings is itself a competitive moat. A customer looking for running shoes, for instance, doesn't just find one pair on Amazon—they find dozens. Some cheaper, some premium, some designed for convenience (next-day Prime shipping), others positioned for trust (hundreds of positive reviews). Amazon knows that buyers come with different value systems, and they've structured their marketplace to meet all of them.

The Cheese Lesson

I once wrote about this idea using a simple metaphor: cheese.

At its most basic, cheese is sold in block-form as the lowest-cost option. But while a block of cheese is cheap, it's not convenient when you need it shredded, sliced, or cubed. That's why grocery stores offer variations. They've diversified the product: pre-sliced, shredded, cubed, individually wrapped, organic, imported, and so on.

Each option speaks to a different buyer's priorities. For some, it's price. For others, it's convenience (saving time and effort). For others, it's experience (fine imported cheese for a wine pairing). For still others, it's trust (organic, hormone-free). The same product, cheese, becomes multiple products when diversified to meet the four pillars of buyer psychology.

The lesson is clear: when companies diversify their offerings, they capture more customers by aligning with individual value systems.

Diversification as Innovation

Product diversification is not separate from innovation; it *is* innovation.

- **Uber** began as a luxury black car service, but soon diversified into UberX (affordable rides), Uber Pool (shared rides), Uber Eats (food delivery), and even Uber Freight. By expanding its options, Uber appealed to more value systems: convenience, price, and user experience.

- **Netflix** started with DVDs by mail, then shifted to streaming, then invested in original content. Each shift expanded its reach and reinforced its position.
- **Airlines** diversify through cabin classes: economy, premium economy, business, and first class. Each level appeals to a different buyer, ensuring the airline captures a wide range of travelers.

Diversification makes companies harder to beat. A competitor might match one offering, but matching the full range is much more difficult.

Innovation and R&D

Innovation doesn't always mean inventing something brand new. Too many companies confuse innovation with invention. Invention is rare—a breakthrough idea like the iPhone or the airplane. Innovation, on the other hand, can be small and incremental, but it's the accumulation of those small improvements that sustains growth.

Innovation happens when you:

- Cut time or effort from a process (Amazon's "1-Click" ordering).
- Make something simpler or easier (Southwest's boarding process).
- Take costs out without sacrificing quality (Walmart's supply chain).
- Make the user experience better (Apple's design and ecosystem).
- Build greater trust (Costco's no-questions-asked return policy).

These are not radical inventions. They are disciplined innovations, constant refinements that align products and services with what buyers truly value.

Toyota revolutionized manufacturing not through a single invention, but through constant innovation. Their famous "andon cord" empowered any worker to stop the assembly line if they saw a defect. That single practice embedded continuous improvement into the culture. Small, incremental innovations, like reducing errors, saving time, improving quality, compounded into a system admired worldwide. Toyota proved that innovation isn't just about new products, but about empowering people to make things simpler, easier, better, and more trustworthy every day.

Intelligence Gathering for Innovation

Where do these ideas come from? Often, from the people closest to the customer.

- **Sales teams** hear directly from buyers about obstacles and frustrations.
- **Customer service staff** see patterns in complaints and requests.
- **Frontline employees** often know where processes break down.
- **Customers themselves** will tell you *if* you ask the right questions.

Too often, companies ask: "How can we grow our business with you?" It's the wrong question. Customers don't exist to help you grow. A few more targeted questions are:

- "How can we make buying from us simpler and easier?"
- "How can we save you time?"
- "How can we make your experience better?"

These questions uncover opportunities for innovation. They shift the focus from the seller's needs to the buyer's needs; the exact shift that leads to organic growth.

Companies like Toyota have built systems for this. Their famous "andon cord" allows any employee to stop the assembly line if they spot a problem. This practice promotes innovation over time, driven by the intelligence of employees closest to the work.

The Risk of Standing Still

The danger of failing to innovate or diversify is simple: competitors will do it for you.

- Blockbuster assumed DVDs and late fees would keep them profitable. Netflix innovated with streaming and subscription models.
- The taxi industry assumed medallions and local control made them untouchable. Uber innovated with apps, ratings, and transparency.
- Sears once dominated American retail. Today, it's a cautionary tale, while Amazon—always diversifying and innovating—sits at the top.

Customers reward the companies that evolve around convenience, price, user experience, and trust. Those that don't eventually lose.

Reflection Checklist

Ask yourself and your leadership team:

1. Do we offer enough product or service options to appeal to different buyer value systems?
2. Are we gathering intelligence from sales, service, and customers to identify new opportunities?

3. Are we innovating consistently in convenience, pricing, user experience, and trust, or waiting for rare breakthroughs?
4. Do we have a formal or informal R&D function dedicated to monitoring competitors, technology, and customer needs?
5. Are we constantly finding ways to remove buyer excuses or leaving gaps for competitors to exploit?

KEY TAKEAWAYS

- Staying ahead requires both diversification and innovation.
- Buyers have different value systems; multiple options ensure more customers say yes.
- Innovation is often incremental by making things simpler, easier, cheaper, or more trustworthy.
- Intelligence gathering is the lifeblood of innovation. Customers and employees know where improvements are needed.
- Companies that fail to innovate or diversify invite competitors to take their place.
- Sustained organic growth comes from constantly evolving around the four pillars.

CHAPTER 12

THE GROWTH CODE IN ACTION

By now, the pattern should be clear. Growth isn't random. It doesn't come from luck, or from shouting louder than the competition. Sustainable, organic growth comes from aligning your company around the principles buyers value most—what I call **The Growth Code.**

At the center of the Growth Code are **The Four Pillars**:

1. **Convenience.** Buyers want things to be simple, easy, effortless and fast. Whether it's one-click ordering from Amazon or an Uber arriving in minutes, convenience removes friction and earns loyalty.
2. **Price.** Price matters, but it's not only about being the cheapest. Buyers want pricing that is competitive, fair, and above all *transparent***.** Hidden fees and surprises destroy trust. Companies that win on price make it clear what something costs and why it's worth it.
3. **User Experience.** Every touchpoint (buying, using, and receiving support) shapes the customer's experience. Clean stores, intuitive websites, responsive service, and proactive communication all send the message of "We value you." User experience is where companies have the most control, and the best seize that opportunity.

4. **Trust.** Buyers want confidence that they will get what's promised, or what they perceive they're buying. Trust is built through guarantees, warranties, testimonials, and recourse when things go wrong. Without trust, nothing else matters.

The best companies constantly improve on these four pillars, *eliminating excuses* for customers to go elsewhere.

Beyond the Pillars

But the Growth Code is more than the four pillars. Pillars are the foundation; they hold up the house. To build a house that lasts, you also need supporting structure disciplines that ensure the pillars remain strong.

- **Strategic Planning.** A clear vision and aligned initiatives keep everyone rowing in the same direction. Without strategy, priorities differ and companies drift.
- **Culture.** Intentional, disciplined cultures—defined by fundamentals and rituals—ensure that everyone behaves consistently in ways that drive growth.
- **Leadership as Coaching.** Managers direct, mentors teach, but coaches inspire. The best leaders uncover values, challenge limiting beliefs, and influence without relying on authority.
- **Communication.** Inspiring companies communicate clearly inside and out. Internally, they engage employees and reduce disengagement costs. Externally, they tell stories that connect to what buyers' value.
- **Staying Ahead.** Growth requires constant innovation, diversification, and intelligence gathering. Standing still is a recipe for being outflanked.

When the four pillars are reinforced by these disciplines, companies become resilient. Competitors may copy a product or lower a price, but it's much harder to replicate a system where everything (product, people, and processes) is aligned around growth.

A CEO's Checklist for Growth

Use this checklist to evaluate where you stand today:

The Four Pillars

- Are we making it simple, easy, fast and effortless for customers to buy from us?
- Is our pricing competitive and transparent?
- Do customers consistently leave with better user experience than they expected?
- Can customers trust us to deliver what we promise and what they expect?

The Disciplines

- Do we have a written strategic plan with clear initiatives and ownership?
- Have we defined and reinforced our cultural fundamentals, acceptable behaviors, and rituals?
- Are our leaders acting more as coaches than as task managers?
- Are we communicating effectively inside (engaging employees) and outside (clear value propositions)?
- Are we innovating constantly and diversifying our offerings to match customer value systems?

A Final Word

The Growth Code is not a secret formula reserved for a few. It is visible in every company that dominates its market. They may not call it by this name, but they live it: they make life easier, price fairly, create user experiences people love, and earn trust. They align strategy, culture, leadership, communication, and innovation to reinforce those pillars every day.

The question is not whether the code works. The question is whether you will apply it.

Growth is not an accident. It is a discipline. It is a choice. And now, you have the framework.

The only thing left is to put it into action.

30-Day Action Plan: Cracking the Growth Code in Your Company

Week 1: Identify Competitors and Alternatives

- List your **top three direct competitors**.
- Include any **do-it-yourself alternatives** customers might choose instead.

Week 2: Compare Across the Four Pillars

- Evaluate yourself and competitors on:
    1. **Convenience** – Simple, easy, fast?
    2. **Price** – Competitive and transparent?
    3. **User Experience** – Memorable buying and product experience?
    4. **Trust** – Confidence in promises delivered?
- Note where competitors are stronger.

Week 3: Diagnose the Gaps

- Pinpoint where you rank lower and identify the buyer excuses this creates.

Week 4: Build Your Strategic Plan

- Choose 2–3 priorities to strengthen weak pillars over the next 6–12 months.

- Assign ownership, set metrics, and create timelines.

Beyond 30 Days: The 90-Day Growth Roadmap

Once you've benchmarked and set priorities, move into building the foundation.

Days 31–60: Leadership & Culture

- Begin **leadership development**, moving managers toward coaching behaviors.
- Define 5–7 **cultural fundamentals** (specific behaviors, not vague values).
- Start reinforcing one fundamental per week through rituals (meetings, shout-outs, recognition).

Days 61–90: Messaging & Engagement

- Audit **internal communication**: newsletters, updates, 1:1s, recognition. Ask: are employees engaged, in-the-know, and inspired?
- Audit **external messaging**: website, sales decks, pitches. Ensure your value proposition emphasizes the Four Pillars and follows a StoryBrand structure.
- Start aligning both internal and external messaging around clarity and inspiration.

6–12 Month Outlook: Embedding the Growth Code

- **Leadership:** Train leaders consistently on the 5 Coaching Steps; build peer coaching into leadership rhythms.
- **Culture:** Roll out a full CultureWise-style system of fundamentals and rituals, non-negotiable and lived daily.
- **Strategic Planning:** Review and update quarterly; adapt as markets shift (pandemics, tariffs, technology).
- **Innovation:** Formalize R&D and customer feedback loops; schedule quarterly competitor reviews.

- **Communication:** Launch refined messaging campaigns internally and externally.

Final Thought

Growth is not a one-time project. It's a discipline. The Four Pillars are your foundation, but leadership, culture, communication, planning, and innovation are the structures that sustain them. Start with 30 days of clarity, extend to 90 days of foundation-building, and commit to a year of embedding the Growth Code across your company.

You might find it advantageous to have a coach or consultant help guide you as finding internal resources to drive the process and provide accountability might prove difficult or costly.

The companies that dominate their markets don't just crack the code once. They live it, refine it, and protect it every day.

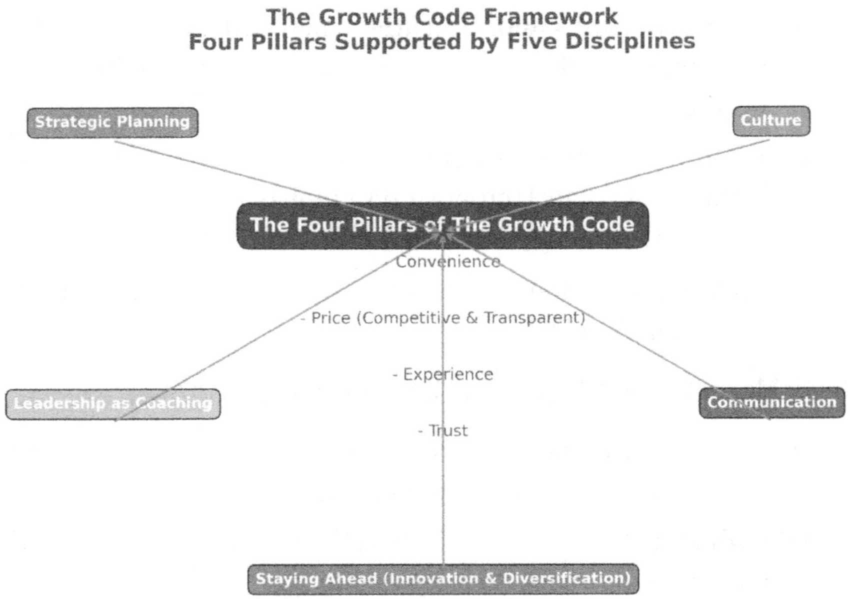

JIM BRAMLETT BIOGRAPHY

With a career spanning over 40 years in the transportation and logistics industry, I have had the opportunity to wear many hats and contribute to the success of various businesses. A serial entrepreneur at heart, I have founded several companies, started new operating divisions for companies and created a multitude of new service offerings.

Most recently, as a Chair for Vistage, I've become an executive coach, guiding and challenging leaders to new heights.

I have also authored two other books, "The Unconventional Thinking of Dominant Companies" and "Stop The Hassle: Simplify, Satisfy & Succeed", providing insights into how businesses can organically grow and dominate their respective markets My entrepreneurial journey and expertise in business growth strategy and logistics have earned me recognition in the industry I frequently share my insights on these topics as a speaker at various events, providing valuable knowledge to the audience.

I currently reside in the Kansas City area, where I continue to explore new business avenues and contribute to the business community's growth. When I'm not wearing my business hat, you'll find me sharing my expertise in business growth strategy and logistics or speaking at events. I call the Kansas City area home.

Made in the USA
Monee, IL
04 November 2026

67384077R00056

A TREATISE

UPON

THE LAW OF EXTRADITION.

WITH

THE CONVENTIONS UPON THE SUBJECT EXISTING BETWEEN ENGLAND AND FOREIGN NATIONS, AND THE CASES DECIDED THEREON.

BY

EDWARD CLARKE,

OF LINCOLN'S INN, BARRISTER-AT-LAW, AND LATE TANCRED STUDENT.

SECOND EDITION.

LONDON:

STEVENS AND HAYNES,

Law Publishers,

BELL YARD, TEMPLE BAR.

1874.

TO

THE GOVERNORS OF THE TANCRED TRUST

This Book

IS WITH ALL RESPECT DEDICATED

BY

THEIR OBLIGED AND FAITHFUL SERVANT,

EDWARD CLARKE.

PREFACE TO THE SECOND EDITION.

SINCE the First Edition of this work was published the law of Great Britain with regard to Extradition has been greatly altered, and several new Conventions have been made with foreign States. That Edition was received with great favour both in this country and in the United States, and was long ago exhausted. In the task of revising the work and adapting it to the present state of the law, I have been much hindered by other engagements, and the delays, for which I alone am responsible, have severely taxed the patience of my publishers. I have, however, spared no pains to make the present volume what I hope and believe my legal brethren will find it—a complete and trustworthy exposition of the law of Great Britain, Canada, France, and the United States, upon a subject of great and of increasing importance.

EDWARD CLARKE.

3, *Garden Court, Temple,*
July 1874.

PREFACE TO THE FIRST EDITION

The Law of Extradition has, until very recently, attracted little attention in England. Various circumstances have of late brought it into frequent public discussion, and it seems advisable that the information upon the subject should be gathered into a convenient form. Several cases, three of them of great importance, have lately been decided in the English Courts; and during a Parliamentary discussion which took place a few months ago, Lord Stanley assured the House of Commons that an opportunity would be afforded next Session for a full and deliberate consideration of the whole subject. The only English book expressly devoted to it is a small pamphlet, published twenty years ago, by Mr. Charles Egan. This pamphlet, written soon after the treaties with the United States and France were concluded, never pretended to be in any sense a text-book, and has long ceased to be of practical utility. Some valuable remarks upon the question were contained in a pamphlet published by the late Sir George Cornewall Lewis in 1859, but he referred almost exclusively to the theory of the subject. No attempt has hitherto been made to collect and compare the cases decided in England and the countries with which in this matter she is most closely connected.

Having been engaged in the three most recent cases in England, I have given a good deal of study to the subject, and I venture to hope that the results of that study, extended for the sake of completeness to the laws of America and France, may not only be useful to the members of my own profession, but may help the public to understand, and the Legislature satisfactorily to deal with, a question which becomes every year of more importance to the world.

EDWARD CLARKE.

3, *Pump Court, Temple,*
December 1, 1866.

CONTENTS.

APPENDIX.

TABLE OF CASES.

A TREATISE

UPON

THE LAW OF EXTRADITION.

CHAPTER I.

THEORY OF THE SUBJECT.

THE subject of extradition has been discussed far more in its political than in its legal aspects. National interest, prejudice, or passion has always governed the deliberations of senates, and has sometimes affected the decisions of the courts. An attempt is made in this volume to ascertain the true principles of the question, and, as briefly as correctness will permit, to trace the history of the law in the United States, England, Canada, and France, and to indicate the rules of practice observed in each of those countries.

In discussion upon this subject it has been often said that the majority of jurists deny the existence of any right to demand extradition. That this assertion is incorrect will be seen by an examination of the opinions of some of the most eminent of early or recent writers.

Beginning with the great jurist who may be considered the founder of modern public law, we find Grotius expressing a very clear opinion as to the existence of this duty :—

"Punishment, as we have said, according to the natural law, may be inflicted by any one who is not open to the like charge; though, no doubt, it is in conformity with civil institutions that the delicts of individuals with regard to their own community should be left to that community, and to its rulers, to be punished or passed over, as they choose. But there is not the same full power left to them in delicts which in any way pertain to human society in general; for these other states may prosecute, as in particular states there is a prosecutor of certain offences which any one may put in motion; and much less have they such power in offences by which another state or its rulers are specially assailed, and in which, consequently, the state or the ruler have, on account of their dignity or security, a right of executing punishment as we have said. This right is not to be impeded by the state in which the offender lives, or its rulers.

"But as states are not accustomed to permit another state to enter their territory armed for the sake of executing punishment, nor is that expedient, it follows that the city where he abides who is found to have committed the offence ought to do one of two things—either itself, being called upon, it should punish the guilty man, or it should leave him to be dealt with by the party which makes the demand; for this is what is meant by giving up, so often spoken of in history. . . . . All which passages, however, are to be understood, that the people or king are not strictly bound to give up the person, but, as we have said, to punish him. . . . . It is a disjunctive obligation." (Bk. ii. c. 21, §§ 3, 4.)

Vattel lays down the same principle of a duty, either to punish the fugitive criminal or to deliver him up to the injured state, in very explicit terms, and adds:

"This is pretty generally observed with respect to great crimes, which are equally contrary to the laws and safety of all nations. Assassins, incendiaries, and robbers are seized everywhere, at the desire of the sovereign in whose territories the crime was committed, and are delivered up to his justice. The matter is carried still further in states that are more closely connected by friendship and good neighbourhood. Even in cases of ordinary transgressions, which are only subjects of civil prosecution, either with a view to the recovery of damages, or the infliction of a slight civil punishment, the subjects of two neighbouring states are reciprocally obliged to appear before the magistrate of the place where they are accused of having failed in their duty. Upon a requisition of that magistrate, called 'letters rogatory,' they are summoned in due form by their own magistrates, and obliged to appear. An admirable institution, by means of which many neighbouring states live together in peace, and seem to form only one republic." (Bk. ii. § 76.)

The principal authority quoted against the existence

of this right is Pufendorf.* The citation, however, is erroneous, as will be seen from the following passages:—

"Among the several ways the governors of a commonwealth are involved in wars from the injuries committed by their subjects, these two, I think, will most deserve

* Story says ('Conflict of Laws,' p. 879) that "Pufendorf explicitly denies it as a matter of right." But in the edition of 1865 this note is appended:—"For this reference to Pufendorf's opinion I must rely on Burlamaqui (part 4, c. 3, §§ 23, 24), not having been able to find it in his 'Treatise on the Law of Nations.' The only reference to the point which I have met with in that work is in book viii. c. 3, §§ 23, 24." In this statement and note there are four errors. Pufendorf does not explicitly deny the right. Burlamaqui does not say so. The passage, book viii. c. 3, §§ 23, 24, does not relate to the matter at all. The passage given in the text, book viii. c. 6, § 12, does expressly refer to it. Sir G. C. Lewis corrected part of the error, and referred to the proper section in the sixth chapter of Pufendorf's eighth book. But, strangely enough, he referred to that passage as an authority for the statement that Pufendorf holds that a state is only bound by treaty engagements, or by some special circumstance, to surrender a fugitive criminal, a proposition which the passage he quotes does not support in the least ('On Foreign Jurisdiction,' &c., 37). Story's mistake has been copied with persistent carelessness. In Wheaton (edition 1863), Phillimore (1854), and Fœlix, the reference to Pufendorf is 'Elementa,' lib. viii. c. 3, §§ 23, 24. In Kent (1854) and Halleck (1861) no reference to Pufendorf is given. Woolsey (1864) gives no references at all. Egan was content to quote Story without verifying. The references of Wheaton, Phillimore, and Fœlix are incorrect. The book Pufendorf published in 1660, entitled "Elementorum Jurisprudentiæ Universalis libri ii." (Cambridge, 1672), only contains two books; the first comprising twenty-one definitions; the second, two axioms and five observations. Of course, no such passage as 'lib. viii. c. 3, §§ 23, 24' can be found in it. The true reference to Pufendorf is given in the text.

our consideration—viz., sufferance and reception. . . . . The guilt of a crime before it hath been judicially tried remains upon them who commit it; but after sentence is passed upon it, they are the criminals who neglect to put the law in execution. The case of reception, and how far the commonwealth gives reason for war against itself by receiving and defending persons who have injured others, may be seen at large in Grot., lib. ii. c. 21, §§ 3, 4, 5, 6." *

The only passage which can possibly be quoted in support of the assertion that Pufendorf denies the duty of extradition, is to be found in the least known of all his works, the treatise, "De Officio Hominis et Civis juxta Legem Naturalem." After saying that a sovereign state is presumed to have power over its subjects, and that knowingly suffering them to commit crimes it shares their guilt; he adds, that the liability to war which a state incurs when it receives and protects fugitive criminals arises rather from special compact than from any general obligation.†

This is very far short of a denial of the duty of extra-

* 'Law of Nature and Nations' (bk. viii. c. 6, § 12). Trans. by Basil Kennett, D.D., Lond. 1749. "Circa receptum autem, et quatenus civitas causam belli contra se præbeat, recipiendo et defendendo eos qui in alios deliquerunt, plene docet." Grotius, d. 1, §§ 3, 4, 5, 6. 'De Jure Naturæ et Gentium.' Ed. Hertius and Barbeyrac. Frankfort and Leipsic, 1744.

† "Ut tamen qui noxium ad se confugientem pœnæ duntaxat declinandæ causa recepit et protegit, bello peti possit: id magis ex peculiari pacto inter vicinos et socios, quam communi aliqua obligatione provenit; nisi iste profugus apud nos hostilia in eam civitatem quam deseruit machinetur." (Lib. ii. c. 16.)

dition; but upon this Burlamaqui says that it was without sufficient reason that Pufendorf made this qualification, and that the rule laid down by Grotius is well established. He himself calls it, "une obligation commune et indispensable." *

Paul Voet is another publicist whose authority has been quoted in favour of considering the rendition of criminals a matter strictly of comity, not of right. It is clear, from his writings, that the passages which have been made to bear this interpretation were caused by his strong opinion in favour of the right of any magistrate to try a criminal found in his jurisdiction, wherever the crime may have been committed. He holds that the magistrate is bound to punish such crimes; that they must be judged by the laws of the place where they were committed; but that, in assigning punishment, the magistrate is not bound to consider either the criminal's domicile, or the place of the crime. He should punish according to the quality of the fault, and the nature of the punishment imposed on that fault in his territory; and if this be not sufficient, the criminal may be given up to the foreign magistrate. By the civil law he must be given up. But now this is hardly ever done, "nisi ex humanitate," and then with letters rogatory, to save the local jurisdiction. (Lib. ii. c. 1.)

Lord Coke's opinion is clearly against the duty of sur-

* 'Principes du Droit de la Nature et des Gens.' Par J. J. Burlamaqui. Ed. Dupin. Paris, 1821. 5 vols. 'Droit des Gens' (part 4, c. 3, § 9).

render. "It is holden, and so it hath been resolved, that divided kingdoms under several kings, in league one with another, are sanctuaries for servants or subjects flying for safety from one kingdom to another; and, upon demand made by them, are not, by the laws and liberties of kingdoms, to be delivered; and this, some say, is grounded upon the law in Deuteronomy, Non trades servum domino suo qui ad te confugerit." (3d Inst., p. 180.) He then gives three instances. But it must be remarked upon this, that the words do not seem to apply to offenders against the criminal law; that the instances he gives are those of political offenders; and that there is no trace of any such resolution as he speaks of in the case of a fugitive criminal.* It must be added, that this dictum does

* "And I scarce understand Lord Coke's doctrine on this point, that foreign kingdoms, even when in league with one another, are sanctuaries for any subjects flying from one to another. How has he supported it? He says, 'It is holden, and so it hath been resolved,' but he neither tells us *when* nor *where* it was resolved. His examples from history are far from proving the point. The first, from Queen Elizabeth's time, shows good political reasons why her demands were not complied with, because she had before done what she complained of. That from Henry VIII. does not seem to prove anything, and that about Pool, the Earl of Suffolk, proves (if anything) the point I am contending for, and consequently is in the teeth of Lord Coke's own assertion."—*Wynne, Eunomus*, Dialogue iii. § 67. Wynne goes on to say that the assertion is directly against the law of nations, and that if a special treaty be made, it operates as a recognition, not a creation, of right. In the judgment in Commonwealth *v.* Deacon, 10 Serj. and Rawl. (U.S.) 145, Chief Justice Tilghman quoted Coke and Wynne's comment, and

not appear ever to have been used as an authority in an English court. Martens says that the extradition of criminals is not a matter of perfect obligation in a free state, whether the criminal be a subject of the state on which the demand is made, or of that which makes it, or of a third state. "Mais l'extradition d'un étranger sujet de l'état qui la reclame pour un crime commis chez lui ou même contre lui, quoique non fondée dans la rigueur de la loi naturelle, s'accorde plus fréquemment soit en vertu de traités, soit même par une simple déférence ou moyennant des réversales; surtout lorsque l'individu se trouve au service de cet état."—*Précis du Droit des Gens,* lib. iii. c. 3, § 101.

This is only a very qualified denial of the right, which, on the other hand, is asserted in express terms by Rutherforth.

"What remains, therefore, for the nation to do is what the injured nation has a right to demand. He ought to be delivered up to those against whom the crime is committed, that they may punish him within their own territories. This is the right. But how far a nation that has been injured in itself or in its members will choose either to insist on this right at first by demanding the criminal,

added, "Although Lord Coke was as great a common lawyer as England ever produced, yet certainly he was not equally proficient in his knowledge of equity or of the law of nations. Perhaps indeed his attachment to the common law gave him a prejudice against all others. Yet when he says a matter has been resolved, I should think he might be relied on, for he certainly was not apt to speak without book."

or to support it afterwards by force if the demand be not complied with, depends upon its own discretion." (Bk. ii. c. 9, § 12.)

The two great jurists of America are in accord upon this subject, for there can be no reason why the opinion of Story upon the operation of a law of extradition among the States of the Union should not be applied to the more general question. He says:—

"However the point may be as to foreign nations, it cannot be questioned that it is of vital importance to the public administration of criminal justice, and the security of the respective states, that criminals who have committed crimes therein should not find an asylum in other states, but should be surrendered up for trial and punishment. It is a power most salutary in its general operation, by discouraging crime, and cutting off the chances of escape from punishment. It will promote harmony and good feelings among the states, and it will increase the general sense of the blessings of the national government. It will, moreover, give strength to the great moral duty which neighbouring states especially owe to each other, by elevating the policy of the mutual suppression of crime into a legal obligation. Hitherto it has proved as useful in practice as it is unexceptionable in its character." ('Story on the Constitution,' § 1803.)

Kent quotes the opinions of Grotius, Vattel, and others, and then adds:—

"The language of these authorities is clear and explicit, and the law and usage of nations as declared by them rests upon the plainest principles of justice. It is the duty of the government to surrender up fugitives upon demand, after the civil magistrate shall have ascertained the existence of reasonable ground for the charge, and sufficient to put the accused upon his trial. The guilty party cannot be tried and punished by any other jurisdiction than the one whose laws have been violated, and therefore the duty of surrendering him applies as well to the case of the subject of the state surrendering as to the case of a subject of the power demanding the fugitives." ('Commentaries,' ed. 1854, p. 40.)

To these citations may be added the opinions of three Englishmen, all, from their position and character, entitled to be listened to upon such a subject.

Lord Brougham said in the House of Lords on the 14th of February 1842:—"He thought the interests of justice required, and the rights of good neighbourhood required, that in two countries bordering upon one another, as the United States and Canada, and even that in England, and in the European countries of France, Holland, and Belgium, there ought to be laws on both sides giving power, under due regulations and safeguards, to each government to secure persons who have committed offences in the territory of one and taken refuge in the territory of the other. He could hardly imagine how nations could maintain the relationship which ought to exist between one civilized country and another without some such power."

Lord Campbell, upon the same occasion, said: "For

his own part, he would like to see some general law enacted, and held binding on all states, that each should surrender to the demands of the others all persons charged with serious offences except political. This, however, he feared, was a rule or law which it would be difficult to get all nations to concur in." *

And in the most valuable of his works Sir George Cornewall Lewis thus laid down the increasing obligation of the duty :—

"A customs league (such as the German Zollverein) and treaties of international postage, copyright, and the extradition of criminals, afford other instances of an infraction of the principle of national exclusiveness, and of an approximation to the formation of all nations into a combined political system. These examples will suffice to show the close connexion which subsists between the progress of civilisation and the relaxation of the national principle, so as to render it consistent with a more enlarged principle of association." ('Methods of Observation and Reasoning in Politics,' ii. 454.)

It has been said by some recent writers that the existence of any duty of extradition is negatived by the treaties which have been made upon the subject. This clearly is a *non sequitur;* a treaty may often be necessary to regulate and limit the performance of a duty of undisputed obligation; and that the granting of extradition is, if not scientifically speaking a matter of perfect obligation, at least a duty of public morality, has not been denied by any

* 60 Hansard, 319, 325.

writer worth notice. It is evident that the reasons assigned by early writers for the performance of this duty have in the progress of society been constantly acquiring greater weight. The complexity of business transactions, the vast extension of credit, the general use of paper-money of various kinds, all make it easy for a modern criminal to commit a fraud which may cause far more wide-spread misery than a similar act could formerly have produced, and to insure at least a few hours' concealment of his guilt. And other improvements—the use of steam, the multiplication of means of locomotion—make it easy for him in those few hours to effect his escape to a foreign country. While the duty of extradition has thus been increasing in weight, the general tendency of European legislation has been to take from the sovereign the right to grant the surrender by his own prerogative. It has thus been found necessary to make provision by treaty or legislative enactment for the performance of this duty; and in no country but England has this been found difficult. In England, however, objections have constantly been raised to the acts and treaties proposed. So far as the objectors bring forward any reason beyond rhetorical and quite inapplicable disquisitions upon national independence, they rely chiefly upon the possibility that a treaty may be abused for the purpose of procuring the rendition of political offenders. That question will be discussed in a later chapter; here it is sufficient to say that no treaty can prevent its own infraction. If a nation cannot be trusted, no treaty is of any use; if it can, it is very easy to agree upon provisions by which the desires of both parties may be met.

It has been recently suggested that, instead of granting the extradition of criminals, the domestic law should be extended to crimes committed abroad. But for this suggestion, the subject of extra-territorial jurisdiction in criminal matters would hardly be worth discussion in England. True it is that many of the Continental states punish crimes committed in other countries by their own subjects, or even by foreigners, and to some slight extent England has adopted the practice. But there are two answers to the argument that its extension would be a substitute for laws of extradition. In the first place, it does not remove the evil. The being made a resort for foreign malefactors is as great a mischief to any country as the escape of offenders against its own laws. The extradition treaty between England and France, for instance, is intended to remedy both these evils. No extension of extra-territorial jurisdiction could have the same effect. Neither country could reclaim its criminals, and Englishmen would wisely think that it was very little advantage to them to be able to try a Frenchman for crimes with which England had nothing to do, or to know that if witnesses were sent over to Paris, the English fugitive might possibly be punished there for the fraud committed in London. The other objection to the system is, that it is ineffective and unjust. It is an indisputable principle of English jurisprudence that crime must be tried by the law of the place at which it was committed; our tribunals would therefore have to administer foreign laws. The expense of prosecution, always heavy, would become prohibitive if witnesses had to be conveyed to a foreign country; and, most serious objection of all, in the great majority of cases, it would be impossible for an innocent man, so accused, to obtain the evidence which he might require for his defence.

From the passages just quoted, and many others of similar import, the following conclusions may be drawn:—

The surrender of fugitive criminals is an international duty. It may not be so plainly a matter of right that the refusal to grant it should subject a nation to the penalty of war, but such refusal is so clearly injurious to the country which refuses, and to the whole world, that it is a serious violation of the moral obligations which exist between civilised communities.

In former times, the surrender was granted by a sovereign in virtue of his own prerogative; but the recent course of European legislation has been to restrain this prerogative, and to cast upon the legislature of a country the task of providing for the performance of this duty.

This provision should be guarded by the exclusion of political offenders, and the requirement of some evidence of guilt before the accused person is delivered up. It would be wise also to restrict the crimes for which surrender should be granted, according to the facility with which criminals could escape from one country to another; but to refuse to make provision at all, would be to inflict an injury upon the whole world, and especially upon the country so refusing.

The surrender, when so restricted, involves no interference with national independence, as the duty of punishing the crime could not be effectively and justly performed by any nation but that whose laws have been broken.

For the only substitute for extradition which has been proposed—the extension of extra-territorial jurisdiction—is contrary to sound and well-established principles of law, is inconvenient in its enforcement, obstructs the course of justice by making the prosecution of crime difficult and expensive, and is unjust to the accused by making it almost impossible for an innocent man to produce the confutation of the charge; thus combining the gravest defects possible in a system of criminal jurisprudence.

CHAPTER II.

EARLY TREATIES AND CASES.

WITHOUT some history of the practice of extradition, so far as it existed, in early times, this book would be incomplete; but the materials for such a history are very scanty, and the few instances produced by different writers in proof or disproof of the duty of rendition are in most cases of doubtful application. The historic origin of the practice is to be found in the relations of the different provinces of the Roman Empire. Under the Republic, a Roman citizen accused of a capital offence might, at any time before decision was pronounced, escape the sentence by going into voluntary exile; and certain of the allied cities were specified by treaty as inviolable places of refuge.* Under the Empire these cities were absorbed into the imperial dominions, and lost their protective character. Few passages of Gibbon have been more often and more deservedly quoted than the splendid sentences in which he described the wide-reaching power of the imperial government:—

"The division of Europe," he says, "into a number of

* Gibbon, 'Decline and Fall,' v. 296; Merivale, 'History of the Romans under the Empire,' iii. 496.

independent states, connected however with each other by the general resemblance of religion, language, and manners, is productive of the most beneficial consequences to the liberty of mankind. A modern tyrant, who should find no resistance either in his own breast or in his people, would soon experience a gentle restraint from the example of his equals, the dread of present censure, the advice of his allies, and the apprehension of his enemies. The object of his displeasure, escaping from the narrow limits of his dominions, would easily obtain, in a happier climate, a secure refuge, a new fortune adequate to his merit, the freedom of complaint, and perhaps the means of revenge. But the empire of the Romans filled the world, and when that empire fell into the hands of a single person, the world became a safe and dreary prison for his enemies. The slave of imperial despotism, whether he was compelled to drag his gilded chain in Rome and the senate, or to wear out a life of exile on the barren rock of Seriphus, or the frozen banks of the Danube, expected his fate in silent despair. To resist was fatal, and it was impossible to fly. On every side he was encompassed with a vast extent of sea and land, which he could never hope to traverse without being discovered, seized, and restored to his irritated master."*

So far, however, as regarded claims of extradition made by the Romans upon independent nations, they seem to have been confined to enemies of the state. Thus, at the end of the war with Antiochus, King of Syria, the Romans

* 'Decline and Fall,' c. 3, *ad fin.*

stipulated by treaty for the delivery up of Hannibal and four Greeks who had been instrumental in promoting the war. Hannibal, however, then escaped.* He was afterwards demanded of the King of Bithynia, and the demand conceded; but he escaped the surrender by death.†

The Roman law, however, required the surrender of citizens who offered violence to foreign ambassadors on Roman territory. Under this law two Romans were surrendered to the Apolloniatæ in 266 B.C., and two others to the Carthaginians in 188 B.C.‡

In the early cases found in modern history, it was always for political offences that the surrender was claimed; indeed, at a time when the transactions of life were comparatively simple, crime was so easily detected, and the criminal had so few means of escape, that there was no necessity for those provisions which the complicated civilisation of the world now renders necessary.

A few treaties have been quoted by writers upon extradition, either as recognitions of the duty, or in disproval of the right. By a treaty concluded as early as 1174, between Henry II. of England and William of Scotland, it was agreed, that if any persons guilty of felony in England should fly into Scotland, they should be immediately seized, and either be tried in the King of Scot-

* Polyb., xxi. 14, xxii. 26.

† Livy, xxxix. 51.

‡ Dig. 50, 5, 17. Rein. 'Criminalrecht der Römer,' p. 175–6. Quoted by Sir G. C. Lewis, 'On Foreign Jurisdiction,' p. 51.

land's courts, or delivered up to the justices of England, and *vice versâ*.*

By the treaty of Paris, concluded in May 1303 between England and France, it was agreed that neither sovereign should grant protection to the enemies of the other.† And by a treaty made by Charles V. of France with the Duke of Savoy in 1378, it was provided that all malefactors who had fled from Savoy to Dauphiny, or from Dauphiny to Savoy, should be delivered up, even if they were subjects of the state surrendering them.‡

The Intercursus Magnus, concluded between Henry VII. and the Flemings in 1497, provided against the harbouring by one power of the rebels of another. Its provisions and effect will best be described in Bacon's words :—

"This is that treaty which the Flemings call to this

* Ward, 'Hist. of the Laws of Nations,' ii. 319; Rymer, i. 39; M. Par., 131, 37.

† Fœlix says he can find no trace of this treaty, ii. 327 *n.* See Hallam, 'Middle Ages,' i. 44. The article is thus printed in Rym., tom. ii. 927, 31 Edw. I., A.D. 1303 :—" Item, accorde est que l'un ne receptera, ne soustendra, ne confortera, ne sera confort, ne ayde aus enemis de l'autre; ne ne souffera qe il aient confort, secours, ne ayde (soit de gents d'armes, ou de vitailles ou d'autres choses, queles qe eles soient) de ses terres, ne de sun poair; mais defendra sur peine de forfaiture de corps et d'avoir, et empeschera a tout sun poair, loialment et en bone foi, qe les ditz enemis ne soient receptez, ne confortez es terres de sa seigneurie, ne de sun poair. Ne que il en aient confort, secours, ne ayde (soit de gents d'armes, de chevaux, d'armeur) anzois les fera vender dedens quarante jours apres ce qe il en ferra requis."

‡ Blondel, 'Monographie Alphabétique de l'Extradition,' 91. Isanbert, 'Collection des Lois,' vol. v. p. 479.

day Intercursus Magnus; both because it is more complete than the precedent treaties of the third and fourth year of the king, and chiefly to give it a difference from the treaty which followed in the one-and-twentieth year of the king, which they call Intercursus Malus.

"In this treaty there was an express article against the reception of the rebels of either prince by other; purporting that if any such rebel should be required by the prince whose rebel he was of the prince confederate, that forthwith the prince confederate should, by proclamation, command him to avoid his country; which if he did not within fifteen days, the rebel was to stand proscribed, and put out of protection. But nevertheless, in this article Perkin (Warbeck) was not named, neither perhaps contained, because he was no rebel. But by this means his wings were clipt of his followers that were English." *

On the 23rd February 1661 a treaty was made between Charles II. and Denmark, by which the latter agreed to deliver up, on requisition, all persons who had been concerned in the murder of Charles I. The States-General of Holland delivered up some of the regicides without any treaty stipulations; but in 1662 (14th September) a treaty was made by which they agreed to give up any persons excepted from the English Act of Indemnity, and all other persons demanded by the English Government.

Under this treaty a demand was made by James II., in 1687, for the extradition of Burnet, who was then acting

* 'Hist. of Henry VII.' 6 Bacon's Works. Ed. Spedding, Ellis & Heath, 173.

as private secretary to the Prince of Orange, and who, for various violent writings against the king, had recently been cited before a Scottish court, and, not appearing, had been outlawed. The circumstances of the case, as related by Burnet himself, and with due allowance made for that fact, are very interesting, and the decision of the States-General may be compared with advantage with some of the recent judgments upon this subject. The English ambassador (Albeville) having demanded Burnet's banishment from the United Provinces, the deputies of the States of Holland called upon him to make answer. He claimed the protection of the States as a naturalised subject.* If he was charged with any offence against the laws of the provinces he would submit to trial. He could not be considered a fugitive or rebel; he had left England three years before, with the king's leave, and had not been in Scotland for fourteen years. As to the sentence which had been passed against him, he could say nothing to that until he saw a copy.

The States hereupon ordered their ambassador to represent to James that naturalisation was a sacred thing, and that if he had anything to lay to Burnet's charge, justice should be done in their courts. Albeville then presented another memorial, in which the article of the treaty was set forth:—

"It was insisted on that, since the States were bound not to give sanctuary to fugitives and rebels, they ought

* He had obtained naturalisation just before, on receiving news of the commencement of proceedings in Scotland.

not to examine the grounds upon which such judgments were given, but were bound to execute the treaty. Upon this it was observed that the words in treaties ought to be explained according to their common acceptation, or the sense given them in the civil law, and not according to any particular forms of courts, where for non-appearance a writ of outlawry or rebellion might lie; the sense of the word 'rebel,' in common use, was a man that had borne arms, or had plotted against his prince; and a 'fugitive' was a man that fled from justice." *

It is obvious that these treaties prove little one way or the other. They mostly relate to political offenders, who were given up, not as criminals but as enemies of the sovereign, and it would be attaching far too much importance to the treaties of 1174 and 1378, to take them as a proof of a necessity for treaty stipulations to justify the demand of the surrender of a criminal.

Most of the cases of extradition, demanded in the absence of treaties, are equally inconclusive.

The delivery up of the Count de St. Pol to Louis XI., by Charles Duke of Burgundy, in violation of his own letters of safe conduct; the surrender of the Earl of Suffolk, by the King of Spain, to Henry VII., upon the ill-kept promise that his life should be spared; and the promise of Elizabeth either to deliver up Bothwell to the Scots, or to send him out of the kingdom, prove as little on one side as the refusal of the King of Scotland to give up Perkin Warbeck; of the King of France, in 1584,

* Burnet, 'History of his own Time' (Ed. 1833), i. 730.

to give up to Elizabeth, Morgan and other Englishmen who were said to be plotting in France against England; and that of France to deliver up Cardinal Pole to Henry VIII., do upon the other.

In 1588 Farnihurst was demanded by Elizabeth from the King of Scotland, he being charged with having been instrumental in the murder of Sir John Russell, the eldest son of the Earl of Bedford. The king refused to deliver him up except upon conviction by a fair trial, but he caused him to enter into ward in the town of Aberdeen." *

After the Restoration the States of Holland gave up some of the regicides before any treaty for that purpose had been made; but others took refuge in Switzerland, which declined to surrender them.

The most notable instance of the surrender of a political offender in recent times is that of Napper Tandy, who, being attainted of treason, was given up by the Senate of Hamburg, on the demand of the English Government in 1792. He was tried in Dublin and acquitted.†

At the present time Spain and other countries, with which England has no treaties of extradition, occasionally give up criminals upon requisition by the British authorities.

As to the common law of England upon the duty of according extradition, five cases have been cited:—Rex *v.* Hutchinson (3 Keble, 785), Rex *v.* Lundy (2 Ventris, 314), Rex *v.* Kimberley (2 Stra. 848), East India Co.

* Sir W. Scott's 'Hist. of Scotland,' ii. 33.

† 27 Howell's 'State Trials,' 1191.

v. Campbell (1 Ves. senr. 246), and Mure *v.* Kaye (4 Taunt. 34).

Of these cases the first three do not touch the subject of extradition at all. In Hutchinson's case the prisoner was accused of murder committed in Portugal, and he was remanded upon the contention of the attorney-general that the offence, being without the dominions of the Crown, was triable by constable and marshal, and not by commission.

In the cases of Lundy and Kimberley, the only point decided was that Ireland came within the proviso of the Habeas Corpus Act, that persons accused of crime in any part of the king's dominions might be sent thither for trial.

In neither of the other cases was a decision as to the legality of extradition necessary, but in each a very clear opinion was expressed. The case of the East India Co. *v.* Campbell was tried in 1749, on the equity side of the Court of Exchequer, Lord Chancellor Hardwicke and Chief Baron Parker taking part in the decision. It was there laid down in the judgment of the whole court, that "the Government may send a prisoner to answer for a crime wherever committed, that he may not involve his country, and to prevent reprisals." Mr. Justice Heath, whose opinion on this point was given in Mure *v.* Kaye (1811), was a judge of very high reputation, and his dictum was not dissented from by the other members of the court.

He said: "As to the first point, it has generally been understood that wheresoever a crime has been committed the criminal is punishable according to the *lex loci* of the country against the law of which the crime was committed, and by the comity of nations the country in which the criminal has been found has aided the police of the country against which the crime was committed in bringing the criminal to punishment. In Lord Loughborough's time the crew of a Dutch ship mastered the vessel, and ran away with her, and brought her into Deal, and it was a question whether we could seize them and send them to Holland, and it was held we might, and the same has always been the law of all civilised countries."

In an opinion given to the Government in 1792, by Serjeant Hill, upon the question of the king's prerogative to expel aliens from the kingdom, the same doctrine is very clearly laid down:—"As to subjects of states in amity, I think the king hath no power over any, if they do not offend his laws, but such as are charged by the states whose subjects they are with high-treason, murder, or defrauding their state, or other atrocious crimes. And as to them, if the sovereign of such state applies to have them delivered up, I think his majesty is, by the constitution, invested with the power of granting or refusing the application, and if granted, may issue a proclamation either to quit his dominions, or else may order them to be apprehended, and sent in safe custody and delivered to such persons as the sovereign of the state to which they belong shall appoint; and if any of them should procure a writ of Habeas Corpus, the special matter might be returned, and they would not be entitled to be discharged, for this is warranted by the practice of nations, and is therefore not part of the legislative, but of the executive, power, which is vested solely in the king, who, as observed by a late learned judge (1 Bl. Comm. 253), with regard to foreign concerns, is representative of his people, and what is done by the royal authority with regard to foreign powers (he adds) is the act of the whole nation; and the prerogative in this respect has always been taken to be so clear that no foreigner ever contested it in the English courts of justice, and the Habeas Corpus appears to have been designedly so penned as not to interfere with it; for the prohibition in that act (sec. 9 and 12) against removing persons from one prison to another, or sending them abroad, is confined to subjects of this realm, whereas all the other provisions of the act extend to all persons and all prisoners, without once mentioning the subjects of the realm, and therefore all the others are intended to extend to aliens, and this not so."*

Upon the authority of E. I. Co. *v.* Campbell, and Mure *v.* Kaye, it is laid down, in 'Chitty on the Criminal Law' (1826), that "an English magistrate may also cause to be arrested, and committed for trial, an offender against the Irish law, or accused of having perpetrated a crime in a foreign country" (p. 14); and "if a prisoner, having committed a felony in a foreign country, come into England, he may be arrested here and conveyed and given up to the magistrates of the country against the laws of which the offence was committed" (p. 16).

* 'Edinburgh Review,' xliii. 141.

These opinions may have been correct, but they have ceased to be law now. If any magistrate were now to arrest a person on this ground, the validity of the commitment would certainly be tested, and, in the absence of special legislative provisions, the prisoner as certainly discharged upon application to one of the superior courts.

CHAPTER III.

HISTORY OF THE LAW IN THE UNITED STATES.

For various reasons, the records of the Acts passed and the cases decided in the United States is entitled to the first place in a history of the modern law and practice of extradition. At the formation of the Union, the question of the rendition of criminals who fled from one state to another to escape the vengeance of the laws they had transgressed, was one of the difficulties with which the founders of the great republic had to deal. The proximity of Canada, and the length of boundary line which made the flight of the criminal so difficult to intercept, soon raised the question from one of local administration to one of national policy. Men were found quite equal to deal with either. The American judicial bench has been adorned by men who added the lawyer's knowledge to the statesman's thought, and who, bringing both to bear on the questions of public law, have left us works of enduring value. In the matter of extradition, the American law was, until 1870, better than that of any country in the world; and the decisions of the American judges are the best existing expositions of the duty of extradition, in its relations at once to the judicial rights of nations and the general interests of the civilisation of the world. A few words will suffice with regard to the domestic aspect of the question in the Union. Before the revolution, a criminal who committed a crime in one of the colonies and fled to another was arrested, wherever found, and sent for trial to the place where the offence was committed.* And the second section of the fourth article of the Constitution of the Union, substantially repealing a clause in the fourth article of Confederation, declared, that "a person charged in any state with treason, felony, or other crime, who shall flee from justice and be found in another state, shall, on demand of the executive authority of the state from which he fled, be delivered up, to be removed to the state having jurisdiction of the crime." In 1791 a demand under this article was made by the governor of Pennsylvania upon the governor of Virginia for the surrender of a fugitive from justice. Doubts were raised as to the person to whom the demand should be addressed and the mode in which it should be made, and the Executive of Virginia refused the surrender, because, as, amongst other reasons, was alleged, Congress had not passed any statute to execute this provision of the supreme law of the land. The opinion of the attorney-general of Virginia assuming that position, and the reply of the Executive of that state sanctioning it, were communicated to Congress by President Washington in October 1791; and to remove the doubts thus raised, the Act of Congress of 12th February 1793

* Chief-Justice Tilghman, 10 Serj. & Rawl. 129.

was passed.* That Act made provision for the rendition of fugitives from justice and of fugitive slaves. The first section concerned criminals only, and declared that on demand made, accompanied with a copy of indictment found or affidavit made before a magistrate, charging the person with having committed "treason, felony, or other crime,"† and certified by the governor or chief magistrate of the demanding state to be authentic, it should be the duty of the executive magistrate of the state to which the person had fled to cause him to be arrested and secured, "and notice thereof given, and the person then to be delivered to the agent of the executive making the demand, if such agent should appear within six months. If no such agent appeared, the prisoner should be discharged." (1 Stat. at Large 302, 2 Congress, Sess. 2, ch. 7.) This still remains the law of the United States. The duty of the governor of the state from which the fugitive is claimed is purely ministerial. No discretion with respect to the nature or character of the crime charged is vested in him. But if he refuses to perform the duty cast upon him, there is no power conferred upon the judicial or any other department of the general government to compel him to do so. The Supreme Court cannot issue a mandamus for this purpose.‡

* Edmonds, J., in Metzger's case, 1 Barbour (S. C. of N. Y.), 257.

† These words include every offence forbidden and made punishable by the laws of the state in which the offence is committed. Sup. Court, 1860. Kentucky *v.* Dennison, 24 Howard, 66.

‡ Sup. Court, 1860. Kentucky *v.* Dennison, 24 Howard, 66.

To authorise the arrest and removal of a fugitive from justice to the state having jurisdiction of the crime, it must distinctly appear from the affidavits before the magistrate upon which the requisition is based that the offence was committed in the state from which the requisition proceeds.* The cases decided upon this statute have for the most part referred to rules of practice and evidence. References are given below † to a few of the most important, but none sufficiently affect the general question of extradition to need discussion here.

The first case in America in which the question of the duty of the extradition of criminals, independently of any treaty obligations, was discussed, was that of the Chevalier de Longchamps in 1784.‡ The circumstances of the case and of the demand of extradition were peculiar. The Chevalier de Longchamps was indicted before the Court of Oyer and Terminer at Philadelphia for threatening bodily harm to M. Marbois, the Consul-General of France in the United States, and Secretary to the French Legation, and also for an assault upon him. It appeared that M. de Longchamps went to M. Marbois, at his official residence, and, using violent language, threatened to dishonour him ("Je vous déshonorerai, Poliçon, Coquin"); and two days later, as they were talking together in a

* Seventh Circuit (Illinois), 1842. *Ex parte* Smith, 3 M'Lean, 121.

† *In re* Leland, 7 Abbott (N. Y.) Practice, N. S., 64. U. S. Digest, N. S., i. 322. *In re* Rutter, 7 Abbott (N. Y.) Practice, N. S., 67. U. S. Digest, N. S., i. 322. *Ex parte* Pfitzer, 28 Indiana, 450.

‡ Respublica *v.* Longchamps, 1 Dallas, 120.

public place, he struck with his stick the cane which M. Marbois held in his hand. The jury at first found the prisoner guilty of the assault only, but being desired by the court to reconsider the matter, they returned a verdict against him on both counts. The president (Washington) and the supreme executive council thereupon informed the judges that the minister of France demanded that M. de Longchamps, having appeared in the uniform of a French officer, and called himself an officer in the service of his majesty, should be delivered up to him for these outrages, to be sent to France. Two questions were submitted to the judges:—1. Could he be lawfully delivered up? 2. If not, whether he ought not to be kept in prison until His Most Christian Majesty should declare the reparation satisfactory?

Sentence was postponed, and these questions were fully argued on the 10th and 12th July 1784. On the 7th October judgment was given, that—1. He could not lawfully be delivered up. The court, however, added, "We think cases may occur where the council could, *pro bono publico*, and to prevent atrocious offenders evading punishment, deliver them up to the justice of the country to which they belong, or where the offences were committed." 2. The demand that he should be kept in prison until the King of France should declare the reparation satisfactory could not be complied with, as, by the law of America, the punishment must be certain and definite. A very heavy sentence was, however, passed. M. de Longchamps was fined one hundred French crowns, and sentenced to imprisonment until the 4th July 1786, making a little over two years. He had further to find security to keep the peace for seven years, to pay the costs of the prosecution, and to remain committed until the sentence was complied with. It must be remembered, in explanation of the president's action in this matter, and perhaps of the severity of the sentence, that at this time there was special political reason in America for the desire to keep on good terms with France. The decision, however, upon the question of extradition was clearly right. No treaty required the rendition of the offender; his offence could only technically be called an offence against the King of France; the assault was committed on American soil, and the whole matter was clearly within the cognisance of American tribunals.

In this same year (1784) the legislature of Virginia passed an Act, which seems to show that the question of the power of an individual State of the Union to grant or demand extradition had already arisen. It provided for the surrender of any of her citizens who should go beyond the limits of the United States, and commit crimes within the jurisdiction of a foreign nation. But it was by this Act left to Congress to decide for what crimes extradition ought to be granted. *

In 1791 the Governor of South Carolina requested the President of the United States to demand of the Governor of Florida certain persons who had fled thither after having committed crimes in South Carolina. Mr. Jeffer-

* 11 Hen. Stat. c. 24, p. 471; Robinson's Practice, i. 7.

son, then Secretary of State, in his report to President Washington, said: "England has no convention with any nation for the surrender of fugitives from justice, and their laws have given no power to the executive to surrender fugitives of any description. They are accordingly constantly refused, and hence England has been the asylum of the Paolis, the La Mottes, the Calonnis; in short, of the most atrocious offenders, as well as of the most innocent victims who have been able to get there. The laws of the United States, like those of England, receive every fugitive, and no authority has been given to our executives to deliver them up. If, then, the United States could not deliver up to General Quesnada (Governor of Florida) fugitives from the laws of his country, we cannot claim as a right the delivery of fugitives from us. And it is worthy of consideration whether the demand proposed to be made in Governor Pinckney's letter, should it be complied with by the other party, might not commit us disagreeably, and perhaps dishonourably." *

These expressions implied a desire for the alteration of the law upon this matter, † and may have helped to bring

* Quoted by Mr. Van Ness, in Holmes *v.* Jennison, 14 Peters, 541.

† A few years later, in 1797, the Attorney-General of the United States gave his official opinion that it was the *duty* of the United States to deliver up, on due demand, heinous offenders, being fugitives from the dominions of Spain; and that as the existing laws of the Union had not made any specific provision for the case the defect ought to be supplied. —1 Opinions of the Att.-Gen., 46.

In 1821 a different opinion was given on similar authority.— 1 Opinions, &c., 384-392.

about the insertion of an article on the subject of extradition in the treaty, often spoken of as Jay's Treaty, which was concluded between the United States and Great Britain in 1794. This article, the 27th, was as follows:—"It is further agreed, that her Majesty and the United States, on mutual requisitions by them respectively, or by their respective ministers or officers authorised to make the same, will deliver up to justice all persons who, being charged with murder or forgery, committed within the jurisdiction of either, shall seek an asylum within any of the countries of the other, provided that this shall only be done on such evidence of criminality as, according to the place where the fugitive or person so charged shall be found, would justify his apprehension and commitment for trial, if the offence had there been committed. The expense of such apprehension and delivery shall be borne and defrayed by those who make the requisition and receive the fugitive." * By the succeeding article it was provided that this clause of the treaty should only exist for twelve years. At the expiration of that time the relations between the two countries were so unfriendly that no attempt was made to renew the treaty. And the circumstances of the only case of importance in which the requisition had been made had aroused feelings in America strongly opposed to any such renewal. This was the case of Jonathan (or Nathan) Robbins, † who

* Public Statutes at Large of the United States. Ed. Richard Peters, viii. 129.

† Wharton's State Trials, 392–456; Bee, Adm. Rep., 267.

was demanded by the British Government in 1799, on a charge of murder. Robbins had been, some years before, one of the crew of H.M.S. *Hermione*, which was taken possession of by mutineers, who, after killing some of the officers, carried the vessel into a Spanish port. On this charge Robbins was imprisoned at Charleston, under a warrant of the district judge of South Carolina. He had been imprisoned six months when he was brought before the court on habeas corpus. The Secretary of State addressed a letter to the judge, mentioning that application had been made by the British minister to the president for the delivery of Robbins according to the treaty, and adding, "the president advises and requests you to deliver him up." The case having been fully heard, the judge ordered the marshal to deliver Robbins to the British consul; and he was thereupon delivered up, carried to Jamaica, tried by court-martial, and hanged in chains. Popular feeling had been greatly excited by the case, it having been alleged that he was an American citizen, that he had been impressed on board a British vessel, and that the crime was committed in endeavouring to escape from his enforced service; and although the evidence of guilt had been overwhelming, and the question carefully tried, a vigorous attack was made upon the president (Adams) for his interference in the matter. He was defended in the House of Representatives by Mr. Marshall (afterwards Chief Justice of the Supreme Court of the United States), in a speech which made the speaker famous, and which is a fine model of close and thoughtful reasoning; but the public feeling was so strong that the incident had a considerable effect on the result of the contest for the presidency between Adams and Jefferson in 1801.

From 1806 to 1842 no treaty provisions as to extradition existed between Great Britain and the United States, but during this period several cases were brought before the American tribunals, which, from the magnitude of the questions involved, and the great repute of some of the judges whose opinions were expressed, are deserving of careful note.

The first was the case of Daniel Washburn,* in 1819. Washburn was arrested in the United States, on a charge of *theft* in Canada, and was brought before Chancellor Kent upon a habeas corpus.

The chancellor held that, irrespective of all treaties, it was the duty of a state to surrender fugitive criminals. It was the duty of a magistrate, irrespective of legislative provisions upon the subject, to commit the fugitive upon due proof of the commission of a crime, so as to afford time to the government to deliver him up, or to the foreign government to claim him. If this claim were not made within a reasonable time, the prisoner would be entitled to his discharge on habeas corpus; the judicial power would have fulfilled its duty by affording the opportunity. It did not matter, he added, whether the prisoner was a subject of the pursuing government or of that under which he had taken refuge. He then reviewed at considerable length the authorities and cases on the

* 3 Wharton's Crim. Trials, 473; 4 Johnson, Ch. Rep., 106.

subject; and with reference to the argument that even if the duty of extradition existed, it must be held to be limited to the cases of murder and forgery, which had been included in the treaty of 1794, he decided that that treaty was merely declaratory, and that, even if during its existence the principle "enumeratio unius est exclusio alterius" applied, at its expiration the general and wider law revived.

This judgment carried the doctrine of the duty of extradition to its fullest possible extent, declaring not only that treaties might declare or limit, but did not create it, but that it was of so high and imperative a nature that in the absence of municipal laws for its enforcement it was itself a law which judges were by virtue of the nature of their office bound to recognise and administer. No later decision has gone quite to this extent; but it is hardly correct to say that the judgment has been overruled by a superior weight of authority. The judgments usually quoted in support of this assertion are rather apparently than really opposed to the ruling of the chancellor, and even where they contradict one of his dicta they leave others of equal or greater importance untouched.* The judgment generally cited as being in clearest contradiction to the decision of Kent is that of Chief Justice Tilghman in the case of Edward Short.†

* The principles laid down in Washburn's case were acted upon by Chief Justice Reid, in Lower Canada, in 1827. See Fisher's case, *post*, p. 77.

† Commonwealth at the instance of Edward Short *v.* Deacon, 10 Serj. & Rawl., 125.

But it will be seen on an examination of that judgment that it is by no means in direct opposition to that of Kent on one or two of the most important points. But before noticing that case it will be well (to keep the order of time) to mention the Act passed by the State of New York on 5th April 1822, and adopted and continued in the New York Revised Statutes i. 164; §§ 8, 9, 10, 11. This law authorised the governor in his discretion, on requisition from a foreign government, to surrender up fugitives charged with murder, forgery, larceny, or other crimes, which by the laws of the state were punishable with death or imprisonment in the state prison, provided the evidence of criminality was sufficient by the laws of the United States to detain the party for trial on a like charge.* The case of Edward Short was tried before the Supreme Court of Pennsylvania in August 1823. Short was charged with having committed murder in Ireland, and was arrested in Pennsylvania at the suit of a private person, without the interference of either the government of Great Britain or that of the United States. The question for the consideration of the court was twofold: 1. Was the evidence sufficient? 2. Was the commitment legal? Upon the first branch of the question the judgment was short and unimportant, but the second branch was fully considered. Chief Justice Tilghman, in delivering judgment, reviewed the old authorities on the subject, not finding in them so strong a concurrence of opinion in favour of the duty of extradition as had been declared by

* See *post*, p. 76.

Chancellor Kent.* He urged the difficulty of establishing any common rule, arising from the different estimation of crimes in different nations, and concluded that upon the whole the safest principle seemed to be that no state had an *absolute* and *perfect* right to demand of another the delivery of a fugitive criminal, although it had what is called an *imperfect* right, that is, a right to ask it as a matter of courtesy, good-will, and mutual convenience. But a refusal to grant such request would be no just cause of war. No state, he said, had a right to ask the delivery of a fugitive for the purpose of wreaking its vengeance upon him. "All that can be said is, that unless he be given up, others may be encouraged to transgress by the hope of escaping punishment, and thus an injury may be sustained. And, indeed, in the case of neighbouring nations the argument is so strong as to be almost irresistible, except in cases attended with peculiar circumstances." He differed from Kent as to the treaty of 1794 being merely declaratory, and laid down that "the treaty gave each nation a right which did not before exist, and which ceased at its expiration." The delivery up of a fugitive was an affair of the executive government, to which the demand of the foreign power must be addressed. The judges could not legally deliver up, nor could they command the executive to do so. No magistrate in Pennsylvania had the right to cause a person to be arrested in order to afford the President of the United States an opportunity to deliver him up, because the

* With reference to Lord Coke's opinion, see *ante*, p. 7.

government had already declared that it would not do so. If the executive hereafter should be of opinion that it had the right, and was bound in duty to give a criminal up, that would be a different case, and one on which the court at present would give no opinion.

Every nation had an undoubted right to surrender fugitives; but the question then would be, whether the President could act in such a case, or must wait for power to be given him by law? Hitherto he had believed he had not the power: if he should change that opinion, the question of his right to act would then be for the judges to decide. "Neither do I give any opinion," said the Chief Justice in conclusion, "whether the executive of the State of Pennsylvania has the power to cause a fugitive criminal to be arrested for the purpose of delivering him up. But confining myself to the case before me, in which the arrest is made at the request of a private person, I am of opinion that there is no law to support it, and therefore the prisoner is entitled to his discharge." It will be seen, on a careful examination of this decision, that the reasons for it may almost be termed technical. The two leading doctrines in Kent's judgment were that the duty of extradition existed independently of any treaties; and that, being a part of international law, it was *ipso facto* a rule of municipal law, and one which judges were bound to administer. Upon the first point, Chief Justice Tilghman, while denying that extradition was a matter of perfect right, conceded that it was an international duty which, between neighbouring nations, was of almost irresistible obligation; and, as to the second point, he went no further than to deny the right of the judges to arrest a fugitive when the executive had already declared that it could not order his extradition. The allusion to the fact that in this case the arrest had been made at the suit of a private person, in no way representing a foreign government, made the decision still less valuable as a precedent.

In 1835 and 1837 two cases came before the courts involving very similar questions, and decided by very able judges, one of them perhaps the greatest jurist America has produced, but the negative conclusions stated in their judgments carried the law no further. The first of these cases was that of José Ferreira dos Santos, which came before Judge Barbour in the Circuit Court of Virginia in the November term of the year 1835. The prisoner, who was a Portuguese subject, was committed for trial under a charge of piracy, and the grand jury threw out the bill. An application was then made by the Portuguese chargé d'affaires, that he might be detained until the government of Portugal should have time to make a demand on that of the United States for his surrender upon the charge of having committed murder in his native country. The question before Judge Barbour was, whether it was proper or competent for the court to detain him in prison for that purpose. He decided in the negative, and discharged the prisoner, saying: "I am of opinion that, without a treaty stipulation, this government is not under any obligation to surrender a fugitive from justice to another government for trial; and that, as a judicial officer of the United States, I have no authority whatsoever either to arrest or detain with a view to such surrender."*

In 1837, in the district court of the United States for the Massachusetts district, a prisoner charged with manslaughter was acquitted upon the ground that the offence was committed within the jurisdiction of a foreign government; and it was then suggested by the district judge, not by any representative of the foreign government (the Society Islands), that the court should remand him to that government for trial. Mr. Justice Story, to whom the suggestion was made, said that he had never known any such authority exercised by the American courts, except where the case was provided for by the stipulations of some treaty. He had great doubts whether, upon principles of international law, and independent of any statutable provisions or treaty stipulations, a court was either bound in duty or authorised in its discretion to surrender any offender to a foreign government. The prisoner was thereupon discharged.†

The general executive having declared its inability to grant extradition, an attempt was now made to use the powers of a state executive for this purpose. In 1840 an application was made to the President of the United States for the extradition of one Holmes, a naturalised citizen of the United States, who was charged

* 2 Brockenborgh and Marshall, 493 (Circ. Court of U. S., Va. 1835).

† U. S. *v.* Davis, 2 Sumner, 485; 1 Opinions of Att.-Gen., 510; 2 Opinions of Att.-Gen., 359.

with having committed murder in Lower Canada. The President declined to act, through an alleged want of power, and the case came back to Governor Jennison of Vermont. Holmes, having been arrested, obtained a writ of habeas corpus from the Supreme Court of Vermont, and the sheriff returned that he was detained under an order of the Governor of Vermont, which commanded the sheriff to deliver him up to the authorities of Lower Canada. The Supreme Court of Vermont held the return sufficient, and remanded Holmes into custody. On appeal to the Supreme Court of the United States, two questions were argued: 1. Whether an appeal would lie. 2. Whether the judgment of the Supreme Court of Vermont was right.

In the result the judges were equally divided, and the appeal was dismissed for want of jurisdiction. But the Supreme Court of Vermont, finding that the majority of the judges of the higher court held that the Governor of Vermont had no authority to arrest and deliver up fugitives, discharged the prisoner.*

After this judgment, it was clear that foreign governments could not, in the absence of treaty stipulations, obtain from the United States the extradition of fugitive criminals.† It had been decided that the delivery up of a fugitive was an act of state within the power of the national executive only; and that the executive having

* Holmes *v.* Jennison, 14 Peters, 540. *Ex parte* Holmes, 12 Verm. Reps., 630. Kent expresses strong disapproval of this decision.—Comm. i. 43.

† 3 Opinions of Att.-Gen., 661 (Legare).

declared itself unable to act in the matter, the judges would not be justified in ordering useless arrests. Whether the President had not, in the absence of special laws, the right to act as the representative of the nation had never been decided; but the effect of Robbins's case was not yet forgotten, and American politicians did not care to risk their popularity merely for the sake of testing a disputed power.

In the circular upon the subject of extradition issued on the 5th April 1841,* the French minister of justice mentioned the four treaties then in existence between France and Spain, Switzerland, Belgium, and Sardinia, and said that from other countries France could obtain extradition, even in the absence of treaties, except from Great Britain and the United States. The first did not grant extradition because its legislation did not allow it; the second because it was not yet settled whether the right of surrender belonged to the different states or to the general government. Both countries soon remedied, at least partially, this grave defect in their laws.

Negotiations had already been commenced between the United States and Great Britain for the conclusion of a convention upon this subject; and in the Ashburton Treaty, which was signed at Washington on the 9th August 1842,† and ratified at London on the 13th October of the same year, a clause was inserted which repeated

* Dalloz, Jurisp. Gén. (1841), iii. 440. Fœlix, ii. 3, and see *post*, p. 159.

† 8 Stats. at Large, 572. 6 Hertslet, Commercial Treaties, 862.

the provisions of the tenth section of the treaty of 1794,* and extended them to other crimes.

By the twenty-seventh article of the Ashburton Treaty, it was "agreed that the United States and her Britannic Majesty shall, upon mutual requisitions by them or their ministers, officers, or authorities,† respectively made, deliver up to justice all persons who, being charged ‡ with the crime of murder, or assault with intent to commit murder or piracy, or arson, or robbery, or forgery, or the utterance of forged paper,§ committed within the juris-

* See *ante*, p. 35.

† The requisition upon Great Britain must now be made by a diplomatic representative of the United States, 33 & 34 Vict., c. 52, §§ 7, 27. That includes a Consul-General, 36 & 37 Vict., c. 60, § 7.

‡ An application by Great Britain under this treaty need not be founded on any indictment found before a British tribunal, nor on any warrant issuing therefrom. It is not necessary that any examination should have taken place in Great Britain. See note to Metzger's case, 1 Barbour, 269. See also *Re* François Farez, 7 Blatchford Circuit Court Reps., 34, 345, 491. 2 Abbott, U. S. Digest, 346.

§ In 1859 the United States Government made a proposal to Great Britain to amend the treaty by adding to it the offences of coining, uttering false money, and embezzlement. The British Government assented, and forwarded draft articles to Washington. The United States Government, however, desired to limit embezzlement to that of public moneys, and as this would have made the amendment of little use, the British Government refused to accept the limitation. On the other hand, the United States objected to the stipulation that the execution of the new arrangement must depend upon the sanction of Parliament being obtained. The negotiations thereupon were abandoned.—Evidence of Rt. Hon. E. Hammond, Report of Select Comm., 1868, 54.

diction of either, shall seek an asylum, or shall be found within the territories of the other: Provided, that this shall only be done upon such evidence of criminality as, according to the laws of the place where the fugitive or person so charged shall be found, would justify his apprehension and commitment for trial, if the crime or offence had been there committed; and the respective judges and other magistrates of the two governments shall have power, jurisdiction, and authority, upon complaint made under oath, to issue a warrant for the apprehension of the fugitive, or person so charged, that he may be brought before such judges or other magistrates respectively—to the end that the evidence of criminality may be heard and considered; and if, on such hearing, the evidence be deemed sufficient to sustain the charge, it shall be the duty of the examining judge or magistrate to certify the same to the proper executive authority, that a warrant may issue for the surrender of such fugitives. The expense of such apprehension and delivery shall be borne and defrayed by the party who makes the requisition and receives the fugitive."

In this clause there is no specific exclusion of political crimes such as will be found in the later convention with France; but in transmitting the treaty to Congress, President Tyler said,—"The article on the subject (extradition) in the proposed treaty is carefully confined to such offences as all mankind agree to regard as heinous, and destructive to the security of life and property.

In this careful and specific enumeration of crimes, the object has been to exclude all political offences or criminal charges arising from wars or intestine commotions."

In England, the common law being held not to permit the surrender of a criminal, this provision could not come into effect without an Act of Parliament; but in the United States a treaty is as binding as an Act of Congress; and this article was immediately put in force. Christiana Cochran (alias Gilmour), a Scotchwoman, accused of having murdered her husband, fled to America by the very ship which conveyed thither the ratifications of the Ashburton Treaty. She was arrested, and her counsel raised a point which has often been discussed since in cases of extradition. He asked to be allowed to prove the prisoner's insanity. After full consideration, the court refused to try the question, and the prisoner was surrendered.*

On the 9th November 1843 a convention was con-

* Egan, 46; St. Alban's Raid, 229; Fœlix, ii. 357, *n.* Fœlix says,—"Une femme accusée d'empoisonnement avait passé de Liverpool à New York; pour refuser l'extradition, on faisait valoir son état d'aliénation mentale." The statement in the text is given upon the authority of Egan; but it would appear from a reference to the case made by Mr. Cushing when Attorney-General, that the court did try the question of the prisoner's sanity. He says that her counsel set up "a plea of insanity, which, after a full and impartial *investigation*, was overruled."—4 Opinions of Att.-Gen., 202 (Cushing). The most instructive case upon the subject of the production of evidence for the prisoner is that of the St. Alban's Raid. See *post*, p. 91.

cluded at Washington between the United States and France,* by which it was agreed:—

"Art. 1. That the high contracting parties shall, on requisitions made in their name, through the medium of their respective diplomatic agents, deliver up to justice persons who, being accused of the crimes enumerated in the next following article, committed within the jurisdiction of the requiring party, shall seek an asylum, or shall be found within the territories of the other: Provided, that this shall be done only when the fact of the commission of the crime shall be so established as that the laws of the country † in which the fugitive or the person so accused shall be found, would justify his or her apprehension and commitment for trial, if the crime had been there committed.

"Art. 2. Persons shall be so delivered up who shall be charged, according to the provisions of this convention, with any of the following crimes, to wit: murder (comprehending the crimes designated in the French penal code by the terms assassination, parricide, infanticide, and poisoning), or with an attempt to commit murder,

* 8 Stats. at Large, 582.

† The word "place" used in the Ashburton Treaty was better than "country," as in America the law is different in different states. "The word 'country,' necessarily under our form of government in carrying out the provisions of the convention, means the special political jurisdiction that has cognisance of the crime. In this case the forms of proceeding that must be observed are those of the State of New York."—Blatchford, J., in *Re* François Farez, 7 Blatchford, Circ. Court Rep., 357.

or with rape, or with forgery, or with arson, or with embezzlement by public officers,* when the same is punishable with infamous punishment.

"Art. 3. On the part of the French government the surrender shall only be by authority of the keeper of the seals, minister of justice; and on the part of the government of the United States, the surrender shall be made only by the authority of the executive thereof.

"Art. 4. The expenses of any detention and delivery effected in virtue of the preceding provisions, shall be borne and defrayed by the government in whose name the requisition shall have been made.

"Art. 5. The provisions of the present convention shall not be applied in any manner to the crimes enumerated in the second article, committed anterior to the date thereof, nor to any crime or offence of a purely political character."

On the 24th of February 1845 the following additional article to the above convention was concluded at Washington:—

"The crime of robbery, defining the same to be the felonious and forcible taking from the person of another, of goods or money to any value, by violence or putting him in fear; and the crime of burglary, defining the same to be, breaking and entering by night into a mansion-house of another, with intent to commit felony; and the

* Persons who discharge the functions of government as such, who are appointed by or officially responsible to it, and who thus enter into the organisation of the government.—8 Opinions of Att.-Gen. (Cushing), 108.

In the French the term is "dépositaires publics."

corresponding crimes included under the French law in the words *vol qualifié crime** not being embraced in the second article of the convention of extradition concluded between the United States and France on the 9th of November 1843, it is agreed by the present article, between the high contracting parties, that persons charged with those crimes shall be respectively delivered up, in conformity with the first article of the said convention; and the present article, when ratified by the parties, shall constitute a part of the said convention, and shall have the same force as if it had been originally inserted in the same."†

It was not at first thought necessary to have an Act of Congress to carry these treaties into effect, and two cases were decided in the absence of any such Act. In the case of Thomas Sheazle and others (known as the "British

* Robbery committed with violence or menaces, or committed in a dwelling-house with circumstances either of night and of escalade or of "effraction."—7 Opinions of Att.-Gen., 643 (Cushing).

† 8 Stats. at Large, 617. 1 Bright, 270. A supplemental convention between the United States and France, signed the 10th February, 1858, extended the provisions of the treaty to principals, accessories, and accomplices in the following crimes: "Forging, or knowingly passing or putting in circulation counterfeit coin or bank-notes, or other paper current as money, with intent to defraud any person or persons; embezzlement by any person or persons in the employ of a society or corporation legally constituted—when these crimes are subject to infamous punishment." 11 Stats. at Large, 741. 2 Bright, 134. It is somewhat singular that fraudulent bankruptcy is excluded from the treaties of extradition of the United States, though included in those of most European nations.

Prisoners' Case"), it was held that, under the authority of the treaty of 1842, persons charged with piracy, committed contrary to Acts of Parliament and on board a British vessel, might be arrested in the United States, examined before a State magistrate, and, if believed guilty, remanded into custody, with a view to their surrender to Great Britain.* The authority of the state judiciary was however, denied in the case of Nicholas Lucien Metzger, who was accused of having committed forgery in France, and whose extradition was demanded by that country in 1847. The French minister first applied to the executive, who declined to interfere in the matter, and referred him to the judicial authorities. Metzger was then arrested and brought before a local magistrate of New York, who decided that he had authority over the case, and committed him to prison; but he was liberated by a circuit judge of that state, who held that the state judiciary had no jurisdiction. He was then brought before Judge Betts, a district judge of the United States, sitting in chambers, who committed him, after hearing a full argument. Judge Betts held that, as the treaty was the supreme law of the land, it was entitled, when coming before the courts, to the same effect as an Act of Congress, though no Act had been passed to define the method of its operation; that under such treaty a fugitive was subject to apprehension and commitment for a crime committed after the date of the signature of the treaty against the laws of the country demanding him, whether such crime were an offence in the

* First Circ. (Mass), 1845. 1 Woodbury and Minot, 66.

country to which he had fled or not; and that whether the *casus fœderis* had arisen, or whether the compact would be executed, was a political question to be decided by the President, the courts having power to direct or contravene his decisions in the first instance.* Whether the judiciary had authority on habeas corpus, after the fugitive was under arrest, to prevent his extradition, if the President decided to make it, was not decided.

The prisoner then petitioned the Supreme Court of the United States for a habeas corpus. After elaborate arguments by Mr. Coxe for the prisoner, and the Attorney-General (Mr. Clifford) against, Mr. Justice M'Lean delivered the judgment of the court. He said that the surrender of fugitives from justice was a matter of conventional arrangement between states, as no such obligation was imposed by the law of nations. Under the provisions of the constitution, the treaty was the supreme law of the land; and, in regard to the rights and responsibilities growing out of it, might become the subject of judicial cognisance. The executive had, therefore, acted rightly in referring the matter to the judicial power. The district judge at chambers exercised a special authority, and the law had made no provision for the revision of his judg-

* "I further adjudge that the said treaty took effect and went into operation on and from the day of the signature thereof.

"I further adjudge that the laws of France are to determine the constituents of the crime of forgery, or *du faux*, of which Metzger is accused, and that the facts in evidence adequately prove the commission of that crime by him in France since the date of the treaty."—Order of Judge Betts, 5 Howard, 117.

ment. The Supreme Court, in issuing the writs asked for, would exercise an original jurisdiction; and that Congress had not given, if, indeed, it had the power to give it. The writs were, therefore, refused.

The president thereupon issued his mandate to the marshal of New York commanding him to surrender Metzger to the diplomatic agents of the French Government. Before, however, the surrender was actually made a writ of habeas corpus was obtained from Judge Edmonds, circuit judge of the Supreme Court of New York. He decided that, in the absence of legislative enactment, neither the executive nor the judicial power had any authority to act upon the treaty of 1843. And that the words in the French treaty being "mis en accusation," the terms "charged" and "accused" in the American version must be so construed as to make them equivalent to that phrase. As that means "indicted" or "arraigned" after examination by the Chambre de Conseil, the prisoner against whom there was simply a complaint made and warrant issued was not within the treaty. He was therefore discharged.*

This decision is obviously quite technical; but it is possible that some of the doubts expressed in the case may have led to the passing, in the following year, of the Act which has since regulated all proceedings in the United States under any extradition treaty. "The Act

* S. District of N. Y. (1847). 1 Barbour, 248. 5 Howard, 176. 5 New York Legal Observer, 83. Wharton's State Trials, 457, *n.* See *Ex parte* Milburn, 9 Peters, 705.

was passed," says Mr. Justice Catron,* "not to give effect to the treaty, but to remove obscurities." The title of the Act is, therefore, clearly a mistake. It is the Act of 12th August 1848, and is entitled, "An Act for giving effect to certain treaty stipulations between this and foreign governments for the apprehension and delivering up of certain offenders." Its provisions are sufficiently important to be given at length:—

"Be it enacted, by the Senate and House of Representatives of America, in Congress assembled:—

"Sect. 1. That in all cases in which there now exists, or hereafter may exist, any treaty or convention for extradition between the government of the United States and any foreign government, it shall and may be lawful for any of the magistrates of the Supreme Court, or judges of the district courts of the United States, and the judges of the several state courts, and the commissioners, authorised to do, by any of the courts of the United States, are hereby severally vested with power, jurisdiction, and authority, upon complaint made under oath or affirmation, charging any person found within the limits of any state, district, or territory, who, having committed within the jurisdiction of any such foreign government, any of the crimes enumerated or provided for by any such treaty or convention, to issue his warrant for the apprehension of the person so charged, that he may be brought before such judge or commissioner, to the end that the evidence of criminality may be heard and considered; and if, on

* In judgment in Kaine's case, 14 Howard, 109.

such hearing, the evidence be deemed sufficient by him to sustain the charge under the provisions of the proper treaty or convention, it shall be his duty to certify the same, together with a copy of all the testimony taken before him, to the Secretary of State, that a warrant may issue upon the requisition of the proper authorities of such foreign government for the surrender of such person, according to the stipulations of the said treaty or convention; and it shall be the duty of the said judge or commissioner to issue his warrant for the commitment of the person so charged to the proper gaol, there to remain until such surrender shall be made.

"Sect. 2. And be it further enacted, That it shall be lawful for the Secretary of State, under his hand and seal of office, to order the person so committed to be delivered to such person or persons as shall be authorised, in the name and on behalf of such foreign government, to be tried for the crime of which such person shall be so accused, and such person shall be delivered up accordingly; and it shall be lawful for the person or persons authorised as aforesaid to hold such person in custody, and to take him or her to the territories of such foreign government, pursuant to such treaty: and if the person so accused shall escape out of any custody to which he or she shall be committed, or to which he or she shall be delivered as aforesaid, it shall be lawful to retake such person in the same manner as any person accused of any crime against the laws in force in that part of the United States to which he or she shall so escape may be retaken on an escape.

"Sect. 4. And be it further enacted, That when any person who shall have been committed under this Act, or any such treaty as aforesaid, to remain until delivered up in pursuance of a requisition as aforesaid, shall not be delivered up pursuant thereto, and conveyed out of the United States within two calendar months after such commitment, over and above the time actually required to convey from the gaol to which he or she shall have been committed, by the readiest way out of the United States, it shall, in every such case, be lawful for any judge of the United States, or of any state, upon application made by or on behalf of the person so committed, and upon proof made to him that reasonable notice of the intention to make such application has been given to the Secretary of State, to order the person so committed to be discharged out of custody, unless sufficient cause shall be shown to such judge why such discharge ought not to be ordered.

"Sect. 5. And be it further enacted, That this Act shall continue in force during the existence of any treaty of extradition with any foreign government, and no longer.

"Sect. 6. And be it further enacted, That it shall be lawful for the courts of the United States, or any of them, to authorise any person or persons to act as a commissioner or commissioners under the provisions of this Act, and the doings of such person or persons, so authorised in pursuance of any of the provisions aforesaid, shall be good and available to all intents and purposes whatever." (9 Stats. at Large, 302; 30 Congress, Sess. 1, ch. 167.)

The principal case which has been decided under the treaty with Great Britain was that of Thomas Kaine in 1852. Kaine was an Irishman, and was charged with an attempt to commit murder in Ireland. In June 1852 Anthony Barclay, the British consul at New York, addressed a requisition and complaint to Judge Betts, stating that it had been represented to Mr. Barclay, and was believed by him, that Kaine did in Ireland, on or about the 5th April 1851, fire a pistol at one James Balfe with intent to murder him; that a warrant to apprehend him was issued by a magistrate of the peace, but that the said Kaine had absconded and fled to the United States. The requisition further stated that the crime of which he had been guilty would have justified his apprehension and commitment for trial if it had been committed in the United States. It then asked that a warrant for his apprehension might be issued, to the end that the evidence of his criminality might be heard and considered; and if on such hearing the evidence should be deemed sufficient, that it should be certified to the proper executive authority, in order that a warrant might issue for his surrender under the treaty between the United States and Great Britain. A warrant was accordingly issued, under which Kaine was brought before Joseph Bridgham, a commissioner of the United States at New York. No witness as to the fact was called, but a policeman produced copies of the warrant of the Irish magistrate, and the deposition on which it was granted, and proved their correctness, and he also proved the identity of the prisoner; on this evidence Kaine was committed. A habeas corpus was then obtained returnable before the Circuit Çourt of the United States for the southern district of New York; but Judge Betts, after hearing arguments, remanded the prisoner into custody. Upon this the Acting Secretary of State issued his warrant directing the marshal to deliver Kaine up to the British consul, but another habeas corpus was obtained from Judge Nelson, and, upon return made, was by him referred to the Supreme Court, where the matter was fully argued. The court, however, refused to decide the case so referred, on the ground that to do so would be to exercise an original jurisdiction which the court did not possess. An application for a writ of habeas corpus was at once made to the Supreme Court by way of appeal from the decision of the Circuit Court. Upon this, the court was divided. Of the judges who took part in the decision, one (Mr. Justice Curtis) held that the Supreme Court had no jurisdiction in the matter; four (Catron, M'Lean, Wayne, and Grier) refused the application for release upon the merits; and the other three (Chief-Justice Taney, and Justices Nelson and Daniel) held that it should be granted. Their reasons were that the commissioner, not being specially appointed for the purposes of the Act, had no jurisdiction; that no judge or commissioner could act on the complaint of a private person; and that, there being no proof of the authority of the Irish magistrate, no competent evidence had been produced. The majority of the court, however, holding these reasons insufficient, the prisoner was remanded. The writ issued by Mr. Justice Nelson, which the Supreme Court had refused to consider, still remained for adjudication, and the matter was argued at chambers. It was there objected, that the decision of Judge Betts sitting in the Circuit Court, upon the return of the writ of habeas corpus before that court, was conclusive, and a bar to any subsequent enquiries into the same matters by virtue of a similar writ. Justice Nelson overruled this objection, and the case was re-argued before him. Opportunity was given to the counsel for the British Government to furnish proof that the prisoner's arrest had been authorised by the President of the United States, but he was not prepared to do so. Justice Nelson accordingly discharged the prisoner upon the three grounds stated in his judgment in the Supreme Court.*

The failure of justice in the case just stated caused an alteration in the practice of the United States. In August 1853 the British Minister requested that the President would issue his mandate to certain magistrates to cause William Calder, charged with forgery in Great Britain, to be arrested and examined, and if the charge should be sustained to certify the same to the President, to the end that the said William Calder should be surrendered. The application was submitted to the Attorney-General (Cushing), who advised that, although the issue of such

* 3 Blatchford Circuit Court Reps., 1. 14 Howard, 103. 10 New York Legal Observer, 257. 1 Robinson's Practice, 10. 6 Opinions of Att.-Gen. 93. 1 Phillimore Comm., 430.

a mandate would be a departure from recent practice, and in his judgment was unnecessary, yet that, considering the opinions expressed by some of the judges in Kaine's case, the request should be granted, and that a mandate should issue whenever desired by the government claiming the surrender. In obedience to the mandate thereupon issued, a warrant of arrest was granted by Judge Edmonds, of the Southern Circuit of the State of New York, Calder was arrested and examined, and the judge certified that there was not sufficient evidence to justify his surrender. The British Minister then applied to the United States Government to give directions that the prisoner should be detained for the time required to produce further evidence. The Attorney-General being again consulted, advised that the President had no power to do this; but that the British Minister could apply at any time for a new warrant of arrest, either with or without a new mandate.*

The judgment of Justice Nelson in the case of Kaine has been referred to in later cases, and by some American writers as deciding that it was within the competence of the court, before which a prisoner might be brought by habeas corpus, to decide upon the sufficiency of the evidence upon which the judge or commissioner taking the examination had acted. The observations of Justice Nelson did no doubt go to this extent. "The proof," he said, "in all cases under the treaty of extradition should be not only complete, but full and satisfactory, that the

* 6 Opinions of Att.-Gen. (Cushing), 91.

offence has been committed by the fugitive in the foreign jurisdiction; sufficiently so to warrant a conviction in the judgment of the magistrate of the offence with which he is charged, if sitting upon the final trial and hearing of the case. No magistrate should order a surrender short of such proof." But the actual decision does not touch this question at all. Justice Nelson held that the commissioner had no authority to commit, as there was before him no evidence at all which could legally be received. It was obviously quite consistent with this decision that the decision of the commissioner should be final as to the sufficiency of any evidence properly before him. And this latter doctrine was expressly affirmed in the next case which came before the court, that of Alexander Heilbronn. In this case Judge Ingersoll, in the District Court of the United States for the southern district of New York, followed the decisions of Judge Judson in the case of Veremaitre,* and Judge Betts in the case of Kaine, and refused to entertain the question of the sufficiency of the evidence upon which the commissioner had acted, remarking, "Where there is legal evidence before the commissioner to establish the charge, and that legal evidence is deemed by him sufficient, no matter how many others may deem it insufficient, and he grants a warrant of commitment, that commitment must stand, and no judge has a right to disregard it, or to render it ineffectual, at least not until the expiration of two calendar months after it shall have been issued. In

* 9 New York Legal Obs., 137.

such a case, no one can revise the opinion of the commissioner except the President. The President has that power. If he should be of opinion that the evidence taken before the commissioner at the hearing was not sufficient to sustain the charge, then it would be his duty to withhold a warrant of extradition. If it should be his opinion that it was sufficient, then it would be his duty to grant such warrant. The necessities of this case, therefore, do not require that I should express an opinion upon the sufficiency of the evidence upon the hearing before the commissioner." *

The necessities of the case did not require these observations about the duty of the President, and they are of little weight. The rights and duties of the President are settled, and limited by the terms of the treaties and the Acts of Congress passed to give them effect, and it clearly is neither his right nor duty to assume a function which those treaties and acts have assigned to the judicial power. Judge Ingersoll's decision was followed in the case of Von Aernam, which occurred very shortly after. The prisoner was charged with uttering forged documents in Canada, and upon examination the commissioner held the evidence sufficient and committed him to prison to await surrender. A writ of habeas corpus was obtained from Judge Betts, District Judge of the Circuit Court of the United States, and upon the return of this writ it was desired on the part of the prisoner to discuss the sufficiency of the evidence before the commissioner. Judge Betts refused to entertain

* 12 New York Legal Obs., 65.

this question, declaring that the courts of the United States had no authority on habeas corpus to enquire into the merits of a decision made by a committing magistrate, or to determine that he erred in the construction of law or the evidence. He added, "In my view of the subject, this court, on the return before it of a writ of habeas corpus, has no further power than to ascertain and determine whether the prisoner stands charged with a criminal offence subjecting him to imprisonment, and whether the commissioner possessed competent authority to inquire into and adjudge upon that complaint." Answering these questions in the affirmative, and holding that he had no authority under the writ to review the justness of the decision of the commissioner, he remanded the prisoner.*

In 1864 occurred the notable case of Franz Müller, who was demanded by Great Britain on a charge of murder. It will be remembered that the police-officer who was in pursuit reached America first, and arrested the fugitive immediately he arrived. Being brought before Commissioner Newton at New York, Müller asked for time to produce witnesses from England to prove an *alibi*, the defence afterwards unsuccessfully set up at the Central Criminal Court. The commissioner refused the request on the ground that it was not his province to determine the question of fact. The evidence before him showed probable

* *Ex parte* Von Aernam, 3 Blatchford Circ. Court Reps., 160. See also Reg. *v.* Van Aernam, U. C. Reps. 4 C. P. 288, *post*, p. 101, Von Aernam was a citizen of the United States.

cause for believing Müller to have committed the crime, and that was the only question he had to try.

The operation of extradition treaties being found to be impaired by the requirements of the American law with regard to evidence, an Act was passed on the 22nd June 1860, similar to that which was afterwards found necessary in England.* It provides, "That in all cases where any depositions, warrants, or other papers, or copies thereof, shall be offered in evidence upon the hearing of an extradition case under the second section of the Act, entitled, 'An Act for giving effect to certain treaty stipulations between this and foreign governments for the apprehension and delivering up of certain offenders,' approved August 12, 1848, such depositions, warrants, or other papers, or copies thereof, shall be admitted and received for the purposes mentioned in the said section, if they shall be properly and legally authenticated, so as to entitle them to be received for similar purposes by the tribunals of the foreign country from which the accused party shall have escaped; and the certificate of the principal diplomatic or consular officer of the United States, resident in such foreign country, shall be proof that any paper or other document so offered, is authenticated in the manner required by this Act," (36 Cong., Sess. 1, ch. 184; 12 U.S. Stats. at Large, 84.)

Since the conclusion of the treaties with Great Britain and France, the United States have entered into many

* 29 & 30 Vict., c. 121. Now repealed by the Extradition Act, 1870, *post*, p. 147, and Appendix, p. xxxvi.

other agreements of a similar nature. In 1845, a treaty with Prussia was negotiated by Mr. Wheaton, but it was rejected by the senate in consequence of the requirement of Prussia that neither power should be required to give up its own subjects. America has never desired to make, or been willing to admit, this reservation,—which, however, is insisted upon by the majority of European states. It was felt that as the United States did not try its citizens for crimes committed abroad, and the other parties to the treaty did, this proviso would produce a want of reciprocity, and that difficulties would probably arise, specially likely in, and important to, the United States, with regard to the case of naturalised subjects. The objection was, however, waived, and a treaty was made in 1852 between the United States and Prussia, acting for herself, and also on behalf of Saxony, Electoral Hesse, Ducal Hesse, Saxe-Weimar, Eisenach, Saxe-Meiningen, Saxe-Altenburg, Saxe-Coburg Gotha, Brunswick, and several of the other petty German states. It provided that the stipulations it contained should apply to any other state of the Germanic confederation which might thereafter declare its accession thereto. This treaty recites, "That whereas the laws and constitution of Prussia, and of the other German states, parties to this convention, forbid them to surrender their own citizens to a foreign jurisdiction, the government of the United States, with a view of making the convention strictly reciprocal, shall be held equally free from any obligation to surrender citizens of the United States;" and its provisions include the crimes of murder, assault with intent to commit murder, piracy, arson, robbery, forgery, the utterance of forged papers, the fabrication or circulation of counterfeit money, whether coin or paper money, and the embezzlement of public money.*

In the year 1863 one Trangott Müller was arrested and brought before Judge Leavitt, Circuit Judge of the United States for the southern district of Ohio, having been charged before the Royal Court of Saxony with one of the crimes included in the Prussian treaty of 16th June 1852. Neither the judge nor the counsel for the Government of Saxony was aware of the Act of June 1860, and after a day's argument, the evidence of criminality was rejected as not sufficient under the second section of the Act of August 1848. The Prussian Government complained of this decision, and the case was referred to the Acting Attorney-General, Mr. T. J. Coffey. Admitting that the Judge was wrong, Mr. Coffey pointed out that there was no appeal from his decision, but he suggested that a fresh authority for Müller's arrest should be issued by the Government of the United States. This was done; Müller was re-arrested and brought before Judge Cadwalader at Philadelphia, under whose decision he was surrendered to the Prussian Government.†

The other treaties into which the United States have entered are thirteen in number. Those with Bavaria,‡ (1853,) Hanover, (1855,)§ the Two Sicilies, (1856,) Austria,

* 10 Stats. at Large of U.S., 965. † 10 Opinions of Att.-Gen., 561.

‡ 10 Stats. at Large of U. S., 1622.

§ 10 Stats. at Large of U. S., 1138. 1 Bright, 271.

(1856,) Baden,* (1857,) Sweden and Norway, (1860,)† and Hayti, (1864,)—contain the exception as to extradition of citizens or subjects; six, those with the Hawaiian Islands, (1849,) the Swiss Confederation, (1850,)‡ Venezuela, (1861,)§ the Dominican Republic, (1867,) Italy, (1868,) and Nicaragua, (1871,)|| omit it. All contain provision as to the evidence required similar to that in the treaties with Great Britain and France.¶

In 1858 a claim of extradition was made upon the United States by Great Britain in the case of William Tyler, a United States Marshal, who, on the 29th Nov. 1858, boarded the United States brig "Concord" when lying in Canadian waters, and in the course of a scuffle shot the master of the vessel. He then arrested him, and had him conveyed to the United States' shore, where the prisoner died. Lord Napier, then the British Ambassador, claimed the surrender of Tyler for murder com mitted within British jurisdiction. But it was answered that the master having died in Michigan, the offence was triable by the United States' courts. The surrender, however, was not absolutely refused, but Lord Napier having consented to await the result of the proceedings about to be instituted in Michigan, a warrant of arrest was granted

* 11 Stats. at Large of U. S., 120. 2 Bright, 135.

† 12 Stats. at Large of U. S., 157. 2 Bright, 135.

‡ 11 Stats. at Large of U. S., 593.

§ 12 Stats. at Large of U. S., 223. 2 Bright, 135.

|| Sanger. Treaties and Postal Conventions between the U. S. and Foreign States, 1872, p. 25.

¶ Wheaton, 6th edit. (Lawrence), 180; 8th edit. (Dana), 190.

to him to be used in case such proceedings should end in the discharge of the accused. Tyler was then tried by the Federal Circuit Court for the district of Michigan, was convicted of manslaughter, and was sentenced to thirty days' imprisonment and a fine of one dollar. The British Government protested against this sentence as inadequate, and at the end of his thirty days' imprisonment, Tyler was again arrested and sent for trial to the State Circuit Court of St. Clair County. He pleaded autrefois convict, and the prosecution replied that the offence charged was the same for which he had been convicted, but that it was not within the jurisdiction of the Federal Court by which he had been tried. Upon demurrer to this replication the question of law was referred by the Circuit judge to the Supreme Court of Michigan, which decided against the prisoner, holding that the Federal Court had acted without jurisdiction. Tyler was accordingly tried in Nov. 1859, and was convicted of murder in the second degree, and sentenced to six years' imprisonment. At this trial a bill of exceptions was tendered to the judge's ruling, and a stay of proceedings obtained. The case was argued before the Supreme Court of Michigan on the 1st May, 1860, and the judge's ruling affirmed. The British Government being satisfied with the second sentence, took no further steps in the matter.*

* The People *v.* William Tyler, 7 Michigan Reps. (Cooley), 161. 8 Michigan Reps. (Cooley), 320. 9 Ops. Att.-Gen., 379 (Black). Evidence of H. T. Holland and Rt. Hon. E. Hammond, Report of Select Committee, 1868, 50, 58.

A remarkable case of extradition, independently of any treaty, occurred in the United States in 1864. One Arguelles, a Spaniard, being governor of a district in Cuba, in which a cargo of Africans had been landed from a slave ship and set free by the authorities, reported to the government that one hundred and forty-one of them had died of the small-pox; but it was discovered that he had sold them into slavery, with the aid of forged papers, and having thus obtained a large sum of money, had escaped to New York. At the request of the captain-general of Cuba and the Spanish minister, Mr. Seward, with the President's sanction, ordered the arrest and delivery up of Arguelles, as a purely executive act. The senate passed a resolution, of 28th May 1864, requesting the President to inform them whether such a surrender had been made, and if so, under what authority of law or treaty it was done. The President enclosed in his reply a report from Mr. Seward, and documents showing the guilt of Arguelles, and the request of the Spanish government. Mr. Seward, in his report, says, "There being no treaty of extradition between the United States and Spain, or any Act of Congress directing how fugitives from justice in Spanish dominions shall be delivered up, the extradition in this case is understood by this department to have been made in virtue of the law of nations and the Constitution of the United States. Although there is a conflict of authorities concerning the expediency of exercising comity towards a foreign government, by surrendering at its request one of its own subjects charged with the commission of crime within its territory, and although it may be conceded that there is no national obligation to make such a surrender upon a demand therefor, unless it is acknowledged by treaty or by statute law, yet a nation is never bound to furnish asylum to dangerous criminals, who are offenders against the human race; and it is believed that if in any case the comity could with propriety be practised, the one which is understood to have called forth the resolution furnished a just occasion for its exercise," (U.S. Dipl. Corr. 1864, part ii. 60–74. Cong. Globe, 1864.)

A resolution, condemning this act as a violation of the Constitution, and in derogation of the right of asylum, was defeated in the House of Representatives by a large majority, and the subject referred to a committee; but Congress took no further action in the matter. Legal proceedings were commenced against the officer who executed the Secretary's warrant on a charge of kidnapping, but these also were abandoned, and the matter has not in any way come under judicial decision.*

It seemed probable that the series of decisions, stated a few pages back, would have been accepted as establishing the inability of the Circuit Court to entertain the question of the sufficiency of the evidence upon which the Commissioner had acted.

* Wheaton, 8th edit. (Dana), 183, *n*. In the recent and notable case of the Bank of England forgeries the Spanish Government acted on this precedent and delivered up Austin Bidwell, who had taken refuge in Cuba, although there is no treaty between Spain and Great Britain.

But in a case which occurred in 1866, these authorities were overruled in a curiously summary way. This was the case of Philip Henrich, who had been claimed by the Prussian government under the treaty of 1852 for forgery, and who had after examination before a Commissioner been committed to prison to await surrender. A writ of habeas corpus was issued from the Circuit Court for the southern district of New York, and the old question as to the competence of the Court to review the evidence of criminality was again fully argued.

Judge Shipman who heard the case quoted the judgments in the successive cases of Veremaitre, Kaine, Heilbronn, and Von Aernam, and overruled them all. The authority upon which he rested his decision was an opinion expressed by Justice Nelson in the case of Kaine, and repeated by that Judge in a private conference upon this particular case. The language of the judgment is somewhat curious. "It is true," said Judge Shipman, "that Justice Nelson in the case of Kaine decided that the commissioner had no competent evidence before him. He therefore did not directly determine the precise question, whether, if the commissioner had had competent evidence presented to him, tending to prove the charge of criminality, it would have been within the rightful power of the court, or the Judge at chambers, to review that evidence; and if he thought it failed to support the charge against the prisoner, to discharge him from custody under the commissioner's warrant. But the whole spirit and scope of his reasoning in the opinion delivered by him in the Supreme Court, as well as in the one delivered by him at chambers, tend toward the assertion and vindication of this power. To set the matter at rest, however, I am authorised by him, after full consultation upon the point, to state that such is his judgment of the law. It is, then, the law of this court, and it is therefore the duty of the court in the present case to look into the evidence upon which the judgment of the commissioner rests, and which he has certified up to this tribunal in compliance with the writ directed to him, and to pass upon its weight as well as upon its competency." Upon examining the evidence, however, Judge Shipman held that it was sufficient, and he laid down as a rule to be observed in similar cases thereafter, that where the commissioner had legal evidence before him, the court would not reverse his judgment except for substantial error in law, or for such manifest error in fact as would warrant a court in granting a new trial for a verdict against evidence.*

In the case of François Farez in 1870, Justice Blatchford while accepting the authority of Henrich's case so far as regarded the examination by the Circuit Court of the sufficiency of the evidence produced before the commissioner, refused to follow the opinion of Justice Nelson as to the quantity of evidence required. Quoting the authority of Chief Justice Marshall, in the case of Aaron Burr, he said "the question for the magistrate is whether, after examination into the matter and a proper oppor-

* 5 Blatchford Circ. Courts Reps., 414. 17 L. T. (N. S.), 55. U. S. Digest (1869), 303.

tunity for the giving of testimony on both sides, there is reasonable ground to hold the accused for trial. The contrary view would destroy the object of such treaties." In this case the prisoner had claimed the right to be examined as a witness on his own behalf, and the commissioner having refused to allow it, the Judge held the commitment invalid. He did not, however, discharge the prisoner, but remanded him into custody under the original warrant of arrest, in order that a further examination might be held.*

This case and that of Henrich are important as laying down rules of practice, and will be referred to in a later chapter.

In the same year occurred the case of Thomas Primrose, who was arrested at Buffalo on a charge of robbery committed in Canada. The case is noticeable for the fact that he was arrested before any mandate had been issued by the President and was remanded upon evidence being given that an application for his surrender had been made by the Canadian Government. The President's mandate afterwards arriving, informations were laid before United States Commissioner Gorham, and he issued a warrant upon which Primrose was brought before him.

The prisoner called witnesses to prove an alibi, but they failed to satisfy the Commissioner, and he was surrendered.†

A very recent and in one respect the most important

* 7 Blatchford Circ. Court Reps., 34, 345, 491. 2 Abbott, N. S. Digest, 346.

† 7 Can. L. J., 109.

case decided in the United States, is that of Richard B. Caldwell, who was indicted for bribing an officer of the United States. He pleaded that the court ought not to take cognizance of the offence charged in the indictment, because at the time when he was arrested and brought within the jurisdiction of the court, he was a resident at Prescott, in the province of Ontario, Dominion of Canada, and was brought into the jurisdiction of the court on a charge of forgery under the provisions of the Ashburton Treaty, and that the offence specified in the indictment was not one of the offences mentioned in that treaty, and that the court had no jurisdiction in the case. His plea was demurred to, and the matter was argued in the Circuit Court of the Southern District of New York, in January 1871. Judge Benedict held that the plea was bad. Whether the prisoner had been extradited in good faith, was, he said, a question for the governments concerned, and not for the Courts of Law; and the prisoner being in fact within the jurisdiction of the court, and charged with a crime committed within that jurisdiction, must be tried for such crime without regard to the matter of extradition at all. In support of this decision he quoted the case of Heilbronn,* who was surrendered to the British Government on a charge of forgery, and was tried and convicted in London for embezzlement, a crime not within the treaty.†

An attempt has lately been made to grant extradition

* See *ante*, p. 62.

† 8 Blatchford Circ. Court Reps., 131. This could not now occur in Great Britain. 33 & 34 Vict. c. 52, § 19.

by virtue of State laws in the case of Carl Vogt, who was arrested in New York on a charge of robbery and murder committed in Belgium. There is no extradition treaty between Belgium and the United States, but a law of the State of New York, passed in 1822 (1 Rev. Stats. 164)* provides that the governor may in his discretion deliver over to justice any person found within the State who shall be charged with having committed without the jurisdiction of the United States any crime except treason, which by the laws of New York, if committed therein, is punishable by death or by imprisonment in the State prison. An application for the surrender of Vogt was made by the Belgian consul, and Governor Hoffman issued his warrant accordingly. A writ of habeas corpus was applied for in the United States' court, but Blatchford, J., dismissed the case for want of jurisdiction. Application was then made to Judge Curtis of the Superior Court, who granted the writ. It was held by the court that the New York statute was unconstitutional, as being in violation of Article 1, § 10, of the Constitution of the United States, which says that no State shall enter into any agreement or compact with another State or with a foreign power. The State could not be constitutionally known to any foreign nation, inasmuch as the whole subject of foreign intercourse is committed to the federal government. This decision came before the Court of Appeal, which unanimously confirmed it upon the same grounds.†

* *Ante*, p. 39. † 7 American Law Review, 186 & 578. See also The People *v.* Curtis, 50 N. Y. 321.

CHAPTER IV.

HISTORY OF THE LAW IN CANADA.

THE law of Canada, with regard to extradition, has been closely connected with that of the United States, and the Canadian provinces were before the mother country in their recognition of international duty upon this subject. In 1827, Joseph Fisher, an alien, was arrested in Lower Canada, charged with larceny in Vermont, and an order was made by the governor of the province for his rendition to that state. A habeas corpus being awarded, Chief-Justice Reid, before whom the case was heard, after full argument and consideration, refused the discharge. In his judgment he adopted the principles laid down by Chancellor Kent in the decision in Washburn's case,* and enforced them by some weighty comments of his own. He said, "The right of surrender is founded on the principle that he who has caused an injury is bound to repair it, and he who has infringed the laws of any country is liable to the punishment inflicted by those laws. If we screen him from that punishment we become parties to his crime, we excite retaliation, we encourage criminals to take refuge among us. We do that as nations which as indi-

* See *ante*, p. 37.

viduals it would be dishonourable, nay criminal, to do. If, on the contrary, we deliver up the accused to the offended nation, we only fulfil our part of the social compact, which directs that the rights of nations as well as individuals shall be respected, and a good understanding maintained between them, and this is the more requisite among neighbouring states, on account of the daily communication which must necessarily subsist between them.* This fugitive was accordingly delivered up, but the government did not accept as conclusive this well-reasoned rule. In 1833 an application was made by the Governor of New York to Lord Aylmer, then Governor of Canada, for the extradition of four men who had crossed the boundary, and barbarously murdered a young woman in the town of Champlain. Lord Aylmer refused the application, saying, in his reply, "It is not competent to the executive, in the absence of any regulation by treaty or legislative enactment on the subject, to dispense with the provision in the Habeas Corpus Act. The subject has received every consideration, and I very much regret to say the opinion of the Attorney-General is confirmed by a majority of those who have been called upon." (Letter of Lord Aylmer to General Marcy, 27th May 1833.)† However, in the same year, the province of Upper Canada remedied this defect in her laws by the passing of a short but comprehensive Act upon the subject. The Act 3 William IV., c. 6, was entitled, "An Act respecting the apprehension

* 1 Stuart, Can. Rep., 245. Quoted Robinson's Practice, i. 9.

† See Holmes *v*. Jennison, 14 Peters, 540.

of fugitive offenders from foreign countries, and delivering them up to justice," and its object was recited to be "for the apprehending and delivering up of felons and other malefactors, who having committed crimes in other countries seek an asylum in Upper Canada."

It enacted—

"1. In case murder, forgery, larceny, or other crimes punishable by the laws of Upper Canada with death or confinement at hard labour, be charged to have been committed within the jurisdiction of a foreign country by a person who has fled to or sought refuge in Upper Canada,—and in case a requisition for the surrender of such person be made by the government of such country, or by its ministers or officers authorised to make the same,—then upon such evidence of criminality as would warrant his apprehension and commitment for trial had the offence been committed in Upper Canada, the Governor may, in his discretion, by and with the advice of the Executive Council, deliver such person up to justice, and direct his transmission to the custody of such foreign government.

"2. For preventing the escape of any person so charged, before an order for his transmission can be obtained from the Governor, any judge or justice of the peace in Upper Canada, acting within his jurisdiction, upon such evidence on oath as satisfies him that the person accused stands charged with some crime of the description hereinbefore specified, or that there is good ground to suspect him to have been guilty thereof, may issue his warrant for the apprehension and commitment of such person, in order that he may be detained in secure custody until application can be made to the Governor for his surrender, and until an order can be made thereon.

"3. But it shall not be incumbent upon the Governor in Council to deliver up any person so charged, if for any reason he deems it inexpedient; and if any person committed under this Act be detained in custody beyond the time reasonably required for carrying the provisions hereof into effect, such person may be discharged upon habeas corpus."

This Act was incorporated in the Consolidated Statutes of Upper Canada, as 22 Vict., c. 96, but was repealed by 23 Vict. c. 41, other legislation extending to the whole of Canada having rendered it unnecessary.

Only one question of difficulty seems to have arisen under this Act, and the case is not reported, but was mentioned by Lord Campbell in the House of Lords.* While, as Sir John Campbell, he was Attorney-General (1834–1841), a slave escaped from his master in the State of New York, and got to Canada. To facilitate his escape, he rode a horse of his master's for a part of the way, but turned it back on reaching the frontier. The authorities of New York, knowing the Canadian government would not give him up as a fugitive slave, took a bill of indictment before the grand jury at New York, and got a true bill returned for felony in stealing the horse, and then

* 60 Hansard, p. 326. See this case referred to in Forsyth's Cases and Opinions on Const. Law, 370.

claimed him. The Canadian government consulted the English government, and the Attorney-General advised that the man could not be given up, as the essential ingredient of the felony, the *animus furandi*, was wanting in his act, and the true bill, where no felony had in fact been committed, did not bring the case within the law.

In the case of Reg. *v.* Tubbee it was held by Macaulay, C.J., that the statute 3 Wm. IV. c. 6 was superseded by the Ashburton treaty so far as concerned Great Britain, Canada, and the United States, but remained in force with respect to other countries. The prisoner, who was charged with bigamy committed in the United States, was therefore discharged, the offence being within the statute, but not the treaty. The chief justice in this case laid down that a judge at chambers has power to review and decide upon the sufficiency of the evidence returned by the committing magistrate, or if necessary to hear further testimony.*

By virtue of the Act of 1833, the treaty between the United States and Great Britain, concluded in 1842,† had immediate operation in the province of Upper Canada; but the Act passed in the following year, to give effect to the treaty in the United Kingdom, was found inconvenient in its application to a territory so extensive as Canada. Accordingly, under the fifth section of the Imperial Act (6 & 7 Vict. c. 76), a Colonial Act was passed (12 Vict. c. 19); and it being left to Her Majesty to fix the day of its coming into operation, an Order in

* 1 Upper Can. Prac. Reps. 98. † See *ante*, p. 46.

Council was made on the 28th March 1850, and proclaimed in May of the same year, by which the operation of the Imperial Act in the colony was suspended. The Canadian Act was afterwards put in the schedule of Repealed Statutes in the Consolidated Statutes (Canada) of 1859, but was re-enacted in terms in those statutes as 22 Vict. c. 89.

The preamble recited that the provision of the Imperial Act, requiring that before the arrest of a fugitive offender, a warrant should issue under the hand and seal of the person administering the government, to certify that a requisition had been made on the authority of the United States, had been found inconvenient, "inasmuch as by the delay occasioned by compliance with the said provision, the offender may have time afforded him for eluding pursuit"; and the first clause of the statute enacted, that upon complaint made, any of the judges of the superior courts in the province, or any of Her Majesty's justices of the peace in the same, might issue a warrant for the apprehension of the person charged;* and if the evidence on the hearing should "be deemed by him sufficient to sustain the charge according to the laws of the province," he should certify the same, with a copy of all the testimony, to

* In the case of Asher Warner (1 U. C., Law Journal 16), the prisoner had been tried in the United States for forgery and found guilty by the jury, but was allowed to be out on bail pending the decision of a point of law. It was decided against him, but no sentence passed, as in the interval he had made his escape to Canada. It was held that he was a person charged or accused within the terms of the treaty and statutes, and might therefore be surrendered to the United States.

the Governor. The other clauses were substantially the same as those of the Imperial Act; but a few alterations were made, which were removed by a later statute. By the 24 Vict. c. 6 (Canada,*) the first three sections of the 22 Vict. c. 89 were repealed, and others substituted for them. In the first of the repealed sections jurisdiction had been given to the justices of the superior courts of the province, and to the justices of the peace. In the new provision the latter were omitted, and jurisdiction was given to "any judge of any of Her Majesty's superior courts of the province, or any judge of a county court in Upper Canada, or any recorder of a city in the province, or any police magistrate or stipendiary magistrate in this province, or any inspector and superintendent of police empowered to act as a justice of the peace in Lower Canada." The former statute had authorised the delivery to the United States, "or any of such states," for crimes committed "within the jurisdiction of the United States or any of such, states." In the amended clauses, the words, "or any of such states," were everywhere struck out. Two other alterations were made in the rules of procedure, in order to bring the law into harmony with that of the United Kingdom. The evidence produced before the magistrate was not to be "sufficient to sustain

* This statute was, as a matter of precaution, sanctioned by the Queen in Council at a Court holden at Balmoral Oct. 11, 1861. 1 Upper Canada, L. J. (N. S.) 60. In the argument in the St. Alban's Raid case, Mr. Abbott said that it was hastily passed, to facilitate the extradition of fugitive slaves. St. Alban's Raid, 164.

the charge according to the laws of this province," but "such as, according to the laws of this province, would justify the apprehension and committal for trial of the person accused;" and in the second clause, which provided that depositions might be produced when "certified under the hand of the person or persons issuing such warrant, *or under the hand of the officer or person having the legal custody thereof*," the latter words were omitted.*

For the sake of clearness, these statutes have been taken together; but in the year before the latest amendments were made, a case had arisen in Canada which caused more excitement, both there and in Great Britain, than had ever been produced by a demand of extradition. This was the case of Anderson.† In September 1853, John Anderson, a negro slave, born in the United States, ran away from his master. About three weeks later, he met and spoke to a planter named Diggs, who recognised him. Anderson asked Diggs where Charles Givens lived, saying he belonged to M'Donald, and wanted Givens to buy him that he might be near his wife. Diggs charged him with being a runaway slave, and refused to let him go. The law of Missouri declares that any slave found more than twenty miles from his home shall be deemed a runaway, and that any person may apprehend a negro being, or suspected of being, a runaway; and it provides

* See now, as to evidence, 31 Vict. c. 94, § 1 of the Dominion (Can. Gaz. 8 Aug. 1868).

† Ann. Reg. (1861), 520, Parliamentary Papers, 1860. 2 Papers of Juridical Society, 452.

a reward for so doing. Diggs, however, told Anderson to come and get his dinner, and he would then go with him to Givens. On the way, Anderson tried to make his escape, and Diggs then called to four negroes who were with him to give chase, saying they should have the reward. Anderson, being overtaken, drew a knife; threatening to kill any one who touched him. The negroes kept off, but Diggs struck at him with a stick, which caught in a bush and broke, and then Anderson stabbed him in the breast. Diggs, turning to flee, caught his foot in a tree and fell, and Anderson then stabbed him in the back, and after being chased a short distance by the negroes, succeeded in making his escape to Canada. Diggs shortly after died of his wounds. Anderson lived unmolested in Canada until 1860, when he was recognised, and was arrested on the application of the officers of the state of Missouri. He was brought before a justice of the peace at Brantford on a charge of murder (under 22 Vict., c. 89,) and the evidence being held sufficient, he was committed to prison, and an application for his extradition was made by General Cass, the United States Secretary of State. A habeas corpus was applied for on behalf of Anderson and the question was argued before the Canadian Court of Queen's Bench.* Chief-Justice Robinson had some doubt whether the court could interfere at all when the justice had made the required certificate.† In his view of the case, however, this

* 20 Upper Canada, Q. B. 164.

† See *Re* Asher Warner, 1 Upper Canada, L. J. (N. S.) 16.

question was unimportant, as, upon the merits, he thought the commitment right. The words of the statute being, "if, on such hearing, the evidence be deemed by him sufficient to sustain the charge according to the laws of this province," the Chief-Justice held that the provision, "according to the laws of this province," referred only to the means and amount of proof, and not to the definition of the offence. By the municipal law of Missouri, Diggs was authorised to arrest Anderson; and by the law of England, the killing of a man legally authorised to arrest the prisoner was murder. Circumstances of justification were for a jury, whose office the justice at Brantford had no right to assume. The fact that, if acquitted, he would be returned to slavery, was not material.* That was a question for the framers of the treaty.

Justice Burns agreed with the Chief-Justice.

Justice M'Lean dissented, and held the commitment bad on three grounds:—

1. The charge was, "did wilfully, maliciously, and feloniously stab and kill," which was not an express charge of murder.

2. The warrant of committal commanded the gaoler to keep the prisoner "until he shall be delivered by due course of law." This was a bad commitment, for the only way in which he could be so delivered was by an order of discharge from that court.†

3. The words, "according to the law of this province,"

* See opinion of Sir F. Pollock, Att.-Gen., 71 Hansard, 56.

† See case of Jacques Besset, 14 L. J. (M. C.), 17; *post*, p. 116.

applied to the nature of the crime, not merely to the quantity of evidence; and as the law of Canada did not recognise slavery, Anderson could not be held to have committed murder in resisting an unlawful detention.

In accordance with the opinion of the majority of the court, the prisoner was remanded; but notice was given of an appeal to the Court of Error and Appeal in Upper Canada. By this time the case had created much excitement in England, and the Secretary for the Colonies addressed a despatch to the Governor of Canada, instructing him not to issue his warrant for the extradition of Anderson, even if the judgment of the Queen's Bench were upheld on appeal. Her Majesty's government, he said, were not satisfied that the decision of the court at Toronto was in conformity with the views of the treaty which had hitherto guided the authorities in this country; and they desired an opportunity of further considering the question, and, if possible, of conferring with the government of the United States upon the subject.

Meanwhile a habeas corpus was moved for in the Queen's Bench at Westminster upon the affidavit (a singularly meagre one) of M. Chamerovzov, the Secretary of the British and Foreign Anti-Slavery Society. The question was argued on behalf of the prisoner by Edwin James, Q.C., Flood, and Gordon Allan, before Chief-Justice Cockburn, and Justices Crompton, Hill, and Blackburn.

The question was whether the Crown, by concurring in the establishment of a separate judicature for Canada, had vested in the courts of that country the exclusive right of issuing a habeas, and the court unanimously held that as the Legislature, in establishing that local judicature, had not expressly abrogated the jurisdiction in this matter possessed by the courts at Westminster, they were, while sensible of the inconvenience which might result from such a course, bound by the precedents quoted to grant the writ.*

It was not however needed. Before it arrived in Canada, the case had been brought by habeas corpus before the Canadian Court of Common Pleas, and that court had, chiefly on technical grounds, overruled the judgment of the Queen's Bench and discharged the prisoner.†

The most important question in the case thus remained without final decision beyond that of the Canadian Queen's Bench. It has, however, been raised in other cases, which will be considered, and the matter discussed in a later chapter of this book.‡ The civil war in the United States gave rise in Canada to two cases of great importance. They were almost contemporaneous, and arose out of very similar circumstances, and involved the same question of law. Slightly the first in order of time was the case of Burley, who was demanded by

* 30 L. J. Q. B., 129; 9 W. R., 225; 7 Jur. N. S. 122; 3 L. T. N. S., 622. In consequence of this decision, the Act 25 Vict. c. 20, was passed, which provides that no writ of habeas corpus shall issue of any court in England to any colony or foreign dominion of the Crown in which any court exists having power to issue and insure the due execution of such writ.

† 10 Canadian C. P., 60. ‡ See *post*.

the United States on a charge of robbery committed on board the steamer 'Philo Parsons' on Lake Erie* on the 19th September 1864. Being brought before the Recorder of Toronto he pleaded in justification that he was a commissioned officer in the service of the Confederate States, that he was entitled to be regarded as a belligerent, and that his object in taking forcible possession of the 'Philo Parsons,' of which act the robbery with which he was charged was part, was to use her as a means to enable his party to effect the release of the Southern prisoners confined on Johnson's Island. He further objected that he was a British subject, and as such could not be surrendered to the United States under the treaty. The Recorder overruled the objection as to nationality, holding that the words "all persons" in the statute were subject to no exception on this ground. He admitted evidence of the matters alleged in justification, granting the adjournments necessary to allow the accused to produce his witnesses. Upon consideration of such evidence, however, he held that the prisoner, having violated neutral territory and been guilty of robbery of a non-combatant, which was not an act of lawful war, was within the treaty, and committed him to prison with a view to his surrender. A writ of habeas corpus was thereupon granted by Hagarty, J., and upon return made, the case was argued before Chief-Justice Draper, (Q. B.,) Chief-Justice Richards,

* 1 Upper Canada, L. J. (N. S.) 20. See also 1 Local Courts and Municipal Gazette, Toronto, 10 (1865).

(C.P.,) (who had been requested by Chief-Justice Draper to sit with him) and Justices Hagarty and Wilson. These judges unanimously remanded the prisoner, saying that the circumstances of the case were so suspicious, that if it had been a case within their own territory, the magistrate would not have been justified in discharging him. Burley had no commission, but his acts were avowed and assumed in a manifesto by President Davis.

Justice Wilson on this point said, "There is an obvious distinction between an order to do a belligerent act, and the recognition and avowal of such act after it has been done. The one is an act of war, the other an act of established government. The one is consistent with what Great Britain acknowledges, the other is not. For us judicially to give effect to the avowal and adoption of these acts would be to recognise the existence of the nationality of the Confederate States, which at present our government refuses to acknowledge."* The

* Burley was surrendered and brought to trial in the State of Ohio. The judge ruled that if the acts complained of had a belligerent object, and were done under the authority of a Confederate Commission, the *animus furandi* was wanting, and he must be found not guilty. The jury disagreed, and the prisoner being released on very moderate bail did not reappear. The minutes of the evidence taken in 1868 by the Select Committee of the House of Commons contain a very singular statement with regard to this case, made by the Right Hon. Edmund Hammond, the permanent Under-Secretary for Foreign Affairs. He said, "It was suggested that the American government contemplated putting him (Burley) on his trial for piracy, which however did not prove to have been the case; but he seems to have been

distinction thus drawn, which has wider and better reasons to support it than can be gathered from the technical manner in which Judge Wilson expressed it, was discussed and illustrated in the other and more valuable case, that of the St. Alban's raiders.* On the 19th October, 1864, Bennett H. Young, with twenty armed followers, entered St. Alban's in Vermont. Declaring themselves Confederate soldiers, they seized the banks, and took possession of the bank-notes and securities they contained. They secured a number of the citizens, and kept them under a guard in a public square. While they were in possession of the St. Alban's bank, a man named Breck entered to pay a note. He was immediately seized, and his money was taken from him

charged in the United States, though not before the Canadian authorities, with assault with intent to commit murder. The question was referred to the law officers in this country, and it was held that, if the United States put him *bonâ fide* on his trial for the offence in respect of which he was given up, it would be difficult to question their right to put him upon his trial also for piracy, or any other offence which he might be accused of committing within their territory, whether or not such offence was a ground of extradition or even within the treaty." Answer 1032. "We admit in this country that if a man is *bonâ fide* tried for the offence for which he was given up, there is nothing to prevent his being subsequently tried for another offence, either antecedently committed or not." Answer 1036.

* The account of this case is taken from a volume published in Montreal in 1865, entitled "The St. Alban's Raid: a Complete and Authentic Report of all the Proceedings. With the Arguments of Counsel, and the Opinions of the Judges, revised by themselves. Compiled by L. N. Benjamin, B.C.L."

by two of the raiders. A skirmish ensued; the raiders failed in an attempt to fire the town, and made their escape, having seized a number of horses belonging to inhabitants of St. Alban's; but on reaching Canada, fifteen of them were arrested without warrants, and without any sworn informations having been taken. One of the prisoners, William H. Hutchinson, was brought before the Recorder of Montreal on a charge of stealing the moneys of the St. Alban's bank and assaulting one of the clerks, and was committed to prison. The warrant of commitment ordered the gaoler to receive "the said William H. Hutchinson and him safely keep for examination." An application was made to Mr. Justice Badgley for a habeas corpus, on the ground that the commital for examination, without mentioning the day, was too general, and also that the information on which the warrant of commitment was issued stated that the prisoner was apprehended on "suspicion of felony," and that this was not a sufficient charge. A writ of certiorari was at the same time moved for to bring up the information, which was sworn to be of the following purport—"That Guillaume Lamothe, chief of police, (by whom it was signed,) arrested the prisoner on suspicion of felony, and found on him ten thousand dollars in Franklin County bank bills, the said bank being situate at St. Alban's, in the State of Vermont, one of the United States of America, and that he had reason to believe that these bills were stolen by Hutchinson, and others with whom he acted in concert." The habeas was granted returnable immediately, but another commitment was at once made out, and returned with the original one. This second commitment was by a justice of the peace for the city of Montreal, and in it both defects were remedied.*

On argument before Judge Badgley, the Recorder's commitment was held too general, and was accordingly quashed, another day being appointed for hearing the application of the prisoner to be discharged from the second warrant. No further separate proceedings were, however, taken in this prisoner's case.

The other prisoners had meanwhile been brought before Justice Coursol, who had signed the second warrant in Hutchinson's case, and were by him remanded for further examination. They immediately petitioned the Court of Queen's Bench for a habeas, on the grounds (1) that the magistrate had no power to remand in cases under the extradition Acts, and (2) that the remand appointed no day for the further examination, and therefore was too general, the statutes giving magistrates power to remand having limited the time to eight days. It appeared, however, that the eight days had not yet expired. The application was peremptorily refused, the judges holding that the power to remand was essential to a magistrate's performance of his duties, and that the irregularity of not

* The validity of a second commitment was discussed and affirmed in the case of Asher Warner—1 Upper Canada, L. J. (N. S.), 16—and in Reg. *v.* Morton and Another, U. C. Reps. 19, C. P. 10, reported as Ex-parte George Henry Martin, 4 Can. L. J. 198. See also observation of Blackburn, J., in Reg. *v.* Tivnan, *post*, p. 128 *n*.

fixing the day was unimportant. They expressed doubts whether they had any jurisdiction until after final commitment.

The examination was then proceeded with by Judge Coursol.

The evidence for the prosecution being closed, the counsel for the prisoners applied for a delay of thirty days to enable them to obtain evidence for the defence.

The petition of the prisoners stated that they desired to prove and could prove that the acts charged against them were done by them as soldiers of the Confederate government, and were duly authorised and directed by the military authorities of the Confederate States, acting under the government thereof, and were acts of warfare committed and performed in conformity with the rules and precedents by which civilised warfare is conducted. The application was opposed on the part of the Crown, and also of the United States, on the ground that it was not the province of the magistrate to receive exculpatory evidence in cases under the extradition treaty, as he would be thereby virtually assuming the jurisdiction of the American courts to try the accused.

Judge Coursol said, "I totally differ from that view, and for this obvious reason, that the Act, to give effect to the treaty, requires that I should be perfectly satisfied of the criminality of the act of the accused according to our own law. The affidavit shows that the accused propose to prove that anything they may have done was an act of legitimate warfare, and as international law is a part of the common law of this country, affecting the character of homicide and other felonies when committed under special circumstances, I cannot be prepared to give my opinion upon the evidence of criminality until I have the whole case before me." He added, that in the 'Chesapeake,'* and other cases, witnesses for the defence were examined without objection. The delay was therefore granted, a promise being given in writing by the prisoners that they would not make any application for release until the month had expired. On the 13th December the inquiry was renewed, and the counsel for the prisoners then made an objection to the jurisdiction of the court. They contended, that in consequence of the alterations made by the 24 Vict., c. 5, in the provisions of the 22 Vict., c. 89, the operation of the Imperial Act 6 & 7 Vict., c. 76, had revived, and that Act requiring a warrant to be issued by the Governor-General in the first instance, which had not been done in this case, the court had no jurisdiction to arrest or detain the prisoners.† Judge Coursol held the objection valid, and at once discharged them.

Immediately after this discharge, Mr. Justice Smith issued a warrant similar to those under which they had been previously in custody, and five of the raiders were re-arrested near Quebec on the 20th December, and brought before him for examination.

At the close of the case for the prosecution the objection which had before succeeded was again raised, but in

* See *post*, p. 123. † See *ante*, p. 82.

an elaborate judgment Mr. Justice Smith overruled it, and held that he had jurisdiction.*

It was then objected that the crime charged was not within the treaty, that it was an offence against the State of Vermont, and as the State jurisdiction of Vermont was separate from, and independent of, the jurisdiction of the United States, it was not covered by the 24 Vict., c. 6, § 1, which only spoke of offences committed "within the jurisdiction of the United States." It was contended that this distinction was recognised by the 22 Vict., c. 89, which spoke of the jurisdiction of the United States, "or of any of such States," and that these words being omitted in the later statute, it intentionally restricted the operation of the treaty to crimes committed solely within the jurisdiction of the United States. Judge Smith held that "jurisdiction" and "territory" were convertible terms when used in the sense of the treaty power. In the treaty and in the law the word "jurisdiction" must mean territorial jurisdiction. The words relied upon were improperly introduced into the earlier Act, and properly rejected from the later one, the law now standing as if they had never been used at all. Upon this decision being pronounced (7th January, 1865) an application was made by the prisoners for another delay of thirty days. Their counsel (Mr. Abbott, Q.C.) thus laid down the principle on which he applied—"If it be really a case of conflicting

* To remove any doubt upon this point an Order in Council was issued, 4th February 1865, declaring the Imperial Act suspended so long as the Provincial Acts should continue in force.

evidence, the fact of the crime being committed being proved, that is no case for a magistrate to try; it is not within his jurisdiction to do so. (*Judge Smith.*—Clearly not; it is none of my business.) But if, on the other hand, the prisoners propose to show that the act committed does not constitute a crime for which extradition could be demanded, that is a question which the judge must investigate and decide. In doing this he does not try the robbery, but the application of the treaty."

Mr. Abbott stated that a delay for a similar purpose had been granted in Burley's case, (for thirty days,) and in another case by Judge Short at Sherbrook.

In spite of the strong opposition of the counsel for the United States, the delay was granted.

On the 10th of February an application for further delay was made on affidavit that the solicitor for the defence had been refused permission to pass the lines to obtain the necessary papers from Richmond, and that Lieutenant Davis, of the Confederate army, who had entered the Federal lines to receive despatches to take to Richmond for this purpose, had been captured and sentenced to death as a spy.

Judge Smith refused further delay. To grant it would, he said, be to decide that the case could not be proceeded with until the war was ended. Witnesses were then called for the defence, chiefly to prove the authenticity of the following documents which were produced: Young's commission as a lieutenant in the Confederate service; his instructions to form a corps of twenty escaped prisoners for special service; the order for the raid signed by Mr. C. C. Clay; the muster rolls of the companies to which the prisoners belonged.

Upon this evidence, after long argument on both sides, Judge Smith, in a very elaborate judgment, discharged the prisoners. He held "that the attack on St. Alban's was a hostile expedition, authorised both expressly and impliedly by the Confederate States, and carried out by a commissioned officer of their army in command of a party of their soldiers. And therefore that no act committed in the course of, or as incident to, that attack can be made the ground of extradition under the Ashburton treaty."

The counsel engaged throughout this case were Mr. Abbott, Q.C., Mr. Laflamme, and Mr. Kerr, for the prisoners; Mr. Johnson, Q.C., for the Crown; and Messrs. Devlin and Ritchie for the United States.

In the year 1866 a case occurred in Lower Canada involving the important question, whether a person who had been surrendered under an extradition treaty could, when put upon his trial, raise the question of the validity and the terms of his extradition. One John Paxton was charged with uttering a forged promissory note, knowing it to be forged. A preliminary plea was put in that the prisoner was a resident in Chicago in the State of Illinois, one of the United States of America, and that he had been thence extradited on a charge of forgery, and could not therefore be legally tried in Canada for any other offence. A replication was filed denying the truth of the plea, and a jury being empannelled to try the issue of fact thus raised, found "that the prisoner was extradited for forgery, whereas he is actually indicted for uttering forged paper."

The Crown prosecutor thereupon moved that the finding and verdict of the jury should be set aside, and a new trial granted upon two grounds, first, that the prisoner had been improperly allowed the right of peremptory challenge; second, that the warrant of the Governor-General authorising the demand of the prisoner from the United States on the charge of forgery did not afford any evidence of the extradition as alleged in the plea. The case was argued before the Crown side of the Queen's Bench (Montreal) on the 20th October 1866. The judges differed in opinion. Drummond, J., was in favour of the prisoner on both points; Badgley, J., in favour of the prisoner on the first point, but against him on the second; Mondelet, Assist.-J., was against the prisoner upon both points. With regard to the more important question involved, Badgley, J., and Mondelet, A.-J., held that the point raised by the plea was not a matter of fact to be submitted to a jury, but was to be determined by the Court itself. In a very powerful judgment, Drummond, J., dissented from and protested against this doctrine. The Court, however, decided that no new trial should be had, inasmuch as no such collateral issue as tendered by the plea should have been submitted to the jury; that the motion therefore should be refused, but that the prisoner should plead and answer to the indictment forthwith, and that the trial thereon should proceed. The prisoner was thereupon again arraigned upon the charge of uttering forged paper, and being called upon to plead to the indictment, said, "I am here by virtue of an Act of Extradition upon the demand made by his Excellency the Governor-General on the United States, charging me with the crime of forgery, and I protest against being called upon to plead to or to answer any other charge than that for which I was so extradited, and I also protest against the unfairness of the Crown in denying the fact of my extradition, which is a violation of the good faith which should mark every proceeding under the treaty, and thus protesting plead not guilty." He was tried and found guilty, but the Court refused to pass sentence until the Court of Appeal should have pronounced upon the validity of the verdict. The Court of Appeal, consisting of the same judges as decided the question before, with the addition of Duval, C.J., affirmed the conviction.* It may be observed that the crime actually charged in this case was within the treaty, but this does not affect the important question involved. The judgment establishes that there is nothing in the law of Canada to prevent the Courts from trying a surrendered prisoner for a crime other than that for which his extradition was granted.†

A further authority upon this point, and in the other

* 10 Lower Canada Jurist, 212, 11, 352.

† See the cases of R. B. Caldwell, *ante*, p. 75; Heilbronn, *ante*, pp. 62, 75; Lamirande, *post*, pp. 102, 168; Renneçon and Faure de Monginot, *post*, pp. 170, 173. See now on this point the Extradition Act, 1870 (33 & 34 Vict., c. 52, §§ 17, 18, 19), *post*, App. XXXVI.

province of Canada, is found in the judgment of Macaulay, C.J., in the case of Von Aernam, who was surrendered to Canada by the United States upon a charge of forgery.* After his committal for trial an application was made for his release on bail, on the grounds that there was no sufficient proof of the *corpus delicti*, or of the instrument being false and fabricated; and it was urged upon his behalf that the offence was at the utmost only a misdemeanour, namely, that of obtaining money by false pretences, which was not an offence within the treaty. Macaulay, C.J., refused the application, saying, "The committing magistrate has transmitted copies of all the depositions, &c. before him, but they are not all that may be reasonably supposed to exist. It is not necessary to express an opinion on the point, but I am much disposed to regard the instrument as a forged bill, and even if the prisoner's offence amounted to false pretences only, I should hesitate to bail him under the circumstances under which he has been taken, surrendered, and received into custody. Being in custody, he is liable to be prosecuted for any offence which the facts may support." †

A notable case which occurred in Lower Canada, and at about the same time as that of Paxton, showed that so far as the safeguards provided by extradition treaties are left to the enforcement of Government officials they are of no great value. In these matters the persons employed to obtain the surrender have generally very strong reasons

* See *ante*, p. 64. † Upper Can. Reps. 4, C. P. 288.

for effecting it whether in accordance with the treaty or in violation of it, and they are aware that the public feeling, without which it is difficult to induce a Secretary of State to act, is not likely to be greatly excited on behalf of a fugitive criminal. One Lamirande, who was cashier to the Bank of France at Poitiers, having abstracted large sums of money from the vaults of the bank, and made entries in the books which he had to keep which were not correct, but represented the sums which would have been in the vaults but for his thefts, fled to Canada, and was claimed by the French Government for the crime of forgery. The warrant of the Governor-General having been issued, the accused was arrested, and after examination before a police magistrate, was, on the 22nd of August, 1866, committed to gaol with a view to his surrender. An application was immediately made to a judge in chambers for a writ of habeas corpus. There could be no question that Lamirande was entitled to his discharge; in the case of Charles Windsor * the Court of Queen's Bench in England had decided that the offence which he had committed was not forgery within the treaty. But at the close of the address of his counsel, the counsel for the Bank of France expressed a desire that the case should be adjourned to the following morning. It was suggested on behalf of the prisoner that as he had been committed by the magistrate to await surrender, advantage might be taken of the delay to remove him from the jurisdiction of the court. This idea was indignantly repudiated by the counsel for

* See *post*, p. 132.

the Bank, and the judge (Drummond, J.) granted the adjournment. When the court sat on the following morning it was found that at the time the adjournment was asked for the French police officers were in possession of the warrant of the Governor-General authorising the surrender; that during the night they had made use of this warrant, and that Lamirande was then on his way to Europe.

The Governor-General telegraphed a statement of the facts to the Secretary of State for Foreign Affairs, but he did not interfere. The friends of the prisoner telegraphed instructions to solicitors in London to endeavour to stop the French police officers while carrying Lamirande through England; but it was vacation time, and there was a difficulty in obtaining or serving a writ of habeas corpus.

The usual diplomatic correspondence followed, with the usual absence of result, and meanwhile Lamirande was convicted in France of forgery upon evidence which in England would clearly not have justified his committal on the charge.*

Of the more recent cases decided in Canada, several refer simply to matters of practice, and do not need any detailed examination.† But three cases in which the questions arose of the amount of evidence to be required

* 10 Lower Canada Reps. 280; 2 Canada L. J. 283, and 4 Canada L. J. 486; Dalloz Juris. Gén. 1867, 2. 171. See *post*, p. 168, and see judgment of Drummond, J., *post*, Appendix, p. xxix.

† Reg. *v.* Robinson, 6 Can. L. J. 98; Reg. *v.* Morton and Another, U. C. Reps. 19, C. P. (N. S. 5) 10, reported as Ex-parte Martin, 4 Can. L. J. 198.

by the committing magistrate and the power of the court to review his decision as to its sufficiency, may properly be quoted here. In the case of John Wesley Kernott, the prisoner was charged with committing forgery in the State of New York, and after examination before the Mayor of Toronto was committed with a view to his surrender. Writs were granted of habeas corpus and of certiorari to remove the proceedings into the Court of Common Pleas. Sullivan, J., sitting in chambers, examined the evidence given, and pronouncing it insufficient, discharged the prisoner. He said, "There are suspicions which may arise from the comparison of handwriting, which probably induced the magistrate to commit the prisoner; but the evidence, on the whole, was not such that I could properly submit to a jury with a charge that if they believed the testimony the offence was made out. It is the duty of all judges and magistrates to be always ready to maintain the public faith with a foreign country; but the citizens of that country, when they come amongst us, are entitled to precisely the same measure of justice as our own people. Neither the treaty nor the statute contemplates the surrender of an accused party upon mere suspicion; and it is well that they do not, for there are so many inducements to procure the extradition of individuals upon pretence of crime falling within the treaty so as to restore them to the foreign jurisdiction for other purposes, that a treaty less guarded than the one under consideration might well lead to great oppression." The counsel for the prosecution having applied that the prisoner might be detained until more perfect evidence could be given, the application was refused, the judge saying he gave no opinion as to whether the magistrate might properly detain the accused on evidence amounting only to ground for suspicion, but he was convinced it would not be right for him to make any such order. The prisoner was fully committed on insufficient evidence, and therefore was entitled to his discharge.* The case of Reno and Anderson, which occurred in 1868, illustrates the necessity of great precaution in surrendering accused persons to a foreign State. They were charged with having attempted to commit murder in the United States. Evidence of an alibi was given on their behalf, and the magistrate having committed them with a view to their surrender, the question of the sufficiency of the evidence was raised before Draper, C.J. He remanded them into custody, saying that the evidence of an alibi was properly received and might be considered by the Governor-General in deciding whether he would grant or refuse extradition, but that if sufficient evidence of criminality was given, the magistrate ought to commit notwithstanding that there was sufficient evidence, if true, to support an alibi.† The two men were accordingly given up, but were never tried. A so-called vigilance committee broke into the gaol at Indiana, where they were confined, brought them out in company with two brothers of Reno, and forthwith hanged them.

* 1 U. C. Chambers Reps. 253.

† Reg. v. Reno and Anderson, 4 Can. L. J. 315.

In 1869 one Albert J. Gould was claimed by the United States on a charge of forgery. In this case there was clearly a *primâ facie* case sufficient to justify the prisoner's commitment, if it remained uncontradicted; but evidence was given to displace it by proving that he had a power of attorney from the person whose name he signed, authorising him so to use the name. Upon this, however, the person in question was called, and said that he signed the power of attorney, believing upon the representations of the prisoner that he was merely witnessing a signature, and that the seal, as indeed appeared from the document itself, was affixed after he had so signed it. The court held that if there were any view of the case which, if submitted to a jury and adopted by them, would warrant a conviction, that would be sufficient. Hagarty, C.J., said, "It is no part of my duty to weigh the evidence or the probably favourable view a jury may take of the prisoner's conduct. I find a decision of the judge before whom the complaint was investigated; I find one view of the evidence adduced in which that decision may be upheld; and whatever opinion I might hold as to the existence of other views, at least as open to adoption, I do not think I am called on to interfere." The prisoner was therefore remanded.*

The important rule that the quality of the offence charged is to be determined by the law of the country where the fugitive is apprehended, was distinctly laid

* Reg. *v.* Albert J. Gould, U. C. Reps. 20, C. P. (N. S. 6), 154.

down in the case of Trueman B. Smith, who was claimed from Canada by the United States in 1869, upon the charge of having in the State of Iowa committed forgery by forging, coining, counterfeiting, and making spurious silver coin of the stamp and imitation of the silver coin of the United States. He was fully committed, but upon return made to a writ of habeas corpus, Adam Wilson, J., said, "This is unquestionably not forgery by the law here, nor from the evidence given can I assume it to be forgery according to the law of the State of Iowa or of the United States of America, if that would make any difference. The statute declares that the offence charged* must be such as would, according to the law of this province, justify the apprehension and committal for trial of the person accused if the crime had been committed here; so that, if not an offence of the character charged according to our law, the person is not to be apprehended, committed, or delivered over to the foreign State."†

In the case of Richard B. Caldwell, claimed from Canada by the United States in 1870, it was held that the uncorroborated evidence of accomplices was sufficient to make a *primâ facie* case, which would justify a committal for extradition. It is difficult to see how on principle or authority this decision can be supported, and the result of the case was a strong warning against so lax a rule. The prisoner was given up to the United States;

* This is obviously a mistake; the words should be "evidence given," not "offence charged."

† 4 Can. L. J. 118; 3 Amer. Law Rev. 178.

he was never tried for the offence for which, upon evidence so unsatisfactory, he had been surrendered; but was tried, convicted, and punished for the offence of bribing an officer of the United States—a matter not of course within the purview of the extradition treaty.*

It only remains to be added that the law of Canada with regard to evidence and practice in extradition cases is now regulated by Stat. 31 Vict., c. 94, § 1, of the Dominion (Can. Gaz. 8 August, 1868), which permits the reception in evidence of copies of the depositions upon which the warrant of arrest has been issued in the United States.

* 6 Can. L. J. 227. See *ante*, p. 74, and 8 Blatchford Circ. Court Reps. 131.

CHAPTER V.

HISTORY OF THE LAW IN ENGLAND.

The history of the subject in England begins with the treaties made with the United States in October, 1842, and with France in 1843. There had been one or two dicta, not decisions, in the English courts, and so far as these went they recognised the duty of the extradition of fugitive criminals; but their authority was very slight, and it was clear that the right to habeas corpus at common law or by statute would, in the absence of treaties or special Acts of Parliament, prevent any proceedings for the rendition of such offenders.

In 1836, certain Spanish convicts were wrecked on the Bahama Islands while proceeding under sentence of transportation from Havannah to Cadiz. The Lieut.-Governor of the Bahamas detained them, and the Attorney-General of the colony advised that such of the convicts as had been convicted of the graver crimes, constituting *mala in se*, should be delivered up to the Spanish Government, and those convicted only of *mala prohibita* set at liberty. But the Attorney-General of England (Sir John Campbell) and the Solicitor-General (Sir R. M. Rolfe) advised that the Lieut.-Governor had no right by the law of England to detain in custody any persons merely on the ground of their having been guilty of offences against the laws of Spain, and that the convicts in question having been wrecked on an island forming part of the territories of His Britannic Majesty were entitled to be dealt with as free agents so long as they conducted themselves in conformity to the laws in force in the Bahama Islands.*

The provision for mutual extradition between the states signing the treaty of Amiens in 1802, contained in that treaty, never came into operation in consequence of the speedy renewal of the war.

And the French Minister of Justice was exactly correct in the statement in his circular of the 5th April 1841, that extradition could not be obtained from Great Britain, because her legislation did not allow it.

Only one demand seems to have been made upon Great Britain before the date of these treaties, and that was by the United States in 1841, in the case of the *Creole*. This case has scarcely received sufficient notice; apart from the question of the necessity of legislative provisions, it is useful in illustrating the cases of Anderson in Canada, and Tivnan in England.†

On the 27th October 1841, the brig *Creole* sailed from Hampton Roads to New Orleans with a cargo of slaves. On the 7th November the negroes rose, murdered a passenger named Hewell, the owner of some of the slaves, wounded the captain and the mate, and took the vessel into Nassau. At the request of the American consul, the

* Forsyth's Cases and Opinions on Const. Law, 341.

† See Anderson's case, *ante*, p. 84. Tivnan's, *post*, p. 126.

Governor put a guard on board, and the matter was investigated by two magistrates.

Nineteen slaves were identified as having participated in the mutiny and murder, and they were placed in confinement, the Governor refusing to give them up to the American Government. The rest were set at liberty. The nineteen were tried at Nassau for piracy and acquitted. The law authorities in England were unanimously of opinion upon this case that they could not be given up in the absence of an Act of the English Parliament giving power to the executive.*

For this reason the extradition clause of the Ashburton treaty, which has already been quoted, while it took immediate effect in America and Canada, did not come into operation in England until August 1843, when the Act 6 & 7 Vict., c. 76, was passed. Some objection was made to this Act in the House of Commons, where fears were expressed that advantage might be taken of the treaty to get back fugitive slaves on pretended charges of robbery. The Attorney-General (Sir F. Pollock), being appealed to on the subject, said that, upon a charge of crime being made against a fugitive, his personal status in the country from which he had fled would be wholly immaterial.

Upon this an amendment was moved by Mr. Hawes, to exclude slaves from the operation of the Act, but it was defeated by 59 to 25.†

The previous chapter, 6 & 7 Vict., c. 75, had made

* Ann. Reg., lxxxiv. 312. Hansard, lx. 27-30, 318-327.

† Hansard, lxxi. 566.

provision for carrying into effect the treaty with France, which had been signed at London on the 13th February, 1843.* The Acts were very similar, differing chiefly in the enumeration of the crimes for which extradition should be accorded to the respective countries.

To France, criminals might be delivered if they were accused of "murder (comprehending the crimes designated in the French penal code by the terms assassination, parricide, infanticide, and poisoning) or of an attempt to commit murder, or forgery, or of fraudulent bankruptcy;" † to the United States, if they were charged with "murder,

* 6 Hertslet's Commercial Treaties, 344.

† As to the meaning of this term in the treaty, refer to 5 & 6 Vict., c. 122, § 32. The following is the definition in the law of France:—"Sera déclaré banqueroutier frauduleux et puni des peines portées au Code pénal tout commerçant failli qui aura soustrait ses livres, détourné ou dissimulé une partie de son actif, ou qui, soit dans ses écritures, soit par des actes publics ou des engagements sous signature privée, soit par son bilan, se sera frauduleusement reconnu débiteur de sommes qu'il ne devait pas."—Code de Commerce, liv. 3, tit. 2, ch. 2, art. 591. It will be observed that this definition does not include the offence of not surrendering to the bankruptcy jurisdiction, and it is clear that such failure to appear cannot properly be called a crime, and ought not to be a ground of extradition. It is simply the making default in a civil proceeding. However, the Act of 1870, and the treaties made since that date, substitute the term "crimes by bankrupts against bankruptcy law," for "fraudulent bankruptcy," referring to the offences mentioned in the Debtors Act, 1869 (32 & 33 Vict., c. 62. Roche and Hazlitt's Bank; Law edit. 1873, p. 207). As no treaty has been made between Great Britain and France but that of 1843, which, by a rather questionable decision of the Court of Queen's Bench, has been held to be

to the United States, if they were charged with "murder, or assault with intent to commit murder, or piracy, or arson, or robbery, or forgery, or the utterance of forged paper."

In both Acts it was provided that, upon requisition duly made, it should be lawful for the Secretary of State to issue his warrant signifying that such requisition had been made, and requiring all justices of the peace and other magistrates and officers of justice to govern themselves accordingly. Thereupon it should be lawful for any such justice of the peace to examine, upon oath, any person or persons touching the truth of the charge, and upon such evidence as, according to the laws of that part of her Majesty's dominions, would justify the apprehension and committal for trial of the person so accused, if the crime of which he or she should be so accused had been there committed, to issue his warrant for the apprehension of such person, and also to commit the person so accused to jail, there to remain until delivered pursuant to the requisition. In every case, "copies of the depositions upon which the original warrant was granted, certified under the hand of the person or persons issuing such warrant, and attested upon the oath of the party producing them, to be true copies of the original depositions," might be received in evidence of criminality.

still in force, a bankrupt cannot be claimed by us from France for the offence of non-surrender although he might be so claimed from Belgium, Germany, Italy. See Oke's Magist. Synopsis, 864. See also Greenwood and Martin's Magisterial and Police Guide, pp. 210–222.

It was provided in the Act relating to France, that no justice of the peace or other person should issue his warrant for the apprehension of any such supposed offender, until it should have been proved to him, upon oath or by affidavit, that the party applying for such warrant was the bearer of a warrant of arrest, or other equivalent judicial document, issued by a judge or competent magistrate in France, authenticated in such manner as would justify the arrest of the supposed offender in France upon the same charge, or unless it should appear to him that the acts charged against the supposed offender were clearly set forth in such warrant of arrest or other equivalent judicial document.

No provision similar to this was inserted in the Act relating to America.

In both Acts it was provided, that any person committed under them might be discharged if he were not delivered up within two months. By the 8 & 9 Vict., c. 120, the powers of these Acts were extended to the police-magistrates of the metropolis; and it was provided that their warrants (forms of which were given in a schedule) might be executed in any part of England.

Attempts were almost immediately made to put these Acts in force. The first case was that of J. C. Clinton, who was claimed by the American Government on a charge of forgery, committed in the United States several years before. The magistrate before whom he was brought thought fit to discharge him, on the ground that the *original* depositions had been produced, whereas the statute only applied to *copies*.* Meanwhile a case had been submitted to the Attorney and Solicitor-General (Sir F. Thesiger and Sir F. Kelly), who advised that the treaty and Act were retrospective, and suggested that Clinton should be re-arrested in term time, and that the judge to whom he might apply for a habeas corpus should be pressed to refer the matter to the full Court.† He was accordingly again arrested, and a habeas corpus was then obtained from Mr. Baron Platt. On its return, Mr. Knowles, Q.C., and Mr. Clarkson for the prisoner, contended that the Act 6 & 7 Vict., c. 76, could not have a retroactive effect. It could not have such effect in America (the United States Const., Art. 3, § 9, providing that no *ex post facto* law should be passed in the United States), and the contracting parties and the British Parliament must be held to have intended perfect reciprocity. Besides, as a Criminal Act, it must be construed strictly. Sir John Bayley, for the prosecution, relied on the fact that the Act, with regard to France (6 & 7 Vict., c. 75), expressly excluded all offences committed antecedently to the date of the treaty, while that relating to America did not. To give the Act retrospective effect would not be to make an *ex post facto* law, as it created no new offence, assigned no new punishment, and did not alter the nature of the evidence required.

Mr. Baron Platt, after short consideration, having no doubt upon the matter, declined to leave it for argument

* Egan on Extradition, 48.

† Forsyth's Cases and Opinions on Const. Law, 366.

before the full Court, and discharged the prisoner. He said that there was much weight in the argument with regard to reciprocity, and, explaining the words of the Act by reference to the terms of the treaty, he was bound to hold that the word "committed" meant "committed after the date of the treaty."*

The next case was that of Jacques Besset, who was claimed by the French Government on a charge of fraudulent bankruptcy, and being brought before Alderman Magnay (then Lord Mayor), was by him committed, 23rd September, 1844.

A writ of habeas corpus was granted by Mr. Justice Wightman at chambers, but stood over until term by consent. It was then argued in the Queen's Bench before Lord Denman, C.-J., and Williams, Coleridge, and Wightman, JJ., by Mr. Montagu Chambers for the prisoner, and Mr. Edwin James against the discharge. Sir F. Thesiger, Att.-Gen., and Mr. Gurney, watched the case for the Lord Mayor. Several objections were taken to the commitment, the chief being, that its conclusion, "until he shall be discharged by due course of law," was bad (Mash's case, 2 W. Bl., 805). Lord Denman, delivering judgment, said, "I regret that on the first application which has come before us under this statute, the warrant is so defective that we cannot allow the Act to take effect. Neither we nor the gaoler have any power but such as the statute

* 6 L. T., 66. See Metzger's case, *ante*, p. 53. See also the case of *Ex parte* Bouvier, *post*, p. 149. The doubts then expressed caused the passing of the Extradition Act, 1873.

gives; and its provisions have not been rightly pursued. We are asked to remand the prisoner on our own authority, as charged with a crime: but we know nothing of the crime, unless as it is brought before us by the warrant; or, I should rather say, we have no authority of the kind in such a case. If we could act in the manner suggested, the statute would have been unnecessary. The prisoner must be discharged.

The other judges concurred.

Lord Denman—"It is proper that it should be understood that this application is at common law. The statute 31 Car. II., c. 2, is not necessary to the right of making it."*

The same result as had occurred in the cases of Clinton and Besset attended almost all the efforts made to put the law in force. Between 1843 and 1852 France claimed fourteen fugitives. In only one case was the extradition obtained, and that was through the person being apprehended in the island of Jersey. This caused a not unnatural dissatisfaction on the part of the French Government, who from time to time made representations to England upon the subject. In 1846, in answer to one of these representations, Lord Aberdeen informed Count St. Aulaire that the note of the French Ambassador had been referred to the Home Department and to the law officers of the Government, and that these authorities

* 6 Adolphus and Ellis, 481. 14 L. J. (M. C.) 17. 1 New Sessions Cases, 337. 9 Jur. 66. See Metzger's Case, 1 Barbour (S. C. of N. Y.), 254.

were of opinion, in which Lord Aberdeen entirely concurred, that to obviate the difficulty complained of by the French Government, a new Convention and a new Act of Parliament were necessary; and that in such new Convention the clause requiring that French subjects should not be delivered up unless the evidence of their guilt was such as to warrant their commitment for trial by the law of the country in which they had taken refuge, ought to be altogether omitted, as being contrary to the real intentions of the contracting powers, and productive of many causes of insuperable difficulty in carrying out the objects of the Convention. A draft of the new Convention was sent to the Count by Lord Aberdeen in the same year. Notwithstanding this expression of opinion, nothing more was done in the matter until May 1852, when the Government of Lord Derby concluded a Convention with France,* and introduced into the House of Lords a Bill to give effect to it in England. This Convention largely increased the list of crimes for which extradition might be granted; the complete list being "murder and attempts to murder; the procuring abortion; rape; manslaughter; sending threatening letters; bigamy; child-stealing; perjury; subornation of perjury; coining or uttering counterfeit coin; counterfeiting the great seal, or using the counterfeit seal; counterfeiting or falsifying of public securities and bank-notes authorised by law; using such counterfeit securities and notes; counterfeiting the puncheons used for marking

* See Appendix, p. vi. 9 Hertslet's Commercial Treaties, 281.

articles of gold and silver, and using the counterfeit puncheons; counterfeiting the public stamps, and using the counterfeit stamps; feloniously forging, and uttering forged instruments; arson; robbery; burglary; stealing in a church or chapel; housebreaking; larceny, or embezzlement by clerks or servants; embezzlement by public officers; fraudulent bankruptcy, and complicity in fraudulent bankruptcy (only in those cases which in the United Kingdom are considered as felony, and punishable by the penalty of transportation); destroying a ship or other merchant vessel; and piracy." In a series of twenty carefully-drawn clauses these crimes were described by the names appropriate to them in the French penal code, in the law of the United Kingdom, and, where necessary, in that of Scotland. And it was agreed that to every demand in extradition the article of the law under which the charge was made should be annexed, and that the demand should only be made by the French Government in those cases in which the acts charged should in France be considered as *crimes*, and be punishable with severe and degrading punishments (*peines afflictives et infamantes*), and by the English Government when the said acts should be considered as felonies, and be punishable with death, or transportation, or imprisonment with hard labour. The Convention applied to persons who had been convicted, as well as to those simply accused.

It was provided, that in the case of a demand by the French Government the ambassador should produce either a sentence of conviction (*arrêt de condamnation*), or a warrant for apprehension (*mandat d'arrêt*), clearly setting forth the nature of the crime with which the fugitive should be charged, and that the Home Secretary, having verified the authenticity of these documents, and ascertained that the crime therein specified was within the Convention, should issue his warrant to a magistrate notifying him of these facts. Thereupon the magistrate should issue his warrant of arrest, and, being satisfied when the accused was brought before him of his identity, should order him to be conveyed to the frontier to be there delivered to the agent of the French Government.

In the Convention of 1843, no exception was made of persons charged with political offences. That omission was remedied in the Convention of 1852, the seventh article of which provided—"No accused or convicted person who may be surrendered, shall, in any case, be proceeded against or punished on account of any political offence committed prior to his being surrendered, nor for any crime or offence not described in the present Convention, which he may have committed previously to his being surrendered; and proof of his having been so surrendered under this Convention shall be a good and valid defence against any proceeding on account of any political offence previously committed, and shall entitle the party to an immediate acquittal." * In introducing into the

* It will be observed that under this Convention a person who had been surrendered could have been tried for other offences than that for which his rendition had been granted, provided that

House of Lords the Bill to give effect to this Convention, Lord Malmesbury, the Foreign Secretary, who had negotiated it, said that he was authorised by the French Ambassador to declare that any Article which the wisdom of Parliament or the ingenuity of our legal profession could invent or draw up, that would perfectly secure political offenders from being surrendered, and prevent any use of the Convention that might fall on such offenders, he was authorised to state the French Government would be willing to accept. This declaration put an end to any serious opposition on this point, but grave question was raised as to the wisdom of abolishing the rule which required evidence of the fugitive's guilt to be produced before the magistrate. The discussion being adjourned, Lord Malmesbury on a later evening proposed certain amendments, the principal of which was that the Secretary of State should not issue his warrant until documentary proof of the accusation was produced, certified under the hand of the *Juge d'Instruction.* The introduction of any amendment, however, caused a serious difficulty, as it would necessitate a supplementary Convention. And attention was called in the House of Lords to the fact, that a law had recently been revived in France which provided for the trial of foreigners before French tribunals for crimes committed out of France. The law was not a new one, and it was similar to the provisions of several European codes; but a strong feeling was expressed in

such other offences were not political, and were within the list of crimes contained in the Convention.

the House of Lords upon the subject, and the discovery, united with the other and more practical difficulties, caused the abandonment of the Bill. The Convention has therefore never come into operation.* It would in many respects have been an improvement upon the former treaty. "It was," says Sir George Cornewall Lewis, "drawn with care and ability, and by it the obstacles which have rendered the Treaty of 1843 inoperative would have been removed." † But it would have been easy to devise a scheme which would have greatly facilitated extradition without dispensing with the requirement that *primâ facie* evidence of guilt should be produced before a magistrate, a safeguard to the fugitive which it is not likely or desirable that an English Parliament will ever consent to take away.

For twenty years (from 1844 to 1864) no case of extradition was argued before English Courts. During this time France had made various demands, (seven between 1854 and 1856, none between the latter year and 1859,) but in no case was the extradition obtained.

The United States were more successful. Between 1854 and 1859, eleven such applications were made, and in six of them the criminal was given up. These six were all cases of murder or attempt to murder; ‡ and they all

* See Debates upon the Bill, Hansard, cxxii. 192, 498, 561.

† On Foreign Jurisdiction, &c., p. 40.

‡ Some of these appear to have been strictly cases of piracy. See U.S. *v.* Gibert, 2 Sumner, 24; and Judge Story's judgment therein.

occurred on the high seas, on American ships which put into Liverpool, so that the witnesses were on board, and could easily appear before the magistrate.*

At the beginning of the year 1864, a case came before the Court of the Province of New Brunswick which arose out of the Civil War in the United States, and involved several important questions of Extradition Law. This was the case of David Collins and another, who were charged with piracy on board the United States' brig 'Chesapeake.' The facts were not disputed. The 'Chesapeake' traded from New York to Portland, Maine, carrying freight and passengers. She left New York on the 5th December, 1863, and upon the 7th, when she was about twenty miles from the United States' coast at Cape Cod, some of the passengers who had come on board at New York took possession of the vessel in the name of the Southern Confederacy. A short conflict took place, in which the second engineer was killed, and the mate and the chief engineer were wounded. The crew were then put ashore in a pilot boat, and the Confederate flag was hoisted, but the vessel was soon afterwards retaken by a United States' gunboat. None of the persons who had been concerned in the seizure of the brig were then taken prisoners, but several of them, including Collins, McKealy and Seeley, were afterwards found in New Brunswick, and the United States' consul at St. John addressed a letter to the

* Sir G. C. Lewis on Foreign Jurisdiction, &c., p. 40. For the result of applications made by England to France, see Appendix, p. xxvi.

Provincial Secretary of New Brunswick, requesting that under the provisions of the Ashburton Treaty these persons should be arrested with a view to their examination on a charge of piracy. A warrant was accordingly issued by the Lieutenant-Governor of the province authorising the arrest. The letter from the United States' consul was accompanied by depositions sworn before the magistrate at St. John, N.B., on the 22nd December, and upon the issuing of the Lieutenant-Governor's warrant, a warrant of arrest was issued by the same magistrate, and the three persons named were apprehended and brought before him on the 4th of January, 1864. The charge proceeded with was that of piracy. The objections afterwards taken before the Court were raised before the magistrate, but were overruled by him. The evidence of the acts of the prisoners being given, and not in fact disputed, witnesses were called on behalf of the defence to show the belligerent character of the acts charged. The Queen's Proclamation of Neutrality was put in, and also a certified copy of the commission establishing a Court in the Province of New Brunswick for the trial of piracy and other offences committed on the high seas, passed at Westminster the 11th day of April, 1829, by writ of Privy Seal. The police-magistrate, however, held that the treaty included piracy committed on an American vessel on the high seas, and that the prisoners had not shown authority from the Confederate Government to commit the acts charged, and added, that looking at the circumstances of the case, he considered the seizure of the

'Chesapeake' was not an act of war, but was done *animo furandi*. He therefore committed the prisoners with a view to their extradition. A writ of habeas corpus was at once sued out, and the case was elaborately argued before Judge Ritchie by Gray, Q.C., and Weldon for the prisoners, and Wetmore, Q.C., and Tuck for the United States. Judge Ritchie took time to consider, and on the 14th March, 1864, delivered a full and very able judgment, discharging the prisoners. He held that the requisition for the surrender was insufficient, as it was not made by a public minister of the United States, but by a consul not claiming any special authority to ask for the surrender, and not indeed asking for it in his letter. The taking of depositions before the police-magistrate was entirely without jurisdiction, as he had no evidence before him that the persons had been legally charged in the United States with the commission of the offence for which their surrender was to be asked. Further, the piracy charged was not municipal piracy, but piracy by the law of nations justiciable wherever the offender might be found, and as the Court of New Brunswick had jurisdiction in the case, the prisoners could not be given up under the treaty. The police-magistrate, he added, had no jurisdiction in cases of piracy,* and the warrant of commitment was bad for showing that the prisoners were

* This was a mistake. The Imperial Statute 12 & 13 Vict., c. 96, gave colonial magistrates jurisdiction in such cases; but it was not brought to the notice of Judge Ritchie. It was not, however, upon this ground that the prisoners were discharged.

examined on charges not included in the warrant of the Lieutenant-Governor, and that upon the face of the warrant no adjudication appeared that the evidence was sufficient according to the law of the province to justify committal for trial.*

In the same year the main question involved in this case came before the Court of Queen's Bench in England, and was similarly decided. This was the case of Tivnan and others,† charged with having "on the high seas, on board a certain American ship, committed the crime of piracy, within the jurisdiction of the United States of America."

The circumstances of the case were briefly these. On 16th November 1863, the United States' steamer 'Joseph L. Gerrity' left Matamoras for New York with cotton. Just before she started, six persons, among whom were the prisoners, came on board as passengers, and on the following night they seized the ship, telling the captain to consider himself a Confederate prisoner. The leader of the party, a person named Hogg, who was believed by the captain to be a major in the Confederate service, said at the time of the seizure that he had proper authority for the act, but did not exhibit any papers.

* "The 'Chesapeake.' The case of David Collins et Al. Compiled from the original documents." Published by J. and A. McMillan, St. John, N.B., 1864. The author is indebted for a copy of this pamphlet to the kindness of an anonymous friend in New Brunswick.

† 5 Best and Smith, 645; 33 L. J., M. C., 201 (Tirnan); 12 W. R., 851 (Turnan); 10 L. T., N. S., 499 (Tivnan).

A few days after the seizure the captain and some of the crew were set adrift in a small boat. The prisoners were afterwards discovered in Liverpool, and on application from the American consul there, the Secretary of State issued his warrant under the 6 & 7 Vict. c. 76. They were thereupon brought before a magistrate at Liverpool, and, the examinations having been taken, were remanded to prison, and it being understood that no further evidence would be taken,* counsel instructed on their behalf by the agents of the Confederate Government moved in the Court of Queen's Bench for a habeas corpus. The writ was granted, and on its return Messrs. Edward James, Q.C., Littler, and J. H. James, moved that the prisoners be discharged.

They contended :—

1. That the Treaty of the 22nd August, 1842, and the Stat. 6 & 7 Vict. c. 76, founded upon it, extended only to acts declared piracy by the municipal law of either of the contracting parties, and not to piracy by the law of nations, which is punishable anywhere. The words of the statute, "delivering up to justice" persons "seeking an asylum," (*i.e.*, a place where they cannot be punished,)

* "Remands were made from time to time, but there has been no final commitment. It is not in general the practice of this Court to interpose before the magistrate has given his final decision, seeing that on a future hearing before him fresh evidence might be adduced. I say this, speaking with reference to the future, for I cannot help seeing that the last of these remands was made in order to ask our assistance."—Compton, J., 5 Best and Smith, 682.

showed that the words "within the jurisdiction" must be taken to mean "within the exclusive jurisdiction" of the respective States. *Re* Kaine, judgment of Nelson, J., 14 Howard, Sup. Court cases, U.S., 137; Marshall's Speech, 5 Wheaton, Sup. Court, U.S., Appendix i.; Opinions of the Attys.-Gen., viii. 84.

2. That the warrant of a justice of the peace under this statute, to apprehend or commit a person for trial, must be founded on one from the Secretary of State, who has no power to issue his except on the view of an original warrant issued and depositions taken in America, which did not appear here. Klüber, § 66. Martens, Précis, § 101. Opinions of Attys.-Gen., vi. 485, and vii. 6. *Re* Kaine, 14 Howard, Sup. Court, U.S., 103.

3. That the warrant of the magistrate was bad for not showing that all the witnesses before him were examined upon oath.* Mash's Case, 2 W. Bl., 805. Kite and Lane's Case, 1 B. and C., 101. Nash's Case, 4 B. and A., 295.

4. That there was no evidence before the magistrate of piracy by the law of nations. The 'Melomane,' 5 Rob. Adm., R 41. The United States *v.* Palmer, 3 Wheaton, 610.

Messrs. Lush, Q.C., Milward, and Vernon Lushington, *contrà*.

* "Suppose the magistrate's warrant defective in this respect, it could be cured by a fresh warrant. We would not discharge on habeas corpus for such a reason."—Blackburn, J., 5 Best and Smith, 668. See St. Alban's Raid, *ante*, p. 93.

1. The term "jurisdiction" has two different significations. First, its primary, natural sense—the right to deal with particular things or persons. Second, its far more common acceptation—the territorial limits within which that authority is exercised. It is in the latter sense that the word is used in the treaty and the statute.

Either of the expressions "jurisdiction" or "territory" in the treaty would extend to all places where the laws of the country have authority, and would therefore include offences committed on shipboard; since for the purposes of law, protection, and punishment, a ship is part of the territory to which she belongs. Wheaton's Int. Law, 7th edition, (Lawrence,) 208. Reg. *v.* Lopez. Dears and B., 525. Marshall's Speech, 5 Wheaton, Sup. Court, U.S., App. i.

On the second and third points they were stopped.

4. The act done was on its face piratical, and not belligerent. There was no proof that the prisoners seized the ship for the Confederate Government, or even that they belonged to the Confederate States.

The second and third points all the judges held to be immaterial, and on the fourth they thought they were not entitled to say that there was no evidence of piracy upon which the magistrate might commit. At the same time they agreed that the establishment of a belligerent character would put an end to the charge.

Upon the main question the court was divided: Crompton, Blackburn, and Shee, JJ., held that the prisoners were either belligerents, and therefore not triable at all, or pirates *jure gentium*, and in that case being triable anywhere they could not be delivered up under the treaty. "Jurisdiction" was held to mean "exclusive jurisdiction," and the word piracy, therefore, meant only "municipal piracy," which alone would be within that exclusive jurisdiction. Cockburn, C.-J., dissented, holding that the term "piracy," there being nothing to limit its operation, must be taken in its comprehensive sense of piracy *jure gentium*. And as this crime was cognisable by the tribunals of all countries, the word "jurisdiction" could not be taken to mean "exclusive jurisdiction." "The language," said the Chief-Justice, "is most comprehensive, and why then is it to be construed in a limited sense? It is said, and with truth, that the primary and original mischief which the statutes of extradition meant to prevent, was that of persons committing crimes in one state, and escaping beyond the reach of the law of that state, and so enjoying impunity; and it is also contended that for that purpose alone were those statutes passed. That that was their primary and principal object there can be no doubt, but that it was the only one I entertain great doubt; for it is impossible not to see that the mischief which it is the object of all civilised states to prevent, is not limited to such cases. An offence may be cognisable, triable, and justiciable in two places, *e.g.*, a murder by a British subject in a foreign country. A British subject who commits a murder in the United States of America may be tried and punished here by our municipal law,* which is made to extend to its citizens in every part of the world. But it would be highly inconvenient, except in certain exceptional cases, that he should be tried in this country for that crime, because criminals escape, not only by being beyond the reach of the law which they have offended, but in consequence of the difficulty, if not impossibility, of proof, unless the offender is brought to justice where the offence has been committed. If, therefore, I find the language of a statute large enough to comprehend both instances, it would be highly inexpedient to restrict it to one alone."

Little notice was taken by the other judges of this point, and it has not since arisen in practice, but it is clear that the case supposed by the Lord Chief-Justice was within the rule laid down by the other judges, and that the English Government would have been bound under that rule to refuse the extradition of the murderer, and to insist that if tried at all he should be tried here, by proceedings which would be at once unfair to the prisoner, and costly and difficult to the prosecution.

The case is now met by the Extradition Act, 1870, § 6., which provides that the surrender may take place whether there is or is not any concurrent jurisdiction in any court of Her Majesty's dominions over the crime charged.

* 24 & 25 Vict., c. 100, § 9, re-enacting 9 Geo. IV., c. 31, § 7. "Murder or manslaughter, or being accessory before the fact to either." See R. *v.* Sawyer, R. and R., 294.

In the following year a case arose, the decision in which was of equal importance with that just cited, and established a very valuable principle.

The prisoner, Charles Windsor, had been the paying teller in the Mercantile Bank of New York, and as such he had the custody of all the money in the vaults of the bank. On the 28th October, 1864, he asked the receiving teller to do duty for him for the next few days, and handed him the "first teller's proofs," where was the following entry:—"Vault, 207,098 dollars reserve." He never returned to the bank, and upon inspection of the vault a large deficiency was discovered, amounting in specie alone to upwards of 30,000 dollars. A warrant was then issued in New York for his apprehension upon the charge of "forgery" under the following section of the New York Forgery Act, 1822:—

"Every person who, with intent to defraud, shall make any false entry, or shall falsely alter any entry made in any books of accounts kept by any *monied* corporation within this state, or in any book of accounts kept by any such corporation or its officers, and delivered, or intended to be delivered, to any person dealing with such corporation, by which any pecuniary obligation, claim, or credit, shall be, or shall purport to be, discharged, diminished, increased, created, or in any manner affected, shall, upon conviction, *be adjudged guilty of forgery* in the third degree."*

* 2 Rev. Stats., New York, 673, § 35. Upon the words italicised some questions were raised; and probably in order to avoid any

Windsor was traced to England, and the Secretary of State having issued his warrant, he was arrested, and after examination before Sir Thomas Henry at Bow Street, was committed to prison to be detained until delivered up according to the Act.

Civil proceedings had also been instituted in this country against the prisoner, and he was in custody for the purpose of compelling him to put in bail, as well as upon the criminal charge. A writ of habeas corpus was granted by Mr. Justice Mellor, and the validity of the return was argued before the Court of Queen's Bench.*

Messrs. M'Mahon and Edward Clarke, for the prisoner, contended that as the offence charged was forgery only by the local law of the State of New York, it did not come within the Extradition Treaty, which applied only to offences which were recognised under the designations

difficulty in future cases, the following provision has been substituted for that stated in the text:—"Every person who with intent to defraud makes any false entry, or falsely alters any entry made in any book of accounts kept by any corporation within this state, or in any book of accounts kept by any such corporation or its officers, and delivered or intended to be delivered to any person dealing with such corporation, by which any pecuniary obligation, claim, or credit is or purports to be discharged, diminished, increased, created, or in any manner affected, is guilty of forgery in the third degree." So far as extradition is concerned, the alteration has no effect.

* 6 B. and S., 522. 34 L. J. M. C., 163. 13 W. R., 655. 12 L. T. N. S., 307. 6 New Rep., 96. 10 Cox. C. C., 118. 11 Jur. N. S., 807.

employed in the treaty and the subsequent statute, as murder, piracy, forgery, &c., by the general law of both countries.

Anderson's Case, 20 Upper Canada Q. B. Rep. 124; Wheaton, Int. Law, 236; Ortolan, Règles Internationales, 327; 1 Phillimore, Int. Law, 413.

Minor points were also raised upon the wording of the New York statute.

Messrs. Hardinge Giffard, Q.C., and Poland, *contrà*.

1. The offence was forgery by the common law of England. This point, however, was abandoned.

2. The constitution and government of the United States recognised the laws of the several States. And in *Re* Tivnan * it had been decided that the treaty applied to municipal or statutable offences.

Cockburn, C.-J., held that the terms of the treaty and statute must be held to apply to offences which in the legislation of both countries have some common element. This act had not the essential character of forgery. It was not forgery by the law of England, nor by the general law of the United States. And where one or the other country, party to an Extradition Treaty, and *à fortiori*, where a component part of one or the other country, thinks proper to make an offence not within the general law of both countries, an offence with a particular designation, that circumstance did not of itself bring the offence within the statute.

Blackburn and Shee, JJ., concurred, and the prisoner,

* 5 Best and Smith. See *ante*, p. 130.

so far as he was detained upon the criminal charge, was discharged.*

In November, 1864, and March, 1865, the French ambassador addressed communications to Earl Russell upon the subject of the failure of the French demands for extradition, the surrender having been obtained in only one case during the twenty-two years that the Convention had been in operation. No action was taken upon the subject by the English Government, and, on the 4th December, 1865, the ambassador gave the six months' notice of the termination of the Convention provided for in the 4th Article. The reason given was twofold—(1) That the English Government declined to surrender persons who had been convicted; and (2) that the requirement of the production before a magistrate of *primâ facie* evidence of the guilt of the person accused was an insuperable obstacle to the execution of the Convention in England, and differed from the general practice of the other European Powers. On the 20th January, 1866, Earl Cowley replied to this notification.

"Her Majesty's Government," he said, "regretted that the Convention had produced so little result; its effect with regard even to the demands made by England having been unsatisfactory. The system could not, however, be altered without having recourse to Parliament, and recent experience had shown that there would be great difficulty

* Compare the case of Lamirande, *ante*, p. 102, and *post*, p. 168. In the treaty with France, "forgery" is used as equivalent to "faux," which latter term includes falsification of accounts.

in obtaining from Parliament any further modification in regard to the requirements of law and the usage of Great Britain in dealing with persons accused of crime."

"The legislature had made a concession in consenting to allow copies of depositions to be received in lieu of parole evidence. And there did not appear to be any insuperable difficulty in the production of evidence of this nature before the English magistrate. This, with evidence of identity, was all that was required for the commitment of a fugitive."

"Her Majesty's Government, however, seeing how serious would be the evil of an abrogation of the Convention, were prepared to consider any suggestions as to the means of making it more effective."

In a conversation with M. Drouyn de Lhuys, of about the same date, Earl Cowley made some remarks on the subject of the surrender of condemned persons. "The concession," he said, "could not be made to France without a fresh Act of Parliament; and indeed it would appear to be of very little use, unless it is intended by the Imperial Government to include among persons condemned those condemned *par contumace.* Criminals condemned after trial seldom find means of escaping the punishment awarded them, but condemnation *par contumace,* or without trial in the presence of the accused, is at such variance with the whole legislation of Great Britain, that it would seem hopeless to expect the sanction of Parliament to such a measure.* On the other hand, it is to be observed

* No exception of persons so condemned was contained in the Convention of 1852. See *ante,* p. 119.

that persons in this position might always be proceeded against in the category of accused persons." *

In the course of the correspondence which ensued, another objection was found to exist to the English practice. By the 6 & 7 Vict., c. 75, § 2, it is provided that the copies of depositions produced shall be certified to be true copies by the person producing them; and the result of this was that some person, usually a police-officer, had to inspect the French proceedings to see if the judge had made a true certificate. This was resented by the French judges as an indignity, and it was agreed that the objection might be removed by a short Act of Parliament, providing that the copies should be accepted in evidence if the signature of the judge who signed them were authenticated by the seal of the French Minister of Justice. A Bill was accordingly prepared, and passed by the legislature with slight opposition.† A clause, however, was introduced, limiting its operation to one year, to insure the full discussion of the subject in the next session of Parliament. In a letter of the 21st May, 1866, the French ambassador stated that it had been agreed that a new attempt should be made to put the treaty in execution, and that with this object a demand in extradition had lately been addressed to the English authorities. In the interest of this experiment, and without withdrawing its objections to the Convention, the French

* See case of Charles Dubois (*alias* Coppin), *post*, p. 140.

† 29 & 30 Vict., c. 121.

Government consented to a prolongation of the treaty for six months.*

This proposal was accepted by the English Government.

The demand referred to was for the extradition of Victor Wideman, on a charge of fraudulent bankruptcy. He was arrested and duly committed; a rule for a writ of habeas corpus was, however, obtained, and the motion to make it absolute was argued before the Queen's Bench on the 12th June, 1866.

Messrs. M'Mahon and Edward Clarke for the prisoner.

The Convention was at an end, and with it the Statute 6 & 7 Vict., c. 75. The Convention provided that it should end at the expiration of six months after notice given by either party; and that notice having been given by France on the 4th December, 1865, the Convention was no longer in existence. No provision had been made for waiver of notice.

2. No proof had been given before the magistrate that the acts charged constituted fraudulent bankruptcy under the French law, or that the prisoner was a French subject, and amenable to that law.

The Solicitor-General (Sir R. P. Collier) and Mr. Hannen, *contrà*.

1. The notice having been waived, the Convention remained in force.

2. There was *primâ facie* evidence of acts of fraudulent

* Correspondence respecting the Extradition Treaty with France, July, 1866.

bankruptcy. The court (Cockburn, C.-J., Mellor and Blackburn, JJ.,) held that the notice must be a continuing notice, and that as there could be no doubt of the nature of the acts charged, the strict proof that they constituted the crime of fraudulent bankruptcy by the French law was unnecessary.*

An application upon similar points was afterwards made to the Lord Chancellor (Cranworth), who granted a writ of habeas corpus, but upon return made and argument thereupon, remanded the prisoner, and he was surrendered.†

In 1866 a case occurred which was of great importance as involving the question whether a fugitive criminal, who had been condemned in a foreign country *par contumace*, was an accused person within the terms of the English treaties. For twenty years after the passing of the first Extradition Act in 1843 the opinion prevailed that a person who had been so condemned could not be surrendered, the treaties with France and the United States not providing for the rendition of persons who had been convicted. When Sir Thomas Henry became chief magistrate of police of the metropolis he requested the Home Secretary to take the opinion of the law officers of the Crown upon this point, and they advised that a person so

* See Taylor on Evidence; §§ 1280, 1281, 1370.

† 12 Jurist., N. S., 536. 14 L. T. N. S., 719. This is said to have been the first instance in which a virtual appeal was made from the Court of Queen's Bench to the Lord Chancellor. The precedent was followed in the case next stated.

condemned *par contumace* could not be surrendered.* Had this opinion been upheld by the courts of law, the advantage to continental nations of entering into extradition treaties with Great Britain would have been but small. In 1866, however, the question was actually raised and received judicial decision. In July of that year a requisition was made by the French Government for the rendition of Charles Dubois, otherwise Coppin, as a person accused of committing within French territory the crime of forgery; and a warrant of arrest having been granted, the prisoner was brought, in the absence of Sir Thomas Henry, before Mr. Vaughan, a police magistrate at Bow Street. In support of the charge a number of depositions were produced which purported to have been taken, some before a *Juge de Paix* of the Canton of Villeneuve-sur-Yonne, and some before the *Juge d'Instruction* at Troyes, and showed that the prisoner had uttered a forged bill of exchange. A copy of the *mise en accusation* signed by the "greffier" of the Cour Impériale at Paris was also put in evidence, and was under the seal of the Cour Impériale, and that of the Minister of Justice. The depositions, which were originals, were under the seals of the Minister of Justice and the Minister of Foreign Affairs. A witness was called to identify the prisoner as the person named in the *mise en accusation*, and he was asked in cross-examination by Mr. Edward Clarke, who appeared for the prisoner, whether Dubois had not been tried and

* Evidence of Sir T. Henry. Report of Select Comm., 1868, p. 17.

convicted *par contumace.* He said he had been so convicted, and sentenced to imprisonment for life. It was then objected on behalf of the prisoner that the evidence did not show forgery, but only the uttering of forged paper, and that this was not an offence within the treaty.* The magistrate held that the uttering of a forged document was forgery. This point, however, became immaterial, and was not finally decided, a letter being produced in which the prisoner confessed the forgeries he had committed. The point was then raised that the prisoner having been convicted and sentenced was not an accused person within the terms of the treaty. Upon this M. Rasul, a French advocate, was called to prove that the conviction was annulled by the surrender of the person accused, and the magistrate said he should hold that the prisoner was within the treaty, and should issue his warrant committing him for the purpose of his surrender. The counsel for the prisoner thereupon applied for a remand such as had been granted in the case of Tivnan,† or that the issue of the warrant should be delayed in order that application might be made for a writ of habeas corpus, but Mr. Vaughan peremptorily refused to accord any delay.‡ Nor would he grant a remand in order that the

* The treaty with the United States was concluded in August 1842, and put in force by 6 & 7 Vict., c. 76; the treaty with France was concluded in February 1843, and put in force by 6 & 7 Vict., c. 75; the two Acts receiving Royal Assent on the same day. The treaty with the United States includes the "utterance of forged paper," that with France does not. † See *ante*, p. 127.

‡ A formal remand or delay in issing the writ need not be

prisoner might give formal evidence of the conviction *par contumace*, saying he did not think the point material. The magistrate's warrant was accordingly issued, but an immediate application to the Home Secretary secured some delay, and the Lord Chancellor (Chelmsford), who came to town for the purpose, and heard the application at his private residence, granted a writ of habeas corpus, which was made returnable on the first day of Michaelmas Term, and was then argued. Mr. Edward Clarke moved for the discharge of the prisoner on the grounds—

1. The depositions produced purported to be authenticated according to the provisions of the Act 29 & 30 Vict., c. 121, whereas they had been taken prior to the passing of that Act. This point was at once overruled.

2. The documents produced were not properly authenticated. The Act 6 & 7 Vict., c. 75, provides that no magistrate shall issue a warrant of arrest with a view to extradition, unless it shall be proved to him upon oath or by affidavit that the person applying for such warrant shall be the bearer of a warrant of arrest, or other equivalent judicial document issued by a judge or competent magistrate in France, authenticated in such manner as would justify the arrest of the supposed offender in France upon the same charge. By the 29 & 30 Vict., c. 121, it is provided that warrants of arrest and copies of depositions may be received in evidence, if the warrant of arrest pur-

asked for now even in vacation time. The Extradition Act secures to the accused the safeguard which Mr. Vaughan so peremptorily refused.

port to be signed by a judge or other competent magistrate of the country in which it was issued, and if the copies of depositions are certified under the hand of such judge or magistrate to be true copies, and the signature of the judge or magistrate be certified by the seal of the Minister of Justice. In this case there is no warrant at all, and the copy of the *mise en accusation* bears no judicial signature whatever, but is simply signed by the clerk to the Cour Impériale. The depositions produced bear no signature of a judge or magistrate who issued or signed any warrant of arrest or other equivalent judicial document.

3. The prisoner, having been condemned *par contumace*, is no longer in the category of accused persons. His status has been changed by the conviction. (Code d'Instr. Crim., §§ 476, 477, 478, 518, 519.)

Sir John Rolt, A.-G., Sir W. Bovill, S.-G., and Mr. Hannen, for the Crown.

The documents produced are sufficient. The copy of the *mise en accusation* is equivalent to a warrant, and is authenticated by the seal of the Cour Impériale, and that of the Minister of Justice. The depositions are originals, not copies, and therefore need not be authenticated according to the provisions of the Acts cited.

As to the condemnation *par contumace*, that is merely provisional, and is intended to operate as a sort of process to compel appearance; and when a person so condemned is arrested or surrenders himself, the condemnation is annulled, and he is tried as if no such conviction had ever taken place. And here there is no sufficient proof of such a conviction.

Mr. Edward Clarke in reply.

It is not the fault of the prisoner if no sufficient proof has been given of the condemnation *par contumace*. The French authorities have refused to supply the necessary evidence.

A person condemned *par contumace* is in the French Code called a "condemned," not an "accused" person (§§ 465, 466); he is in a less favourable position at his subsequent trial (§§ 518, 519); the sentence at once alters his civil status, and becomes irrevocable at the expiration of twenty years.

There is no power to authenticate a seal, or to receive original depositions unless they are properly certified.

The Lord Chancellor at once gave judgment, remanding the prisoner for the purpose of his being surrendered; and, while acknowledging the importance of the questions raised, he said he felt no doubt upon either of them. With regard to the documents, he held that as the originals had been produced the Acts above cited did not apply, but that even if they did, all the formalities required had been substantially fulfilled. Upon the question of the character and effect of a conviction *par contumace*, the judgment was full and clear, although comment was made on the inadequacy of the proof that in this case any such conviction had taken place. His Lordship quoted the evidence given by the French advocate, M. Rasul: "If a man is accused of forgery in France, and a judgment *par contumace* obtained against him, it would be a sentence of the court without the assistance of a jury. If that man is arrested or surrenders himself, that judgment is annulled, so that it is exactly the same as if no proceedings had been taken against him, and then he undergoes his trial for the offence with which he was charged," and continued,—" Without this evidence it would have been impossible for the magistrate to have any competent knowledge upon the subject; for, as Lord Brougham said in *The Sussex Peerage Case* (11 Cl. and Fin. 115), 'The judge has not organs to know and to deal with the text of the foreign law, and therefore requires the assistance of a lawyer who knows how to interpret it.' But, having this assistance, and being referred by M. Rasul to the Code Napoléon, we may venture to look into the text and to the Article 476 of the Code d'Instruction Criminelle, upon which he founds his opinion, which is in these terms:—'Si l'accusé se constitue prisonnier ou s'il est arrêté avant que la peine soit éteinte par prescription, le jugement rendu par contumace et les procédures faites contre lui depuis l'ordonnance de prise de corps ou de se représenter, seront anéantis de plein droit et il sera procédé à son égard dans la forme ordinaire.' It will be observed that the article commences by calling the alleged offender, after a judgment *par contumace*, the *accused* and not the *condemned*. And as upon his appearance or upon his apprehension judgment against him is annulled, and he is to be put upon his trial for the offence, I do not see how he can be described otherwise than as an accused person."

"But it is said that the judgment *par contumace* places the party who afterwards surrenders himself, or is apprehended and brought before the court, in a less favourable position upon the trial which ensues, and Articles 518 and 519 of the Code d'Instruction Criminelle were referred to to establish this assertion. I ought, perhaps, to refuse to look at these articles without a skilled interpreter, but I am so anxious that the case should be thoroughly investigated, that I am disposed to permit this further irregularity in the proceedings."

"It appears to me that the object and effect of these articles have been entirely misunderstood. The title of the chapter under which they are merged is, 'De la Reconnoissance de l'Identité d'un individu condamné évadé et repris;' and Article 18 is to this effect:—'La reconnoissance de l'identité d'un individu condamné évadé et repris sera faite par la cour qui aura prononcé sa condamnation.' It merely provides for establishing the identity of the party before he is sent to his trial. And in a note to this article in the edition of the Code which I have, it is said, 'Au reste, cette identité reconnue comme l'arrêt de condamnation se trouve anéanti de plein droit, l'accusé devrait être soumis à de nouveaux débats devant les jurés.' The 519th Article merely provides that all the judgments with regard to the identification of an accused party shall be without the assistance of a jury. It does not appear, therefore, that the trial of a person condemned *par contumace* differs at all from that of a party who is put upon his trial without any previous condemnation."

"But in order that no part of the argument for the

prisoner may be disregarded, I will assume that it has been established that the judgment *par contumace* does work some prejudice to the party upon the trial, either by reducing the amount of necessary proof, or by changing its character, or by making him liable to costs; but how could that possibly take him out of the category of accused persons? He has ceased to be a person condemned, because his condemnation is annulled upon his appearance, and he is to take his trial for offences with which he stands charged. What better, I ought rather to say what other, description of him could be given than that of a person accused?" *

In the year 1868, a Committee of the House of Commons, very strongly constituted, was appointed to consider the whole matter of Extradition Law. It held many meetings, and examined a number of witnesses who had practical experience of the working of the existing treaties, and of the faults and defects which had so seriously impaired their usefulness; and the result of the recommendations of the Committee was the passing in 1870 of the Extradition Act (33 & 34 Vict. c. 52), for which the country is indebted chiefly to the ability of Sir Thomas Henry, and which is in itself a comprehensive and ably-drawn code of law upon this subject. The principal defect of the law before 1870, was that, while requiring formalities before the arrest, which often gave warning to the criminal, and enabled him to escape, it did not secure to him, when actually arrested, any opportunity of testing before one of the superior courts of law the legality of the arrest and

* L. R. 2 Ch. App. 47. 36 L. J. Ch. 80. 12 Jur. (N.S.) 867. 15 L. T. (N.S.) 165.

surrender. In the great majority of cases in which the British Government had consented to grant extradition, the police-officers, when actually armed with the warrant of arrest, had been unable to find the fugitive; and, on the other hand, the danger existed that, as in Lamirande's case, a person might be given up who was not guilty of any offence within the treaties. There were other and serious defects. Neither the then existing treaties nor the Acts of Parliament by which they had been put in force, contained any exception as to political offenders, or any provision preventing the trial of a fugitive when once surrendered for offences other than that for which his rendition had been claimed. And very great difficulty was found in negotiating fresh treaties with foreign powers, in consequence of the necessity of obtaining from the British Parliament, after each treaty was signed, an Act of Parliament embodying and enforcing its provisions. This requirement was strongly objected to by foreign states, and had prevented the conclusion of several treaties with regard to which negotiations had commenced; while it had prevented the treaty actually made with Prussia in 1864 from being put in force. These defects were pointed out in the first edition of this work, and the remedies there suggested were all contained in the Extradition Act of 1870. The practice under that Act will be fully dealt with in a later chapter, but the general principles of the statute may be shortly stated. It laid down a complete system of Extradition Law, defining the persons who might be the subjects of extradition, and the crimes for which surrender might be granted; dispensed with formalities antecedent to the arrest, but required every magistrate on committing a prisoner for the purpose of surrender, to tell him that he would not be given up for fifteen days, and that during that time he could apply for a writ of habeas corpus in order to test the validity of the commitment. It made provision for the non-surrender of political offenders, and for the insertion in the treaties, whenever necessary, of a stipulation that the person whose surrender should be granted should only be tried for the offence for which he had been claimed. And subject to the limitations contained in the statute, power was given to the Executive Government to make fresh treaties, and to put them in force by an Order in Council instead of a special Act of Parliament. The first case which came before the English courts under this Act was that of a man named Bouvier, who was in September, 1872, claimed by the French Government as having been convicted, *par contumace*, of the offences of *abus de confiance*, fraudulent bankruptcy and forgery. He was arrested in Jersey, and the warrant by which he was there committed to prison with a view to his surrender made mention of all three offences. A writ of habeas corpus was obtained, and the case argued before the Court of Queen's Bench; the important question being raised whether the effect of the Extradition Act, 1870, had not been to render the treaty with France entirely inoperative.

That treaty was originally put in force in Great Britain by the Act 6 & 7 Vict. c. 75, but that statute was repealed by the Extradition Act, 1870, and the obligation of the treaty has since depended on the terms of Section 27 of the Act of 1870. That section provides that the Act "(with the exception of anything contained in it which is inconsistent with the treaties referred to in the Acts so repealed) shall apply (as regards crimes committed either before or after the passing of this Act) in the case of the foreign states with which those treaties are made in the same manner as if an Order in Council referring to such treaties had been made in pursuance of this Act, and as if such order had directed that every law and ordinance which is in force in any British possession, with respect to such treaties, should have effect as part of this Act."

Two points were raised on behalf of the prisoner by Mr. George Browne, his counsel:—

1. As a judgment is indivisible, the surrender of the prisoner to the French authorities on a judgment including *abus de confiance*, an offence not within the treaty or the Act of 1870, would be a surrender for an offence not contemplated by the Act, and therefore would be illegal.

2. The treaty with France has ceased to have any legal effect, as neither by it nor the French law is any provision made for preventing the trial of a prisoner surrendered under it for an offence other than that for which the rendition was demanded.

It was further suggested that the diplomatic correspondence which had taken place between the British and French Governments amounted to a termination of the treaty by six months' notice, as provided by Article 4 of that treaty. It, however, appeared that its operation had been continued by mutual agreement between the two Governments, and by such agreement it was declared to be in force until September, 1873. It is not clear that under the provisions of the Extradition Act, 1870, a convention once renounced could be continued by an informal agreement between the Governments concerned, but the point was not pressed and would probably have been held to be decided by the case of Wideman.*

Sir J. D. Coleridge, A.-G., and Mr. C. Bowen appeared for the Crown, and upon the second point, which indeed included the first, relied upon an affidavit made by M. Adolphe Moreau, the officially-appointed counsel to the French Embassy in London. The most material parts of this affidavit were the following paragraphs:—"I say, speaking from my own knowledge, that according to the law of France provision is made that a fugitive criminal shall not, until he has been restored or had an opportunity of returning to Her Majesty's dominions, be detained or tried in France for any offence committed by him prior to such surrender other than the extradition crime proved by the facts upon which the surrender is granted; and I say, speaking from my own knowledge and experience, that this law is observed in practice by the French tribunals and authorities. . . . . It is a principle of French and of international law, that the individual whose extradition has been granted can only be prosecuted and tried for the very crime for which his extradition has been

* See *ante*, p. 138.

obtained; and I say, speaking from my own knowledge and actual experience, that this is the invariable practice of the French tribunals." The full account of the French law contained in the next chapter will enable the reader to put its proper value upon this affidavit. It was, however, uncontradicted, and was accepted by the court as decisive of the question. Cockburn, C.-J., Blackburn, J., and Mellor, J., accordingly remanded the prisoner to custody, holding that provision was made by the French law that he should be tried only for the offence for which the surrender was asked. Upon the other question, whether in the absence of any such provision the 27th section of the Extradition Act, 1870, would have the effect of keeping the Convention in force, they expressed very serious doubts. Cockburn, C.-J., said if it were necessary to decide the point he should say that the language used was sufficient to have that effect; Blackburn, J., said he had very serious doubts whether the Legislature had effected by that section what was intended, and that he, if required to decide the point, should take time to consider; Mellor, J., said he was inclined to agree with the argument of the Attorney-General, but felt some doubt; and all the judges expressed a strong opinion that it was desirable to set the question at rest by further legislation.* As this was the

* *Ex parte* Bouvier, 27 L. T. (N.S.) 844. It is curious that this point has not yet been taken in any case under the American treaty. It is quite clear that neither that treaty nor the law of the United States contains the provision required by the Extradition Act, 1870. The question is a very important one, and deserves to be fully argued. Nor can the case of Bouvier be

only point on which further legislation was really wanted, it is not easy to see why it was entirely neglected when the amending Act was passed in 1873.

In the following year occurred the case of Elise Counhaye, who was claimed by the Belgian Government under the Treaty of July 31, 1872, charged with complicity in the fraudulent bankruptcy of her husband. This case also came before the Court of Queen's Bench, and was argued on behalf of the prisoner by Sir J. Karslake, Q.C., and Messrs. Day, Q.C., and R. V. Williams. They contended:

1. That the treaty applied only to "crimes by bankrupts against the Bankruptcy Law, and therefore not to the act charged against the prisoner, who was not a bankrupt.

2. The definition of "extradition crime" in Section 26 of the Act of 1870 is "a crime which, if committed in England or within English jurisdiction would be one of the crimes described in the first schedule to the Act; and the Debtors' Act, 1869 (32 & 33 Vict. c. 62), sect. 11, which contains the law relating to the punishment of fraudulent debtors, only renders criminal the offence of fraudulent removal of property in contemplation of bankruptcy when committed by the bankrupt, and does not include accomplices.

3. The crime charged against the prisoner was committed before the Extradition Act, 1870, was passed, and it is contrary to principle in the absence of express provision to give retrospective effect to a criminal statute.

4. The depositions taken in Belgium, and received in

accepted as conclusive even with regard to France. The point may be raised again upon more satisfactory affidavits as to the law of France than were before the court in that case.

evidence against the prisoner by the police-magistrate, should not have been so received, as they were taken in the absence of the prisoner, and she had no opportunity of cross-examining the witnesses.

5. The treaty provides that the requisition for the surrender shall be made to Her Majesty's Principal Secretary of State for Foreign Affairs, accompanied by a warrant of arrest or other equivalent judicial document issued by a judge or magistrate duly authorised to take cognizance of the acts charged against the accused in Belgium, together with duly authenticated depositions or statements taken on oath before such judge or magistrate. Here the warrant of arrest, if it discloses any crime at all, discloses one committed in France, and not in Belgium, and the depositions were not taken before the judge who issued the warrant.

Sir J. D. Coleridge, A.-G., and Mr. C. Bowen appeared for the Crown, but were not heard upon all the points raised, the Court, consisting of Blackburn, Quain, and Archibald, JJ., being clearly of opinion that the prisoner not being a bankrupt was not within the terms of the treaty, and must be discharged. They, however, held that the depositions were admissible against the prisoner, it being for the magistrate to decide what weight he would attach to statements so taken. They also held that the provisions of Article 2 of the treaty might be waived by the Secretary of State, and that therefore the fact that the depositions were not signed by the magistrate who issued the warrant was immaterial. With regard to the question of the retrospective operation of the statute, Blackburn, J., said he considered the point so doubtful, that it was desirable the Legislature should cause the Act to be amended.*

The only other case of importance which has arisen under the Act of 1870 is that of Huguet, who was claimed by the French Government in 1872 on a charge of fraudulent bankruptcy. The warrant of arrest having been issued, he was apprehended and brought before Mr. Vaughan, one of the police-magistrates at Bow Street. Certain evidence was then taken, and the case was adjourned. At the adjournment Sir Thomas Henry presided, and further evidence was produced, but the witness who had been called on the first occasion did not appear, and on evidence being given by the clerk to the police-court that his deposition had been taken in the presence of the accused, and that the latter had been allowed to cross-examine, Sir Thomas Henry received in evidence the deposition so taken. In the Court of Exchequer, Barons Martin and Pollock held that the deposition was properly admitted. Kelly, C.-B., expressed great doubt upon the subject, but it was not necessary to decide the point, as all the learned barons were of opinion that without this deposition there was sufficient evidence against the prisoner. Mr. Montagu Chambers, Q.C., and Mr. Besley appeared for the prisoner, and Sir J. D. Coleridge, A.-G., and Mr. C. Bowen for the Crown. The very important question was in this case raised, whether the Court would examine the sufficiency of the evidence before the police-

* *Re* Elise Counhaye, L. R. 8 Q. B., 410; 42 L. J., 217; 28 L. T. (N.S.) 761.

magistrate, and the Court held that it was not called upon to do so. Upon this point Baron Martin said, "The question is, was this proceeding within the jurisdiction of Sir Thomas Henry? I don't say that if there had been no evidence before him, or he had acted contrary to law, we would not have discharged the prisoner, but it appears to me that all the proceedings have been properly taken. This is not a court of appeal from his decision, and it is for him to decide whether or not the evidence is sufficient."* This question of the power of the Court to examine the weight as well as the competency of the evidence before the police-magistrate, has been much argued, and variously decided in the United States, and will probably be further discussed in England. The case mentioned above is obviously not conclusive of the matter. In the year 1873 a further Extradition Act was passed (36 & 37 Vict. c. 60), upon which the reader will find some observations in the concluding chapter of this book. It is only necessary here to say that it gave retrospective effect to the Act of 1870 and the treaties made thereunder, and that it extended the list of crimes for which extradition might be accorded, and included accomplices within the provisions which previously applied only to the principal offenders. Since the passing of the Extradition Act, 1870, the British Government has entered into treaties upon this subject with Germany, Belgium, Italy, Sweden and Norway, Brazil and Austria. The full text of these treaties will be found in the Appendix to this work.

* *Ex parte* Huguet. 29 L. T. (N.S.) 41.

CHAPTER VI.

HISTORY OF THE LAW IN FRANCE.

THE law of extradition in France differs in every respect from that of the countries already treated of. The question of the propriety of delivering up a demanded fugitive has never been discussed before a French tribunal. That is held to be a purely political question with which courts of justice have no concern.* On the other hand, the questions with which the French courts have dealt have seldom arisen in proceedings in England or America. All the cases which are found in the French reports are those of criminals who, having been delivered up to

* The principle of extradition does not depend upon treaties, but upon the sovereign rights residing in the ruler of each State in virtue of which he maintains good relations with his neighbours; to put in action the power of extradition is a measure of international right emanating from the will of the executive power. See Faustin Helie, Tr. de l'Inst. Crim. t. 2, § 132, p. 667; Mangin. Tr. de l'Action Publique, No. 75; Trebutien. Cours Élémentaire de Droit Crim., t. 2, p. 132; Le Sellyar, Tr. du Droit Crim., t. 5, No. 1952; Dalloz, Jurisp. Gén., 1867, i. 281.

Governments can extend or modify treaties at their will, and can grant or receive the extradition of criminals whether any treaty exist or not. Comtesse de la Grandville; Dalloz, Jurisp. Gén., 1827, i., 288; Sirey, Collect. Nouv. 8, 1, 628; Rep. Gén., vii., 141.

France, have tried there to dispute the legality of their surrender, or have raised some objection to the manner of their trial.

These cases are very simple, and require no detailed analysis, but they have considerable interest as illustrating another side of the Law of Extradition. A convenient starting-place for this part of the history is found in a Circular of the French Minister of Justice which was issued in 1841, and lays down with great fulness the theory of French law upon the subject.

The only question of any importance arising before this time seems to have been as to the right of the Government to surrender a French subject. That this right was possessed by the Kings of France until 1830 seems to be acknowledged, but it was contended later, that it was a right which existed in the persons of the kings of France, and that in the absence of positive law, the chief of the Government which issued from the revolution of that year did not inherit it. Dalloz, however, maintains that it existed by virtue of the Circular of the 25th October, 1811, which recognised the right of the Government to grant the extradition of a Frenchman, and regulated its exercise.* The question, however, is now of no importance, as by the year 1841 it had been thoroughly established that no French subject could be given up.†

* Dalloz, Dict. Gén. Suppl., 229.

† See Correspondence respecting Extradition, 1866, p. 14. Case of the Baron de Vidil, Rep. Gén. de Jurisp., vii., 140, *post*, Appendix, p. xxvi.

It is stated by several French authors, that in 1831 the French Government declared that for the future it would neither grant nor demand extradition, and notified to the Swiss Confederation its renunciation of the then existing treaties,* but the fact that fresh treaties were made in 1834 and 1838 makes this statement appear improbable; it is discredited by Fœlix;† and the silence of the French Minister upon the matter, when he is mentioning treaties which had been in existence long before 1831, seems conclusive as to the incorrectness of the statement.

In the Circular of 1841 the French Minister of Justice mentioned that France had four treaties with foreign powers:—with Spain (29th September, 1765), Switzerland (18th July, 1828), Belgium (29th November, 1834), and Sardinia (23rd May, 1838).‡ He added, that even in the absence of treaties she could obtain the extradition of criminals from other countries except from Great Britain and the United States. He then, after stating the principles of justice and expediency on which the practice of extradition was founded, mentioned two important

* Mangin, Tr. de l'Act., publ., No. 74; Ortolan and Ledeau, Tr. de Min., publ., 231.

† Fœlix, 2, 329.

‡ It would appear that other treaties had formerly existed, but had either been renounced or allowed to fall into disuse. In Mr. Jefferson's letter of 1791, referred to at p. 32 of this work, he says:—"I know that such conventions exist between France and Spain, France and Sardinia, France and Germany, France and the United Netherlands; between the several sovereigns constituting the Germanic body, and I believe very generally between co-terminous States on the continent of Europe."

limitations. It should never, he said, be claimed or granted for trifling offences. They were not sufficiently injurious to the welfare of the state, and he added, "Il faut une raison puissante pour faire rechercher sur la terre étrangère l'homme qui s'est puni par l'éloignement volontaire de sa patrie."

The other exception regarded political offences.

"Les crimes politiques s'accomplissent dans des circonstances si difficiles à apprécier, ils naissent de passions si ardentes, qui souvent sont leur excuse, que la France maintient le principe que l'extradition ne doit pas avoir lieu pour fait politique. C'est une règle qu'elle met son honneur à soutenir. Elle a toujours refusé, depuis 1830, de pareilles extraditions; elle n'en demandera jamais."*

Of the remainder of the Circular, which deals with the rules to be observed in all cases of extradition, the following is a summary:†—

1. Extradition does not apply to persons who have taken refuge in their own country; consequently France can only demand the extradition of a Frenchman, or of a foreigner, who has taken refuge in a country other than that to which he belongs.‡

* The treaty between France and Switzerland of the 18th July, 1828, Art. 5, includes specifically "les crimes contre la sûreté de l'Etat." This provision has, however, never been acted upon, nor reproduced (Blondel, Monog. Alphabétique, 42), and is considered to be tacitly abrogated. Letter of M. Nestor Treitt, Report on Extradition, 1868; Appendix.

† The Circular is given in full in Dalloz, Jurisp. Gén., 1841, iii. 440.

‡ There is no such limitation in the treaty between Great

2. Extradition can only be admitted with regard to a person accused of an act punishable with severe and degrading punishment (*peine afflictive ou infamante*), that is to say, of a crime other than a political crime, and not of a misdemeanour (*délit*). It follows that if the extradition has been obtained of a person accused at once of a crime and a misdemeanour, he ought not to be put upon his trial for the misdemeanour.

So in the case of the surrender of a person accused of an ordinary crime, and a political crime, he should only be tried for the former, and if acquitted, or after the expiration of his punishment, he must leave France within a time fixed by the Government.

Britain and France, but under this rule France in 1861 refused the surrender of Baron de Vidil. England it seems would not refuse a surrender upon the ground of nationality. See the judgment of Cockburn, L.C.-J., in Windsor's case, *ante*, p. 130; and Burley's case, *ante*, p. 89. As to the rule in the United States, see pp. 37, 44.

Martens says that a State should not surrender its own subjects. Droit des Gens, § 101. Faustin Helie is of opinion that such a surrender is quite proper. Droit Intern. 672. Kluit holds the surrender legitimate, but says that political convenience will generally prevent it. De Deditione Profugorum, 61. There is some difference of opinion among foreign writers as to whether a fugitive should be given up to any country but his own. Martens, Droit des Gens., § 101, says not; Faustin Helie, Tr. de l'Inst. Crim., 2, 672; and Kluit, De Deditione Profugorum, 61, say that such a surrender would be perfectly legitimate. The question was mooted recently in the case of Marguerite Diblanc, a Belgian subject, who committed murder in London, and fled to Paris, but she was surrendered without any formal decision upon the point.

3. The order of extradition states the act upon which it is founded, and that act alone should be investigated.

Whence it follows, that if, during the trial of the crime for which extradition has been granted, proofs are discovered of another crime, a new demand in extradition must be made.*

4. The Government alone is competent to decide the scope of an order of extradition, and to interpret its terms; the courts must suspend proceedings until that decision is given.†

5. The Government alone is entitled to make a demand of extradition upon a foreign power; the *procureurs-généraux* can only correspond with the magistrates of neighbouring and friendly states in order to obtain information.

6. The *Procureur-Général* should forward to the department of the Ministry of Justice, with an explanatory letter, the demand of extradition, accompanied by a warrant of arrest, or by a decree of the *chambre des mises en accusation,* or by a decree of condemnation, either after jury trial or *par contumace*, according to the state of the proceedings.

The Belgian and Spanish Governments are in the habit of only granting extradition upon the production of the decree of the *chambre des mises en accusation.*

* See Lesellyer, Traité du Droit Crim., 5, 1954; Fœlix, Droit Intern., 580; Rep. Gén. de Jurisp., vii., 143.

† Comtesse de Granville, Dalloz, Jurisp. Gén., 1827, i., 288; Burgerey, Dalloz, J. G., 1841, i., 440; Davia, Dalloz, J. G., 1847, iv., 249; Dareau, Dalloz, J. G., 1853, v., 215; Chardon, Dalloz, J. G., 1865, i., 248; Renneçon, Dalloz, J. G., 1867, i. 281.

7. If, pending the demand of extradition, the act which has prompted it has lost the character of a crime, and become a misdemeanour, or if the accusation has been annulled (*s'il est intervenu un arrêt de non lieu*), the minister should be informed without delay, that the demand may be withdrawn, or the accused set at liberty and conducted to the frontier.

8. When the accused is delivered up, he is at first in the charge of the administrative authority, then received by the *Procureur-Général*, who takes measures for sending him to the place where the accusation should be prosecuted.

9. The Government has the exclusive right of deciding upon demands of extradition made by foreign Governments, although the magistrates of these countries sometimes forward warrants, orders of arrest, or records of conviction, directly to the magistrates of the French tribunals; these documents should immediately be transmitted to the department of the Ministry of Justice.

10. In France the execution of a Royal Decree of Extradition is intrusted to the administrative authority.

11. If the foreigner whose extradition has been granted is at the time under accusation, or undergoing a sentence, the execution of the order of extradition must be postponed until the decision upon the charge or the expiration of the sentence. Nevertheless, the extradition cannot be hindered by anything but the requirements of public justice, as, for instance, if the foreigner were detained for debt.

The Circulars upon Extradition of 6th October, 1810,

12th June, 1816, and 31st July, 1821, were abrogated by that of 1841.

The rule that a prisoner surrendered upon a charge of crime, but accused also of misdemeanour, should only be tried for the crime, had been acted upon in the case of Dermenon, who was given up by Geneva in 1840 on a charge of fraudulent bankruptcy. The *renvoi* of the *chambre des mises en accusation* ordered that, if acquitted on this charge, he should be tried for simple bankruptcy and breach of trust. He was so acquitted, and the Minister of Justice held himself bound to re-deliver him to Geneva. That state refused to receive him; but the question whether this operated as a new extradition, or whether he ought to be liberated at the French frontier, was held to be purely a political matter.*

The rule was also recognised in the case of Sauve, a deserter from the French army, accused of theft. He was delivered up by Switzerland on the express condition that he should not be tried as a deserter, but only for the theft for which he had been condemned *par contumace.* It was held in this case, that the judges empowered according to the information, to judge of the misdemeanour as well as the crime, ought to declare themselves without jurisdiction over the former. Sauve was tried and condemned as a deserter; but this judgment was overruled by the Conseil de Révision de Paris, and he was sent back to be allowed to purge his contumacy, and to be tried for the thefts charged against him.†

* Dalloz, Jurisp. Gén., 1840, i. 438.

† *Ibid.*, 1862, v. 159.

Other cases, however, show that the principle must be taken with some modifications.

In the case of Wolf Cromback in 1845, the prisoner was delivered up by Switzerland for *faux en écriture de commerce.* The order of extradition was general, but this was the only description of forgery specified in the treaty under which he was claimed. On his trial the writings proved not to be of a commercial character, and he was convicted of *faux en écriture privée.* He thereupon prayed the court that he might be sent back to Switzerland, quoting Dermenon's case; but this point was overruled, and he was sentenced to five years of *réclusion*, and to *l'exposition.* He appealed to the Cour de Cassation, which, after deliberation in Chambre de Conseil, decided, that as the treaty provided for the delivery up, not only of those declared guilty, but of those pursued as such, in virtue of warrants certified by the proper legal authority, the legality of the extradition and of its consequences must be tested, not by reference to the gravity and legal character of the crime as described in the sentence of condemnation, but with regard to the original charge against him upon which he was pursued. The appeal was therefore rejected.*

In the same year the Abbé Grandvaux, charged with *faux en écriture privée et d'enlèvement de mineure,* was given up by Tuscany, with an express stipulation that he should not be tried for the latter offence. The

* Dalloz, Jurisp. Gén., 1845, i. 111. See some observations upon this singular decision in Rep. Gén. de Jurisp., vii. 143.

chambre des mises en accusation, however, finding there were no sufficient grounds for the heavier charge, remanded him, and instructed the Cour d'Assises to try him for the smaller offence. On appeal against this *arrêt*, the Cour de Cassation held that the criminal courts must proceed without regard to the conditions of extradition. That was a matter for the consideration of the Government, which might prevent the execution of the sentence, and re-deliver the criminal.*

In a much more recent case, that of Pascal, surrendered by Spain in 1858, the Cour de Cassation held that if the appellant, whose extradition had been granted upon a charge of rape, and of an indecent assault, with violence, had only been convicted of an indecent assault, without violence, upon a child of less than eleven years, it was clear that it was the same act differently described, and therefore there was no ground for a reference to the limitations in the order of extradition.†

It has been decided that the conditions in a grant of extradition are stipulations in favour of the accused, which he may waive if he thinks it advisable. Upon such waiver he may be tried not merely for a crime not within the extradition treaty under which he was surrendered, but for a crime entirely unconnected with the matter which has been the ground of his extradition.‡ But if, being accused of fraudulent bankruptcy and simple bank-

* Dalloz, Jurisp. Gén., 1845, i. 405. † *Ibid.*, 1863, v. 176.

‡ Legraverend, Législ. Crim., i. 112; Blondel, Monog. Alphabétique, 33; and see the Lamirande case, *post*, p. 168.

ruptcy, and given up for the former, he allows himself to be tried for fraudulent bankruptcy only, without renouncing the benefit of the terms of the order of extradition, he cannot afterwards complain that the question of simple bankruptcy was not left to the jury.*

The other French decisions refer chiefly to the incompetence of the tribunals to consider the legality of the surrender which has been made. The doctrine was fully laid down in the case of Burgerey in 1841. He was given up by the Republic of Berne on a charge which did not come within the treaty. He appealed against his conviction, but the Cour de Cassation held that the two countries might have extended or modified the Convention by subsequent agreements, according to the requirements and obligations of the friendly relations which subsisted between them: that the French tribunals were not called upon to inquire into the reasons which had determined the Republic of Berne, the sole guardian of its own independence and dignity, to grant the extradition; and that whether it had been demanded, or spontaneously accorded, the prisoner had been legally remitted to the jurisdiction of the law by which his crime was punishable.†

The Cour d'Assises of the Seine also decided in 1846 (December 13) that as the right of extradition was

* Le Sieur Pascal, Dalloz, Jurisp. Gén., 1847, i. 202.

† Dalloz, Jurisp. Gén., 1841, i. 440. And see the cases of L'Abbé Laugé, Dalloz, J. G., 1845, i. 223; Bastianesi, *ibid.*, 405; Cruveillé, Dalloz, J. G., 1847, i. 94; Viremaitre, J. G., 1851, v. 248; Dareau, J. G., 1853, v. 215; Chardon, J. G., 1865, i. 248.

inherent in every Government, and treaties only regulated this pre-existent right, it was not giving a retrospective operation to a treaty to try a fugitive surrendered under it for an offence committed before the treaty was concluded.*

Since the first edition of this work was published, three very important cases have come before the French courts. They were fully discussed and reported, and the decisions may be taken to have established the law in France with regard to the respective functions of the executive and judicial authorities in respect of matters of extradition. Slightly the first in order of time was that of Lamirande, who was surrendered by Canada, or rather was kidnapped in Canada by the French police-officers under the circumstances stated in a former chapter.† He was sent for trial before the Cour d'Assises de Vienne by the *chambre des mises en accusations* on charges of forgery, theft, and breach of trust. The Minister of Justice had addressed a letter to the *Procureur-Général* directing him to bring Lamirande to trial for forgery only, unless he voluntarily accepted the decision of the jury upon the other charges. The President of the Court informed the prisoner of this, and called upon him to declare if he consented to be tried for theft and breach of trust. Lamirande refused to consent, but the court nevertheless decided that he should be tried upon all the charges. It held that the fundamental principle of the separation of powers forbade

* Davia, Dalloz, Jurisp. Gén., 1847, iv. 249.

† See *ante*, p. 102; and *post*, Appendix, p. xxix.

the French tribunals to concern themselves with the interpretation or application of the acts of government by which the accused had been submitted to their jurisdiction; that by the mere fact of the sending an accused person for trial before his natural judges, the Government had guaranteed the regularity of his extradition, and that this decision, which was in the exclusive competence of the executive power, could not be the subject of any appeal to the courts, and further, that the letter of the Minister of Justice was simply one of instruction to the *Procureur-Général*, and could not in any way hinder the execution of a decree of the *chambre des mises en accusation.* Upon the day after this decision was given (December 4, 1866,) Lamirande consented in case of his acquittal for forgery to be tried on the charge of theft, but the *Procureur-Général* appealed against the decree above stated, and the question was re-argued before the same court, which reversed its former decison, holding now that it was bound by the requisition of the Minister of Justice. This decree recited that it was a matter of principle that an accused should only be tried for the offence for which he was surrendered except with his express consent. Lamirande was accordingly tried for forgery only, and being convicted was sentenced to ten years' solitary confinement.* The other two cases occurred

* Dalloz, Jurisp. Gén., 1867, ii., 171. See also two very able articles by M. Ducrocq in the Revue Critique, t. 29, p. 481 (Dec. 1866), and t. 30, p. 1 (Jan. 1867). "Après les contestations de son avocat en date du 3 Décembre, Lamirande a accepté, le 4, le

in the early part of 1867, and were very similar in the questions of law involved. One, Renneçon, who had been a wine merchant at Avize (Marne) was claimed from Belgium under the treaty of the 22nd November, 1834, upon a charge of fraudulent bankruptcy. A regular demand was made by the French Government, but before it was finally completed he consented to be sent to France. The *Procureur-Impérial* of Epernay was informed by the Belgian authorities that the prisoner demanded to be given up without waiting for the completion of the preliminary legal forms, and he was accordingly given up at the frontier to the French gendarms. Upon his examination by the *Juge d'Instruction* at Epernay, it was found that the charge of fraudulent bankruptcy could not be sustained, but he was sent for trial for the misdemeanour of simple bankruptcy. He objected before the Cour d'Assises that he ought only to be tried for the offence for which his extradition had been claimed, and the court adjourned the trial in order that a copy might be obtained of the demand to be given up which he had addressed to the Belgian Government. The document was supplied by the Belgian Minister of Justice, and on the 1st of February, 1867, the Cour Impériale

débat sur les faux, et en cas d'acquittement même sur les vols, de sorte que son acquiescement nous aurait obligér à le garder, s'il eût été acquitté, et à le juger sur les accusations que le respect des Traités nous empêchait de soumettre au jury dès l'ouverture de la session." Letter of M. de Moustier, Lamirande Correspondence, 2, 84. See also Blondel, Monog. Alphab. de l'Extradition, 33, and Rep. Gén., vii. 143.

at Paris, having considered its terms, ordered that the prisoner should be reconducted to the frontier and there set at liberty. The *Procureur-Général* did not appeal in time against this decree, and it was accordingly carried into effect. But M. Baroche, the Minister of Justice, considered the case of so much importance that, although the prisoner had been set free, he ordered the *Procureur-Général* to apply to the Cour de Cassation to annul the decree of the Cour Impériale. In his despatch to the *Procureur-Général*, M. Baroche laid down in the most distinct terms the doctrine that the courts of law had nothing to do with the control or interpretation of proceedings in extradition, and referred fully to cases in support of this proposition.* All such questions were, he said, matters for the decision of the Government alone. The only discretion permitted to the courts was, that if the prisoner raised difficulties on which it appeared the Government had not been asked to decide, the trial might be postponed until such decision had been given. He declared that the Court mistook the principles of extradition when it recognised on behalf of a fugitive a right arising from the treaty, the right of being tried only for a

* "Les questions qui peut soulever une extradition étant uniquement internationales un accusé n'a pas qualité pour invoquer dans un intérêt exclusivement personnel les vices prétendus d'une extradition, soit en la forme, soit au fond (Cruveillé, Dalloz, Jurisp. Gén, 1847, i. 94. Viremaître, Dalloz, J. G., 1851, v. 248. Dareau, Dalloz, J. G., 1853, v. 215. Lamirande, Dalloz, J. G., 1867, ii. 171)." See the despatch in full in Dalloz, 1867, i. 281. See also the case of Quesson, Dalloz, J. G., 1867, i. 463.

certain crime or misdemeanour. A criminal could acquire no right against the justice of his country; the tribunal had nothing to do but to try the facts; it could not take cognizance of the conditions upon which extradition had been granted except upon a notification from the Minister of Justice.*

And he quoted the case of Bastianesi, who was given up by a foreign state without any demand of extradition having been made. In this case the court postponed the trial, and the French Government made application to the foreign state, which ratified the surrender, and the prisoner was then tried.†

The Cour de Cassation accepted the doctrines laid down in this despatch, but in annulling the decree of the court below rested its judgment in great measure upon

* It is notable with what emphatic distinctness the doctrine is laid down in the despatch. "Que l'appréciation et l'exécution des actes d'extradition tenant à l'interprétation des traités, rentrent dans le pouvoir du Gouvernement (Aff. Grandvaux), que les traités de l'extradition sont des actes de haute administration intervenus, entre deux puissances, et que ces puissances, et que ces puissances seules peuvent de concert expliquer ou interpréter; qu'il n'appartient en aucune manière à l'autorité judiciaire de s'immiscer dans ces explications ou interprétations (Affs. Viremaître, Dareau), et que ces actes de haute administration échappent a tout contrôle de l'autorité judiciaire (Aff. Chardon). Enfin l'arrêt Dermenon (Dalloz, Jurisp. Gén., 1840, i. 438) défend aux tribunaux de décider si des actes d'une autorité étrangère constituent ou non une extradition virtuelle sans en référer à l'interprétation du Gouvernement."

† Bastianesi; Dalloz, J. G., 1845, i. 405; Blondel, Monog. Alphab., 8.

the special circumstances of the case. It stated as the grounds of the annulment, (1) that in case of a dispute between the public prosecutor and the accused as to whether the circumstances of his extradition implied a convention regulated by treaty between the two powers, there is ground for adjournment until the competent authority has decided the question. (2) That the court acts without authority if it decides that the giving up should involve the consequences of an extradition; especially if it founds its decision exclusively on documents coming from the foreign country. (3) That Renneçon, having consented to be sent to France before the completion of the formalities consequent upon a regular demand, could not complain of the non-observance of conditions applicable to cases of extradition; and (4) that the judge who holds an accused to be detained contrary to the provisions of the treaty cannot order him to be reconducted to the frontier, that right belonging to the executive power only.*

In the other case, that of Faure de Monginot, there was nothing in the special circumstances which rendered unnecessary a distinct decision of the main question. He was claimed from Belgium under the same treaty for complicity in fraudulent bankruptcy, and was regularly surrendered. It being found by the *chambre des mises en accusation* that there was no evidence against him upon the charge on which his surrender had been obtained, he was sent for trial before the *tribunal correc-*

* Aff. Renneçon; Dalloz, Jurisp. Gén., 1867, i. 281.

tionnel de la Seine for misdemeanour in embezzling and breach of trust.

Upon objection being made that the surrender had been granted for a different offence, the tribunal held that the stipulations of treaties were matters of international law, and decided that the accused should be taken to the frontier and set at liberty. On the 24th May, 1867, the Cour Impériale de Paris affirmed this judgment; there being no question as to the facts. But the prisoner was not so fortunate as Renneçon, for the decision was not carried into effect. An appeal was lodged, and acting on the doctrines laid down by M. Baroche in his despatch, the Court reversed its judgment on 25th July, 1867.

The result of the cases is that there is nothing in the French law to prevent the courts from trying a prisoner for crimes other than that for which his surrender has been granted.* The Minister of Justice may interpose and re-deliver the accused to the state which has surrendered him if he is acquitted of the offence for which he was given up, but this interposition is a political not a judicial act, and cannot be compelled by any process known to the French law.

* In arguing the Lamirande case, Doutre, Q.C. said:—" In 1855 Carpentier, Grelet, and Parot, were obtained from the United States for a particular crime; none of them was ever tried in France for that crime; two were found guilty of another crime, one died in gaol, the other is still there undergoing his sentence."

CHAPTER VII.

RULES OF PRACTICE IN THE DIFFERENT COUNTRIES.

IT may be useful to gather up in a short chapter the various rules mentioned in the foregoing pages, with regard to the practical proceedings on demands made upon each of the countries whose law upon this subject has been considered. Demands by Great Britain upon France are always made by the ambassador in Paris in the name of the English Government directly upon the French Government, and are supported by a warrant of arrest issued by a magistrate in England, and copies of the depositions upon which it was founded. These last, however, are not necessary, the French authorities being contented to deliver up the fugitive upon the production of the warrant of the arrest only. The papers are always taken to France by a police-officer able to speak to the identity of the accused. Upon this, the demand is considered by the French Government, and if it be granted, the fugitive is arrested and given up without any investigation by a French court. The matter is purely one of state, with which no legal tribunal is competent to deal.*

* See *ante*, p. 157.

In the case of criminals surrendered to France, an *arrêt de renvoi* is issued by the *chambre des mises en accusation,* directing the court within whose jurisdiction the offence was committed to bring the prisoner to trial. If this *arrêt* directs a trial upon a charge other than that for which he was surrendered, it is in the discretion of the Government to interfere and prevent the trial. Or the prisoner himself may appeal to the Cour de Cassation against the *arrêt.* The cases show, however, that the court will not upon this ground annul it.* If this appeal be not made, the trial takes place upon the charge named in the *arrêt de renvoi,* and no objection raised by the prisoner during its continuance, as to the legality of the surrender, is a reason for the postponement of judgment upon the facts which have been submitted to the jury. This judgment can only be suspended by the appeal just mentioned against the *arrêt de renvoi.* After trial and sentence, an appeal lies to the Cour de Cassation. Upon the acquittal of the prisoner, or if he be convicted, upon the expiration of his sentence he is conducted to the frontier and there set at liberty.

The practice with respect to demands in extradition made upon Great Britain for the surrender of a person suspected of being in the United Kingdom, is now regulated by the Extradition Act, 1870 (33 & 34 Vict. c. 52).† The requisition must be made upon one of the principal Secretaries of State by some person recognised by him as a diplomatic representative of the foreign state (§ 7).

* See *ante,* p. 172. † Appendix, p. xxxvi.

This includes any person recognised as a Consul-General of the foreign State (Extradition Act, 1873,—36 and 37 Vict. c. 60, § 7).* The demand need not be accompanied by any copies of depositions, or even of a warrant of arrest issued in the foreign State, but it is usual for the Secretary of State to require some *primâ facie* evidence of guilt, or some proof of the conviction in the foreign State, to be laid before him. If he thinks the offence is not one of a political character, and that the surrender should be granted, he by order under his hand and seal signifies to the chief magistrate of the metropolitan police courts, or one of the other magistrates of the metropolitan police court in Bow Street (§ 26), that such requisition has been made, and requires him to issue his warrant for the apprehension of the fugitive criminal (§ 7). Upon receiving such an order and being furnished with such evidence as would in his opinion justify the issue of the warrant if the crime had been committed or the criminal convicted in England, the police magistrate issues a warrant for the apprehension of the fugitive (§ 8), and this warrant may be executed in any part of the United Kingdom (§ 13). When the fugitive is apprehended he is brought before the police magistrate, who hears the case in the same manner, and has the same jurisdiction and powers, as near as may be, as if the prisoner were charged with an indictable offence committed in England; but by a special clause in the Act it is provided that he shall receive any evidence which may be tendered to show that the crime of which

* Appendix, p. liii.

the prisoner is accused or of which he is alleged to have been convicted, is an offence of a political character or is not an extradition crime (§ 9). The term "extradition crime" is defined (§ 26) to mean a crime which, if committed in England, or within English jurisdiction, would be one of the crimes described in the first schedule to the Extradition Act, 1870, now enlarged by the schedule to the Extradition Act, 1873. But the police magistrate must have before him the Order in Council by which the Act has been applied in the case of the foreign State by which the requisition has been made, as the Act itself is only operative so long as such Order remains in force, and subject to the limitations, restrictions, conditions, exceptions, and qualifications, if any, contained in the Order (§ 5).* In the case of a fugitive alleged to have been convicted of an extradition crime, the police magistrate only requires proof of the conviction and of the identity of the person brought before him. This, however, only applies to persons who have been convicted after a trial of the ordinary kind, and have then made their escape; not to those condemned *par contumace*, erroneously rendered in the Act "convicted for contumacy;" these latter are included in the category of "accused persons" (§ 26).† In the case of an accused person, an original foreign warrant authorising the arrest of the criminal must be produced (§ 10). It must purport

* Thus, for instance, no British subject can be surrendered to Denmark, Germany, Belgium, or Italy. Appendix, p. xxix.

† See the case of Dubois (*alias* Coppin), *ante*, p. 140.

to be signed by a judge, magistrate, or officer of the foreign State where the same was issued, and it must be authenticated by the oath of some witness, or by being sealed with the official seal of the Minister of Justice or some other Minister of State (§ 15). Evidence must of course be given of the identity of the prisoner with the person named in such warrant. If, in addition to this, such evidence is produced as (subject to the provisions of the Act) would, according to the law of England, justify the committal for trial of the prisoner if the crime of which he is accused had been committed in England, the police magistrate is required to commit him to the Middlesex House of Detention, or to some other prison in Middlesex, there to await the warrant of a Secretary of State for his surrender, and must forthwith send to a Secretary of State a certificate of the committal, and such report upon the case as he may think fit (§ 10). At the time of the committal the police magistrate must inform the criminal that he will not be surrendered until after the expiration of fifteen days, and that he has a right to apply for a writ of habeas corpus (§ 11). Upon the expiration of the fifteen days, or, if a writ of habeas corpus is obtained, upon the decision of the court remanding the prisoner, a Secretary of State may by warrant order the surrender to any person in his opinion duly authorised by the foreign State to receive the criminal; but if he be not conveyed out of the United Kingdom within two months after the expiration of the fifteen days, or the decision of the court, any judge of one of the Superior Courts at

Westminster may order his discharge, unless a Secretary of State, on having reasonable notice of the application, shall show sufficient cause to the contrary (§ 12). One of the chief defects in the law as it existed prior to 1870 was then remedied by Section 8 of the Act, which provides that a police magistrate * or any justice of the peace, in any part of the United Kingdom, may issue a warrant of arrest without any previous order from a Secretary of State, on such information or complaint, and such evidence, or after such proceedings as would, in the opinion of the person issuing the warrant, justify the issue of a warrant if the crime had been committed or the criminal convicted in that part of the United Kingdom in which he exercises jurisdiction. The person issuing such warrant must forthwith send a report of the fact, together with the evidence and information or complaint, or certified copies thereof, to a Secretary of State, who may, if he think fit, order the warrant to be cancelled and the person apprehended to be discharged. Any person arrested on such a warrant must be sent to London and brought before a police magistrate. If the magistrate shall not, within such reasonable time as, having reference to the circumstances of the case, he shall fix, receive an order from the Secretary of State

* This term is by the interpretation clause of the Act (§ 26) limited to "a chief magistrate of the metropolitan police courts or one of the other magistrates of the metropolitan police court in Bow Street," so that the other police magistrates of the metropolis and the stipendiary magistrates in different parts of the country have no jurisdiction of any kind in matters of extradition, except when the crime is alleged to have been committed on the high seas." (§ 16).

signifying that a requisition has been made for the surrender of the person so arrested, he must discharge him, otherwise the case proceeds in the way just described. The evidence of criminality may consist wholly or in part of depositions, or copies of depositions, or certificates, which must be authenticated in the manner provided by the Act (§ 14). The depositions are admissible whether taken in the presence or absence of the accused, or whether taken in the particular charge or not. It is for the magistrate to give to them what weight he thinks proper.*

The practice in Canada is similar to that in England. In the United States, in the case of demands made by Great Britain, the proceedings are commenced by a complaint of the commission of the offence being made on oath by the proper consular officer before some one of the magistrates specified in the treaty. This complaint need not be founded upon personal knowledge, but it must be specific as to the commission and locality of the crime charged, and must allege that the person accused is a fugitive from justice. A copy of this complaint is then presented to the State Department at Washington, which thereupon issues a mandate directed to some one of the qualified magistrates, usually a commissioner of the State of New York, requiring him "to issue a warrant for the apprehension of the fugitive or person so charged, that he may be brought before such magistrate, to the end that the evidence of criminality may be heard and considered." It is not necessary that any warrant of arrest should have been issued or any other proceedings taken in Great

* *Per* Blackburn, J. *In re* Counhaye, L. R. 8 Q. B., 416.

Britain. The State Department requires *primâ facie* evidence of the guilt of the person accused, but the complaint by the British consular officer is sufficient. In the case of demands made by France, it must be shown that the fugitive has been charged in that country,* but the production of a mere *mandat d'arrêt* without any evidence to support it has been accepted as sufficient.† The mandate issued by the State Department is not a warrant of arrest, and cannot be used for that purpose, but under the power which it confers the magistrate may issue a second warrant of arrest if the prisoner, through any defect in the first warrant, or in the proceedings thereunder, shall be discharged.‡ The magistrate to whom the mandate is addressed issues his warrant of arrest, and the fugitive being brought before him, evidence of identity and of criminality must be produced. The latter may consist of depositions taken in Great Britain, and these must be authenticated as required by the American statutes,§ which very closely correspond with that now in force in Great Britain. If the depositions show that documents alleged to have been forged have been produced to the deponent, such documents need not be pro-

* See Metzger's case. 1 Barbour (S. C. of N. Y.), 248, *ante*, p. 54.

† 7 Opinions of Atty.-Gen., 285 (Cushing).

‡ See the opinion of Stanbury, A.-G., upon the case of Robert Vance, who was discharged in consequence of delay in appointing an agent to receive him. 12 Opinions of Atty.-Gen., 75.

§ Act, Aug. 12, 1848, § 2; 9 U. S. Stats. at Large, 302; Act, June 22, 1860, § 1; 12 U. S. Stats. at Large, 84; 2 Bright, 134.

duced before the magistrate. Witnesses are to be examined on both sides, and in the State of New York the prisoner is entitled to give evidence on oath in his own defence.* If the magistrate deems the evidence sufficient to sustain the charge, he certifies that fact, together with a copy of the proceedings before him, to the Secretary of State, who thereupon issues his warrant ordering the Marshal of the United States having the prisoner in custody to surrender him to some person named in the warrant. Should the evidence at first produced before the magistrate be informal or insufficient, the applying Government is entitled to have an adjournment for a time reasonably sufficient to enable it to remedy the defect. After an adjudication by the magistrate, a writ of habeas corpus can only be obtained from the United States Court, the courts of the different States having no power to interfere in matters of extradition. Upon the return to the writ the court will inquire into the competence and sufficiency of the evidence before the magistrate. If, however, it appears that he was duly authorised to hear the case, and that competent evidence was before him, the court will only set aside the commitment if there has been manifest error in the adjudication as to its sufficiency. And if the commitment be set aside, the prisoner may be remanded back to custody that a further examination may be held upon the original warrant of arrest. But pending proceedings upon habeas corpus, the prisoner cannot be the subject of a second arrest upon an extradition warrant.

* Sess. Laws of N. Y., 1869, c. 678.

All the proceedings are at the expense of the Government applying for the surrender,* and it is not necessary that they should be carried on or approved by the United States district attorney.† The rule requiring the surrender to be made within two months after final commitment is the same as in Great Britain.‡

The only important question which has arisen upon the rules of practice in England, the United States, and Canada, relates to the evidence upon which the magistrate is to commit. It is necessary that the evidence shall be such as would justify a commitment for trial if the crime had been committed in the country upon which the demand is made. Upon this a question has been much discussed as to the duty of the magistrate to receive evidence for the prisoner.

In the minutes of a conference upon the subject of an amendment of the existing treaty, held at Paris on February 8, 1866, the following paragraph occurs:—

"The question was then considered, how far the impression apparently entertained in France, that in a case

* 7 Opinions of Atty.-Gen., 396, 612; 9, 497.

† *Ibid.*, 9, 246 (Black).

‡ The fullest statement of the rules of practice in the United States will be found in the cases of Phillip Henrich, 7 Blatchford, Circ. Court Reps. 414; 17 L. T. (N.S.) 55; and *Re* Farez, 7 Blatchford, Circ. Court Reps. 34, 345, 491. See also an excellent letter by Mr. Peter Williams, who was engaged in obtaining the rendition of Macdonnell and others for the recent Bank Forgeries, published in the 'Solicitors' Journal and Reporter' of July 5, 1873. Also *Ex parte* Ross. 2 U. S. Circ. Court Reps. (Ohio), 252.

of extradition the English magistrate actually tried the prisoner, was well founded; and it appeared that the impression was unfounded. The prisoner brought before a magistrate on an extradition warrant would be entitled, indeed, to deny his identity with the person named in the warrant, and would further be entitled to have read in his presence the depositions on which he was charged; but he would not be permitted to controvert the truth of the depositions, or to produce before the magistrate exculpatory evidence." *

On the other hand, it was said in debate in the House of Commons by the Attorney-General (Sir Hugh Cairns), that as to an accused person being precluded from entering into any other defence than a denial of his identity, he differed entirely from that view, for he apprehended that it would be quite open to him to produce any evidence in his power to controvert the allegations made in the depositions.† Neither of these conflicting propositions is exactly correct. It must be remembered that the magistrate investigating a case of demanded extradition, is not quite in the same position as if he were deciding on a charge of crime committed within his own jurisdiction. In the latter case he has full discretion. He may, and often does, discharge a prisoner because, although there is *primâ facie* evidence of guilt, the circumstances are so obscure, the intent so doubtful, the testimony so con-

* Correspondence respecting the Extradition Treaty with France, July 1866, p. 18.

† Speech in the House of Commons, 3rd August, 1866.

flicting, that he thinks a jury would not be likely to convict. But in a case of extradition he cannot consider these matters. If he find sufficient evidence of guilt to justify a commitment, the question of a probability of a conviction is not one for his consideration. But it naturally follows from this that he should be strict in requiring proof of the criminality of the acts which are charged. In an ordinary case he can commit the prisoner upon bail, and leave difficult questions of law to be dealt with by the Court above. But in an extradition case he is to ascertain, not the commission of certain acts upon whose character another and higher tribunal may decide, but that there is sufficient evidence that the crime specified in a foreign warrant has by the prisoner been committed.

The words of the statutes are peculiar. "Such evidence as would, according to the law of England, justify the committal for trial of the prisoner if the crime of which he is accused had been committed in England." The language of the former statute was only slightly different. "Such evidence as, according to the laws of that part of her Majesty's dominions, would justify the apprehension and committal for trial of the person so accused if the crime of which he or she shall be so accused had been there committed."

The question was raised in Anderson's case whether the proviso, "according to the laws of that part of her Majesty's dominions," applied only to the nature and amount of evidence required, or extended to the nature of the crime,* and this has been much discussed in other cases noticed in the foregoing pages. To those cases the reader is referred for illustrations. It will suffice here to note the principles which apply to this subject.

It is clear, in the first place, that the proviso does relate to the nature and amount of evidence required. Thus, although by the English statute depositions may be received in lieu of oral testimony, the general English rules of evidence must be observed. Thus no hearsay evidence, no statements of the prisoner after threats or

* In Anderson's case this question did not necessarily arise. The crime charged against him upon the facts stated was murder by the law of England as well as by that of the United States. The question, whether the circumstances showed sufficient provocation to reduce it to manslaughter, was one for the jury, and one with which the Canadian courts had nothing to do. Nor had these courts any right to inquire into the justice or policy of the legislative enactment under which the arrest was attempted to be made. That was a matter for the consideration of the foreign country, and could not, however it was resolved, affect the nature of the crime. An illustration may be given in the English Act, 14 & 15 Vict., cap. 19, by which if three poachers are out together at night armed, any person is authorised to apprehend them. It is very probable that American judges would disapprove of that Act, as part of what they might consider an iniquitous system of game laws; but so long as it remains upon the English Statute-book, a poacher killing a person so attempting to apprehend him would unquestionably be guilty of murder, and England would have an indisputable right to claim him under the treaty. So far as this question was decided in the case of Anderson, it was decided rightly. This was in the decision of the Queen's Bench (Canada) in favour of the surrender, *ante*, p. 86. See also Reg. v. Sattler, 1 Dears and Bell, C. C., 525.

promises held out to him, could be received. Supposing sufficient unexceptionable evidence to be produced as to the facts, it cannot be the duty of the magistrate to receive evidence in contradiction on the part of the prisoner. However strong the contradiction might be, there would be a conflict of evidence on a matter of fact sufficient to go to a jury, and in that case the magistrate has no option but to commit.

This rule appears to govern the case of a denial of identity. That is a question of fact which could properly be submitted to a jury, and which is only decided by a magistrate in ordinary cases in the exercise of a discretion which he does not possess in matters of extradition. The American rules of practice are the same as those of England, and in Franz Müller's case the commissioner at New York refused to receive evidence of the *alibi* which was afterwards unsuccessfully attempted in England,* nor can there be any doubt of the propriety of his decision.

But the prosecution must produce sufficient evidence of criminality; that is, they must not only prove the commission of the acts described in the depositions, but also that they come within the definition of one of the crimes named in the Act under which proceedings are taken. It is equally well established that if on examination the magistrate finds that the acts are not disputed, but that a justification is established, antecedent to, and independent of, the acts themselves, he must discharge the prisoner. This is seen in the various cases previously cited where

* See *ante*, p. 64.

murder or robbery has been charged on account of acts committed as belligerents.* If the belligerent character, or any similar justification (such, for instance, in a case of forgery, as the authority to sign †) be established, the magistrate cannot commit the prisoner. In the case of the *Roanoke* at Bermuda, the prisoners were charged with piracy. They produced a commission from Jefferson Davis, the President of the Confederate States, and were immediately released; and upon complaint by the Government of the Northern States, the English Government upheld the decision of the magistrate.

There can be no doubt that the magistrate is bound to afford the prisoner a reasonable opportunity of producing this class of evidence. But it will be observed that this rule applies only to evidence as to the quality of the act charged; removing it altogether from the class of crimes, by the operation of a rule of law, by showing that it had an antecedent justification. It is otherwise when it is desired by evidence as to the acts themselves to show a justification arising out of the circumstances, or to reduce the amount of guilt which is involved.

This question will arise most frequently upon charges of murder. In this case it is necessary to have *primâ facie* evidence of a wilful killing. It may be that an antecedent justification may be shown of the class just noticed, and then the prisoner will be entitled to his

* See *ante*, pp. 90, 98.

† See Reg. *v.* Gould, 20 Upp. Can. C. P. (N.S. 6), 154, *ante*, p. 106.

release. But if not, the question upon the facts of the case whether the act charged is really murder, manslaughter, or homicide justified by the circumstances of the case, depends upon evidence of fact which is proper for the consideration of a jury, and upon which, therefore, the magistrate is not entitled to decide. If the prisoner be charged upon the foreign warrant with murder, and the evidence for the prosecution shows a *primâ facie* case of wilful killing, it is not for the magistrate to decide how far provocation, terror, or accident affected the guilt of the act.*

At the same time, it would only be reasonable, considering that the deportation to another country for trial is in itself a severe penalty, that the magistrate should allow anything to appear upon the depositions which the prisoner's advisers might believe would be useful to him in an appeal to a higher Court against the commitment.

* This view of the limits of the duty of the committing magistrate was acted upon by Commr. C. W. Newton, of the Southern District of New York, in the case of John C. Bennett. 11 L. T. (N.S.), 489. See also Story on the Const. of the U. S., § 1812.

CHAPTER VIII.

CONCLUSION.

It has, the author hopes, been sufficiently established in the foregoing pages that the extradition of criminals is an international duty. It may not be scientifically described as a duty of perfect obligation, but it is certainly a duty of political morality. And in countries like England, where it can only be performed in accordance with legislative provisions, it becomes the duty of the legislature to afford the means of its fulfilment. To refuse to do this in obedience to some fancied requirement of national independence and dignity is to pervert a valuable principle into a means of mischief to the whole world. But at the same time every possible precaution should be taken that the privilege thus accorded to foreign nations shall not be improperly used.

In the concluding chapter of the first edition of this work the author pointed out the defects then existing in the law of Great Britain. He referred especially to the delay and formalities which took place before the issue of a warrant of arrest, and which served frequently to warn the fugitive and enable him to escape pursuit; to the want of any security that a prisoner should have an opportunity of testing before a superior court of law the validity of his arrest and commitment; to the absence from the treaties and statutes of any provision that a fugitive should not be surrendered for a political offence or tried upon any other charge than that for which his rendition was obtained; and he expressed a hope that in the course of the discussions then impending, a scheme might be devised which, while affording every proper safeguard to the fugitive, should at the same time remove from England the reproach of being one of the least ready of all the nations of the world to perform her duty in this matter as a member of the family of civilised communities. This hope was realised, and the Extradition Act of 1870 included the amendments proposed, and made the law in every respect satisfactory. One further step has been taken since, and that in a wrong direction. The Act of 1873 was carelessly or ignorantly drawn, and its three chief provisions were far from being improvements on the law they altered. It should be remembered that extradition cannot safely be allowed to become a matter of ordinary police. A person who is found living in Great Britain is *primâ facie* entitled to the protection of her laws, and should not be delivered over to a foreign jurisdiction except upon a serious charge, and after strict precautions taken against injustice being done. The Act of 1873 so extends the schedule of crimes that a treaty might now be made and put in force, under which persons should be surrendered for doing wilful damage to a tree or for boxing a boy's ears in the street. Of course, it is not likely that such a treaty will be made, but there was no occasion to pass an Act of Parliament to make such a folly possible. The Act moreover gave a retrospective effect to the provisions of the principal Act, that of 1870. And here again it was worse than useless to pass a bill through Parliament in order to enable Great Britain to give up, after 1873, persons who were charged with having committed crimes abroad before 1870. The lapse of time very often diminishes the means of defence more than those of prosecution, and the pursuit of a fugitive three years after the alleged offence looks rather like revenge than justice. Again, the person who drew the Act was not acquainted with English law, and made it recite that a person who is accessory before *or after* the fact is by English law liable to be tried and punished as if he were the principal offender. Then followed a provision that extradition should apply to accessories before or after the fact as if they were principals. So far as the English law does consider accessories as principals, they were already included in the terms of the principal Act, and it had been so held,* with the exception that where the offence defined was "Crimes *by bankrupts* against bankruptcy laws," it was held that the bankrupt's wife, not herself a bankrupt, could not be surrendered for complicity. This trivial exception could not justify the passing of an Act with the monstrous provision that accessories after the fact should be liable to extradition as if they were the principal criminals.

* *In re* Elise Counhaye, L. R. 8 Q. B., 410.

But a still worse provision is found in Section 5 of this unfortunate Act, which provides that a Secretary of State may by order under his hand and seal require a police magistrate or justice of the peace to take evidence for the purposes of criminal matters pending in foreign States, whether any person is charged or not, and that witnesses may be compelled to give evidence and produce documents at such a proceeding as in the case of an ordinary charge of an indictable offence. This is in conflict with the whole spirit of our law. To allow depositions to be used here for the purpose of justifying the surrender of a fugitive, that he may be tried where the offence was committed by the law of which it was a violation, and where the witnesses can easily be obtained, is just and reasonable; but to alter the law of England in order that a person may be convicted abroad on the evidence of witnesses who may never be confronted with him, of whom he may never have heard until their depositions are produced against him, and who may have given their evidence before any charge was made against him, is a blunder which ought not to be allowed to soil our statute-book. It may be urged that it is not likely to be acted on, but the excuse condemns it. A useless law is a bad law, and the sooner it is repealed the better.

APPENDIX.

APPENDIX.

FRANCE.

CONVENTION BETWEEN GREAT BRITAIN AND FRANCE, FOR THE MUTUAL SURRENDER, IN CERTAIN CASES, OF PERSONS FUGITIVE FROM JUSTICE.—*Signed at London, February* 13, 1843.

[Ratifications exchanged at London, March 13, 1843.]

HER Majesty the Queen of the United Kingdom of Great Britain and Ireland, and His Majesty the King of the French, having judged it expedient, with a view to the better administration of justice, and to the prevention of crime within their respective territories and jurisdictions, that persons charged with the crimes hereinafter enumerated, and being fugitives from justice, should, under certain circumstances, be reciprocally delivered up;

Their said Majesties have named as their Plenipotentiaries to conclude a Convention for this purpose, that is to say:—

Her Majesty the Queen of the United Kingdom of Great Britain and Ireland, the Right Honourable George Earl of Aberdeen, Viscount Gordon, Viscount Formartine, Lord Haddo, Methlick, Tarvis, and Kellie, a Peer of the United Kingdom, a Member of Her Majesty's Most Honourable Privy Council, Knight of the Most Ancient and Most Noble Order of the Thistle, and Her Majesty's Principal Secretary of State for Foreign Affairs;

And His Majesty the King of the French, the Sieur Louis de Beaupoil, Count of Sainte Aulaire, a Peer of France, Grand Officer of the Royal Order of the Legion of Honour, Grand Cross of the Order of Leopold of Belgium, his Ambassador Extraordinary to Her Britannic Majesty;

Who, after having communicated to each other their respective full powers, found in good and due form, have agreed upon and concluded the following Articles:—

ARTICLE I.

It is agreed that the High Contracting Parties shall, on requisitions made in their name through the medium of their respective

La Convention conclue, le 13 Fév. 1843, entre la France et la Grande Bretagne, pour l'Extradition Réciproque des Malfaiteurs.

Sa Majesté la Reine du Royaume Uni de la Grande Bretagne et d'Irlande, et Sa Majesté le Roi des Français, ayant jugé convenable, en vue d'une meilleure administration de la justice, et pour prévenir les crimes dans leurs territoires et juridictions respectives, que les individus accusés des crimes ci-après énumérés, et qui se seraient soustraits par la fuite aux poursuites de la justice, fussent, dans certaines circonstances, réciproquement extradés;

Leurs dites Majestés ont nommé pour leurs Plénipotentiaires à l'effet de conclure dans ce but une Convention, savoir:—

Sa Majesté la Reine du Royaume Uni de la Grande Bretagne et d'Irlande, le Très-Honorable George Comte de Aberdeen, Vicomte Gordon, Vicomte Formartine, Lord Haddo, Methlick, Tarvis, et Kellie, Pair du Royaume Uni, Conseiller de Sa Majesté en son Conseil Privé, Chevalier du Très-Ancien et Très-Noble Ordre du Chardon, et Principal Secrétaire d'État de Sa Majesté pour les Affaires Étrangères;

Et Sa Majesté le Roi des Français, le Sieur Louis de Beaupoil, Comte de Sainte-Aulaire, Pair de France, Grand Officier de l'Ordre Royal de la Légion d'Honneur, Grand Croix de l'Ordre de Léopold de Belgique, son Ambassadeur Extraordinaire près Sa Majesté Britannique;

Lesquels, après s'être communiqué leurs pleins pouvoirs respectifs, trouvés en bonne et dûe forme, ont arrêté et conclu les Articles suivants:—

Article I.

Il est convenu que les Hautes Parties Contractantes, sur les réquisitions faites en leur nom par l'intermédiaire de leurs Agents

Diplomatic Agents, deliver up to justice persons who, being accused of the crimes of murder (comprehending the crimes designated in the French Penal Code by the terms assassination, parricide, infanticide, and poisoning,) or of an attempt to commit murder, or of forgery, or of fraudulent bankruptcy, committed within the jurisdiction of the requiring party, shall seek an asylum, or shall be found within the territories of the other: provided that this shall be done only when the commission of the crime shall be so established as that the laws of the country where the fugitive or person so accused shall be found would justify his apprehension and commitment for trial, if the crime had been there committed.

Consequently, on the part of the French Government, the surrender shall be made only by the authority of the Keeper of the Seals, Minister of Justice, and after the production of a warrant of arrest or other equivalent judicial document, issued by a Judge, or other competent authority in Great Britain, clearly setting forth the acts for which the fugitive shall have rendered himself accountable; and on the part of the British Government, the surrender shall be made only on the report of a Judge or Magistrate duly authorised to take cognizance of the acts charged against the fugitive in the warrant of arrest or other equivalent judicial document, issued by a Judge or competent Magistrate in France, and likewise clearly setting forth the said acts.

Article II.

The expenses of any detention and surrender made in virtue of the preceding Article shall be borne and defrayed by the Government in whose name the requisition shall have been made.

Article III.

The provisions of the present Convention shall not apply in any manner to crimes of murder, forgery, or fraudulent bankruptcy, committed antecedently to the date thereof.

Article IV.

The present Convention shall be in force until the 1st of January 1844, after which date either of the High Contracting Parties shall be at liberty to give notice to the other of its intention to put an end to it; and it shall altogether cease and determine at the expiration of six months from the date of such notice.

Diplomatiques respectifs, seront tenues de livrer en justice les individus qui, accusés des crimes de meurtre (y compris les crimes qualifiés dans le Code Pénal Français d'assassinat, de parricide, d'infanticide, et d'empoisonnement,) ou de tentative de meurtre, ou de faux, ou de banqueroute frauduleuse, commis dans la juridiction de la partie requérante, chercheront un asile, ou seront rencontrés dans les territoires de l'autre : pourvu que cela n'ait lieu que dans le cas ou l'existence du crime sera constatée de telle manière que les lois du pays où le fugitif ou individu ainsi accusé sera rencontré justifieraient sa détention, et sa mise en jugement, si le crime y avait été commis.

En conséquence, l'extradition ne sera effectuée, de la part du Gouvernement Français, que sur l'avis du Garde des Sceaux, Ministre de la Justice, et après production d'un mandat d'arrêt ou autre acte judiciaire équivalent, émané d'un Juge ou d'une autorité compétente de la Grande Bretagne, énonçant clairement les faits dont le fugitif se sera rendu coupable; et elle ne sera effectuée de la part du Gouvernement Britannique, que sur le rapport d'un Juge ou Magistrat commis à l'effet d'entendre le fugitif sur les faits mis à sa charge par le mandat d'arrêt ou autre acte judiciaire équivalent, émané d'un Juge ou Magistrat compétent en France, et énonçant également d'une manière précise les dits faits.

Article II.

Les frais de toute détention et extradition opérées en vertu de l'Article précédent seront supportés et payés par le Gouvernement au nom duquel la réquisition aura été faite.

Article III.

Les dispositions de la présente Convention ne s'appliqueront en aucune manière aux crimes de meurtre, de faux, ou de banqueroute frauduleuse, commis antérieurement à sa date.

Article IV.

La présente Convention sera en vigueur jusqu'au 1 Janvier 1844; après cette époque l'une des Hautes Parties Contractantes pourra déclarer à l'autre son intention de la faire cesser; et elle cessera en effet à l'expiration des six mois qui suivront cette déclaration.

Article V.

The present Convention shall be ratified, and the ratification shall be exchanged at London at the expiration of three weeks from its date, or sooner if possible.

In witness whereof, the respective Plenipotentiaries have signed the same, and have affixed thereto the seals of their arms.

Done at London, the 13th day of February, in the year of our Lord 1843.

(L.S.) Aberdeen.
(L.S.) Ste. Aulaire.

Convention between Her Majesty and the French Republic, for the Mutual Surrender of Criminals.—*Signed at London, May* 28, 1852.

[Ratifications exchanged at London, June 2, 1852.]

Her Majesty the Queen of the United Kingdom of Great Britain and Ireland, and the Prince President of the French Republic, having found that the Convention concluded between Great Britain and France, on the 13th of February 1843, for the mutual surrender of criminals, has not completely attained its intended object, have deemed it expedient to conclude a new Convention on the subject, and have for that purpose named as their respective Plenipotentiaries, that is to say:

Her Majesty the Queen of the United Kingdom of Great Britain and Ireland, the Right Honourable James Howard, Earl of Malmesbury, Viscount Fitzharris, Baron Malmesbury, a Peer of the United Kingdom, a Member of Her Britannic Majesty's Most Honourable Privy Council, and Her Britannic Majesty's Principal Secretary of State for Foreign Affairs;

And the Prince President of the French Republic, the Sieur Alexander Colonna Count Walewski, Commander of the National Order of the Legion of Honour, Grand Cross of the Order of St. Januarius of the Two Sicilies, Grand Cross of the Order of Merit of St. Joseph of Tuscany, Ambassador of the French Republic to Her Britannic Majesty;

Who, after having communicated to each other their respective

ARTICLE V.

La présente Convention sera ratifiée, et les ratifications seront échangées à Londres à l'expiration de trois semaines à partir de sa date, ou plus tôt si faire se peut.

En foi de quoi les Plénipotentiaires respectifs l'ont signée, et y ont apposé les cachets de leurs armes.

Fait à Londres, le 13 Février, l'an de grâce 1843.

(L.S.) ABERDEEN.
(L.S.) STE. AULAIRE.

LA CONVENTION CONCLUE, LE 28 MAI 1852, ENTRE LA RÉPUBLIQUE FRANÇAISE ET LA GRANDE BRETAGNE POUR L'EXTRADITION RÉCIPROQUE DES MALFAITEURS.

SA Majesté la Reine du Royaume Uni de la Grande Bretagne et d'Irlande, et le Prince Président de la République Française, ayant reconnu que la Convention conclue, le 13 Février 1843, entre la Grande Bretagne et la France, pour l'extradition réciproque des malfaiteurs, n'a point complétement atteint le but proposé, ont jugé convenable de conclure à ce sujet une nouvelle Convention, et ont nommé à cet effet pour leurs Plénipotentiaires respectifs, savoir:

Sa Majesté la Reine du Royaume Uni de la Grande Bretagne et d'Irlande, le Très-Honorable Jacques Howard, Comte de Malmesbury, Vicomte Fitzharris, Baron Malmesbury, Pair du Royaume Uni, Membre du Très-Honorable Conseil Privé de Sa Majesté Britannique, et Principal Secrétaire d'État de Sa Majesté Britannique pour les Affaires Étrangères;

Et le Prince Président de la République Française, le Sieur Alexandre Colonna Comte Walewski, Commandeur de l'Ordre National de la Légion d'Honneur, Grand-Croix de l'Ordre de Saint Janvier des Deux Siciles, Grand-Croix de l'Ordre du Mérite de Saint Joseph de Toscane, Ambassadeur de la République Française près Sa Majesté Britannique;

Lesquels, après s'être réciproquement communiqué leurs pleins

full powers, found in good and due form, have agreed upon and concluded the following Articles:—

ARTICLE I.

The Government of Her Britannic Majesty and the French Government shall, on requisition made in their name by their respective Diplomatic Agents, deliver up to each other reciprocally, any persons, except native subjects or citizens of the Party upon whom the requisition may be made, who, being convicted or accused of any of the crimes hereinafter specified, committed within the jurisdiction of the requiring Party, shall be found within the territories of the other Party.

ARTICLE II.

The surrender shall be made on account of the following crimes, which, however differently denominated in the respective legislations, are punishable under both with grave penalties, namely:—

1. The crime provided for and punished in France under the denomination of *homicide volontaire*, and in the United Kingdom under that of *murder*; whatever may be the means, the instrument, or the substance employed for the commission thereof.

It is understood that the surrender shall be made for an attempt to commit murder (*homicide volontaire*) as well as for that crime itself.

2. The crime of *procuring abortion:* provided for and punished in France and in the United Kingdom under the same denomination.

3. The crime provided for and punished in France under the denomination of *viol*, and in the United Kingdom under that of *rape;* including the crime of having carnal knowledge without violence of a girl under ten years of age, which is also provided for by the French Penal Code, and is punished in the same manner as *rape* in the United Kingdom.

4. *Blows and wounds followed by death:* a crime provided for and punished by the French Penal Code; and punished also in England and Ireland under the denomination of *manslaughter*, and in Scotland under the denomination of *culpable homicide.*

5. *Menaces in writing*, with an order to deposit a sum of money, or to perform any other condition: a crime provided for and punished by the French Penal Code; in England and Ireland under the denomination of *sending or delivering a letter or writing*

pouvoirs respectifs, trouvés en bonne et dûe forme, sont convenus des Articles suivans :—

Article I.

Le Gouvernement de Sa Majesté Britannique et le Gouvernement Français se livreront réciproquement, chacun à l'exception de ses nationaux, sur la demande faite en leur nom par leurs Agens Diplomatiques respectifs, les individus qui, étant condamnés ou poursuivis pour l'un des crimes ci-après énumérés, commis dans la juridiction de la Partie requérante, seraient trouvés sur le territoire de l'autre Partie.

Article II.

L'extradition sera accordée à raison des crimes suivans, lesquels, quelle que soit d'ailleurs leur dénomination différente dans les deux législations, sont également punis par l'une et par l'autre de peines graves, savoir :—

1° Le crime prévu et puni en France sous la dénomination de *homicide volontaire*, et dans le Royaume Uni sous celle de *murder*; quels que soient d'ailleurs le moyen, l'instrument, ou la substance employés pour le commettre.

Il est entendu que la tentative d'homicide volontaire (*murder*) pourra, comme le crime lui-même, donner lieu à l'extradition.

2° Le crime de *procurer l'avortement*: prévu et puni en France et dans le Royaume Uni sous une pareille dénomination.

3° Le crime prévu et puni en France sous la dénomination de *viol*, et dans le Royaume Uni sous celle de *rape*; y compris l'attentat consommé sans violence si la victime a moins de dix ans; crime également prévu par le Code Pénal Français, et puni comme *rape* dans le Royaume Uni.

4° Les *coups et blessures suivis de mort*: crime prévu et puni par le Code Pénal Français; et puni aussi en Angleterre et en Irlande sous la dénomination de *manslaughter*, et en Écosse sous la dénomination de *culpable homicide*.

5° Les *menaces par écrit*, avec ordre de déposer une somme d'argent, ou de remplir toute autre condition: crime prévu et puni par le Code Pénal Français; en Angleterre et en Irlande sous la dénomination de *sending or delivering a letter or writing demanding*

demanding with menaces, &c.; and in Scotland under the denomination of *sending threatening or incendiary letters.*

6. *Bigamy:* a crime provided for and punished in France and in the United Kingdom under the same denomination.

7. *Carrying off a child:* a crime provided for and punished in France under that denomination by the Penal Code; in England and Ireland under the denomination of *child-stealing;* and in Scotland under the denomination of *theft or child-stealing.*

8. *False evidence:* a crime provided for and punished in France under that denomination by the Penal Code; by the English and Irish law under the denomination of *perjury;* and in Scotland under the denomination of *perjury or false affirmation.*

9. *Subornation of witnesses:* a crime provided for and punished under that denomination by the French Penal Code, and by the law of the United Kingdom under the denomination of *subornation of perjury.*

10. *Counterfeiting or altering money,* or *uttering* counterfeit or altered money: crimes provided for and punished in France and in the United Kingdom under the same denominations.

11. *Counterfeiting the Seal of the State,* or *using the counterfeit Seal; counterfeiting or falsifying of public securities and bank-notes authorised by law; using such counterfeit securities and notes,* or *introducing such counterfeit securities and notes:* crimes provided for and punished in France by the Penal Code; in the United Kingdom under similar denominations; and in Scotland also under the denomination of *falsehood and forgery.*

12. *Counterfeiting the puncheons used for marking articles of gold and silver;* and *using the counterfeit puncheons:* crimes provided for and punished in France by the Penal Code; and in the United Kingdom under the same denominations.

13. *Counterfeiting the public stamps;* and *using the counterfeit stamps:* crimes provided for and punished in France and in the United Kingdom under the same denominations.

14. *Forgery of public written instruments,* or *written instruments of commerce or banking,* or *private written instruments,* and *using such forged instruments:* crimes provided for and punished in France by the Penal Code; in England and Ireland under the denomination of *feloniously forging and uttering forged instruments;* and in Scotland under the denomination of *falsehood, forgery, and uttering.*

15. *Burning:* a crime provided for and punished in France by the Penal Code; in England and Ireland under the denomination

with menaces, &c.; et en Écosse sous la dénomination de *sending threatening or incendiary letters.*

6° *La bigamie:* crime prévu et puni en France et dans le Royaume Uni sous une pareille dénomination.

7° *L'enlèvement d'un enfant:* crime prévu et puni en France sous cette dénomination par le Code Pénal; en Angleterre et en Irlande (*sic*) sous la dénomination de *child-stealing*; et en Écosse sous la dénomination de *theft or childstealing.*

8° Le *faux témoignage:* crime prévu et puni en France dans cette dénomination par le Code Pénal; par la loi Anglaise et Irlandaise sous la dénomination de *perjury;* et en Écosse sous la dénomination de *perjury or false affirmation.*

9° La *subornation de témoins:* crime prévu et puni sous cette dénomination par le Code Pénal Français, et par la loi du Royaume Uni sous la dénomination de *subornation of perjury.*

10° La *contrefaçon ou l'altération des monnaies*, ou *l'émission* de monnaies contrefaites ou altérées: crimes prévus et punis en France et dans le Royaume Uni sous une pareille dénomination.

11° La *contrefaçon du Sceau de l'Etat*, ou *l'usage du Sceau contrefait; la contrefaçon ou la falsification des effets publics et des billets de banque autorisés par la loi; l'usage de ces effets et billets contrefaits*, ou *l'introduction des mêmes effets et billets contrefaits;* crimes prévus et punis en France par le Code Pénal; dans le Royaume Uni sous une pareille dénomination; et en Écosse aussi sous la dénomination de *falsehood and forgery.*

12° La *contrefaçon des poinçons servant à marquer les matières d'or et d'argent;* et *l'usage de ces poinçons contrefaits:* crimes prévus et punis en France par le Code Pénal; et dans le Royaume Uni sous une pareille dénomination.

13° La *contrefaçon des timbres nationaux;* et *l'usage de ces timbres contrefaits:* crimes prévus et punis en France et dans le Royaume Uni sous une pareille dénomination.

14° Le *faux en écriture authentique*, ou *en écriture de commerce ou de banque*, et *en écriture privée;* et *l'usage de ces actes faux:* crimes prévus et punis en France par le Code Pénal; en Angleterre et en Irlande sous la dénomination de *feloniously forging and uttering forged instruments;* et en Écosse sous la dénomination de *falsehood, forgery, and uttering.*

15° *L'incendie;* crime prévu et puni en France par le Code Pénal; en Angleterre et en Irlande sous la dénomination de *arson*

of *arson and felonious burning*; and in Scotland under the denomination of *wilful fire-raising.*

16. *Stealing, when attended with violence or intimidation* towards the person whose property is stolen: a crime provided for and punished in France by the Penal Code, (including the case of extortion provided for in Article 400, § 1, of the said Code;) and in the United Kingdom under the denomination of *robbery.* The attempt to commit this crime shall not be placed upon the same footing as the crime itself, in regard to surrender, unless it shall have been made by at least two persons, or by a single person armed.

Stealing or attempting to steal, by night, in an inhabited house, into which the robber has effected an entrance by breaking, scaling, false keys, or any guilty contrivance: a crime provided for and punished in France by the Penal Code; in England and Ireland under the denomination of *burglary;* and in Scotland under the denomination of *theft when committed by housebreaking, or housebreaking with intent to steal.*

Stealing in a building devoted to Divine worship: a crime provided for and punished in France by the Penal Code; in England and Ireland under the denomination of *stealing in a church or chapel;* and in Scotland under the denomination of *theft.*

Stealing in the day-time in an inhabited house, or in any place attached (*dépendance*) to an inhabited house: a crime provided for and punished in France by the Penal Code; in England and Ireland under the denomination of *housebreaking and stealing in a dwelling-house;* and in Scotland under the denomination of *theft.*

The crimes provided for and punished in France under the denomination of *vol domestique et abus de confiance domestique;* in England and Ireland under that of *larceny or embezzlement by clerks or servants;* and in Scotland under those of *theft, breach of trust, and embezzlement.*

17. The crimes provided for and punished in France under the denomination of *soustractions commises par des comptables ou par des dépositaires publics;* in England and Ireland under that of *embezzlement by public officers;* and in Scotland under the same denomination, and also under those of *theft, breach of trust, and embezzlement.*

18. *Fraudulent bankruptcy,* and *participation in fraudulent bankruptcy:* crimes provided for and punished in France by the Code of Commerce and the Penal Code; and in the United Kingdom under

and felonious burning; et en Écosse sous la dénomination de *wilful fire-raising*.

16° Le *vol commis à l'aide de la violence ou de l'intimidation* exercée sur la personne volée: crime prévu et puni en France par le Code Pénal, (y compris le cas d'extorsion prévu par l'Article 400, § 1, du même Code;) et dans le Royaume Uni sous la dénomination de *robbery*. La tentative de ce crime ne sera considérée comme le crime lui-même, en ce qui concerne l'extradition, qu'autant qu'elle aura eu lieu par deux personnes au moins, ou par une seule personne armée.

Le *vol commis ou tenté la nuit dans une maison habitée*, dont le voleur s'est procuré l'entrée à l'aide d'effraction, d'escalade, de fausses clefs, ou par une manœuvre coupable: crime prévu et puni en France par le Code Pénal; en Angleterre et en Irlande sous la dénomination de *burglary*; et en Écosse sous la dénomination de *theft when committed by housebreaking, or housebreaking with intent to steal*.

Le *vol commis dans un édifice consacré au Culte*: crime prévu et puni en France par le Code Pénal; en Angleterre et en Irlande sous la dénomination de *stealing in a church or chapel*; et en Écosse sous la dénomination de *theft*.

Le *vol commis le jour dans une maison habitée*, ou dans la dépendance d'une maison habitée: crime prévu et puni en France par le Code Pénal; en Angleterre et en Irlande sous la dénomination de *housebreaking and stealing in a dwelling-house*; et en Écosse sous la dénomination de *theft*.

Les crimes prévus et punis en France sous la dénomination de *vol domestique et abus de confiance domestique*; en Angleterre et en Irlande sous celle de *larceny or embezzlement by clerks or servants*; et en Écosse sous celles de *theft, breach of trust, and embezzlement*.

17° Les crimes prévus et punis en France sous la dénomination de *soustractions commises par des comptables ou par des dépositaires publics*; en Angleterre et en Irlande sous celle de *embezzlement by public officers*; et en Écosse sous une pareille dénomination, comme aussi sous celles de *theft, breach of trust, and embezzlement*.

18° La *banqueroute frauduleuse*, et *la complicité de banqueroute frauduleuse*: crimes prévus et punis en France par le Code de Commerce et le Code Pénal; et dans le Royaume Uni sous une pareille

the same denomination; but in those cases only which in the United Kingdom are considered as felony, and punished by the penalty of transportation.

19. The crime of *destroying a ship or other merchant-vessel*, effected by any means whatever, in the cases where it shall have been committed by the captain, master, or pilot charged with the navigation of such ship or vessel: a crime provided for and punished in France by the Law of the 10th of April 1825; and in the United Kingdom under the same denomination.

The crime provided for and punished in France under the denomination of *baraterie*, and in the United Kingdom under that of *piracy*.

20. The crime of *mutiny among the crew of a ship*; in the case where persons forming part of the crew of a sea-going ship or vessel shall have taken possession thereof by fraud or violence committed upon the captain or commander; and also in the case where they shall have delivered over such ship or vessel to pirates: a crime provided for and punished in France by the Law of the 10th April 1825, and in the United Kingdom under the denomination of *piracy*.

The surrender shall, however, be demanded by either of the two Contracting Parties only in the following cases, that is to say: by the French Government, in those cases in which the acts hereinbefore enumerated shall in France be considered as *crimes*, and be punishable with severe and degrading punishments, (*peines afflictives et infamantes*;) and by the British Government, in those cases in which the said acts shall be considered as *felonies*, and be punishable with death, or transportation, or imprisonment with hard labour. It shall be sufficient for each Government, in order to prove that its demand is in this respect well founded, to annex thereto the article or articles, clause or clauses, of the law applicable to the act which may give rise to the surrender.

ARTICLE III.

On the part of the French Government, the surrender shall be made in the following manner:

The Ambassador or other Diplomatic Agent of Her Britannic Majesty at Paris, shall produce, in support of any demand for surrender, an authentic and duly legalised copy of a certificate of conviction, or of a warrant to apprehend a person indicted, or of a warrant to apprehend a person charged, clearly setting forth the

dénomination; mais seulement dans les cas qui sont considérés dans le Royaume Uni comme *felonies*, et punis de la peine de la transportation.

19° Le crime de *destruction d'un navire ou autre bâtiment de commerce*, opérée par des moyens quelconques, dans le cas où il aurait été commis par le capitaine, maître, patron, ou pilote chargé de la conduite du dit navire ou bâtiment: crime prévu et puni en France par la Loi du 10 Avril 1825; et dans le Royaume Uni sous une pareille dénomination.

Le crime prévu et puni en France sous la dénomination de *baraterie*, et dans le Royaume Uni sous celle de *piracy*.

20° Le crime de *sédition parmi l'équipage d'un navire;* dans le cas où des individus faisant partie de l'équipage d'un navire ou bâtiment de mer, se seraient emparés du dit bâtiment par fraude ou violence envers le capitaine ou commandant; et aussi dans le cas où ils auraient livré le dit bâtiment ou navire à des pirates: crime prévu et puni en France par la Loi du 10 Avril 1825, et dans le Royaume Uni sous la dénomination de *piracy*.

Toutefois, l'extradition ne pourra être demandée par chacune des deux Parties Contractantes que dans les cas ci-après, savoir: par le Gouvernement Français, dans le cas où les actes ci-dessus énumérés seront en France réputés *crimes*, et punissables de peines afflictives ou infamantes; et par le Gouvernement Britannique, dans les cas ou les mêmes actes seront considérés comme *felonies*, et punissables de la peine de mort, ou de la transportation, ou de l'emprisonnement avec travail forcé. Il suffira à chaque Gouvernement, pour établir la légitimité de sa demande à cet égard, d'y joindre l'article ou les articles, la clause ou les clauses, de loi applicables au fait qui motivera l'extradition.

Article III.

De la part du Gouvernement Français, l'extradition aura lieu ainsi qu'il suit:

L'Ambassadeur ou autre Agent Diplomatique de Sa Majesté Britannique à Paris, joindra à l'appui de chaque demande d'extradition, l'expédition authentique et dûment légalisée soit d'un certificat de condamnation, (*certificate of conviction,*) soit d'un mandat d'arrêt contre une personne accusée, (*warrant to apprehend a person indicted,*) ou d'un mandat d'arrêt contre une personne poursuivie, (*warrant to apprehend a person charged,*) faisant clairement connaître

nature of the crime with which the fugitive is charged. The judicial document thus produced shall be accompanied by the description of the person claimed, and by any particulars which may serve to identify him.

The Keeper of the Seals, Minister of Justice, shall examine the demand in the documents in support thereof; he shall forthwith address a report thereon to the President of the Republic; and, if there be found due cause, a presidential decree shall grant the surrender of the individual claimed, and shall order that he be arrested and delivered up to the English authorities.

In consequence of such decree, the Minister of the Interior shall give orders that the individual claimed may be sought for, and when arrested, may be conducted to the frontier of France, in order to be there delivered to the person appointed to receive him on the part of the English Government.

If it should happen that the documents produced by the English Government in order to identify the person claimed, and the par ticulars collected by the agents of the French police for the same purpose, should prove insufficient, notice thereof shall immediately be given to the Ambassador or other Diplomatic Agent of Her Britannic Majesty at Paris; and the individual claimed shall, if he is in custody, continue to be detained until the English Government shall be enabled to produce further proof of his identity.

ARTICLE IV.

On the part of the English Government, the surrender shall be made in the following manner:

The Ambassador or other Diplomatic Agent of France at London, shall produce to the Government of Her Britannic Majesty either a sentence of conviction (*arrêt de condamnation*) or a warrant for apprehension (*mandat d'arrêt*), clearly setting forth the nature of the crime with which the fugitive is charged. Such document shall be accompanied by the description of the person convicted or accused, and by any other particulars which may serve to identify him.

The said document, when legalised by the Ambassador or other Diplomatic Agent of France at London, shall be considered as proof positive that the individual therein named has been convicted, or is lawfully accused, of having committed a crime cognisable by the French tribunals. Her Britannic Majesty's Secretary of State for the Home Department shall examine the judicial acts to be pro-

la nature du crime à raison duquel le fugitif est poursuivi. Le document judiciaire ainsi produit sera accompagné du signalement et des autres renseignemens pouvant servir à constater l'identité de l'individu réclamé.

M. le Garde des Sceaux, Ministre de la Justice, examinera la demande et les pièces à l'appui; il en fera l'objet d'un rapport immédiat au Président de la République; et, s'il y a lieu, un décret présidentiel accordera l'extradition de l'individu réclamé, et ordonnera qu'il soit arrêté et livré aux autorités Anglaises.

En conséquence de ce décret, M. le Ministre de l'Intérieur donnera des ordres pour que l'individu poursuivi soit recherché, et, en cas d'arrestation, conduit jusqu'à la frontière de France, pour y être livré à la personne chargée de le recevoir de la part du Gouvernement Anglais.

S'il arrivait que les documens produits par le Gouvernement Anglais pour constater l'identité, et les renseignemens recueillis par les agens de la police Française pour le même objet, fussent reconnus insuffisans, avis en sera donné immédiatement à l'Ambassadeur ou autre Agent Diplomatique de Sa Majesté Britannique à Paris; et l'individu poursuivi, s'il a été arrêté, continuera à être détenu, en attendant que le Gouvernement Anglais ait pu produire de nouveaux élémens de preuve pour constater son identité.

Article IV.

De la part du Gouvernement Anglais, l'extradition aura lieu de la manière suivante:

L'Ambassadeur ou autre Agent Diplomatique de France à Londres, produira au Gouvernement de Sa Majesté Britannique soit un arrêt de condamnation, soit un mandat d'arrêt, faisant clairement connaître la nature du crime à raison duquel le fugitif est poursuivi. A ce document seront joints le signalement du condamné ou du prévenu, et les autres renseignemens et indications pouvant servir à faire reconnaître son identité.

Le même document, revêtu de la légalisation de l'Ambassadeur ou autre Agent Diplomatique de France à Londres, sera considéré comme une preuve positive que l'individu qui s'y trouve nommé a été condamné, ou qu'il est légitimement poursuivi, comme ayant commis un crime justiciable des tribunaux Français. Le Secrétaire d'État de Sa Majesté Britannique pour le Ministère de l'Intérieur

duced, as above provided, in the name of the French Government; and after having verified the authenticity of those documents, and ascertained that the crime therein specified is one of those described in the present Convention, he shall issue his warrant to a magistrate, in order to notify to him that the surrender of the person named in the documents produced has been regularly demanded by the French Government conformably to the Convention; and that in consequence such person is to be arrested, in whatever part of the United Kingdom he may have taken refuge, and delivered up to the French authorities.

On receipt of such warrant, the magistrate shall immediately issue his warrant directing the police to seek for and arrest such person, and to bring him before himself or some other magistrate. The person who may be in consequence arrested by the police shall be brought before the magistrate; and the magistrate, after having satisfied himself as to the identity of the individual arrested, either by the confession or acquiescence of such individual, or by other sufficient proof, which may be either direct, or presumptive and circumstantial, shall order that such individual shall be conducted to the frontier of the United Kingdom, in order to be there delivered to the person appointed to receive him on the part of the French Government.

If, in those cases where there may be no direct proof, it should happen that after an attentive examination on the part of the magistrate, the circumstantial proof should be found insufficient, notice thereof shall immediately be given to the Ambassador or other Diplomatic Agent of France; and the individual claimed shall be detained in custody a sufficient time for the French Government to furnish to the Government of Her Britannic Majesty any further proof which it may be able to produce, in order to identify such individual.

Article V.

Any person claimed who may be detained in custody in either of the two countries, in conformity with the stipulations of the two preceding Articles, shall be set at liberty if, within one month after the day of his arrest, the Government which claims his surrender shall not have furnished the further evidence which it has been required to produce in proof of his identity.

The period of such detention shall be lengthened to a reasonable extent, in case the individual who shall have taken refuge in one of

examinera les actes judiciaires produits, ainsi qu'il vient d'être dit, au nom du Gouvernement Français; et après avoir vérifié l'authenticité de ces documens, et avoir reconnu que le crime qui s'y trouve spécifié est un de ceux prévus dans la présente Convention, il adressera son warrant à un magistrat pour lui notifier que l'extradition de la personne désignée dans les documens produits a été régulièrement demandée par le Gouvernement Français conformément à la Convention; et qu'en conséquence cette personne doit être arrêtée, quel que soit le lieu du Royaume Uni où elle se soit réfugiée, et remise aux autorités Françaises.

A la réception de ce warrant, le magistrat devra immédiatement délivrer son warrant ordonnant à la police de rechercher et d'arrêter cette personne, et de la conduire devant lui ou devant un autre magistrat. La personne qui sera arrêtée par la police en conséquence, sera amenée devant le magistrat; et ce magistrat, après s'être assuré de l'identité de l'individu arrêté, soit par le propre aveu ou l'acquiescement de cet individu, soit par d'autres preuves suffisantes, lesquelles pourront être ou directes, ou présomptives et circonstantielles, ordonnera que cet individu soit conduit à la frontière du Royaume Uni, pour y être livré à la personne chargée de le recevoir de la part du Gouvernement Français.

Dans les cas où il n'y aura pas de preuves directes, s'il arrivait qu'après un examen attentif de la part du magistrat, les preuves circonstantielles fussent reconnues insuffisantes, avis en sera donné immédiatement à l'Ambassadeur ou autre Agent Diplomatique de France; et l'individu réclamé sera maintenu en arrestation pendant le temps nécessaire pour que le Gouvernement Français fournisse à celui de Sa Majesté Britannique les nouveaux élémens de preuve qui seraient en son pouvoir, à l'effet de constater du même individu.

Article V.

L'individu poursuivi qui sera maintenu en arrestation dans l'un des deux pays contractans, conformément aux dispositions des deux Articles précédens, sera mis en liberté si, dans le mois à compter du jour de son arrestation, le Gouvernement réclamant l'extradition n'a pas fourni les nouveaux élémens de preuve qui lui auront été demandés à l'effet de constater l'identité.

La durée de cette détention sera augmentée dans une proportion raisonnable, dans le cas où l'individu réfugié dans l'un des deux

the two countries shall have committed his crime in a colonial possession of the other, or in a country placed under its protectorate; and reciprocally, in case he shall have committed his crime in one of the two countries, and have taken refuge in a colonial possession of the other.

ARTICLE VI.

In any case where an individual convicted or accused in France of any of the crimes described in the present Convention, and who shall have taken refuge in the United Kingdom, shall have obtained naturalisation in England subsequently to his conviction or accusation, such naturalisation shall not prevent the search for, arrest, and surrender of such individual to the French authorities, in conformity with the said Convention.

In like manner the surrender shall take place on the part of France in any case where an individual accused or convicted in England of any of the same crimes, who shall have taken refuge in France, shall under the same circumstances have obtained naturalisation in France.

ARTICLE VII.

No accused or convicted person who may be surrendered, shall in any case be proceeded against or punished on account of any political offence committed prior to his being surrendered, nor for any crime or offence not described in the present Convention, which he may have committed previously to his being surrendered; and proof of having been so surrendered under this Convention shall be a good and valid defence against any proceeding on account of any political offence previously committed, and shall entitle the party to an immediate acquittal.

ARTICLE VIII.

The surrender shall not take place if, since the commission of the acts charged, the accusation, or the conviction, exemption from prosecution or punishment has been acquired by lapse of time, according to the laws of the country where the accused shall have taken refuge.

ARTICLE IX.

If the individual claimed should be under prosecution, or in custody, for a crime or offence committed in the country where he may have taken refuge, his surrender may be deferred until he shall have suffered his punishment.

pays aurait commis son crime dans une des possessions coloniales de l'autre, ou dans un des pays placés sous son protectorat; et réciproquement, dans le cas où, ayant commis son crime dans l'un des deux pays, il se serait réfugié dans une des possessions coloniales de l'autre.

ARTICLE VI.

Dans le cas où un individu condamné ou accusé en France pour un des crimes prévus dans la présente Convention, et réfugié dans le Royaume Uni, serait parvenu à se faire naturaliser sujet Anglais postérieurement à la condamnation ou à l'accusation dont il est l'objet, cette naturalisation ne mettra aucun obstacle à ce que la recherche, l'arrestation, et la remise de cet individu aux autorités Françaises aient lieu conformément à la même Convention.

L'extradition aura lieu pareillement de la part de la France dans le cas où un individu poursuivi ou condamné en Angleterre pour un des mêmes crimes, et réfugié en France, aurait obtenu dans les mêmes circonstances la naturalisation Française.

ARTICLE VII.

Le prévenu ou le condamné dont l'extradition aura été accordée, ne pourra être dans aucun cas poursuivi ou puni pour aucun délit politique antérieur à l'extradition, ni pour aucun des crimes ou délits non prévus par la présente Convention, qu'il aurait commis antérieurement à l'extradition; et la preuve qu'on a été extradé en vertu de la présente Convention sera considérée comme un moyen de défense bon et valable contre les poursuites qui seraient exercées en raison d'un délit politique antérieurement commis, et entraînera l'acquittement immédiat du prévenu.

ARTICLE VIII.

L'extradition ne pourra avoir lieu si, depuis les faits imputés, la poursuite, ou la condamnation, la prescription de l'action ou de la peine est acquise, d'après les lois du pays où le prévenu s'est réfugié.

ARTICLE IX.

Si l'individu réclamé est poursuivi ou se trouve détenu pour un crime ou délit qu'il a commis dans le pays où il s'est réfugié, son extradition pourra être différée jusqu'à ce qu'il ait subi sa peine.

In case he should be proceeded against or detained in such country, on account of obligations contracted towards private individuals, his surrender shall nevertheless take place, the injured party retaining his right to prosecute his claims before the competent authority.

ARTICLE X.

If the person accused or convicted should not be the subject of that one of the two States by which he is claimed, he shall not be surrendered until after the Government to which he belongs shall have been consulted, and have had sufficient opportunity to state any reasons which it may have for opposing the surrender. In every such case, the Government upon which the demand is made shall be free to take such decision as it may think fit, and to deliver up the accused to be tried either in his native country, or in the country where the crime shall have been committed.

If the individual claimed by one of the two Contracting Parties, in pursuance of the present Convention, should be also claimed by one or several other Powers, on account of other crimes committed upon their territory, his surrender shall, in preference, be granted in compliance with that demand which is earliest in date: unless any other arrangement should be made between the Governments which have claimed him, either on account of the gravity of the crimes committed, or for any other reasons.

ARTICLE XI.

Every article found in the possession of the individual claimed at the time of his arrest, shall be seized, in order to be delivered up with his person at the time when the surrender shall be made. Such delivery shall not be limited to the property or articles obtained by stealing or by fraudulent bankruptcy, but shall extend to everything that may serve as proof of the crime. It shall take place even when the surrender, after having been ordered, shall be prevented from taking place by reason of the escape or death of the individual claimed.

ARTICLE XII.

Each of the two Contracting Parties shall defray the expenses occasioned by the arrest within its territories, the detention, and the conveyance to its frontier, of the persons whom it may consent to surrender in pursuance of the present Convention.

Dans le cas où il serait poursuivi ou détenu dans le même pays, à raison d'obligations par lui contractées envers des particuliers, son extradition aura lieu néanmoins, sauf à la partie lésée à poursuivre ses droits devant l'autorité compétente.

ARTICLE X.

Si le prévenu ou le condamné n'est pas sujet de celui des deux États qui le réclame, il ne pourra être livré qu'après que le Gouvernement auquel il appartient aura été consulté, et mis en demeure de faire connaître les motifs qu'il pourrait avoir de s'opposer à l'extradition. Dans tous les cas, le Gouvernement saisi de la demande restera libre d'y donner la suite qui lui paraîtra convenable, et de livrer le prévenu pour être jugé soit à son pays natal, soit au pays où le crime aura été commis.

Si l'individu réclamé par l'une des deux Parties Contractantes, aux termes de la présente Convention, se trouvait également réclamé par une ou plusieurs autres Puissances, à raison d'autres crimes commis sur leur territoire, son extradition sera préférablement accordée à la demande qui sera la première en date; à moins qu'il n'en soit différemment disposé entre les Gouvernemens réclamans par des motifs tirés, soit du degré de gravité du crime, soit d'autres considérations.

ARTICLE XI.

Tous les objets trouvés en la possession de l'individu réclamé lors de son arrestation, seront saisis, pour être livrés avec sa personne au moment où s'effectuera l'extradition. Cette remise ne se bornera pas aux valeurs ou aux objets quelconques provenant de vol ou de banqueroute frauduleuse, mais elle comprendra tous ceux qui pourraient servir à la preuve du crime. De plus elle sera effectuée dans le cas même où l'extradition, ayant été ordonnée, ne pourrait avoir lieu néanmoins par suite de l'évasion ou de la mort de l'individu réclamé.

ARTICLE XII.

Chacune des deux Parties Contractantes supportera les frais occasionnés par l'arrestation sur son territoire, la détention, et le transport à sa frontière, des individus dont elle accordera l'extradition en vertu de la présente Convention.

Article XIII.

The stipulations of the present Convention shall be applicable as well to the respective colonial possessions of the two Contracting Parties, as to the countries placed under their protectorate. Article IX. of the Treaty of the 7th of March 1815, shall, however, continue in force in regard to the respective possessions of the said Parties in the East Indies.

It is further agreed that any demands for surrender which may be made in pursuance of the present Article, may be disposed of by the respective Governors of the said possessions or countries; such Governors being, however, bound ultimately to report the affair to their respective Governments at home.

Article XIV.

The stipulations of the present Convention shall in no wise be applicable to crimes committed previously to the 13th of February 1843, the date of the former Convention concluded between the Contracting Parties.

Article XV.

Her Britannic Majesty engages to recommend to Parliament to pass an Act to enable her to carry into execution the arrangements of the present Convention. When such an Act shall have been passed, the Convention shall come into operation from and after a day to be then fixed upon by the two High Contracting Parties; and due notice shall be given beforehand by the Government of each country, of the day which may be so fixed upon.

The Convention shall continue in force until six months after either of the two Contracting Parties shall have given notice to the other of its intention to terminate its operation. Such notice, however, shall not be given before the 1st of January 1854.

Article XVI.

The present Convention shall be ratified, and the ratifications shall be exchanged at London as soon as may be within three weeks from the date of signature.

In witness whereof, the respective Plenipotentiaries have signed the same, and have affixed thereto the seals of their arms.

Done at London, the twenty-eighth day of May, in the year of our Lord one thousand eight hundred and fifty-two.

(L.S.) Malmesbury.
(L.S.) A. Walewski.

ARTICLE XIII.

Les dispositions de la présente Convention sont applicables, tant aux possessions coloniales respectives des deux Parties Contractntes, qu'aux pays placés sous leur protectorat. Toutefois l'Article IX. du Traité du 7 Mars 1815, continuera à être en vigueur en ce qui concerne les possessions respectives des dites Parties dans les Indes Orientales.

Il est de plus convenu que les demandes d'extradition qui seraient formées en exécution du présent Article, pourront être traitées entre les Gouverneurs respectifs des dites possessions ou des dits pays; sauf aux dits Gouverneurs à rendre ultérieurement compte de l'affaire aux Gouvernemens métropolitains respectifs.

ARTICLE XIV.

Les dispositions de la présente Convention ne seront en aucune manière applicables aux crimes commis antérieurement au 13 Février 1843, date de la Convention précédemment conclue entre les Parties Contractantes.

ARTICLE XV.

Sa Majesté Britannique s'engage à recommander au Parlement d'adopter une loi qui l'autorise à mettre en vigueur les dispositions de la présente Convention. Lorsque cette loi aura été adoptée, la Convention sera mise à exécution à partir d'un jour qui sera alors fixé par les deux Hautes Parties Contractantes; et dans chaque pays le Gouvernement fera dûment connaître d'avance le jour ainsi convenu.

La Convention ne cessera que six mois après que l'une des deux Parties Contractantes aura notifié à l'autre son intention d'y mettre fin, sans que cette dénonciation puisse avoir lieu néanmoins avant le 1er Janvier 1854.

ARTICLE XVI.

La présente Convention sera ratifiée, et les ratifications en seront échangées à Londres le plus tôt que faire se pourra dans le délai de trois semaines à compter du jour de la signature.

En foi de quoi, les Plénipotentiaires respectifs l'ont signée, et y ont apposé les cachets de leurs armes.

Fait à Londres, le vingt-huit Mai, l'an de grâce mil huit cent cinquante-deux.

(L.S.) MALMESBURY.
(L.S.) A. WALEWSKI.

Memorandum respecting Cases of Extradition of British Subjects from France between the Years 1852 and 1865.

1. Case of James Howie, fraudulent bankrupt, whose extradition is applied for, October 8, 1852, but the French Government, though consenting to the extradition, does not succeed in finding him, as recorded in a despatch dated October 29, 1852.

2. Case of Alexander Heilbronn, accused of forgery, September 12, 1853. The French Government consents to the same, October 1, 1853.

3. Case of Harry Arthur Allen, accused of forgery, whose extradition was requested December 3, 1853. To this request no reply from the French Government is to be found.

4. Case of David Landrigan, an English deserter, June 15, 1854, whose extradition the French Government refused on the ground of desertion not being one of the crimes mentioned in the Treaty, June 30, 1854.

5. Case of Charles Healy, whose extradition is requested March 8, 1857, he being accused of fraudulent bankruptcy. The French Government consent to give him up, March 24, 1857, but the original request is withdrawn, owing to the fact of Healy's compounding with his creditors, April 24, 1857.

6. Case of Thomas Glass, whose extradition is requested, February 28, 1857, and granted March 30, 1857.

7. Case of Michael Clarke, whose extradition is asked for, June 22, 1859. The French Government reply that search will be made for him with a view to the above result, but a final despatch, dated August 22, 1859, states that no trace of him can be found.

8. Case of Baron de Vidal, whose extradition is requested, July 10, 1861, and refused, July 11, 1861, because he is a French subject.

9. Case of Francis James Leah, whose extradition is requested, September 12, 1865, but refused, September 14, 1865, because theft, the crime of which the above was accused, does not come within the scope of the Treaty.

DENMARK.

CONVENTION BETWEEN HER MAJESTY AND THE KING OF DENMARK, FOR THE MUTUAL SURRENDER OF CRIMINALS.—*Signed at London, April* 15, 1862.

(Ratifications exchanged at London, May 27, 1862.)

HER Majesty the Queen of the United Kingdom of Great Britain and Ireland, and His Majesty the King of Denmark, having judged it expedient, with a view to the better administration of justice, and to the prevention of crime within their respective territories and jurisdictions, that persons charged with or convicted of the crimes hereinafter enumerated, and being fugitives from justice, should, under certain circumstances, be reciprocally delivered up; their said Majesties having named as their Plenipotentiaries to conclude a Convention for this purpose; that is to say:—

Her Majesty the Queen of the United Kingdom of Great Britain and Ireland, the Right Honourable John Earl Russell, Viscount Amberley of Amberley and Ardsalla, a Peer of the United Kingdom, a Member of Her Majesty's Most Honourable Privy Council, Her Principal Secretary of State for Foreign Affairs;

And His Majesty the King of Denmark, M. Torben de Bille, His Chamberlain, Commander of the Order of Dannebrog, and decorated with the Cross of Honour of the same Order, his Envoy Extraordinary and Minister Plenipotentiary to Her Britannic Majesty;

Who, after having communicated to each other their respective full powers, found in good and due form, have agreed upon and concluded the following Articles:—

ARTICLE I.

It is agreed that the High Contracting Parties shall, on requisition made in their name through the medium of their respective Diplomatic Agents, deliver up to justice persons who, being accused or convicted of murder, (comprehending the crimes of assassination, parricide, infanticide, and poisoning,) or attempt to commit murder, or of forgery, (comprehending the counterfeiting of bank-notes, or public securities, or money,) or of fraudulent bankruptcy, committed within the jurisdiction of the requiring Party, shall be found within the territories of the other, provided that such persons are not subjects of the Party upon which the requisition is made. Provided also, that in the case of a person accused, the surrender shall be made only when the commission of the crime shall be so established as that the laws of the country where the fugitive or person so accused shall be found would justify his apprehension and commitment for trial if the crime had been there committed, and in the case of a person convicted, the surrender shall be made only on the production of an authenticated copy of his conviction and on proof of his identity.

Consequently, on the part of the Danish Government, the surrender shall be made only by the consent of the Minister to whose department appertains the administration of justice, and after the production, in the case of a person accused, of a warrant of arrest or other equivalent judicial document issued by a Judge or other competent authority in the United Kingdom, clearly setting forth the acts for which the fugitive shall have rendered himself accountable, or in the case of a person convicted, on the production of an authenticated copy of his conviction and on proof of his identity.

On the part of the British Government, the surrender in the case of a person accused shall be made only on the warrant or other equivalent judicial document for the arrest of a fugitive issued by a Judge or Magistrate duly authorised to take cognizance of the acts charged against the fugitive in Denmark, and on duly authenticated depositions or statements on oath before such Judge or Magistrate, clearly setting forth the said acts, or on such other evidence thereof as, according to the laws of England, would warrant the apprehension of the said fugitive and his committal for trial for the said acts, if they had been therein committed, or in the case of a person convicted, on the production of an authenticated copy of his conviction and on proof of his identity.

Article II.

In the case of the person accused or convicted of any of the crimes mentioned in the preceding Article, who may have fled from a colony or possession of one of the High Contracting Parties and be found in a colony or possession of the other, the surrender shall be made subject always to the conditions prescribed in the preceding Article, on a requisition addressed by the Governor of the one colony directly to the Governor of the other. The Governor upon whom the requisition is made shall be at liberty either to grant the surrender or to refer the matter to his Government.

Article III.

The expenses of any detention and surrender made in virtue of the preceding Articles shall be borne and defrayed by the Government in whose name the requisition shall have been made.

ARTICLE IV.

The present Convention shall come into operation as soon as the necessary legislative Acts shall have been passed. Either of the High Contracting Parties shall be at liberty to give notice to the other at any time for its termination; and in such case it shall altogether cease and determine at the expiration of six months from the date of such notice.

ARTICLE V.

The present Convention shall be ratified, and the ratifications shall be exchanged at London in one month, or sooner if possible.

In witness whereof, the respective Plenipotentiaries have signed the present Convention, and have affixed thereto the seal of their arms.

Done at London, the fifteenth day of April, in the year of our Lord One thousand eight hundred and sixty-two.

(L.S.) RUSSELL.
(L.S.) TORBEN BILLE.

CANADA.

THE LAMIRANDE EXTRADITION CASE.

A complete account of this will be found in the following judgment delivered by Mr. Justice Drummond:—"On the 26th July last (1866) a document under the signature of his Excellency the Governor-General, purporting to be a warrant for the extradition of the petitioner, issued under the authority vested in his Excellency by the provisions of 6 & 7 Vict., intituled 'An Act to give effect to a Convention between Her Majesty and the King of the French for the apprehension of certain offenders,' setting forth that the said petitioner stood accused of the crime of 'forgery by having, in his capacity of cashier of the Bank of France at Poitiers, made false entries in the books of the said bank, and thereby defrauded the said bank of the sum of seven hundred thousand francs;' that a requisition had been made to his Excellency by the Consul-

General of France in the province of British North America to issue his warrant for the arrest of the said prisoner, and requiring all the justices of the peace and other magistrates and officers of justice within their several jurisdictions to aid in apprehending the petitioner and committing him to jail. Under this document the prisoner was arrested, and after examination before William H. Brehaut, Esq., police-magistrate and justice of the peace, was fully committed to the common jail of this district on the 22nd day of the current month of August. On the following day, between the hours of eleven and twelve o'clock in the forenoon, notice was given in due form by the prisoner's counsel to the counsel charged with the criminal prosecutions in this district, that he (the counsel for the prisoner) would present a petition to any one of the judges of the Court of Queen's Bench who might be present in chambers at one o'clock in the afternoon of the following day (the 24th), praying for a writ of habeas corpus and the discharge of the prisoner. At the time appointed this petition was submitted to me. Mr. J. Doutre appeared for the petitioner, Mr. T. K. Ramsay for the Crown, and Mr. Pominville for the private prosecutor. A preliminary objection, raised on the ground of insufficient notice, was overruled. Mr. Doutre then set forth his client's case in a manner so lucid that I soon convinced myself, after perusing the statute cited in the warrant of extradition, that the warrant itself, the pretended warrant of arrest alleged to have been issued in France—*arrêt de renvoi*—and all the proceedings taken with a view to obtain the extradition of the petitioner, were unauthorised by the above cited statute, illegal, null and void, and that the petitioner was therefore entitled to his discharge from imprisonment. But as Mr. Pominville, whom I supposed to be acting as counsel for the Bank of France, wished to be heard, I adjourned the discussion of the case until the following morning. I would have issued the writ before adjourning had the counsel for the prisoner insisted upon it. But that gentleman was no doubt lulled into a sense of false security by the indignation displayed by the counsel for the Crown when Mr. Doutre signified to me his apprehension that a *coup de main* was in contemplation to carry off the petitioner before his case had been decided. On the following morning, Saturday, the 25th of this month, I ordered the issuing of a writ of habeas corpus to bring the petitioner before me with a view to his immediate discharge. My determination to discharge him was founded upon the reasons following:—1. Because it is provided by the 1st section of the Act of the British Parliament to give effect to a Convention between Her Majesty and the King of the French for the apprehension of certain offenders (6 & 7 Vict., c. 75), that every requisition to deliver up to justice any fugitive accused of any of the crimes enumerated in the said Act shall be made by an ambassador of the Government of France or by an accredited diplomatic agent; whereas the requisition made to deliver up the petitioner to justice has been made by Abel Frederic Gautier, Consul-General of France in the provinces of British North America, who is neither an ambassador of the Government of France nor an accredited diplomatic agent of that Government, according to his own avowal upon oath. 2. Because, by the 3rd section of the said statute it is provided that no justice of the peace, or any other person, shall issue his warrant for any such supposed offender until it shall have been proved to him upon oath or affidavit that the person applying for such warrant is the bearer of a warrant of arrest or other equivalent judicial document, issued by a judge or competent magistrate in France, authenticated in such manner as would justify the arrest of the supposed offender in France upon the same charge, or unless it shall appear to him that the act charged against the supposed offender is clearly set forth in such warrant of arrest or other judicial document; whereas the justice of the peace who issued his warrant against the petitioner issued the same without having any such proof before him, the only document produced before him, as well as before me, in lieu of such warrant of arrest or other equivalent judicial documents, being a paper writing alleged to be a translation into English of a French document made by some unknown or unauthorised person in the office of the counsel for the prosecutor at New York, and bearing no authenticity whatever. 3. Because, supposing the said document, purporting to be a translation of an *acte d'accusation* or indictment, accompanied by a pretended warrant for arrest, and designated as an *arrêt de renvoi*, to be authentic, it does not contain the designation of any crime comprised in the number of the various crimes for or by reason of the alleged commission of which any fugitive can be extradited under the said statute. 4. Because by the 1st section of the said Act it is provided that no justice of the peace shall commit any person accused of any of the crimes mentioned in the said Act (to wit, murder, attempt to commit murder, forgery, and fraudulent bankruptcy) unless upon such evidence as according to the laws of that part of Her Majesty's dominions in which the supposed offender shall be found would justify the apprehension and committal for trial of the person so accused, if the crime of which he shall be accused had been there committed; whereas the evidence produced against the petitioner upon the accusation of forgery brought against him before the committing magistrate would not have justified him in apprehending or committing the petitioner for the crime of forgery had the acts charged against him been committed in that part of Her Majesty's dominions where the petitioner was found—to wit, in Lower Canada. 5. Because the said warrant for the extradition of the petitioner, as well as the warrant for his apprehension, does not charge him with the commission of any one of the crimes for which a warrant of extradition can be issued under the said statute; inasmuch as in both of the said warrants the alleged offence is charged against the petitioner as 'forgery by having in the capacity of cashier of the branch of the Bank of France at Poitiers made false entries in the books of the bank, and thereby defrauded the said bank of the sum of seven hundred thousand francs.' Whereas the said offence as thus designated does not constitute the crime of forgery according to the laws of England and Lower Canada, for, to use the words of Judge Blackburn when he pronounced judgment concurrently with Chief-Justice Cockburn and Judge Shee, in a case analogous to this (*Ex parte Charles Windsor*, Court of Queen's Bench, May 1865, 13 W.R., 655), 'Forgery is the false making of an instrument purporting to be that which it is not; it is not the making of an instrument purporting to be that which it is; it is not the making of an instrument which purports to be what it really is, but which contains false statements. Telling a lie does not become a forgery because it is reduced to writing.' The gaoler's return to this writ of habeas corpus was that he had delivered over the prisoner to Edme Justin Melin, *Inspecteur Principal de Police de Paris*, on the night of the 24th instant, at twelve o'clock, by virtue of an order signed by M. H. Sanborn, Deputy-Sheriff, grounded upon an instrument signed by his Excellency the Governor-General. It appears that the petitioner thus delivered up to this French policeman is now on his way to France, although his extradition was illegally demanded, and although he was accused of no crime under which he could have been legally extradited; and although, as I am credibly informed, his Excellency the Governor-General had promised, as he was bound in honour and justice, to grant him an opportunity of having his case decided by the first tribunal of the land before ordering his extradition. It is evident that his Excellency has been taken by surprise, for the document signed by him is a false record, purporting to have been signed on the 23rd instant at Ottawa, while his Excellency was at Quebec, and falsely certified to have been recorded at Ottawa before it had been signed by the Governor-General. In so far as the petitioner is concerned, I have no further order to make, for he who was to have been brought before me is now probably on the high seas, swept away by one of the most audacious and hitherto successful attempts to frustrate the ends of justice which has yet been heard of in Canada. The only action I can take, in so far as he is concerned, is to order that a copy of this judgment be transmitted by the Clerk of the Crown to the Governor-General, for the adoption of such measures as his Excellency may be advised to take to maintain that respect which is due to the courts of Canada and to the laws of England. As to the public officers who have been connected with this matter, if any proceedings are to be adopted against them they will be informed thereof on Monday the 24th day of September next, in the Court of Queen's Bench, holding criminal jurisdiction, to which day I adjourn this case for further consideration."

NOTE ON POLITICAL OFFENCES.

"With regard to political offences there is no great difficulty. It should be provided, that no surrender should be granted except on the declaration of the minister of the foreign power that the fugitive is wanted for trial for the offence charged in the depositions used against him and no other. If treaties are made, there are abundant models for a clause which would protect political offenders from rendition. The clause lately proposed in the House of Commons was probably hastily drawn up, and was obviously faulty. It provided:—

"'Nothing in this Act, or in any previous Acts relating to Treaties of Extradition, shall be construed to authorise the extradition of any person in whose case there shall be reasonable grounds for believing that his offence, if any, had for its motive or purpose the promotion or prevention of any political object; nor to authorise the extradition of any person the requisition for the delivery of whom shall not contain an undertaking on the part of the sovereign or government making such requisition that such person shall not be proceeded against, or punished on account of, any offence which he shall have committed before he shall be delivered up other than the offence specified in the requisition.'

"This assumed that a political crime could be correctly defined as a crime committed from political motives. As was pointed out in the debate, the murder of President Lincoln, and the shooting of a policeman in Ireland by Fenian assassins, were both crimes committed for political reasons; but no one would pretend that they were any the less murders; and murders, the perpetrators of which it would be a disgrace to any nation to harbour. If Booth had escaped to England, there would have been little debate as to the propriety of giving him up to be tried for murder.

"The killing of a man in civil war, the seizure of property by the leaders of an armed rebellion, are examples of true political crimes. So far as rules upon the subject can be laid down, the provision of the Convention of 1852, and the clauses inserted in treaties made by France with other foreign nations, afford good models for imitation. But the line is a narrow one, and it would be well to leave to the Secretary of State a discretion which he would exercise in responsibility to Parliament. The existence of slavery in some countries causes another difficulty which might be got over either by a provision similar to that in the treaty between the United States and Mexico, which stipulated that no slave should be surrendered, or which would be far better, by limiting the rendition of slaves to cases of the most atrocious crimes."—*Extract from concluding chapter of First Edition.*

The following are the clauses upon this subject inserted in the most recent French treaties:—

"Il est expressément stipulé que le prévenu ou le condamné dont l'extradition aura été accordée ne pourra être, dans aucun cas, poursuivi ou puni pour aucun crime ou délit politique antérieur à l'extradition.

"Ne sera pas réputé crime politique ni fait connexe à un semblable crime, l'attentat contre la personne du chef d'un gouvernement étranger, ou contre celle d'un des membres de sa famille, lorsque cet attentat constituera le fait, soit de meurtre, soit d'assassinat, soit d'empoisonnement."

Article 8 of Convention between France and Saxe-Weimar, 7 Aug. 1858.

"9. § 1. Il est expressément stipulé que le prévenu ou le condamné dont l'extradition aura été accordée, ne pourra, dans aucun cas, être poursuivi ou puni pour un délit politique antérieur à l'extradition, ni pour un des crimes ou délits non prévus par la présente Convention.

"§ 2. Mais il est entendu que les crimes contre la personne du souverain, ou des membres de sa famille, et respectivement des cardinaux de la Sainte Eglise, ne sont point compris dans le § 1 du présent Article."

Convention between France and the Pontifical States, 19 July, 1859.

"Ses tentatives d'assassinat, d'homicide, ou d'empoisonnement contre le chef d'un gouvernement étranger ne seront pas réputés crimes politiques pour l'effet de l'extradition. Ne seront pas non plus considérés comme crimes politiques ceux énumérés dans cet Article, lorsqu'ils seront commis contre l'héritier immédiat de la couronne de France."

Convention between France and Chili, 11 April, 1860.

"Il est bien entendu que ne sera pas réputé délit politique, ni fait connexe à un semblable délit, l'attentat contre la personne d'un souverain étranger ou contre celle des membres de sa famille, lorsque cet attentat constituera le fait, soit d'assassinat, soit d'empoisonnement, soit de meurtre."

Additional Convention between France and the Low Countries, 2 Aug. 1860.

"I see a notice has been given that when the Bill goes into committee a clause will be proposed, the purpose of which is to exclude all offences which are considered to be of a political character. I do not say that on principle I should have any objection to that, provided you define what is to be treated as a political offence. I take it that, in a rough and popular way, it would not be difficult to do that. For instance, if a man were killed in a riot, or in an attempt to excite a tumult or popular insurrection, that probably would be regarded as a political offence. But a difficulty would arise where you have to deal with attempts at assassination.

"It does seem to me that, while on the one hand we desire to retain inviolate the right of exemption from arrest for political offences, it is monstrous to say, on the other hand, that if any private person is assassinated in the streets of Paris for example, and the murderer escapes to England, he may be punished; but that if the person so assassinated is invested with any political character, then the offence becomes a political offence, and the law of England declares that he shall not be given up to justice. This position appears to me to be utterly untenable. There is, I apprehend, a discretionary power given to the Secretary of State as to the application of the Act, and all I can say on this point is, that if any honourable gentleman can succeed in establishing a distinction between the case of a purely political offence and an offence against morality, I shall be willing to consider the proposal to insert a clause to meet such a case."—*Speech of Lord Stanley in the House of Commons*, 3rd August, 1866.

On the same occasion Mr. J. S. Mill suggested that the political offences excluded from the operation of the law should be defined as, "Any offence committed in the course of or furthering of civil war, insurrection, or political commotions."

---

33 & 34 Vict. c. 52

(EXTRADITION ACT, 1870).

An Act for amending the Law relating to the Extradition of Criminals. [9th August, 1870.]

Whereas it is expedient to amend the law relating to the surrender to foreign States of persons accused or convicted of the commission of certain crimes within the jurisdiction of such States, and to the trial of criminals surrendered by foreign States to this country:

Be it enacted by the Queen's Most Excellent Majesty, by and with the advice and consent of the Lords Spiritual and Temporal, and Commons, in this present Parliament assembled, and by the authority of the same, as follows:

Preliminary.

Short title.

1. This Act may be cited as "The Extradition Act, 1870."

Where arrangement for surrender of criminals made, Order in Council to apply Act.

2. Where an arrangement has been made with any foreign State with respect to the surrender to such State of any fugitive criminals, Her Majesty may, by Order in Council, direct that this Act shall apply in the case of such foreign State.

Her Majesty may, by the same or any subsequent Order, limit the operation of the Order, and restrict the same to fugitive criminals who are in or suspected of being in the part of Her Majesty's dominions specified in the Order, and render the operation thereof subject to such conditions, exceptions, and qualifications as may be deemed expedient.

Every such Order shall recite or embody the terms of the arrangement, and shall not remain in force for any longer period than the arrangement.

Every such Order shall be laid before both Houses of Parliament within six weeks after it is made, or, if Parliament be not then sitting, within six weeks after the then next meeting of Parliament, and shall also be published in the "London Gazette."

Restrictions on surrender of criminals.

3. The following restrictions shall be observed with respect to the surrender of fugitive criminals:—

(1.) A fugitive criminal shall not be surrendered if the offence in respect of which his surrender is demanded is one of a political character, or if he prove to the satisfaction of the police magistrate or the court before whom he is brought on habeas corpus, or to the Secretary of State, that the requisition for his surrender has in fact been made with a view to try or punish him for an offence of a political character:

(2.) A fugitive criminal shall not be surrendered to a foreign State unless provison is made by the law of that State, or by arrangement, that the fugitive criminal shall not, until he has been restored or had an opportunity of returning to Her Majesty's dominions, be detained or tried in that foreign State for any offence committed prior to his surrender other than the extradition crime proved by the facts on which the surrender is grounded:

(3.) A fugitive criminal who has been accused of some offence within English jurisdiction not being the offence for which his surrender is asked, or is undergoing sentence under any conviction in the United Kingdom, shall not be surrendered until after he has been discharged, whether by acquittal or on expiration of his sentence or otherwise:

(4.) A fugitive criminal shall not be surrendered until the expiration of fifteen days from the date of his being committed to prison to await his surrender.

Provisions of arrangement for surrender.

4. An Order in Council for applying this Act in the case of any foreign State shall not be made unless the arrangement—

(1.) Provides for the determination of it by either party to it after the expiration of a notice not exceeding one year; and,

(2.) Is in conformity with the provisions of this Act, and in particular with the restrictions on the surrender of fugitive criminals contained in this Act.

Publication and effect of Order.

5. When an Order applying this Act in the case of any foreign State has been published in the "London Gazette," this Act (after the date specified in the Order, or if no date is specified, after the date of the publication,) shall, so long as the Order remains in force, but subject to the limitations, restrictions, conditions, exceptions, and qualifications, if any, contained in the Order, apply in the case of such foreign State. An Order in Council shall be conclusive evidence that the arrangement therein referred to complies with the requisitions of this Act, and that this Act applies in the case of the foreign State mentioned in the Order, and the validity of such Order shall not be questioned in any legal proceedings whatever.

Liability of criminal to surrender.

6. Where this Act applies in the case of any foreign State, every fugitive criminal of that State who is in or suspected of being in any part of Her Majesty's dominions, or that part which is specified in the Order applying this Act (as the case may be), shall be liable to be apprehended and surrendered in manner provided by this Act, whether the crime in respect of which the surrender is sought was committed before or after the date of the Order, and whether there is or is not any concurrent jurisdiction in any court of Her Majesty's dominions over that crime.

Order of Secretary of State for issue of warrant in United Kingdom if crime is not of a political character.

7. A requisition for the surrender of a fugitive criminal of any foreign State, who is in or suspected of being in the United Kingdom, shall be made to a Secretary of State by some person recognised by the Secretary of State as a diplomatic representative of that foreign State. A Secretary of State may, by order under his hand and seal, signify to a police magistrate that such requi-

sition has been made, and require him to issue his warrant for the apprehension of the fugitive criminal.

If the Secretary of State is of opinion that the offence is one of a political character, he may, if he think fit, refuse to send any such order, and may also at any time order a fugitive criminal accused or convicted of such offence to be discharged from custody.

Issue of warrant by police magistrate, justice, &c.

8. A warrant for the apprehension of a fugitive criminal, whether accused or convicted of crime, who is in or suspected of being in the United Kingdom, may be issued—

(1.) By a police magistrate on the receipt of the said order of the Secretary of State, and on such evidence as would in his opinion justify the issue of the warrant if the crime had been committed or the criminal convicted in England; and

(2.) By a police magistrate or any justice of the peace in any part of the United Kingdom, on such information or complaint and such evidence or after such proceedings as would in the opinion of the person issuing the warrant justify the issue of a warrant if the crime had been committed or the criminal convicted in that part of the United Kingdom in which he exercises jurisdiction.

Any person issuing a warrant under this section without an order from a Secretary of State shall forthwith send a report of the fact of such issue, together with the evidence and information or complaint, or certified copies thereof, to a Secretary of State, who may if he think fit order the warrant to be cancelled, and the person who has been apprehended on the warrant to be discharged.

A fugitive criminal, when apprehended on a warrant issued without the order of a Secretary of State, shall be brought before some person having power to issue a warrant under this section, who shall by warrant order him to be brought and the prisoner shall accordingly be brought before a police magistrate.

A fugitive criminal apprehended on a warrant issued without the order of a Secretary of State shall be discharged by the police magistrate, unless the police magistrate, within such reasonable time as, with reference to the circumstances of the case, he may fix, receives from a Secretary of State an order signifying that a requisition has been made for the surrender of such criminal.

Hearing of case and evidence of political character of crime.

9. When a fugitive criminal is brought before the police magis-

trate, the police magistrate shall hear the case in the same manner, and have the same jurisdiction and powers, as near as may be, as if the prisoner were brought before him charged with an indictable offence committed in England.

The police magistrate shall receive any evidence which may be tendered to show that the crime of which the prisoner is accused or alleged to have been convicted is an offence of a political character or is not an extradition crime.

Committal or discharge of prisoner.

10. In the case of a fugitive criminal accused of an extradition crime, if the foreign warrant authorising the arrest of such criminal is duly authenticated, and such evidence is produced as (subject to the provisions of this Act) would, according to the law of England, justify the committal for trial of the prisoner if the crime of which he is accused had been committed in England, the police magistrate shall commit him to prison, but otherwise shall order him to be discharged.

In the case of a fugitive criminal alleged to have been convicted of an extradition crime, if such evidence is produced as (subject to the provisions of this Act) would, according to the law of England, prove that the prisoner was convicted of such crime, the police magistrate shall commit him to prison, but otherwise shall order him to be discharged.

If he commits such criminal to prison, he shall commit him to the Middlesex House of Detention, or to some other prison in Middlesex, there to await the warrant of a Secretary of State for his surrender, and shall forthwith send to a Secretary of State a certificate of the committal, and such report upon the case as he may think fit.

Surrender of fugitive to foreign State by warrant of Secretary of State.

11. If the police magistrate commits a fugitive criminal to prison, he shall inform such criminal that he will not be surrendered until after the expiration of fifteen days, and that he has a right to apply for a writ of habeas corpus.

Upon the expiration of the said fifteen days, or, if a writ of habeas corpus is issued, after the decision of the court upon the return to the writ, as the case may be, or after such further period as may be allowed in either case by a Secretary of State, it shall be lawful for a Secretary of State, by warrant under his hand and seal, to order the fugitive criminal (if not delivered on the decision of the court) to be surrendered to such person as may in his opinion be duly authorised to receive the fugitive criminal by the foreign State from which the requisition for the surrender proceeded, and such fugitive criminal shall be surrendered accordingly.

It shall be lawful for any person to whom such warrant is directed and for the person so authorised as aforesaid to receive, hold in custody, and convey within the jurisdiction of such foreign State the criminal mentioned in the warrant; and if the criminal escapes out of any custody to which he may be delivered on or in pursuance of such warrant, it shall be lawful to retake him in the same manner as any person accused of any crime against the laws of that part of Her Majesty's dominions to which he escapes may be retaken upon an escape.

Discharge of persons apprehended if not conveyed out of United Kingdom within two months.

12. If the fugitive criminal who has been committed to prison is not surrendered and conveyed out of the United Kingdom within two months after such committal, or, if a writ of habeas corpus is issued, after the decision of the court upon the return to the writ, it shall be lawful for any judge of one of Her Majesty's Superior Courts at Westminster, upon application made to him by or on behalf of the criminal, and upon proof that reasonable notice of the intention to make such application has been given to a Secretary of State, to order the criminal to be discharged out of custody, unless sufficient cause is shown to the contrary.

Execution of warrant of police magistrate.

13. The warrant of the police magistrate issued in pursuance of this Act may be executed in any part of the United Kingdom in the same manner as if the same had been originally issued or subsequently indorsed by a justice of the peace having jurisdiction in the place where the same is executed.

Depositions to be evidence.

(6 & 7 Vict., c. 76.)

14. Depositions or statements on oath, taken in a foreign State, and copies of such original depositions or statements, and foreign

certificates of or judicial documents stating the fact of conviction, may, if duly authenticated, be received in evidence of proceedings under this Act.

Authentication of depositions and warrants.

(29 & 30 Vict., c. 121.)

15. Foreign warrants and depositions or statements on oath, and copies thereof, and certificates of or judicial documents stating the fact of a conviction, shall be deemed duly authenticated for the purposes of this Act if authenticated in manner provided for the time being by law or authenticated as follows:—

(1.) If the warrant purports to be signed by a judge, magistrate, or officer of the foreign State where the same was issued;

(2.) If the depositions or statements or the copies thereof purport to be certified under the hand of a judge, magistrate, or officer of the foreign State where the same were taken to be the original depositions or statements, or to be true copies thereof, as the case may require; and

(3.) If the certificate of or judicial document stating the fact of conviction purports to be certified by a judge, magistrate, or officer of the foreign State where the conviction took place; and

if in every case the warrants, depositions, statements, copies, certificates, and judicial documents (as the case may be) are authenticated by the oath of some witness or by being sealed with the official seal of the Minister of Justice, or some other Minister of State: And all courts of justice, justices, and magistrates shall take judicial notice of such official seal, and shall admit the documents so authenticated by it to be received in evidence without further proof.

CRIMES COMMITTED AT SEA.

Jurisdiction as to crimes committed at sea.

16. Where the crime in respect of which the surrender of a fugitive criminal is sought was committed on board any vessel on the high seas which comes into any port of the United Kingdom, the following provisions shall have effect:—

(1.) This Act shall be construed as if any stipendiary magistrate in England or Ireland, and any sheriff or sheriff substitute in Scotland, were substituted for the police magistrate throughout this Act, except the part relating to the execution of the warrant of the police magistrate:

(2.) The criminal may be committed to any prison to which the person committing him has power to commit persons accused of the like crime:

(3.) If the fugitive criminal is apprehended on a warrant issued without the order of a Secretary of State, he shall be brought before the stipendiary magistrate, sheriff, or sheriff substitute who issued the warrant, or who has jurisdiction in the port where the vessel lies, or in the place nearest to that port.

FUGITIVE CRIMINALS IN BRITISH POSSESSIONS.

Proceedings as to fugitive criminals in British possessions.

17. This Act when applied by Order in Council, shall, unless it is otherwise provided by such Order, extend to every British possession in the same manner as if throughout this Act the British possession were substituted for the United Kingdom or England, as the case may require, but with the following modifications; namely,

(1.) The requisition for the surrender of a fugitive criminal who is in or suspected of being in a British possession may be made to the Governor of that British possession by any person recognised by that Governor as a consul-general, consul, or vice-consul, or (if the fugitive criminal has escaped from a colony or dependency of the foreign State on behalf of which the requisition is made) as the Governor of such colony or dependency:

(2.) No warrant of a Secretary of State shall be required, and all powers vested in or acts authorised or required to be done under this Act by the police magistrate and the Secretary of State, or either of them, in relation to the surrender of a fugitive criminal, may be done by the Governor of the British possession alone:

(3.) Any prison in the British possession may be substituted for a prison in Middlesex:

(4.) A judge of any court exercising in the British possession the like powers as the Court of Queen's Bench exercises in England may exercise the power of discharging a criminal when not conveyed within two months out of such British possession.

Saving of laws of British possessions.

18. If by any law or ordinance, made before or after the passing of this Act by the Legislature of any British possession, provision is made for carrying into effect within such possession the surrender of fugitive criminals who are in or suspected of being in such British possession, Her Majesty may, by the Order in Council applying this Act in the case of any foreign State, or by any subsequent Order, either

Suspend the operation within any such British possession of this Act, or of any part thereof, so far as it relates to such foreign State, and so long as such law or ordinance continues in force there, and no longer;

Or direct that such law or ordinance, or any part thereof, shall have effect in such British possession, with or without modifications and alterations, as if it were part of this Act.

General Provisions.

Criminal surrendered by foreign State not triable for previous crime.

19. Where, in pursuance of any arrangement with a foreign State, any person accused or convicted of any crime which, if committed in England, would be one of the crimes described in the first schedule to this Act is surrendered by that foreign State, such person shall not, until he has been restored or had an opportunity of returning to such foreign State, be triable or tried for any offence committed prior to the surrender in any part of Her Majesty's dominions other than such of the said crimes as may be proved by the facts on which the surrender is grounded.

As to use of forms in second schedule.

20. The forms set forth in the second schedule to this Act, or forms as near thereto as circumstances admit, may be used in all matters to which such forms refer, and in the case of a British possession may be so used, *mutatis mutandis*, and when used shall be deemed to be valid and sufficient in law.

Revocation, &c. of Order in Council.

21. Her Majesty may, by Order in Council, revoke or alter, subject to the restrictions of this Act, any Order in Council made in pursuance of this Act, and all the provisions of this Act with respect to the original Order shall (so far as applicable) apply, *mutatis mutandis*, to any such new Order.

Application of Act in Channel Islands and Isle of Man.

22. This Act (except so far as relates to the execution of warrants in the Channel Islands) shall extend to the Channel Islands and Isle of Man in the same manner as if they were part of the United Kingdom; and the Royal Courts of the Channel Islands are hereby respectively authorised and required to register this Act.

Saving for Indian treaties.

23. Nothing in this Act shall affect the lawful powers of Her Majesty or of the Governor-General of India in Council to make treaties for the extradition of criminals with Indian native states, or with other Asiatic States conterminous with British India, or to carry into execution the provisions of any such treaties made either before or after the passing of this Act.

Power of foreign State to obtain evidence in United Kingdom.

24. The testimony of any witness may be obtained in relation to any criminal matter pending in any court or tribunal in a foreign State in like manner as it may be obtained in relation to any civil matter under the Act of the session of the nineteenth and twentieth years of the reign of Her present Majesty, chapter one hundred and thirteen, intituled "An Act to provide for taking evidence in Her "Majesty's dominions in relation to civil and commercial matters "pending before foreign tribunals;" and all the provisions of that Act shall be construed as if the term "civil matter" included a criminal matter, and the term "cause" included a proceeding against a criminal: Provided that nothing in this section shall apply in the case of any criminal matter of a political character.

Foreign State includes dependencies.

25. For the purposes of this Act, every colony, dependency, and constituent part of a foreign State, and every vessel of that State, shall (except where expressly mentioned as distinct in this Act) be deemed to be within the jurisdiction of and to be part of such foreign State.

DEFINITION OF TERMS.

"British possession."

26. In this Act, unless the context otherwise requires,—

The term "British possession" means any colony, plantation,

island, territory, or settlement within Her Majesty's dominions, and not within the United Kingdom, the Channel Islands, and Isle of Man; and all colonies, plantations, islands, territories, and settlements under one legislature, as hereinafter defined, are deemed to be one British possession:

"Legislature."

The term "legislature" means any person or persons who can exercise legislative authority in a British possession, and where there are local legislatures as well as a central legislature, means the central legislature only:

"Governor."

The term "Governor" means any person or persons administering the government of a British possession, and includes the Governor of any part of India:

"Extradition crime."

The term "extradition crime" means a crime which, if committed in England or within English jurisdiction, would be one of the crimes described in the first schedule to this Act:

"Conviction."

The terms "conviction" and "convicted" do not include or refer to a conviction which under foreign law is a conviction for contumacy, but the term "accused person" includes a person so convicted for contumacy:

"Fugitive criminal." *"Fugitive criminal of a foreign State."*

The term "fugitive criminal" means any person accused or convicted of an extradition crime committed within the jurisdiction of any foreign State who is in or is suspected of being in some part of Her Majesty's dominions; and the term "fugitive criminal of a foreign State" means a fugitive criminal accused or convicted of an extradition crime committed within the jurisdiction of that State:

"Secretary of State."

The term "Secretary of State" means one of Her Majesty's Principal Secretaries of State:

"Police magistrate."

The term "police magistrate" means a chief magistrate of the metropolitan police courts or one of the other magistrates of the metropolitan police court in Bow Street:

"Justice of the peace."

The term "justice of the peace" includes in Scotland any sheriff, sheriff substitute, or magistrate:

"Warrant."

The term "warrant," in the case of any foreign State, includes any judicial document authorising the arrest of a person accused or convicted of crime.

Repeal of Acts.

Repeal of Acts in third schedule.

27. The Acts specified in the third schedule to this Act are hereby repealed as to the whole of Her Majesty's dominions; and this Act (with the exception of anything contained in it which is inconsistent with the treaties referred to in the Acts so repealed) shall apply (as regards crimes committed either before or after the passing of this Act), in the case of the foreign States with which those treaties are made, in the same manner as if an Order in Council referring to such treaties had been made in pursuance of this Act, and as if such Order had directed that every law and ordinance which is in force in any British possession with respect to such treaties should have effect as part of this Act.

Provided that if any proceedings for or in relation to the surrender of a fugitive criminal have been commenced under the said Acts previously to the repeal thereof, such proceedings may be completed, and the fugitive surrendered, in the same manner as if this Act had not passed.

Schedules.

FIRST SCHEDULE.

List of Crimes.

The following list of crimes is to be construed according to the law existing in England, or in a British possession (as the case may be), of the date of the alleged crime, whether by common law or by statute made before or after the passing of this Act:—

Murder, and attempt and conspiracy to murder.

Manslaughter.

Counterfeiting and altering money and uttering counterfeit or altered money.

Forgery, counterfeiting, and altering, and uttering what is forged or counterfeited or altered.

Embezzlement and larceny.

Obtaining money or goods by false pretences.

Crimes by bankrupts against bankruptcy law.

Fraud by a bailee, banker, agent, factor, trustee, or director, or member, or public officer of any company made criminal by any Act for the time being in force.

Rape.

Abduction.

Child-stealing.

Burglary and housebreaking.

Arson.

Robbery with violence.

Threats by letter or otherwise with intent to extort.

Piracy by law of nations.

Sinking or destroying a vessel at sea, or attempting or conspiring to do so.

Assaults on board a ship on the high seas with intent to destroy life, or to do grievous bodily harm.

Revolt or conspiracy to revolt by two or more persons on board a ship on the high seas against the authority of the master.

SECOND SCHEDULE.

Form of Order of Secretary of State to the Police Magistrate.

To the chief magistrate of the metropolitan police courts *or* other magistrate of the metropolitan police court in Bow Street [*or* the stipendiary magistrate at].

WHEREAS, in pursuance of an arrangement with referred to in an Order of Her Majesty in Council dated the day of , a requisition has been made to me, , one of Her Majesty's Principal Secretaries of State, by , the diplomatic representative of , for the surrender of , late of , accused [*or* convicted] of the commission of the crime of , within the jurisdiction of Now I hereby, by this my order under my hand and seal, signify to you that such requisition has been made, and require you to issue your warrant for the apprehension of such fugitive, provided that the conditions of The Extradition Act, 1870, relating to the issue of such warrant, are in your judgment complied with.

Given under the hand and seal of the undersigned, one of Her Majesty's Principal Secretaries of State, this day of 18 .

Form of Warrant of Apprehension by Order of Secretary of State.

Metropolitan police district [*or* county *or* borough of] to wit. — To all and each of the constables of the metropolitan police force [*or* of the county *or* borough of].

WHEREAS the Right Honourable , one of Her Majesty's Principal Secretaries of State, by order under his hand and seal, hath signified to me that requisition hath been duly made to him for the surrender of , late of , accused [*or* convicted] of the commission of the crime of within the jurisdiction of : This is therefore to command you in Her Majesty's name forthwith to apprehend the said , pursuant to The Extradition Act, 1870, wherever he may be found in the United Kingdom or Isle of Man, and bring him before me or some other [* magistrate sitting in this court], to show cause why he should not be surrendered in pursuance of the said Extradition Act, for which this shall be your warrant.

Given under my hand and seal at [*Bow Street, one of the police courts of the metropolis] this day of 18 .

J. P.

Form of Warrant of Apprehension without Order of Secretary of State.

Metropolitan police district [*or* county *or* borough of] to wit. — To all and each of the constables of the metropolitan police force [*or* of the county *or* borough of].

Whereas it has been shown to the undersigned, one of Her Majesty's justices of the peace in and for the metropolitan police district [*or* the said county *or* borough of], that late of is accused [*or* convicted] of the commission of the crime of within the jurisdiction of : This is therefore to command you in Her Majesty's name forthwith to apprehend the said and to bring him before me or some other magistrate sitting at this court [*or* one of Her Majesty's justices of the peace in and for the county [*or* borough] of], to be further dealt with according to law, for which this shall be your warrant.

Given under my hand and seal at Bow Street, one of the police courts of the metropolis [*or* in the county *or* borough aforesaid], this day of 18 .

J. P.

Form of Warrant for bringing Prisoner before the Police Magistrate.

County [*or* borough] of to wit. — To constable of the police force of and to all other police officers in the said county [*or* borough] of

Whereas late of accused [*or* alleged

* *Note.*—Alter as required.

to be convicted of] the commission of the crime of within the jurisdiction of , has been apprehended and brought before the undersigned, one of Her Majesty's justices of the peace in and for the said county [*or* borough] of ; And whereas by The Extradition Act, 1870, he is required to be brought before the chief magistrate of the metropolitan police court, or one of the police magistrates of the metropolis sitting at Bow Street, within the metropolitan police district [*or* the stipendiary magistrate for]: This is therefore to command you the said constable in Her Majesty's name forthwith to take and convey the said to the metropolitan police district [*or* the said], and there carry him before the said chief magistrate or one of the police magistrates of the metropolis sitting at Bow Street within the said district [*or* before a stipendiary magistrate sitting in the said] to show cause why he should not be surrendered in pursuance of The Extradition Act, 1870, and otherwise to be dealt with in accordance with law, for which this shall be your warrant.

Given under my hand and seal at in the county [*or* borough] aforesaid, this day of 18 .

J. P.

Form of Warrant of Committal.

Metropolitan police district [*or* the county *or* borough of] to wit. — To one of the constables of the metropolitan police force [*or* of the police force of the county *or* borough of], and to the keeper of the

Be it remembered, that on this day of in the year of our Lord late of is brought before me the chief magistrate of the metropolitan police courts [*or* one of the police magistrates of the metropolis] sitting at the police court in Bow Street, within the metropolitan police district, [*or* a stipendiary magistrate for ,] to show cause why he should not be surrendered in pursuance of The Extradition Act, 1870, on the ground of his being accused [*or* convicted] of the commission of the crime of within the jurisdiction of , and forasmuch as no sufficient cause has been shown to me why he should not be surrendered in pursuance of the said Act:

This is therefore to command you the said constable in Her Majesty's name forthwith to convey and deliver the body of the said into the custody of the said keeper of the at , and you the said keeper to receive the said into your custody, and him there safely to keep until he is thence delivered pursuant to the provisions of the said Extradition Act, for which this shall be your warrant.

Given under my hand and seal at Bow Street, one of the police courts of the metropolis [*or* at the said], this day of 18

J. P.

Form of Warrant of Secretary of State for Surrender of Fugitive.

To the keeper of and to

WHEREAS late of accused [*or* convicted] of the commission of the crime of within the jurisdiction of , was delivered into the custody of you the keeper of by warrant dated pursuant to The Extradition Act, 1870:

Now I do hereby, in pursuance of the said Act, order you the said keeper to deliver the body of the said into the custody of the said , and I command you the said to receive the said into your custody, and to convey him within the jurisdiction of the said , and there place him in the custody of any person or persons appointed by the said to receive him, for which this shall be your warrant.

Given under the hand and seal of the undersigned, one of Her Majesty's Principal Secretaries of State, this day of

THIRD SCHEDULE.

Year and Chapter.	Title.
6 & 7 Vict. c. 75.	An Act for giving effect to a Convention between Her Majesty and the King of the French for the apprehension of certain offenders.
6 & 7 Vict. c. 76.	An Act for giving effect to a Treaty between Her Majesty and the United States of America for the apprehension of certain offenders.
8 & 9 Vict. c. 120.	An Act for facilitating execution of the Treaties with France and the United States of America for the apprehension of certain offenders.
25 & 26 Vict. c. 70.	An Act for giving effect to a Convention between Her Majesty and the King of Denmark for the mutual surrender of criminals.
29 & 30 Vict. c. 121.	An Act for the Amendment of the Law relating to Treaties of Extradition.

---

36 & 37 Vict. c. 60
(EXTRADITION ACT, 1873).

An Act to amend The Extradition Act, 1870.

[5th August, 1873.]

Be it enacted by the Queen's most Excellent Majesty, by and with the advice and consent of the Lords Spiritual and Temporal, and Commons, in this present Parliament assembled, and by the authority of the same, as follows:

Construction of Act and short title.

(33 & 34 Vict., c. 52.)

1. This Act shall be construed as one with The Extradition Act, 1870, (in this Act referred to as the principal Act,) and the principal Act and this Act may be cited together as The Extradition Acts, 1870 and 1873, and this Act may be cited alone as The Extradition Act, 1873.

Explanation of sect. 6 *of* 33 & 34 Vict. c. 52.

2. Whereas by section six of the principal Act it is enacted as follows:

"Where this Act applies in the case of any foreign State, every fugitive criminal of that State who is in or suspected of being in any part of Her Majesty's dominions, or that part which is specified in the Order applying this Act (as the case may be), shall be liable to be apprehended and surrendered in manner provided by this Act, whether the crime in respect of which the surrender is sought was committed before or after the date of the Order, and whether there is or is not any concurrent jurisdiction in any court of Her Majesty's dominions over that crime."

And whereas doubts have arisen as to the application of the said section to crimes committed before the passing of the principal Act, and it is expedient to remove such doubts, it is therefore hereby declared that—

A crime committed before the date of the Order includes in the said section a crime committed before the passing of the principal Act, and the principal Act and this Act shall be construed accordingly.

Liability of accessories to be surrendered.

3. Whereas a person who is accessory before or after the fact, or counsels, procures, commands, aids, or abets the commission of any indictable offence, is by English law liable to be tried and punished as if he were the principal offender, but doubts have arisen whether such person as well as the principal offender can be surrendered under the principal Act, and it is expedient to remove such doubts; it is therefore hereby declared that—

Every person who is accused or convicted of having counselled, procured, commanded, aided, or abetted the commission of any extradition crime, or of being accessory before or after the fact to any extradition crime, shall be deemed for the purposes of the principal Act and this Act to be accused or convicted of having committed such crime, and shall be liable to be apprehended and surrendered accordingly.

Explanation of sect. 14 *of* 33 & 34 Vict. c. 52 *as to statements on oath including affirmations.*

4. Be it declared, that the provisions of the principal Act relating to depositions and statements on oath taken in a foreign State, and

copies of such original depositions and statements, do and shall extend to affirmations taken in a foreign State, and copies of such affirmations.

Power of taking evidence in United Kingdom for foreign criminal matters.

5. A Secretary of State may, by order under his hand and seal, require a police magistrate or a justice of the peace to take evidence for the purposes of any criminal matter pending in any court or tribunal in any foreign State; and the police magistrate or justice of the peace, upon the receipt of such order, shall take the evidence of every witness appearing before him for the purpose in like manner as if such witness appeared on a charge against some defendant for an indictable offence, and shall certify at the foot of the depositions so taken that such evidence was taken before him, and shall transmit the same to the Secretary of State; such evidence may be taken in the presence or absence of the person charged, if any, and the fact of such presence or absence shall be stated in such deposition.

Any person may, after payment or tender to him of a reasonable sum for his costs and expenses in this behalf, be compelled, for the purposes of this section, to attend and give evidence and answer questions and produce documents, in like manner and subject to the like conditions as he may in the case of a charge preferred for an indictable offence.

Every person who wilfully gives false evidence before a police magistrate or justice of the peace under this section shall be guilty of perjury.

Provided that nothing in this section shall apply in the case of any criminal matter of a political character.

Explanation of sect. 16 *of* 33 & 34 Vict. c. 52.

6. The jurisdiction conferred by section sixteen of the principal Act on a stipendiary magistrate, and a sheriff or sheriff substitute, shall be deemed to be in addition to, and not in derogation or exclusion of, the jurisdiction of the police magistrate.

Explanation of diplomatic representative and consul.

7. For the purposes of the principal Act and this Act a diplomatic representative of a foreign State shall be deemed to include any person recognised by the Secretary of State as a consul-general

of that State, and a consul or vice-consul shall be deemed to include any person recognised by the Governor of a British Possession as a consular officer of a foreign State.

Addition to list of crimes in schedule.

8. The principal Act shall be construed as if there were included in the first schedule to that Act the list of crimes contained in the schedule to this Act.

SCHEDULE.

List of Crimes.

The following list of crimes is to be construed according to the law existing in England or in a British Possession (as the case may be) at the date of the alleged crime, whether by common law or by statute made before or after the passing of this Act:

Kidnapping and false imprisonment.

Perjury, and subornation of perjury, whether under common or statute law.

(24 & 25 *Vict.* c. 96, *&c.*)

Any indictable offence under the Larceny Act, 1861, or any Act amending or substituted for the same, which is not included in the first schedule to the principal Act.

Any indictable offence under the Act of the session of the twenty-fourth and twenty-fifth years of the reign of Her present Majesty, chapter ninety-seven, "To consolidate and amend the statute law of England and Ireland relating to malicious injuries to property," or any Act amending or substituted for the same, which is not included in the first schedule to the principal Act.

Any indictable offence under the Act of the session of the twenty-fourth and twenty-fifth years of the reign of Her present Majesty, chapter ninety-eight, "To consolidate and amend the statute law of England and Ireland relating to indictable offences by forgery," or any Act amending or substituted for the same, which is not included in the first schedule to the principal Act.

Any indictable offence under the Act of the session of the twenty-fourth and twenty-fifth years of the reign of Her present Majesty, chapter ninety-nine, "To consolidate and amend the statute law of the United Kingdom against offences relating to the coin," or any Act amending or substituted for the same, which is not included in the first schedule to the principal Act.

Any indictable offence under the Act of the session of the twenty-fourth and twenty-fifth years of the reign of Her present Majesty, chapter one hundred, "To consolidate and amend the statute law of England and Ireland relating to offences against the person," or any Act amending or substituted for the same, which is not included in the first schedule to the principal Act.

Any indictable offence under the laws for the time being in force in relation to bankruptcy which is not included in the first schedule to the principal Act.

GERMANY.

TREATY BETWEEN HER MAJESTY AND THE EMPEROR OF GERMANY, FOR THE MUTUAL SURRENDER OF FUGITIVE CRIMINALS.—*Signed at London, May* 14, 1872.

[Ratifications exchanged at London, June 21, 1872.]

HER Majesty the Queen of the United Kingdom of Great Britain and Ireland, and His Majesty the Emperor of Germany, having judged it expedient, with a view to the better administration of justice and to the prevention of crime within the two countries and their jurisdictions, that persons charged with or convicted of the crimes hereinafter enumerated, and being fugitives from justice, should, under certain circumstances, be reciprocally delivered up; Their said Majesties have named as their Plenipotentiaries to conclude a Treaty for this purpose, that is to say:

Her Majesty the Queen of the United Kingdom of Great Britain and Ireland, the Right Honourable Granville George Earl Granville, Lord Leveson, a Peer of the United Kingdom, Knight of the Most Noble Order of the Garter, a Member of Her Majesty's Privy Council, Lord Warden of the Cinque Ports and Constable of Dover Castle, Chancellor of the University of London, Her Majesty's Principal Secretary of State for Foreign Affairs;

And His Majesty the Emperor of Germany, His Minister of State and Chamberlain, Albert Count of Bernstorff-Stintenburg, Knight of the Exalted Order of the Black Eagle, Grand Cross of the Order of the Red Eagle with oak leaves, Grand Commander of the Order of the Imperial and Royal House of Hohenzollern in diamonds, and Knight of the Order of the Crown with the Red Cross; Grand Cross of the Order of Civil Merit of the Crown of Bavaria, and of the Order of the Ernestine Branch of the House of Saxony, Knight of the Order of the Golden Lion of the House of Nassau, &c., &c., &c., Ambassador Extraordinary and Plenipotentiary of His Imperial and Royal Majesty to Her Britannic Majesty;

Nachdem Ihre Majestät die Königin des Vereinigten Königreichs von Grossbritannien und Irland, und Seine Majestät der Deutsche Kaiser, behufs besserer Verwaltung der Rechtspflege und zur Verhütung von Verbrechen innerhalb der beiden Reiche und deren Gerichtsbarkeiten es für zweckmässig befunden haben, dass Personen, welche der in diesem Vertrage aufgeführten strafbaren Handlungen beschuldigt oder wegen solcher verurtheilt und vor der Justiz flüchtig geworden sind, unter bestimmten Umständen gegenseitig ausgeliefert werden sollen; so haben Ihre eben gedachten Majestäten behufs Abschliessung eines desfallsigen Vertrags zu Ihren Bevollmächtigten ernannt:

Ihre Majestät die Königin des Vereinigten Königreichs von Grossbritannien und Irland den sehr ehrenwerthen Granville George Grafen Granville, Lord Leveson, Pair des Vereinigten Königreichs, Ritter des Höchstedlen Ordens vom Hosenband, Mitglied Ihrer Majestät Höchstehrenwerthen Geheimenrathes, Lord Wardein der fünf Häfen, Schlosshauptmann von Dover, Kanzler der Universität London, Allerhöchstihren Haupt-Staatssekretair für die Auswärtigen Angelegenheiten;

Und Seine Majestät der Deutsche Kaiser Allerhöchstseinen Staats-Minister und Kämmerer, Albrecht Grafen von Bernstorff-Stintenburg, Ritter des hohen Ordens vom Schwarzen Adler, Grosskreuz des Rothen Adler-Ordens mit Eichenlaub, Gross-Komthur des Kaiserlichen und Königlichen Haus-Ordens von Hohenzollern in Brillanten, Ritter des Kronen-Ordens dritter Klasse mit dem rothen Kreuz; Grosskreuz des Ordens der Bayerischen Krone und des Sachsen-Ernestinischen Haus-Ordens, Ritter des Ordens vom Goldenen Löwen des Hauses Nassau, &c., &c., &c., ausserordentlichen und bevollmächtigten Botschafter Seiner Kaiserlichen und Königlichen Majestät bei Ihrer Grossbritannischen Majestät;

Who, after having communicated to each other their respective full powers, found in good and due form, have agreed upon and concluded the following Articles :—

ARTICLE I.

The High Contracting Parties engage to deliver up to each other those persons who, being accused or convicted of a crime committed in the territory of the one Party, shall be found within the territory of the other Party, under the circumstances and conditions stated in the present Treaty.

ARTICLE II.

The crimes for which the extradition is to be granted are the following :—

(1). Murder, or attempt to murder.

(2). Manslaughter.

(3). Counterfeiting or altering money, uttering or bringing into circulation counterfeit or altered money.

(4). Forgery or counterfeiting or altering, or uttering what is forged or counterfeited or altered; comprehending the crimes designated in the German Penal Code as counterfeiting or falsification of paper money, bank notes, or other securities, forgery or falsification of other public or private documents, likewise the uttering or bringing into circulation or wilfully using such counterfeited, forged, or falsified papers.

(5). Embezzlement or larceny.

(6). Obtaining money or goods by false pretences.

(7). Crimes by bankrupts against bankruptcy law; comprehending the crimes designated in the German Penal Code as bankruptcy liable to prosecution.

(8). Fraud by a bailee, banker, agent, factor, trustee, or director, or member or public officer of any company, made criminal by any law for the time being in force.

(9). Rape.

Welche, nachdem sie sich gegenseitig ihre Vollmachten mitgetheilt und dieselben in guter und gehöriger Form befunden, die folgenden Artikel vereinbart und abgeschlossen haben:

Artikel I.

Die hohen vertragenden Theile verpflichten sich einander diejenigen Personen auszuliefern, welche wegen einer, auf dem Gebiete des einen Theils begangenen strafbaren Handlung beschuldigt oder verurtheilt sind und in dem Gebiete des anderen Theiles aufgefunden werden, sofern die in dem gegenwärtigen Vertrage angegebenen Fälle und Voraussetzungen vorhanden sind.

Artikel II.

Die strafbaren Handlungen, wegen deren die Auslieferung zu gewähren ist, sind folgende:

(1). Mord, Mordversuch.

(2). Todtschlag.

(3). Nachmachen oder Verfälschen von Metallgeld, Verausgabung oder In-Verkehr-Bringen nachgemachten oder verfälschten Metallgeldes.

(4). Nachmachen oder Verfälschen von Papiergeld, Banknoten oder anderen Werthpapieren, Fälschung oder Verfälschung anderer öffentlicher oder Privat-Urkunden, imgleichen Verausgabung oder In-Verkehr-Bringen oder wissentliches Gebrauchen solcher nachgemachten oder gefälschten Papiere.

(5). Diebstahl und Unterschlagung.

(6). Erlangung von Geld oder anderen Sachen durch falsche Vorspiegelungen..

(7). Strafbarer Bankerrutt, unter welchen Begriff alle diejenigen strafbaren Handlungen fallen, die nach den bezüglichen Bestimmungen des deutschen Strafgesetzbuchs gerichtlich geahndet werden.

(8). Untreue Seitens eines Verwalters und Beauftragten, Banquiers, Agenten, Prokuristen, Vormundes oder Kurators, Vorstandes, Mitgliedes oder Beamten irgend einer Gesellschaft, soweit dieselbe nach den bestehenden Gesetzen mit Strafe bedroht ist.

(9). Nothzucht.

(10). Abduction.
(11). Child-stealing.
(12). Burglary or housebreaking.

(13). Arson.
(14). Robbery with violence.
(15). Threats by letter, or otherwise, with intent to extort.
(16). Sinking or destroying a vessel at sea, or attempting to do so.
(17). Assaults on board a ship on the high seas with intent to destroy life or to do grievous bodily harm.

(18). Revolt, or conspiracy to revolt, by two or more persons on board a ship on the high seas, against the authority of the master.

The extradition is also to take place for participation in any of the aforesaid crimes, provided such participation be punishable by the laws of both the Contracting Parties.

ARTICLE III.

No German shall be delivered up by any of the Governments of the Empire to the Government of the United Kingdom; and no subject of the United Kingdom shall be delivered up by the Government thereof to any German Government.

ARTICLE IV.

The extradition shall not take place if the person claimed on the part of the Government of the United Kingdom, or the person claimed on the part of any of the Governments of the German Empire, has already been tried and discharged or punished, or is still under trial, in one of the States of the German Empire or in the United Kingdom respectively, for the crime for which his extradition is demanded.

If the person claimed on the part of the Government of the United Kingdom, or if the person claimed on the part of any of the Governments of the German Empire, should be under examination for any other crime in one of the States of the German Empire or

(10). Entführung.

(11). Kinderraub.

(12). Einbrechen und Eindringen in ein Wohnhaus oder dazu gehöriges Nebengebäude mit der Absicht, ein Verbrechen zu begehen, zur Tages-(housebreaking) oder Nachtzeit (burglary).

(13). Vorsätzliche Brandstiftung.

(14). Raub mit Gewaltthätigkeiten.

(15). Erpressung.

(16). Vorsätzliche Versenkung oder Zerstörung eines Schiffes zur See, oder Versuch dieses Verbrechens.

(17). Angriffe auf Personen an Bord eines Schiffes auf hoher See in der Absicht zu tödten oder eine schwere Körperverletzung zu verüben.

(18). Widerstand mit Thätlichkeiten (revolt) gegen den Schiffsführer an Bord eines Schiffes auf hoher See, wenn dieser von zwei oder mehreren Personen verübt wird, oder Verschwörung zu einem solchen Widerstande.

Die Auslieferung findet auch wegen Theilnahme an einer der vorbezeichneten strafbaren Handlungen statt, sofern diese nach der Gesetzgebung beider vertragenden Theile mit Strafe bedroht ist.

Artikel III.

Kein Deutscher wird von Seiten der Regierungen des Deutschen Reichs an die Regierung des Vereinigten Königreichs und von Seiten dieser kein englischer Unterthan an eine Regierung des Deutschen Reichs ausgeliefert werden.

Artikel IV.

Die Auslieferung soll nicht stattfinden, wenn die von einer Regierung des Deutschen Reichs verfolgte Person im Vereinigten Königreich, oder die Seitens der Regierung des Vereinigten Königreichs verfolgte Person in einem der Staaten des Deutschen Reichs wegen derselben strafbaren Handlung, wegen deren die Auslieferung beantragt wird, in Untersuchung gewesen und ausser Verfolgung gesetzt worden, oder sich noch in Untersuchung befindet, oder bereits bestraft worden ist.

Wenn die von einer Regierung des Deutschen Reichs verfolgte Person im Vereinigten Königreich, oder wenn die Seitens der Regierung des Vereinigten Königreichs verfolgte Person in einem der Staaten des Deutschen Reichs wegen einer anderen strafbaren

in the United Kingdom respectively, his extradition shall be deferred until the conclusion of the trial and the full execution of any punishment awarded to him.

Article V.

The extradition shall not take place if, subsequently to the commission of the crime, or the institution of the penal prosecution, or the conviction thereon, exemption from prosecution or punishment has been acquired by lapse of time, according to the laws of the State applied to.

Article VI.

A fugitive criminal shall not be surrendered if the offence in respect of which his surrender is demanded is one of a political character, or if he prove that the requisition for his surrender has in fact been made with a view to try or punish him for an offence of a political character.

Article VII.

A person surrendered can in no case be kept in prison or be brought to trial in the State to which the surrender has been made, for any other crime or on account of any other matters than those for which the extradition shall have taken place.

This stipulation does not apply to crimes committed after the extradition.

Article VIII.

The requisition for extradition shall be made through the Diplomatic Agents of the High Contracting Parties respectively.

The requisition for the extradition of an accused person must be accompanied by a warrant of arrest issued by the competent authority of the State requiring the extradition, and by such evidence as, according to the laws of the place where the accused is found, would justify his arrest if the crime had been committed there.

If the requisition relates to a person already convicted, it must be accompanied by the sentence of condemnation passed against the

Handlung in Untersuchung ist, so soll ihre Auslieferung bis zur Beendigung dieser Untersuchung und vollendeter Vollstreckung der etwa gegen sie erkannten Strafe aufgeschoben werden.

Artikel V.

Die Auslieferung soll nicht stattfinden, wenn seit der begangenen strafbaren Handlung, oder der Einleitung der strafgerichtlichen Verfolgung, oder der erfolgten Verurtheilung nach den Gesetzen des ersuchten Staats Verjährung der strafgerichtlichen Verfolgung oder der erkannten Strafe eingetreten ist.

Artikel VI.

Ein flüchtiger Verbrecher soll nicht ausgeliefert werden, wenn die strafbare Handlung, wegen deren seine Auslieferung verlangt wird, einen politischen Character an sich trägt, oder wenn er beweisen kann, dass der Antrag auf seine Auslieferung in Wirklichkeit mit der Absicht gestellt worden ist, ihn wegen eines Verbrechens oder Vergehens politischer Natur zu verfolgen oder zu bestrafen.

Artikel VII.

Die ausgelieferte Person darf in dem Staate, an welchen die Auslieferung erfolgt ist, keinenfalls wegen einer anderen strafbaren Handlung oder auf Grund anderer Thatsachen, als derjenigen, wegen deren die Auslieferung erfolgt ist, in Haft gehalten oder zur Untersuchung gezogen werden.

Auf strafbare Handlungen, welche nach erfolgter Auslieferung verübt sind, findet diese Bestimmung keine Anwendung.

Artikel VIII.

Die Anträge auf Auslieferung sollen durch die diplomatischen Agenten der hohen vertragenden Theile gestellt werden.

Mit dem Antrage auf Auslieferung eines Beschuldigten müssen ein Haftbefehl, welcher von der zuständigen Behörde des die Auslieferung begehrenden Staates erlassen ist, und solche Beweise beigebracht werden, welche nach den Gesetzen des Ortes, wo der Beschuldigte aufgefunden wird, dessen Verhaftung rechtfertigen würden, wenn die strafbare Handlung dort begangen wäre.

Betrifft der Antrag eine bereits verurtheilte Person, so muss das Straf-Urtheil beigebracht werden, welches von dem zuständigen

convicted person by the competent Court of the State that makes the requisition for extradition.

A requisition for extradition cannot be founded on sentences passed *in contumaciam*.

Article IX.

If the requisition for extradition be in accordance with the foregoing stipulations, the competent authorities of the State applied to shall proceed to the arrest of the fugitive.

The prisoner is then to be brought before a competent Magistrate, who is to examine him and to conduct the preliminary investigation of the case, just as if the apprehension had taken place for a crime committed in the same country.

Article X.

The extradition shall not take place before the expiration of fifteen days from the apprehension, and then only if the evidence be found sufficient, according to the laws of the State applied to, either to justify the committal of the prisoner for trial, in case the crime had been committed in the territory of the said State, or to prove that the prisoner is the identical person convicted by the Courts of the State which makes the requisition.

Article XI.

In the examinations which they have to make in accordance with the foregoing stipulations, the authorities of the State applied to shall admit as entirely valid evidence the sworn depositions or statements of witnesses taken in the other State, or copies thereof, and likewise the warrants and sentences issued therein, provided such documents are signed or certified by a Judge, Magistrate, or Officer of such State, and are authenticated by the oath of some witness, or by being sealed with the official seal of the Minister of Justice, or some other Minister of State.

Article XII.

If sufficient evidence for the extradition be not produced within two months from the date of the apprehension of the fugitive, he shall be set at liberty.

Gericht des die Auslieferung begehrenden Staates gegen den Verurtheilten erlassen ist.

Auf Straf-Urtheile, welche von Ungehorsams wegen (*in contumaciam*) erlassen sind, kann der Auslieferungs-Antrag nicht gegründet werden.

Artikel IX.

Wenn das Auslieferungsgesuch nach den vorstehenden Bestimmungen begründet ist, so sollen die zuständigen Behörden des ersuchten Staates zur Festnahme des Flüchtlings schreiten.

Der Ergriffene wird sodann vor den dazu gesetzlich berufenen richterlichen Beamten gebracht, welcher ihn ebenso zu verhören und den Straffall vorläufig zu untersuchen hat, als wenn die Ergreifung wegen einer im Inlande begangenen strafbaren Handlung erfolgt wäre.

Artikel X.

Die Auslieferung erfolgt nicht vor Ablauf von fünfzehn Tagen seit der Ergreifung und nur dann, wenn die Beweise für genügend befunden worden sind, um nach den Gesetzen des ersuchten Staats entweder die Verweisung des Ergriffenen zur Hauptuntersuchung zu rechtfertigen, falls die strafbare Handlung im Gebiet dieses Staats begangen wäre, oder darzuthun, dass der Ergriffene mit der von den Gerichten des ersuchenden Staats verurtheilten Person identisch ist.

Artikel XI.

Die Behörden des ersuchten Staats haben bei der Prüfung, welche ihnen nach den vorstehenden Bestimmungen obliegt, den beeidigten Zeugen-Aussagen, welche in dem anderen Staate zu Protokoll genommen sind, imgleichen den Abschriften solcher Original-Zeugen-Aussagen, und ebenso den Haftbefehlen und Straf-Urtheilen volle Beweiskraft beizulegen, vorausgesetzt, dass diese Schriftstücke durch einen Richter, eine obrigkeitliche Person oder einen anderen Beamten dieses Staates unterzeichnet oder bescheinigt und durch einen beeidigten Zeugen oder durch Beidrückung des Amtssiegels des Justiz- oder eines anderen Staatsministers beglaubigt sind.

Artikel XII.

Wenn die zur Auslieferung genügenden Beweise nicht binnen zwei Monaten von dem Tage der Ergreifung des Flüchtigen an beigebracht werden, so ist der Ergriffene auf freien Fuss zu setzen.

Article XIII.

All articles seized, which were in the possession of the person to be surrendered at the time of his apprehension, shall, if the competent authority of the State applied to for the extradition has ordered the delivery thereof, be given up when the extradition takes place; and the said delivery shall extend not merely to the stolen articles, but to everything that may serve as a proof of the crime.

Article XIV.

The High Contracting Parties renounce any claim for the reimbursement of the expenses incurred by them in the arrest and maintenance of the person to be surrendered, and his conveyance till placed on board ship; they reciprocally agree to bear such expenses themselves.

Article XV.

The stipulations of the present Treaty shall be applicable to the Colonies and foreign Possessions of Her Britannic Majesty.

The requisition for the surrender of a fugitive criminal who has taken refuge in any of such Colonies or foreign Possessions shall be made to the Governor or chief authority of such Colony or Possession by the chief consular officer of the German Empire in such Colony or Possession.

Such requisitions may be disposed of, subject always, as nearly as may be, to the provisions of this Treaty, by the said Governor or chief authority, who, however, shall be at liberty either to grant the surrender or to refer the matter to his Government.

Her Britannic Majesty shall, however, be at liberty to make special arrangements in the British Colonies and foreign Possessions for the surrender of German criminals who may take refuge within such Colonies and foreign Possessions, on the basis, as nearly as may be, of the provisions of the present Treaty.

The requisition for the surrender of a fugitive criminal from any Colony or foreign Possession of Her Britannic Majesty shall be

ARTIKEL XIII.

Alle in Beschlag genommenen Gegenstände, welche sich zur Zeit der Ergreifung im Besitze des Auszuliefernden befinden, sollen, wenn die zuständige Behörde des um die Auslieferung ersuchten Staats die Ausantwortung derselben angeordnet hat, bei Vollziehung der Auslieferung mit übergeben werden, und es soll sich diese Ueberlieferung nicht blos auf die entfremdeten Gegenstände, sondern auf Alles erstrecken, was zum Beweise der strafbaren Handlung dienen kann.

ARTIKEL XIV.

Die hohen vertragenden Theile verzichten darauf, die Erstattung derjenigen Kosten, welche ihnen aus der Festnahme und dem Unterhalt des Auszuliefernden und seinem Transport bis zur Einschiffung erwachsen, in Anspruch zu nehmen, willigen vielmehr gegenseitig darin, diese Kosten selbst zu tragen.

ARTIKEL XV.

Die Bestimmungen des gegenwärtigen Vertrages sollen auf die Colonien und auswärtigen Besitzungen Ihrer Grossbritannischen Majestät Anwendung finden.

Der Antrag auf Auslieferung eines flüchtigen Verbrechers, welcher in einer dieser Colonien oder auswärtigen Besitzungen Zuflucht gefunden hat, soll an den Statthalter oder die oberste Behörde dieser Colonie oder Besitzung durch den obersten Consular-Beamten des Deutschen Reichs in dieser Colonie oder Besitzung gerichtet werden.

Ueber solche Anträge soll der gedachte Statthalter oder die gedachte oberste Behörde so viel als möglich nach den Bestimmungen des gegenwärtigen Vertrages befinden, jedoch soll denselben freistehen, entweder die Auslieferung zu bewilligen oder über den Fall an ihre Regierung zu berichten.

Ihrer Grossbritannischen Majestät soll es jedoch freistehen, in den Brittischen Colonien und auswärtigen Besitzungen über die Auslieferung Deutscher Verbrecher, welche innerhalb dieser Colonien und auswärtigen Besitzungen Zuflucht gefunden haben, auf möglichst gleicher Grundlage mit den Bestimmungen des gegenwärtigen Vertrages besondere Anordnungen zu treffen.

Anträge betreffend die Auslieferung von Verbrechern, welche aus einer Colonie oder auswärtigen Besitzung Ihrer Grossbritannischen

governed by the rules laid down in the preceding Articles of the present Treaty.

Article XVI.

The present Treaty shall come into force ten days after its publication in conformity with the forms prescribed by the laws of the High Contracting Parties. It may be terminated by either of the High Contracting Parties, but shall remain in force for six months after notice has been given for its termination.

The Treaty shall be ratified, and the ratifications shall be exchanged at London in four weeks, or sooner if possible.

In witness whereof the respective Plenipotentiaries have signed the same, and have affixed thereto the seal of their arms.

Done at London, the 14th day of May, in the year of our Lord One thousand eight hundred and seventy-two.

(L.S.) Granville.
(L.S.) Bernstorff.

Protocol.

The undersigned Plenipotentiaries of Her Majesty the Queen of the United Kingdom of Great Britain and Ireland, and of His Majesty the Emperor of Germany, in proceeding this day to the signature of the Treaty concluded between their said Majesties for the mutual surrender of fugitive criminals, have agreed that the Convention of the same purpose which was signed between Her Britannic Majesty and His Majesty the King of Prussia on the 5th of March, 1864, shall be cancelled from and after the day on which the Treaty signed this day shall come into operation, after having been ratified by the High Contracting Parties.

London, the 14th of May, 1872.

Granville.
Bernstorff.

Majestät geflüchtet sind, sollen nach den Bestimmungen der vorstehenden Artikel des gegenwärtigen Vertrags behandelt werden.

ARTIKEL XVI.

Der gegenwärtige Vertrag soll zehn Tage nach seiner, in Gemässheit der durch die Gesetzgebung der hohen vertragenden Theile vorgeschriebenen Formen erfolgten Veröffentlichung in Kraft treten. Der Vertrag kann von jedem der beiden hohen vertragenden Theile aufgekündigt werden, bleibt jedoch nach erfolgter Aufkündigung noch sechs Monate in Kraft.

Der Vertrag wird ratifizirt und die Ratifikationen werden nach vier Wochen, oder wo möglich früher, in London ausgewechselt werden.

Zu Urkund dessen haben die beiderseitigen Bevollmächtigten die gegenwärtige Uebereinkunft unterzeichnet und mit ihren Wappen untersiegelt.

So geschehen zu London am vierzehnten Mai, im Jahre des Herrn Ein tausend achthundert und zwei und siebenzig.

(L.S.) GRANVILLE.
(L.S.) BERNSTORFF.

Protokoll.

Die unterzeichneten Bevollmächtigten Ihrer Majestät der Königin des Vereinigten Königreichs von Grossbritannien und Irland, und Seiner Majestät des Deutschen Kaisers sind, indem sie am heutigen Tage zur Unterzeichnung des Vertrages geschritten sind, welcher zwischen Ihren genannten Majestäten für die gegenseitige Auslieferung flüchtiger Verbrecher abgeschlossen worden ist, übereingekommen, dass die zu demselben Zwecke unter dem 5ten März 1864, zwischen Ihrer Grossbritannischen Majestät und Seiner Majestät dem Könige von Preussen abgeschlossene Convention von und an dem Tage aufgehoben sein soll, an welchem der heute unterzeichnete Vertrag nach erfolgter Ratifikation durch die beiden hohen vertragenden Theile in Kraft tritt.

London, den 14ten May 1872.

GRANVILLE.
BERNSTORFF.

BELGIUM.

ORDER IN COUNCIL, DATED OCTOBER 15, 1872, FOR CARRYING INTO EFFECT A TREATY BETWEEN HER MAJESTY AND THE KING OF THE BELGIANS, FOR THE MUTUAL SURRENDER OF CRIMINALS.—*Signed at Brussels, July* 31, 1872.

At the Court at Balmoral, the 15th day of October, 1872.

Present:

THE QUEEN'S MOST EXCELLENT MAJESTY IN COUNCIL.

WHEREAS by an Act of Parliament made and passed in the Session of Parliament holden in the thirty-third and thirty-fourth years of the reign of Her present Majesty, intituled "An Act for Amending the Law relating to the Extradition of Criminals," it was amongst other things enacted, that where an arrangement has been made with any foreign State with respect to the surrender to such State of any fugitive criminals, Her Majesty may, by Order in Council, direct that the said Act shall apply in the case of such foreign State; and that Her Majesty may, by the same or any subsequent Order, limit the operation of the Order, and restrict the same to fugitive criminals who are in or suspected of being in the part of Her Majesty's dominions specified in the Order, and render the operation thereof subject to such conditions, exceptions, and qualifications as may be deemed expedient:

And whereas a Treaty was concluded on the thirty-first day of July last between Her Majesty and the King of the Belgians, for the Mutual Extradition of Fugitive Criminals, which Treaty is in the terms following:—

Her Majesty the Queen of the United Kingdom of Great Britain and Ireland, and His Majesty the King of the Belgians, having judged it expedient, with a view to the more complete prevention of crime within their respective territories, that persons charged with or convicted of the crimes hereinafter enumerated, and being fugitives from the justice of their country, should, under certain circumstances, be reciprocally delivered up; Their said Majesties have named as their Plenipotentiaries to conclude a Treaty for this purpose, that is to say:—

Her Majesty the Queen of the United Kingdom of Great Britain and Ireland, John Savile Lumley, Esquire, Her Envoy Extraordinary and Minister Plenipotentiary to His Majesty the King of the Belgians;

And His Majesty the King of the Belgians, the Count d'Aspremont Lynden, Officer of His Order of Leopold, Commander of the Order of the Ernestine Branch of the House of Saxony, Grand Cross of the Orders of Charles III., of the Medjidie, and of the Saviour, Member of the Senate, His Minister of Foreign Affairs;

Who, after having communicated to each other their respective full powers, found in good and due form, have agreed upon the following Articles:—

Article I.

It is agreed that Her Britannic Majesty and His Majesty the King of the Belgians shall, on requisition made in their name by their respective Diplomatic Agents, deliver up to each other reciprocally any persons, except, as regards Great Britain, native born and naturalised subjects of Her Britannic Majesty, and except as regards Belgium, those who are by birth or who may have become citizens of Belgium, who, being accused or convicted as principals or accessories before the fact, of any of the crimes hereinafter specified, committed within the territories of the requiring Party, shall be found within the territories of the other Party:

1. Murder (including assassination, parricide, infanticide, and poisoning), or attempt to murder.
2. Manslaughter.
3. Counterfeiting or altering money, or uttering counterfeit or altered money.
4. Forgery, counterfeiting, or altering, or uttering what is forged or counterfeited or altered.
5. Embezzlement or larceny.
6. Obtaining money or goods by false pretences.

Sa Majesté la Reine du Royaume Uni de la Grande Bretagne et d'Irlande, et Sa Majesté le Roi des Belges, ayant jugé opportun, afin de mieux assurer la répression des crimes dans leurs territoires respectifs, de se livrer réciproquement, sous certaines conditions, les personnes accusées ou condamnées du chef des crimes ci-après énumérés et qui auraient fui la justice de leur pays; leurs dites Majestés ont nommé pour leurs Plénipotentiaires, à l'effet de conclure un Traité dans ce but, savoir:—

Sa Majesté la Reine du Royaume Uni de la Grande Bretagne et d'Irlande, John Savile Lumley, Esquire, Son Envoyé Extraordinaire et Ministre Plénipotentiaire près Sa Majesté le Roi des Belges;

Et Sa Majesté le Roi des Belges, le Comte d'Aspremont Lynden, Officier de Son Ordre de Léopold, Commandeur de l'Ordre de la Branche Ernestine de la Maison de Saxe, Grand Cordon des Ordres de Charles III, du Medjidié, et du Sauveur, Sénateur, Son Ministre des Affaires Etrangères;

Lesquels, après s'être communiqué réciproquement leurs pleins pouvoirs, reconnus en bonne et dûe forme, sont convenus des Articles suivants:—

Article I.

Il est convenu que Sa Majesté Britannique et Sa Majesté le Roi des Belges, sur la demande faite en leur nom par leurs Agents Diplomatiques respectifs, se livreront réciproquement tous les individus, sauf relativement à l'Angleterre les sujets de Sa Majesté Britannique par naissance ou naturalisation, et relativement à la Belgique ceux qui sont nés ou naturalisés citoyens Belges, qui étant accusés ou condamnés comme auteurs ou complices avant l'acte, pour l'un des crimes ci-après spécifiés, commis sur le territoire de la Partie requérante, seront trouvés sur le territoire de l'autre Partie:

1. Meurtre (y compris l'assassinat, le parricide, l'infanticide et l'empoisonnement) ou tentative de meurtre.
2. Homicide commis sans préméditation ou guet-apens.
3. Contrefaçon ou altération de monnaie, ainsi que mise en circulation de la monnaie contrefaite ou altérée.
4. Faux, contrefaçon, ou altération, ou mise en circulation de ce qui est falsifié, contrefait, ou altéré.
5. Soustraction frauduleuse ou vol.
6. Escroquerie d'argent, valeurs, ou marchandises sous de faux prétextes.

7. Crimes by bankrupts against bankruptcy law.

8. Fraud by a bailee, banker, agent, factor, trustee, or director, or member or public officer of any company, made criminal by any law for the time being in force.

9. Rape.
10. Abduction.
11. Child-stealing.
12. Burglary or housebreaking.
13. Arson.
14. Robbery with violence (including intimidation).
15. Threats by letter or otherwise with intent to extort.
16. Piracy by law of nations.

17. Sinking or destroying a vessel at sea, or attempting or conspiring to do so.

18. Assaults on board a ship on the high seas with intent to destroy life or to do grievous bodily harm.

19. Revolt or conspiracy to revolt by two or more persons on board a ship on the high seas against the authority of the master.

Provided that the surrender shall be made only when, in the case of a person accused, the commission of the crime shall be so established as that the laws of the country where the fugitive or person accused shall be found would justify his apprehension and commitment for trial if the crime had been there committed; and, in the case of a person alleged to have been convicted, on such evidence as, according to the laws of the country where he is found, would prove that he had been convicted.

In no case can the surrender be made unless the crime shall be punishable according to the laws in force in both countries with regard to extradition.

Article II.

In the dominions of Her Britannic Majesty other than the Colonies or foreign Possessions of Her Majesty, the manner of proceeding shall be as follows:—

I. In the case of a person accused—

7. Crimes des banqueroutiers frauduleux prévus par la loi.

8. Détournement ou dissipation frauduleux au préjudice d'autrui, des effets, deniers, marchandises, quittances, écrits de toute nature, contenant ou opérant obligation ou décharge, et qui avaient été remis à la condition de les rendre et d'en faire un usage ou un emploi déterminé.

9. Viol.

10. Enlèvement de mineurs.

11. Enlèvement d'enfant.

12. Vol avec effraction ou escalade.

13. Incendie.

14. Vol avec violence (comprenant intimidation).

15. Menaces d'attentat punissable d'une peine criminelle.

16. Prise d'un navire par les marins ou passagers par fraude ou violence envers le capitaine.

17. Echouement, perte, destruction, ou tentative d'échouement, de perte, ou de destruction d'un navire à la mer par le capitaine ou les officiers et gens de l'équipage.

18. Attaque ou résistance à bord d'un navire en haute mer avec violence et voies de fait envers le capitaine par plus du tiers de l'équipage.

19. Révolte ou complot de révolte par deux ou plusieurs personnes à bord d'un navire en haute mer, contre l'autorité du capitaine.

Toutefois, l'extradition ne sera accordée, dans le cas d'une personne accusée, que si la perpétration du crime est établie de telle façon que les lois du pays où le fugitif accusé sera trouvé justifieraient son arrestation et son emprisonnement si le crime avait été commis dans ce pays; et dans le cas d'une personne prétenduement condamnée, que sur la production d'une preuve qui, d'après les lois du pays où le fugitif a été trouvé, établirait suffisamment qu'il a été condamné.

En aucun cas l'extradition ne pourra avoir lieu que lorsque le crime sera prévu par la législation sur l'extradition en vigueur dans les deux pays.

ARTICLE II.

Dans les Etats de Sa Majesté Britannique, autres que les Colonies ou les possessions étrangères de Sa Majesté, la manière de procéder sera la suivante :—

I. S'il s'agit d'une personne accusée—

The requisition for the surrender shall be made to Her Britannic Majesty's Principal Secretary of State for Foreign Affairs by the Minister or other Diplomatic Agent of His Majesty the King of the Belgians, accompanied by a warrant of arrest or other equivalent judicial document, issued by a Judge or Magistrate duly authorized to take cognizance of the acts charged against the accused in Belgium, together with duly authenticated depositions or statements taken on oath before such Judge or Magistrate, clearly setting forth the said acts, and containing a description of the person claimed, and any particulars which may serve to identify him. The said Secretary of State shall transmit such documents to Her Britannic Majesty's Principal Secretary of State for the Home Department, who shall then, by order under his hand and seal, signify to some Police Magistrate in London that such requisition has been made, and require him, if there be due cause, to issue his warrant for the apprehension of the fugitive.

On the receipt of such order from the Secretary of State, and on the production of such evidence as would, in the opinion of the magistrate, justify the issue of the warrant if the crime had been committed in the United Kingdom, he shall issue his warrant accordingly.

When the fugitive shall have been apprehended, he shall be brought before the police magistrate who issued the warrant, or some other police magistrate in London. If the evidence to be then produced shall be such as to justify, according to the law of England, the committal for trial of the prisoner, if the crime of which he is accused had been committed in England, the police magistrate shall commit him to prison to await the warrant of the Secretary of State for his surrender; sending immediately to the Secretary of State a certificate of the committal and a report upon the case.

After the expiration of a period from the committal of the prisoner, which shall never be less than fifteen days, the Secretary of State shall, by order under his hand and seal, order the fugitive criminal to be surrendered to such person as may be duly authorized to receive him on the part of the Government of His Majesty the King of the Belgians.

II. In the case of a person convicted—

The course of proceeding shall be the same as in the case of a person accused, except that the warrant to be transmitted by the

La demande d'extradition sera adressée au Premier Secrétaire d'Etat de Sa Majesté pour les Affaires Etrangères par le Ministre ou autre Agent Diplomatique de Sa Majesté le Roi des Belges. A cette demande seront joints un mandat d'arrêt ou autre document judiciaire équivalent, délivré par un Juge ou Magistrat dûment autorisé à prendre connaissance des actes imputés à l'accusé en Belgique, ainsi que les dépositions authentiques ou les déclarations faites sous serment devant ce Juge ou Magistrat, énonçant clairement les dits actes, et contenant, outre le signalement de la personne réclamée, toutes les particularités qui pourraient servir à établir son identité.

Le dit Secrétaire d'Etat transmettra ces documents au Premier Secrétaire d'Etat de Sa Majesté Britannique pour les Affaires Intérieures, qui, par un ordre de sa main et muni de son sceau, signifiera à l'un ou l'autre Magistrat de Police à Londres que la demande d'extradition a été faite, et le requerra, s'il y a lieu, de délivrer un mandat pour l'arrestation du fugitif.

A la réception d'un semblable ordre du Secrétaire d'Etat, et sur la production de telle preuve qui, dans l'opinion de ce Magistrat, justifierait l'émission du mandat si le crime avait été commis dans le Royaume Uni, il délivrera le mandat requis.

Lorsqu'alors le fugitif aura été arrêté, il sera amené devant le Magistrat de Police qui a lancé le mandat, ou devant un autre Magistrate de Police à Londres. Si la preuve qu'on produira est de nature à justifier, selon la loi Anglaise, la mise en jugement du prisonnier dans le cas où le crime dont il est accusé aurait été commis en Angleterre, le Magistrat de Police l'enverra en prison pour attendre le mandat du Secrétaire d'Etat, nécessaire à l'extradition, et il adressera immédiatement au Secrétaire d'Etat une attestation de l'emprisonnement avec un rapport sur l'affaire.

Après l'expiration d'un certain temps, qui ne pourra jamais être moindre de quinze jours depuis l'emprisonnement de l'accusé, le Secrétaire d'Etat, par un ordre de sa main et muni de son sceau, ordonnera que le criminel fugitif soit livré à telle personne qui sera dûment autorisée à le recevoir au nom du Gouvernement de Sa Majesté le Roi des Belges.

II. S'il s'agit d'une personne condamnée—

La marche de la procédure sera la même que dans le cas d'une personne accusée, sauf que le mandat à transmettre par le Ministre

Minister or other Diplomatic Agent in support of his requisition shall clearly set forth the crime of which the person claimed has been convicted, and state the fact, place, and date of his conviction. The evidence to be produced before the police magistrate shall be such as would, according to the law of England, prove that the prisoner was convicted of the crime charged.

After the police magistrate shall have committed the accused or convicted person to prison to await the order of a Secretary of State for his surrender, such person shall have the right to apply for a writ of *habeas corpus;* if he should so apply, his surrender must be deferred until after the decision of the Court upon the return to the writ, and even then can only take place if the decision is adverse to the applicant. In the latter case the Court may at once order his delivery to the person authorised to receive him, without the order of a Secretary of State for his surrender, or commit him to prison to await such order.

Article III.

In the dominions of His Majesty the King of the Belgians other than the Colonies or foreign Possessions of His said Majesty, the manner of proceeding shall be as follows:—

I. In the case of a person accused—

The requisition for the surrender shall be made to the Minister for Foreign Affairs of His Majesty the King of the Belgians by the Minister or other Diplomatic Agent of Her Britannic Majesty, accompanied by a warrant of arrest issued by a Judge or Magistrate duly authorized to take cognizance of the acts charged against the accused in Great Britain, together with duly authenticated depositions or statements taken on oath before such Judge or Magistrate, clearly setting forth the said acts, and containing a description of the person claimed, and any other particulars which may serve to identify him.

The Minister for Foreign Affairs shall transmit the warrant of arrest, with the documents thereto annexed, to the Minister of Justice, who shall forward the same to the proper judicial authority, in order that the warrant of arrest may be put in course of execution by the Chamber of the Council (*Chambre du Conseil*) of the Court of First Instance of the place of residence of the accused, or of the place where he may be found.

After issue of the order for arrest, and on exhibition of the warrant of arrest, the foreigner may be provisionally arrested, and

ou autre Agent Diplomatique, à l'appui de la demande d'extradition, énoncera clairement le crime pour lequel la personne réclamée aura été condamnée, et mentionnera le fait, le lieu, et la date du jugement. La preuve à produire devant le Magistrat de Police sera telle que d'après la loi Anglaise elle établirait que le prisonnier a été condamné pour le crime dont on l'accuse.

Après que le Magistrat de Police aura envoyé la personne accusée ou condamnée en prison pour attendre l'ordre d'extradition du Secrétaire d'Etat, cette personne aura le droit de réclamer une ordonnance d'*habeas corpus;* l'extradition doit alors être différée jusqu'après la décision de la Cour sur le renvoi de l'ordonnance, et elle ne pourra avoir lieu que si la décision est contraire au demandeur. Dans ce dernier cas, la Cour peut immédiatement ordonner la remise de celui-ci à la personne qui est autorisée à le recevoir, sans qu'il soit besoin d'attendre l'ordre d'extradition du Secrétaire d'Etat, ou bien l'envoyer en prison pour attendre cet ordre.

ARTICLE III.

Dans les Etats de Sa Majesté le Roi des Belges, autres que les Colonies ou possessions étrangères de Sa dite Majesté, on procédera de la façon suivante :—

I. S'il s'agit d'une personne accusée—

La demande d'extradition sera adressée au Ministre des Affaires Etrangères de Sa Majesté le Roi des Belges par le Ministre ou autre Agent Diplomatique de Sa Majesté Britannique ; à cette demande seront joints un mandat d'arrêt délivré par un Juge ou Magistrat dûment autorisé à prendre connaissance des actes imputés à l'accusé dans la Grande Bretagne, ainsi que les dépositions authentiques ou les déclarations faites sous serment devant ce Juge ou Magistrat, énonçant clairement les dits actes, et contenant, outre le signalement de la personne réclamée, toutes les particularités qui pourraient servir à établir son identité.

Le Ministre des Affaires Etrangères transmettra le mandat d'arrêt, avec les pièces annexées, au Ministre de la Justice, qui fera parvenir les documents à l'autorité judiciaire, à l'effet de voir rendre le dit mandat d'arrêt exécutoire par la Chambre du Conseil du Tribunal de Première Instance du lieu de la résidence de l'inculpé, ou du lieu où il pourra être trouvé.

Après l'ordonnance d'arrestation et sur l'exhibition du mandat d'arrêt, l'étranger pourra être provisoirement arrêté, et le Juge

the *Juge d'Instruction* is authorized to proceed according to the rules prescribed by the *Code d'Instruction Criminelle.*

The foreigner may claim to be provisionally set at liberty in any case in which a Belgian enjoys that right, and under the same conditions. The application shall be submitted to the Chamber of the Council (*Chambre du Conseil*).

The surrender shall not be granted unless on production of the order of the Chamber of the Council (*Chambre du Conseil*), of the decree of the Chamber of Indictments or Investigation (*Chambre des Mises en Accusation*), or of the act of criminal procedure (*acte de procédure criminelle*), issued by the competent Judge, formally decreeing or necessarily involving the sending of the accused before a criminal court (*la juridiction répressive*), delivered in original or in an authenticated copy, and after having taken the opinion of the Chamber of Indictments or Investigation (*Chambre des Mises en Accusation*) of the Court of Appeal within whose jurisdiction the foreigner shall have been arrested.

The hearing of the case shall be public, unless the foreigner should demand that it should be with closed doors.

The public authorities and the foreigner shall be heard. The latter may obtain the assistance of counsel.

Within a fortnight from the receipt of the documents, they shall be returned, with a reasoned opinion, to the Minister of Justice, who shall decide and may order that the accused be delivered to the person duly authorized on the part of the Government of Her Britannic Majesty.

II. In the case of a person convicted—

The course of proceeding shall be the same as in the case of a person accused, except that the conviction or sentence of condemnation issued in original or in an authenticated copy, to be transmitted by the Minister or other Diplomatic Agent in support of his requisition, shall clearly set forth the crime of which the person claimed has been convicted, and state the fact, place, and date of his conviction. The evidence to be produced before the magistrate charged with the investigation of the case shall be such as would, according to the Belgian laws, prove that the prisoner was convicted of the crime charged.

Article IV.

A fugitive criminal may, however, be apprehended under a warrant issued by any police magistrate, justice of the peace, or

d'Instruction est autorisé à procéder suivant les règles prescrites par le Code d'Instruction Criminelle.

L'étranger pourra réclamer la liberté provisoire dans le cas où un Belge jouit de cette faculté et dans les mêmes conditions. La demande sera soumise à la Chambre du Conseil.

L'extradition ne sera accordée que sur la production de l'ordonnance de la Chambre du Conseil, de l'arrêt de la Chambre des Mises en Accusation, ou de l'acte de procédure criminelle émané du Juge compétent, décrétant formellement ou opérant de plein droit le renvoi du prévenu ou de l'accusé devant la juridiction répressive, délivrés en original ou en expédition authentique, et après avoir pris l'avis de la Chambre des Mises en Accusation de la Cour d'Appel dans le ressort de laquelle l'étranger aura été arrêté.

L'audience sera publique, à moins que l'étranger ne réclame le huis-clos.

Le Ministère public et l'étranger seront entendus. Celui-ci pourra se faire assister d'un Conseil.

Dans la quinzaine à dater de la réception des pièces, elles seront renvoyées avec l'avis motivé au Ministre de la Justice, qui statuera et pourra ordonner que l'inculpé soit livré à la personne qui sera dûment autorisée au nom du Gouvernement de Sa Majesté Britannique.

II. S'il s'agit d'une personne condamnée—

Le cours de la procédure sera le même que dans le cas d'une personne accusée, sauf que le jugement ou l'arrêt de condamnation délivré en original ou en expédition authentique, à transmettre par le Ministre ou l'Agent Diplomatique à l'appui de la demande d'extradition, énoncera clairement le crime pour lequel la personne réclamée aura été condamnée, et mentionnera le fait, le lieu, et la date du jugement. La preuve à produire devant le magistrat chargé de l'investigation du cas sera telle que, conformément aux lois Belges, elle établirait que le prisonnier a été condamné pour le crime dont on l'accuse.

Article IV.

Un criminel fugitif peut, cependant, être arrêté sur un mandat délivré par tout Magistrat de Police, Juge de Paix, ou autre auto-

other competent authority in either country, on such information or complaint, and such evidence, or after such proceedings as would, in the opinion of the person issuing the warrant, justify the issue of a warrant, if the crime had been committed or the prisoner convicted, in that part of the dominions of the two Contracting Parties in which he exercises jurisdiction: Provided however that, in the United Kingdom, the accused shall, in such case, be sent as speedily as possible before a police magistrate in London. He shall be discharged, as well in the United Kingdom as in Belgium, if within fourteen days a requisition shall not have been made for his surrender by the Diplomatic Agent of his country, in the manner directed by Articles II and III of this Treaty.

The same rule shall apply to the cases of persons accused or convicted of any of the crimes specified in this Treaty, committed on the high seas, on board any vessel of either country which may come into a port of the other.

Article V.

If the fugitive criminal who has been committed to prison be not surrendered and conveyed away within two months after such committal (or within two months after the decision of the Court upon the return to a writ of *habeas corpus* in the United Kingdom), he shall be discharged from custody, unless sufficient cause be shown to the contrary.

Article VI.

When any person shall have been surrendered by either of the High Contracting Parties to the other, such person shall not, until he has been restored or had an opportunity of returning to the country from whence he was surrendered, be triable or tried for any offence committed in the other country prior to the surrender, other than the particular offence on account of which he was surrendered.

Article VII.

No accused or convicted person shall be surrendered, if the offence in respect of which his surrender is demanded shall be deemed by the party upon which it is made to be a political offence, or to be an act connected with (*connexe à*) such an offence, or if he prove to the satisfaction of the police magistrate, or of the Court before which he is brought on *habeas corpus*, or to the

rité compétente dans chaque pays, à la suite d'un avis, d'une plainte, d'une preuve, ou de tout autre acte de procédure qui, dans l'opinion de la personne délivrant le mandat, justifierait ce mandat, si le crime avait été commis ou la personne condamnée dans la partie des Etats des deux Contractants où il exerce juridiction : pourvu que, cependant, s'il s'agit du Royaume Uni, l'accusé soit, dans un pareil cas, envoyé aussi promptement que possible devant un Magistrat de Police à Londres. Il sera relâché, tant dans le Royaume Uni qu'en Belgique, si dans les quatorze jours une demande d'extradition n'a pas été faite par l'Agent Diplomatique de son pays, suivant le mode indiqué par les Articles II et III de ce Traité.

La même règle s'appliquera aux cas de personnes accusées ou condamnées du chef de l'un des crimes spécifiés dans ce Traité et commis en pleine mer, à bord d'un navire de l'un des deux pays et qui viendrait dans un port de l'autre.

Article V.

Si le criminel fugitif qui a été arrêté n'est pas livré et emmené dans les deux mois après son arrestation (ou dans les deux mois après la décision de la Cour sur le renvoi d'une ordonnance d'*habeas corpus* dans le Royaume Uni), il sera mis en liberté, à moins qu'il n'y ait un motif suffisant de le retenir en prison.

Article VI.

Lorsqu'une personne aura été extradée par l'une des Hautes Parties Contractantes, cette personne, jusqu'à ce qu'elle soit rentrée dans le pays d'où elle a été extradée, ou qu'elle ait eu occasion de le faire, ne sera poursuivie pour aucun délit commis dans l'autre pays avant l'extradition, autre que celui pour lequel l'extradition a eu lieu.

Article VII.

Aucune personne accusée ou condamnée ne sera extradée, si le délit pour lequel l'extradition est demandée est considéré par la Partie requise comme un délit politique ou un fait connexe à un semblable délit, ou si la personne prouve, à la satisfaction du Magistrat de Police ou de la Cour devant laquelle elle est amenée pour l'*habeas corpus*, ou du Secrétaire d'Etat, que la demande

Secretary of State, that the requisition for his surrender has in fact been made with a view to try or to punish him for an offence of a political character.

ARTICLE VIII.

Warrants, depositions, or statements on oath, issued or taken in the dominions of either of the two High Contracting Parties, and copies thereof, and certificates of or judicial documents stating the fact of conviction, shall be received in evidence in proceedings in the dominions of the other, if purporting to be signed or certified by a Judge, Magistrate, or officer of the country where they were issued or taken.

Provided such warrants, depositions, statements, copies, certificates, and judicial documents are authenticated by the oath of some witness, or by being sealed with the official seal of the Minister of Justice, or some other Minister of State.

ARTICLE IX.

The surrender shall not take place if, since the commission of the acts charged, the accusation, or the conviction, exemption from prosecution or punishment has been acquired by lapse of time, according to the laws of the country where the accused shall have taken refuge.

ARTICLE X.

If the individual claimed by one of the two High Contracting Parties in pursuance of the present Treaty should be also claimed by one or several other Powers, on account of other crimes committed upon their respective territories, his surrender shall be granted to that State whose demand is earliest in date; unless any other arrangement should be made between the Governments which have claimed him, either on account of the gravity of the crimes committed, or for any other reasons.

ARTICLE XI.

If the individual claimed should be under prosecution, or condemned for a crime or offence committed in the country where he may have taken refuge, his surrender may be deferred until he shall have been set at liberty in due course of law.

In case he should be proceeded against or detained in such

d'extradition a été faite, en réalité, dans le but de la poursuivre ou de la punir pour un délit d'un caractère politique.

ARTICLE VIII.

Les mandats, dépositions, déclarations sous serment, délivrés ou recueillis dans les Etats de l'une des deux Hautes Parties Contractantes, les copies de ces pièces, ainsi que les certificats ou les documents judiciaires établissant le fait de la condamnation, seront reçus comme preuve dans la procédure des Etats de l'autre Partie, s'ils sont revêtus de la signature ou accompagnés de l'attestation d'un Juge, Magistrat, ou fonctionnaire du pays où ils ont été délivrés ou recueillis.

Pourvu que ces mandats, dépositions, déclarations, copies, certificats, et documents judiciaires soient rendus authentiques par le serment d'un témoin, ou par le sceau officiel du Ministre de la Justice ou d'un autre Ministre d'Etat.

ARTICLE IX.

L'extradition n'aura pas lieu si, depuis les faits imputés, les poursuites, ou la condamnation, la prescription de l'action ou de la peine est acquise d'après les lois du pays où le prévenu s'est réfugié.

ARTICLE X.

Si l'individu réclamé par l'une des Hautes Parties Contractantes, en exécution du présent Traité, est aussi réclamé par une ou plusieurs autres Puissances, du chef d'autres crimes commis sur leurs territoires respectifs, son extradition sera accordée à l'Etat dont la demande est la plus ancienne en date, à moins qu'il n'existe entre les Gouvernements qui l'ont réclamé un arrangement qui déciderait de la préférence, soit à raison de la gravité des crimes commis, soit à raison de tout autre motif.

ARTICLE XI.

Si l'individu réclamé est poursuivi ou condamné pour un crime ou un délit commis dans le pays où il s'est réfugié, son extradition pourra être différée jusqu'à ce qu'il ait été mis en liberté selon le cours régulier de la loi.

Dans le cas où il serait poursuivi ou détenu dans le même pays à

country, on account of obligations contracted towards private individuals, his surrender shall nevertheless take place, the injured party retaining his right to prosecute his claims before the competent authority.

Article XII.

Every article found in the possession of the individual claimed at the time of his arrest, shall, if the competent authority so decide, be seized, in order to be delivered up with his person at the time when the surrender shall be made. Such delivery shall not be limited to the property or articles obtained by stealing or by fraudulent bankruptcy, but shall extend to everything that may serve as proof of the crime. It shall take place even when the surrender, after having been ordered, shall be prevented from taking place by reason of the escape or death of the individual claimed.

The rights of third parties with regard to the said property or articles are nevertheless reserved.

Article XIII.

Each of the High Contracting Parties shall defray the expenses occasioned by the arrest within its territories, the detention, and the conveyance to its frontier, of the persons whom it may consent to surrender in pursuance of the present Treaty.

Article XIV.

The stipulations of the present Treaty shall be applicable to the Colonies and foreign Possessions of the two High Contracting Parties.

The requisition for the surrender of a fugitive criminal who has taken refuge in a Colony or foreign Possession of either Party, shall be made to the Governor or chief authority of such Colony or Possession by the chief consular officer of the other in such Colony or Possession; or, if the fugitive has escaped from a Colony or foreign Possession of the Party on whose behalf the requisition is made, by the Governor or chief authority of such Colony or Possession.

Such requisitions may be disposed of, subject always, as nearly as may be, to the provisions of this Treaty, by the respective Governors or chief authorities, who, however, shall be at liberty either to grant the surrender or to refer the matter to their Government.

raison d'obligations par lui contractées envers des particuliers, son extradition n'en aura pas moins lieu, sauf à la partie lésée à faire valoir ses droits devant l'autorité compétente.

Article XII.

Tout objet trouvé en la possession de l'individu réclamé au moment de son arrestation sera, si l'autorité compétente en a ainsi ordonné, saisi pour être livré avec sa personne lorsque l'extradition aura lieu. Cette remise ne sera pas limitée aux objets acquis par vol ou banqueroute frauduleuse, mais elle s'étendra à toute chose qui pourrait servir de pièce de conviction. Elle se fera même si l'extradition, après avoir été accordée, ne peut s'accomplir par suite de l'évasion ou de la mort de l'individu réclamé.

Sont, cependant, réservés les droits des tiers sur les objets susmentionnés.

Article XIII.

Chacune des Hautes Parties Contractantes supportera les frais occasionnés par l'arrestation sur son territoire, la détention, et le transport à la frontière des personnes qu'elle consentirait à extrader en exécution du présent Traité.

Article XIV.

Les stipulations du présent Traité seront applicables aux Colonies et Possessions étrangères des deux Hautes Parties Contractantes.

La demande d'extradition d'un criminel fugitif qui s'est réfugié dans une Colonie ou Possession étrangère de l'une des Parties sera faite au Gouverneur ou au fonctionnaire principal de cette Colonie ou Possession par le principal Agent Consulaire de l'autre dans cette Colonie ou Possession; ou, si le fugitif s'est échappé d'une Colonie ou Possession étrangère de la Partie au nom de laquelle l'extradition est demandée, par le Gouverneur ou le fonctionnaire principal de cette Colonie ou possession.

Ces demandes seront faites ou accueillies en suivant toujours, aussi exactement que possible, les stipulations de ce Traité par les Gouverneurs ou premiers fonctionnaires, qui, cependant, auront la faculté ou d'accorder l'extradition ou d'en référer à leur Gouvernement.

Her Britannic Majesty shall, however, be at liberty to make special arrangements in the British Colonies and foreign Possessions for the surrender of Belgian criminals who may there take refuge, on the basis, as nearly as may be, of the provisions of the present Treaty.

ARTICLE XV.

The present Treaty shall come into operation ten days after its publication in conformity with the laws of the respective countries.

Either Party may at any time terminate the Treaty on giving to the other six months' notice of its intention.

ARTICLE XVI.

The present Treaty shall be ratified, and the ratifications shall be exchanged at Brussels as soon as may be within six weeks from the date of signature.

In witness whereof the respective Plenipotentiaries have signed the same, and have affixed thereto the seals of their arms.

Done at Brussels, the thirty-first day of July, in the year of Our Lord one thousand eight hundred and seventy-two.

(L.S.) J. SAVILE LUMLEY.

And whereas the ratifications of the said Treaty were exchanged at Brussels on the twenty-ninth day of August last:

Now, therefore, Her Majesty, by and with the advice of Her Privy Council, and in virtue of the authority committed to her by the said recited Act, doth order, and it is hereby ordered, that from and after the twenty-eighth day of October, one thousand eight hundred and seventy-two, the said Act shall apply in the case of the said Treaty with the King of the Belgians.

EDMUND HARRISON.

Sa Majesté Britannique se réserve, cependant, le droit de faire des arrangements spéciaux dans les Colonies Anglaises ou Possessions étrangères pour l'extradition de criminels Belges qui y auraient cherché refuge, en se conformant, aussi exactement que possible, aux stipulations du présent Traité.

Article XV.

Le présent Traité entrera en vigueur dix jours après sa publication dans les formes prescrites par la législation des pays respectifs.

Chaque Partie peut en tout temps mettre fin au Traité, en donnant à l'autre, six mois à l'avance, avis de son intention.

Article XVI.

Le présent Traité sera ratifié, et les ratifications seront échangées à Bruxelles le plus tôt possible dans les six semaines de la date de la signature.

En foi de quoi les Plénipotentiaires respectifs ont signé ce même Traité, et y ont apposé le sceau de leurs armes.

Fait à Bruxelles, le trentième et unième jour de Juillet, dans l'année de grâce mil huit cent soixante-douze.

(L.S.) Cte. d'Aspremont-Lynden.

ITALY.

Order in Council, dated March 24, 1873, for carrying into effect a Treaty between Her Majesty and the King of Italy for the Mutual Surrender of Fugitive Criminals. —*Signed at Rome, February* 5, 1873.

At the Court at Windsor, the 24th day of March, 1873.

Present:

The Queen's Most Excellent Majesty in Council.

Whereas by an Act of Parliament made and passed in the Session of Parliament holden in the thirty-third and thirty-fourth years of the reign of Her present Majesty, intituled "An Act for amending the Law relating to the Extradition of Criminals," it was amongst other things enacted, that where an arrangement has been made with any foreign State with respect to the surrender to such State of any fugitive criminals, Her Majesty may, by Order in Council, direct that the said Act shall apply in the case of such foreign State; and that Her Majesty may, by the same or any subsequent Order, limit the operation of the Order, and restrict the same to fugitive criminals who are in or suspected of being in the part of Her Majesty's dominions specified in the Order, and render the operation thereof subject to such conditions, exceptions, and qualifications as may be deemed expedient:

And whereas a Treaty was concluded on the fifth day of February last between Her Majesty and the King of Italy for the Mutual Extradition of Fugitive Criminals, which Treaty is in the terms following:—

Her Majesty the Queen of the United Kingdom of Great Britain and Ireland, and His Majesty the King of Italy, having judged it expedient, with a view to the better administration of justice, and to the prevention of crime within their respective territories, that persons charged with or convicted of the crimes hereinafter enumerated, and being fugitives from justice, should, under certain circumstances, be reciprocally delivered up; Their said Majesties have named as their Plenipotentiaries to conclude a Treaty for this purpose, that is to say:—

Her Majesty the Queen of the United Kingdom of Great Britain and Ireland, Sir Augustus Berkeley Paget, Her Majesty's Envoy Extraordinary and Minister Plenipotentiary to His Majesty the King of Italy;

And His Majesty the King of Italy, the Noble Emilio Visconti Venosta, Deputy in the Parliament, and Minister Secretary of State for Foreign Affairs;

Who, after having communicated to each other their respective full powers, found in good and due form, have agreed upon and concluded the following Articles:—

Article I.

The High Contracting Parties engage to deliver up to each other reciprocally any persons who, being accused or convicted of any of the crimes specified in the Article following, committed within the territory of either of the said Parties, shall be found within the territory of the other, in the manner and under the conditions determined in the present Treaty.

Article II.

The crimes for which the extradition is agreed to are the following:—

1. Murder, or attempt or conspiracy to murder, comprising the crimes designated by the Italian Penal Code as the association of criminals for the commission of such offences.

2. Manslaughter, comprising the crimes designated by the Italian Penal Code as wounds and blows wilfully inflicted which cause death.

3. Counterfeiting or altering money, and uttering or bringing into circulation counterfeit or altered money.

4. Forgery, counterfeiting or altering, or uttering of the thing or document that is forged or counterfeited or altered.

Sua Maestà la Regina del Regno Unito della Gran Bretagna ed Irlanda, e Sua Maestà il Re d'Italia, avendo giudicato conveniente per la migliore amministrazione della giustizia e per prevenire i reati nei loro rispettivi territori, che le persone imputate o condannate per i reati quì appresso enumerati, e che cerchino sottrarsi alla giustizia, sieno, in certi casi, reciprocamente consegnate; le Loro prefate Maestà hanno nominato come Loro Plenipotenziari per conchiudere un Trattato a questo scopo, cioè:—

Sua Maestà la Regina del Regno Unito della Gran Bretagna ed Irlanda, Sir Augustus Berkeley Paget, Sua Inviato Straordinario e Ministro Plenipotenziario presso Sua Maestà il Re d'Italia;

E Sua Maestà il Re d'Italia, il Nobile Emilio Visconti Venosta, Deputato al Parlamento, Suo Ministro Segretario di Stato per gli Affari Esteri;

I quali, dopo essersi communicati i loro respettivi pieni poteri, trovati in buona e debita forma, hanno convenuto e conchiuso gli Articoli seguenti:—

Articolo I.

Le Alte Parti Contraenti si obbligano di consegnarsi reciprocamente coloro i quali essendo imputati o condannati per uno dei reati indicati nel seguente Articolo, commesso nel territorio di una di esse Parti, saranno trovati nel territorio dell'altra, nei modi e con le condizioni stabilite nel presente Trattato.

Articolo II.

I reati pei quali è convenuta la estradizione sono i seguenti:—

1. Assassinio, o tentativo o cospirazione per assassinare, comprendente i reati designati dal Codice Penale Italiano siccome associazione di malfattori per la perpetrazione di tali reati.
2. Omicidio volontario, comprendente i reati indicati dal Codice Penale Italiano colla designazione di percosse e ferite volontarie che producano la morte.
3. Contraffazione o alterazione di moneta, e spaccio od emissione di moneta contraffata o alterata.
4. Falsificazione, contraffazione o alterazione, o emissione della cosa o documento falso, o contrafatto o alterato.

5. Larceny, or unlawful abstraction or appropriation.

6. Obtaining money or goods by false pretences (cheating or fraud).

7. Fraudulent bankruptcy.

8. Fraud, abstraction, or unlawful appropriation by a bailee, banker, agent, factor, trustee, director, or member or officer of any public or private company or house of commerce.

9. Rape.

10. Abduction.

11. Child-stealing.

12. Burglary and housebreaking, comprising the crimes designated by the Italian Penal Code as entry by night, or even by day, with fracture or escalade, or by means of false key or other instrument, into the dwelling of another person with intent to commit a crime.

13. Arson.

14. Robbery with violence.

15. Threats by letter or otherwise, with intent to extort money or anything else.

16. Piracy, according to international law, when the pirate, a subject of neither of the High Contracting Parties, has committed depredations on the coasts, or on the high seas, to the injury of citizens of the requiring Party, or when, being a citizen of the requiring Party, and having committed acts of piracy, to the injury of a third State, he may be within the territory of the other Party without being subjected to trial.

17. Sinking or destroying, or attempting to sink or destroy, a vessel at sea.

18. Assaults on board a ship on the high seas with intent to kill or to do grievous bodily harm.

19. Revolt, or conspiracy by two or more persons on board a ship on the high seas, against the authority of the master.

Accomplices before the fact in any of these crimes shall, moreover, also be delivered up, provided their complicity be punishable by the laws of both the Contracting Parties.

Article III.

The Italian Government shall not deliver up any Italian to the United Kingdom; and no subject of the United Kingdom shall be delivered up by it to the Italian Government.

5. Furto od indebita sottrazione o appropriazione.

6. L'ottenuta consegna di danaro o di oggetti col mezzo di raggiro truffa o frode).

7. Bancarotta dolosa.

8. Frode, sottrazione o appropriazione indebita, commessa da un depositario, banchiere, agente, amministratore, curatore (*trustee*), direttore o membro o ufficiale di qualsiasi pubblica o privata compagnia o casa di commercio.

9. Ratto (*rape*).

10. Rapimento di persona (*abduction*).

11. Sottrazione di fanciulli.

12. *Burglary* e *house-breaking*, comprendendosi sotto queste designazioni secondo la nomenclatura del Codice Penale Italiano, l'atto di chi, di notte tempo o anche di giorno, s'introduce mediante rottura o scalata o per mezzo di chiave falsa od altro strumento, nell'altrui abitazione per commettere un reato.

13. Incendio volontario.

14. Depredazione con violenza.

15. Minacce per lettera o per altro modo per estorcere danaro o altra cosa.

16. Pirateria, secondo il diritto internazionale, quando il pirata, straniero alle due Alte Parti Contraenti, abbia commesso delle depredazioni sulle coste o in alto mare a danno dei cittadini della parte richiedente, ovvero quando, essendo cittadino della parte richiedente ed avendo commesso atti di pirateria in danno di un terzo Stato, egli si trovi nel territorio dell' altra parte senza esservi sottoposto a giudizio.

17. Sommersione o distruzione, o tentativo di sommersione o distruzione di nave in mare.

18. Assalto a bordo di una nave in alto mare col fine di uccidere o di produrre gravi danni corporali.

19. Rivolta, o cospirazione di due o più persone a bordo di una nave in alto mare contro l'autorità del capitano.

Sarà pure accordata l'estradizione di coloro i quali avranno partecipato prima del fatto ad alcuno di questi reati (complici), purchè tale partecipazione sia punita dalle leggi di ambedue le Parti Contraenti.

ARTICOLO III.

Dal Governo Italiano non sarà consegnato alcun Italiano al Regno Unito, e verun suddito del Regno Unito sarà da esso consegnato al Governo Italiano.

Article IV.

In any case where an individual convicted or accused shall have obtained naturalisation in either of the two Contracting States after the commission of the crime, such naturalisation shall not prevent the search for, arrest, and delivery of the individual. The extradition may, however, be refused if five years have elapsed from the concession of naturalisation, and the individual has been domiciled, from the concession thereof, in the State to which the application is made.

Article V.

No accused or convicted person shall be given up if the offence for which he is claimed is political, or if he proves that the demand for his surrender has been made with the intention of trying and punishing him for a political offence.

Article VI.

The extradition shall not be granted if, since the commission of the crime, the commencement of proceedings, or the conviction, such a length of time has elapsed as to bar the penal prosecution or the punishment, according to the laws of the State to which application is made.

Article VII.

The accused or convicted person who has been given up shall not, until he has been liberated, or had an opportunity of returning to the country in which he was living, be imprisoned or subjected to trial in the State to which he has been given up, for any crime or on any charge other than that on account of which the extradition took place.

This does not apply to offences committed after the extradition.

Article VIII.

If the individual claimed is under prosecution or in custody for a crime committed in the country where he has taken refuge, his surrender may be deferred until the law has taken its course.

In case he should be proceeded against or detained in such country on account of obligations contracted with private individuals, or any other civil claim, his surrender shall nevertheless take place, the injured party retaining his right to prosecute his claims against him before the competent authority.

ARTICOLO IV.

La naturalità ottenuta in uno dei due Stati Contraenti, dall'imputato o condannato, dopo il commesso reato, non impedirà la ricerca, l'arresto e la consegna dello stesso. Può tuttavia essere ricusata la estradizione, ove siano trascorsi cinque anni dalla concessa naturalità, e l'individuo abbia, dalla concessione di questa, tenuto il suo domicilio nello Stato richiesto.

ARTICOLO V.

Non sarà consegnato un imputato o condannato, se il reato pel quale egli è domandato sia politico; ovvero se egli prova che la domanda della sua consegna sia stata fatta con l'intendimento di giudicarlo o punirlo per un reato politico.

ARTICOLO VI.

Non sarà accordata la estradizione, se dal commesso reato, dall'iniziato procedimento, o dalla condanna, sia decorso tanto tempo che l'azione penale o la pena secondo la legge dello Stato richiesto sia estinta.

ARTICOLO VII.

L'imputato o condannato consegnato, finchè non sia stato liberato, o non abbia avuto l'opportunità di tornare nel paese dove dimorava, non potrà essere carcerato, o sottoposto a giudizio nello Stato, a cui fu consegnato, per reato o per altra imputazione diversa da quella per la quale avenne la estradizione.

Ciò non si applica ai reati commessi dopo l'estradizione.

ARTICOLO VIII.

Se l'individuo domandato è sotto processo o carcerato per un reato commesso nel paese dove si è refugiato, la sua estradizione può essere differita finchè la legge abbia avuto il suo corso.

In caso si debba procedere contro di lui o sia egli detenuto nello stesso paese per obbligazioni contratte con privati o per ogni altra azione civile, la sua consegna, ciò non ostante, avverrà, salvo alla parte di far valere i suoi diritti contro di lui innanzi all'autorità competente.

Article IX.

The requisitions for extradition shall be made respectively by means of the Diplomatic Agents of the High Contracting Parties.

The demand for the extradition of an accused person must be accompanied by a warrant of arrest issued by the competent authority of the State applying for the extradition, and by such proof as, according to the law of the place where the fugitive is found, would justify his arrest if the crime had been committed there.

If the requisition relates to a person convicted, it must be accompanied by the sentence of condemnation of the competent Court of the State applying for the extradition.

The demand for extradition must not be founded upon a sentence *in contumaciam.*

Article X.

If the demand for extradition be made according to the foregoing stipulations, the competent authorities of the State to which the requisition is made shall proceed to arrest the fugitive.

The prisoner shall be taken before the competent magistrate, who shall examine him, and make the preliminary investigations of the affair, in the same manner as if the arrest had taken place for a crime committed in the same country.

Article XI.

In the examinations to be made in conformity with the proceding stipulations, the authorities of the State to which the demand is addressed shall admit, as entirely valid evidence, the documents and depositions taken on oath in the other State, or copies of them, and likewise the warrants and sentences issued there: provided that such documents are signed or certified by a Judge, Magistrate, or officer of such State, and are authenticated by the oath of some witness, or stamped with the official seal of the Department of Justice or some other Department of State.

Article XII.

If, within two months from the arrest of the accused, sufficient evidence be not produced for his extradition, he shall be liberated.

Article XIII.

The extradition shall not take place until the expiration of fifteen

ARTICOLO IX.

Le domande di estradizione saranno fatte rispettivamente per mezzo degli Agenti Diplomatici delle Alte Parti Contraenti.

La domanda per la estradizione di un imputato dev' essere accompagnata da un mandato di cattura, rilasciato dalla competente autorità dello Stato che richiede la estradizione, e con tale prova che, secondo la legge del luogo dove il fuggitivo è trovato giustificherebbe il suo arresto, se il reato fosse stato quivi commesso.

Se la domanda riguarda un condannato, dev' essere accompagnata dalla sentenza di condanna della Corte competente dello Stato che fa la domanda di estradizione.

La domanda di estradizione non può fondarsi sopra una sentenza in contumacia.

ARTICOLO X.

Se la domanda di estradizione è fatta secondo gli anzidetti patti, le autorità competenti dello Stato richiesto procederanno alla cattura del fuggitivo.

Il catturato sarà condotto innanzi al Magistrato competente, il quale lo interrogherà, e fara le preliminari indagini sul fatto nel modo stesso che se la cattura fosse avvenuta per un reato commesso in quel paese.

ARTICOLO XI.

Le autorità dello Stato richiesto, negli esami che debbono fare, giusta le precedenti stipulazioni, ammetteranno, come prova intieramente valida, i documenti e le deposizioni testimoniali raccolte con giuramento nell' altro Stato, o copie di esse, e similmente i mandati e le sentenze ivi emanate, purchè tali documenti siano firmati o certificati da un giudice o Magistrato o Ufficiale dello Stato medesimo, e siano autenticati col giuramento di qualche testimone, o contrassegnati col sigillo uffiziale del Ministero di Giustizia, o di qualche altro Ministero di Stato.

ARTICOLO XII.

Se nel termine di due mesi dalla data della cattura del imputato, non sarà esibita sufficiente prova per la estradizione, egli sarà liberato.

ARTICOLO XIII.

Non sarà eseguita la estradizione prima che siano decorsi quindici

days after the arrest, and then only if the evidence has been found sufficient, according to the laws of the State to which the demand is addressed, to justify the committal of the prisoner for trial in case the crime had been committed in the territory of that State; or to show that the prisoner is the identical person condemned by the Tribunals of the State which demands him.

ARTICLE XIV.

If the prisoner be not given up and taken away within two months from his apprehension or from the decision of the Court upon the demand for a writ of *habeas corpus* in the United Kingdom, he shall be set at liberty, unless sufficient cause be shown for the delay.

ARTICLE XV.

If the individual claimed by one of the two Contracting Parties in conformity with the present Treaty, should be also claimed by another or by other States on account of crimes committed in their territories, his surrender shall, in preference, be granted according to priory of demand, unless an agreement be made between the Governments which make the requisition, either on account of the gravity of the crimes committed or for any other reason.

ARTICLE XVI.

Every article found in the possession of the prisoner at the time of his arrest shall be seized, in order to be delivered up with him.

Such delivery shall not be limited to the property or articles obtained by the robbery or fraudulent bankruptcy, but shall include everything that may serve as evidence of the crime; and it shall take place even when the extradition, after having been ordered, cannot take effect, either on account of the escape or the death of the delinquent.

ARTICLE XVII.

The High Contracting Parties renounce all claim for repayment of the expenses incurred for the arrest and maintenance of the person to be given up, and for his conveyance on board a ship; such expenses shall be borne by themselves respectively.

ARTICLE XVIII.

The stipulations of the present Treaty shall be applicable to the Colonies and foreign Possessions of the two High Contracting Parties.

giorni dal dì della cattura, e solamente quando la prova sia stata trovata sufficiente, secondo le leggi dello Stato richiesto, a giustificare il rinvio del detenuto al giudizio nel caso che il reato fosse stato commesso nel territorio del suddetto Stato, od a dimostrare che il catturato è l' identica persona condannata dai Tribunali dello Stato che lo richiede.

ARTICOLO XIV.

Se l' arrestato non sia consegnato e condotto via fra due mesi dall' arresto, o dalla decisione della Corte sopra la domanda di un ordinanza di *habeas corpus* nel Regno Unito, sarà liberato, tranne il caso che sia sufficientemente dimostrata la cagione del ritardo.

ARTICOLO XV.

Se l' individuo domandato da una delle due Parti Contraenti in conformità del presente Trattato, sia anche chiesto da un altro o da altri Stati, per reati commessi nei loro territori, la consegna di lui sarà di preferenza accordata secondo l' anteriorità della domanda, tranne che fra i Governi richiedenti non si sia stabilito un accordo o per riguardo alla gravità dei reati commessi o per qualunque altra ragione.

ARTICOLO XVI.

Ogni oggetto di cui l' arrestato sarà trovato possessore al momento dell' arresto sarà sequestrato, per essere poi con lui consegnato. La consegna non si restringerà alle cose od oggetti provenienti dal furto o dalla bancarotta dolosa, ma comprenderà qualunque cosa che può servire di prova del reato, e sarà eseguita anche quando, dopo ordinata la estradizione, non potrà questa avere effetto, o per la fuga o per la morte del delinquente.

ARTICOLO XVII.

Le Alte Parti Contraenti rinunziano ad ogni domanda per rimborso delle spese occorse per la cattura e sostentamento della persona da consegnare, e per la sua traduzione sino sul bordo di una nave; le quali spese rimarranno a rispettivo lora carica.

ARTICOLO XVIII.

Le disposizioni del presente Trattato si applicheranno alle colonie e possedimenti stranieri (*foreign possessions*) delle due Alte Parti Contraenti.

The requisition for the surrender of a person accused or condemned who has taken refuge in any such Colony or Possession of either Party, shall be made to the Governor or chief authority of such Colony or Possession by the chief Consular Officer of the other residing in such Colony or Possession; or, if the accused or condemned person has escaped from a Colony or foreign Possession of the Party on whose behalf the requisition is made, the requisition shall be made by the Governor or chief authority of such Colony or Possession.

Such requisitions may be disposed of, in accordance as far as possible with the stipulations of this Treaty, by the respective Governors or chief authorities, who, however, shall be at liberty either to grant the extradition or to refer the matter to their own Government.

Her Britannic Majesty shall nevertheless be at liberty to make special arrangements in the British Colonies and foreign Possessions for the surrender to His Italian Majesty of criminals who may have taken refuge in such Colonies or Possessions, always in conformity, so far as possible, with the provisions of the present Treaty.

Finally, it is agreed that this stipulation does not apply to the Island of Malta, the Ordinance of the Maltese Government of May 3, 1863 (No. 1230), remaining in full force.

Article XIX.

The High Contracting Parties declare that the present stipulations apply as well to persons accused or convicted, whose crimes, on account of which the extradition is demanded, may have been committed previously, as to those whose crimes may be committed subsequently to the date of this Treaty.

Article XX.

The present Treaty shall come into operation ten days after its publication according to the forms prescribed by the laws of the High Contracting Parties.

Either Party may at any time put an end to this Treaty, which, however, shall remain in force for six months after the notice for its termination.

This Treaty shall be ratified, and the ratifications shall be exchanged at Rome within six weeks, or sooner if possible.

In witness whereof the respective Plenipotentiaries have signed in

La domanda di estradizione per la consegna di un imputato o condannato, il quale sia fuggito in una delle dette colonie o possedimenti di una delle due parti, sarà fatta al Governatore, o all' autorità suprema di detta colonia o possedimento, dal principale ufficiale Consolare dell' altra residente nella colonia o possedimento; o se l' imputato o il condannato sia fuggito da una colonia o possedimento straniero della parta nell' interesse della quale è fatta la domanda, essa sarà fatta dal Governatore o dall' autorità suprema di tale colonia o possedimento.

Su tali domande potrà essere provveduto in conformità, per quanto è possibile, dei patti di questo Trattato dai rispettivi Governatori o dalle autorità supreme, le quali tuttavia avranno la facoltà o di accordare la estradizione o di riferirne al proprio Governo.

Sua Maestà Britannica nondimeno potrà dare speciali provvedimenti nelle Colonie Britanniche e possedimenti stranieri, per la consegna dei delinquenti rifugiati in dette colonie o possedimenti, a Sua Maestà Italiana, sempre in conformità, per quanto sia possibile, alle disposizioni del presente Trattato.

Resta infine convenuto che questo patto non si applica all' Isola di Malta, rimanendo in pieno vigore l' Ordinanza del Governo Maltese del 3 Maggio 1863, No. 1,230.

Articolo XIX.

Le Alte Parti Contraenti dichiarano che le presenti stipulazioni si applicano tanto agli imputati o condannati, il cui reato, pel quale è chiesta l' estradizione, sia stato commesso prima quanto a quelli che l' abbiano commesso posteriormente alla data di questo Trattato.

Articolo XX.

Il presente Trattato andrà in vigore dieci giorni dopo la sua pubblicazione, secondo le forme prescritte dalle leggi delle Alte Parti Contraenti.

Ciascuna delle Alte Parti potrà in ogni tempo por fine a questo Trattato, il quale però rimarrà in vigore sei mesi dopo la denunzia.

Questo Trattato sarà ratificato, e le ratificazioni saranno scambiate a Roma fra sei settimane, o più sollicitamente se sarà possibile.

In fede di che i rispettivi Plenipotenziari hanno firmato in doppio

duplicate, in English and Italian, the present Treaty, and have affixed thereto their respective seals.

Done at Rome, the 5th day of February, in the year of our Lord one thousand eight hundred and seventy-three.

(L.S.) A. B. Paget.
(L.S.) Visconti Venosta.

And whereas the ratifications of the said Treaty were exchanged at Rome on the 18th of March last:

Now, therefore, Her Majesty, by and with the advice of Her Privy Council, and in virtue of the authority committed to Her by the said recited Act, doth order, and it is hereby ordered, that from and after the eleventh day of April, one thousand eight hundred and seventy-three, the said Act shall apply in the case of the said Treaty with the King of Italy.

Edmund Harrison.

Declaration rectifying an Error in Article XVIII. of the Treaty between Her Majesty and the King of Italy of the 5th February, 1873, for the Mutual Surrender of Fugitive Criminals.—*Signed at Rome, May* 7, 1873.

The Envoy Extraordinary and Minister Plenipotentiary of Her Majesty the Queen of Great Britain and Ireland to His Majesty the King of Italy, and His Italian Majesty's Minister for Foreign Affairs, having concurrently recognised a material error in the date of the Ordinance of the Maltese Government of the 21st of February, 1863, as it is mentioned at the end of the XVIIIth Article of the Extradition Treaty of the 5th of February, 1873, between Great Britain and Italy, have, by common consent, declared that the words:—

"Finally, it is agreed that this stipulation does not apply to the Island of Malta, the Ordinance of the Maltese Government of May 3, 1863 (No. 1230), remaining in full force," shall be read:—

"Finally, it is agreed that this stipulation does not apply to the Island of Malta, the Ordinance of the Maltese Government of the 21st of February, 1863, remaining in full force."

The present Declaration is signed in duplicate at Rome, this 7th day of May, 1873.

(L.S.) A. B. Paget.
(L.S.) Visconti Venosta.

esemplare, in Inglese e in Italiano, il presente Trattato e vi hanno apposto il rispettivo sigillo.

Fatto a Roma il giorno cinque di Febbraio, l'anno del Signore mille ottocento settantatre.

(L.S.) VISCONTI VENOSTA.
(L.S.) A. B. PAGET.

L'INVIATO Straordinario e Ministro Plenipotenziario di Sua Maestà la Regina della Gran Bretagna ed Irlanda presso Sua Maestà Italiana ed il Ministro degli Affari Esteri di Sua Maestà il Re d'Italia, avendo concordemente riconosciuto essere occorso un materiale errore nella indicazione della data dell'Ordinanza del Governo Maltese del 21 Febbraio 1863, che si trova menzionata in fine dell'Articolo XVIII della Convenzione d'Estradizione del 5 Febbraio 1873, fra la Gran Bretagna e l'Italia, hanno di comune consenso dichiarato che dove si legge:—

"Resta in fine convenuto che questo patto non si applica all'Isola di Malta, rimanendo in pieno vigore l'Ordinanza del Governo Maltese del 3 Maggio 1863 (No. 1230)," debba invece leggersi:—

"Resta in fine convenuto che questo patto non si applica all'Isola di Malta, rimanendo in pieno vigore l'Ordinanza del Governo Maltese del 21 Febbraio 1863."

Fatta la presente Dichiarazione in doppio originale a Roma il dì 7 Maggio 1873.

(L.S.) A. B. PAGET.
(L.S.) VISCONTI VENOSTA.

DENMARK.

TREATY BETWEEN HER MAJESTY AND THE KING OF DENMARK, FOR THE MUTUAL SURRENDER OF FUGITIVE CRIMINALS.—*Signed at Copenhagen, March* 31, 1873.

[Ratifications exchanged at Copenhagen, April 26, 1873.]

HER Majesty the Queen of the United Kingdom of Great Britain and Ireland, and His Majesty the King of Denmark, having judged it expedient, with a view to the better administration of justice, and to the prevention of crime within their respective territories and jurisdictions, that persons charged with or convicted of the crimes hereinafter enumerated, and being fugitives from justice, should, under certain circumstances, be reciprocally delivered up; Their said Majesties have named as their Plenipotentiaries to conclude a Treaty for this purpose, that is to say:

Her Majesty the Queen of the United Kingdom of Great Britain and Ireland, Sir Charles Lennox Wyke, Knight Commander of the Most Honourable Order of the Bath, Her Envoy Extraordinary and Minister Plenipotentiary to His Majesty the King of Denmark;

And His Majesty the King of Denmark, Baron Otto Ditlev Rosenörn-Lehn, Knight Commander of the Order of the Danebrog and Danebrogsmand, His Majesty's Minister for Foreign Affairs;

Who, after having communicated to each other their respective full powers, found in good and due form, have agreed upon the following Articles:—

ARTICLE I.

It is agreed that Her Britannic Majesty and His Majesty the King of Denmark shall, on requisition made in their name by their respective Diplomatic Agents, deliver up to each other reciprocally any persons, except native born or naturalised subjects of the Party upon whom the requisition may be made, who, being accused or

DA Hans Majestæt Kongen af Danmark og Hendes Majestæt Dronningen af det forenede Kongerige Storbritannien og Irland, til bedre Haandhævelse af Retspleien og til Forebyggelse af Forbrydelser indenfor deres respektive Territorer og Statsgebeter, have anseet det for gavnligt, at Personer, som ere anklagede for eller overbeviste om at have gjort sig skyldige i de nedenfor angivne Forbrydelser og ved Flugt have unddraget sig Retsforfölgning, blive under visse Omstændigheder gjensidigen udleverede, saa have bemeldte Majestæter til i dette Öiemed at afslutte en Traktat udnævnt til deres Befuldmægtigede:

Hans Majestæt Kongen af Danmark, Baron Otto Ditlev Rosenörn-Lehn, Kommandeur af Danebrog og Danebrogsmand, Hans Majestæts Udenrigsminister;

Og Hendes Majestæt Dronningen af det forenede Kongerige Storbritannien og Irland, Sir Charles Lennox Wyke, Kommandeur af Bath-Ordenen, Hendes Majestæts overordentlige Gesandt og befuldmægtigede Minister hos Hans Majestæt Kongen af Danmark;

Hvilke, efter gjensidig Meddelelse af deres respektive Fuldmagter, der befandtes i god og rigtig Form, ere komne overeens om fölgende Artikler:--

ARTIKEL I.

Hans Majestæt Kongen af Danmark og Hendes Britiske Majestæt forpligte sig til, paa derom i deres Navn gjennem deres respektive diplomatiske Agenter fremsat Begjæring, gjensidigen at udlevere til hinanden Personer, som, anklagede for eller overbeviste om at have begaaet nogen af de nedenfor angivne Forbrydelser indenfor den

convicted of any of the crimes hereinafter specified, committed within the territory of the requiring Party, shall be found within the territories of the other Party :—

1. Murder, or attempt or conspiracy to murder.

2. Manslaughter.

3. Counterfeiting or altering money, or uttering counterfeit or altered money.

4. Forgery or counterfeiting or altering, or uttering what is forged or counterfeited or altered.

5. Embezzlement or larceny.

6. Obtaining money or goods by false pretences.

7. Crimes by bankrupts against bankruptcy law.

8. Fraud by a bailee, banker, agent, factor, trustee, or director, or member or public officer of any company, made criminal by any law for the time being in force.

9. Rape.

10. Abduction.

11. Child-stealing.

12. Burglary or housebreaking.

13. Arson.

14. Robbery with violence.

15. Threats by letter or otherwise with intent to extort.

16. Piracy by law of nations.

17. Sinking or destroying a vessel at sea, or attempting or conspiring to do so.

18. Assaults on board a ship on the high seas with intent to destroy life or to do grievous bodily harm.

19. Revolt or conspiracy to revolt by two or more persons on board a ship on the high seas against the authority of the master.

Provided that the surrender shall be made only when, in the case of a person accused, the commission of the crime shall be so established as that the laws of the country where the fugitive or person so accused shall be found would justify his apprehension and commitment for trial if the crime had been there committed; and in the case of a person alleged to have been convicted, on such

Parts Territorium, der begjærer Udleveringen, maatte blive antrufne indenfor den anden Parts Territorium, dog med Undtagelse af det Tilfælde, at saadanne Personer have Indfödsret ifölge Födsel eller Naturalisation i den Stat, til hvilken Begjæringen om Utleveringen er rettet :—

1. Mord eller Forsög paa Mord eller Samraad om Mord.

2. Drab.

3. Eftergjörelse eller Forfalskning af Penge eller Udgivelse af eftergjorte eller forfalskede Penge.

4. Dokumentfalsk eller anden Eftergjörelse eller Forfalskning eller svigagtig Brug af et falsk Dokument eller af anden eftergjort eller forfalsket Gjenstand.

5. Tilegnelse af betroet Gods eller Tyveri.

6. Tilvendelse af Penge eller Gods ved falske Foregivender.

7. Forbrydelser af Fallenter imod Fallitlovgivningen.

8. De efter den til enhver Tid gjældende Lovgivning strafbare svigagtige Handlinger, der begaaes af en Depositarius, Bankier, Agent, Faktor, Værge, Kurator eller af et Selskabs Bestyrer, Medlem eller offentlige Betjente.

9. Voldtægt.

10. Bortförelse.

11. Barnerov.

12. Indbrudstyveri.

13. Brandstiftelse.

14. Röveri.

15. Trusler, som i Breve eller paa anden Maade fremföres for at aftvinge Penge eller Gods.

16. Söröveri i folkeretlig Forstand.

17. Sænkning eller Tilintetgjörelse af et Skib i Söen eller herpaa rettet Forsög eller Komplot.

18. Voldsgjerninger ombord paa et Skib i rum Sö, udövede i den Hensigt at dræbe eller tilföie en större Legemsbeskadigelse.

19. Mytteri ombord paa et Skib i rum Sö mod Skibsförerens Myndighed eller derpaa rettet Sammenrottelse af to eller flere Personer.

Udleveringen af en Person, der er anklaget for en Forbrydelse, skal dog ikkun da finde Sted, naar der er tilveiebragt et saadant Bevis for Udförelsen af denne, at der efter det Lands Love, hvor den Undvegne eller Anklagede antræffes, deri vilde indeholdes tilstrækkelig Hjemmel til at paagribe ham og stille ham for Retten, hvis Forbrydelsen var begaaet i dette Land. Ligeledes skal

evidence as, according to the laws of the country where he is found, would prove that he had been convicted.

Article II.

In the dominions of Her Britannic Majesty other than the Colonies or foreign Possessions of Her Majesty, the manner of proceeding shall be as follows:—

I. In the case of a person accused—

The requisition for the surrender shall be made to Her Britannic Majesty's Principal Secretary of State for Foreign Affairs by the Minister or other Diplomatic Agent of His Majesty the King of Denmark at London, accompanied by (1) a warrant or other equivalent judicial document for the arrest of the accused, issued by a Judge or Magistrate duly authorized to take cognizance of the acts charged against him in Denmark; (2) duly authenticated depositions or statements taken on oath before such Judge or Magistrate, clearly setting forth the acts on account of which the fugitive is demanded; and (3) a description of the person claimed, and any other particulars which may serve to identify him. The said Secretary of State shall transmit such documents to Her Britannic Majesty's Principal Secretary of State for the Home Department, who shall then, by order under his hand and seal, signify to some police magistrate in London that such requisition has been made, and require him, if there be due cause, to issue his warrant for the apprehension of the fugitive.

On the receipt of such order from the Secretary of State, and on the production of such evidence as would, in the opinion of the magistrate, justify the issue of the warrant if the crime had been committed in the United Kingdom, he shall issue his warrant accordingly.

When the fugitive shall have been apprehended in virtue of such warrant, he shall be brought before the police magistrate who

Udleveringen af en Person, der angives at være domfældt, alene finde Sted efter Forelæggelse af et saadant Retsdokument, som ifölge det Lands Love, hvor han antræffes, vilde afgive Bevis for hans Domfældelse.

ARTIKEL II.

Hendes Britiske Majestæts Lande, med Undtagelse af Hendes Majestæts Kolonier eller Bilande, skal fölgende Fremgangsmaade anvendes:—

I. I det Tilfælde, at den Person, der fordres udleveret, er anklaget,

Skal Begjæringen om Udlevering skee til Hendes Britiske Majestæts förste Stats-secretair for de udenlandske Anliggender ved Hans Majestæt Kongen af Danmarks Gesandt eller diplomatiske Agent i London, og denne Begjæring skal være ledsaget (1) af en Fængslingskjendelse eller et andet tilsvarende Retsdokument angaaende den Paagjældendes Fængsling, udstedt af en Dommer eller anden Retsembedsmand, som er behörig bemyndiget til at gjöre de Handlinger, der lægges den Paagjældende til Last i Danmark, til Gjenstand for Undersögelse; (2) af behörig legaliserede Udsagn og Forklaringer, som under Eed ere afgivne for en saadan Dommer eller Retsembedsmand, og som give en klar Fremstilling af de Handlinger, paa Grund af hvilke Udleveringen er begjært, samt endelig (3) af en Beskrivelse af den Person, der fordres udleveret, og af en Meddelelse af andre Data, som kunne tjene til at godtgjöre hans Identitét. Bemeldte Stats-secretair skal fremsende disse Dokumenter til Hendes Britiske Majestæts förste Stats-secretair for de indenrigske Forhold, og denne skal da ved en med sin Underskrift og sit Segl forsynet Ordre meddele en Politimyndighed i London, at en Begjæring som den ovennævnte er fremsat, og paalægge ham, hvis han finder den behörig begrundet, at udstede en Befaling om den Undvegnes Paagribelse.

Naar den nævnte Politimyndighed har modtaget en saadan Befaling fra Statssecretairen, og naar den finder det Bevis, der fremlægges for den, at være af saadan Beskaffenhed, at det vilde retfærdiggjöre Udstedelsen af en Anholdelsesbefaling, hvis Forbrydelsen var bleven begaaet i det Forenede Kongerige, skal den udstede en saadan Anholdelsesbefaling i Overeensstemmelse dermed.

Naar den Undvegne er bleven anholdt ifölge denne Anholdelsesbefaling, skal han stilles for den Politimyndighed, som udstedte

issued it, or some other police magistrate in London. If the evidence to be then produced shall be such as to justify, according to the law of England, the committal for trial of the prisoner if the crime of which he is accused had been committed in England, the police magistrate shall commit him to prison to await the warrant of the Secretary of State for his surrender; sending immediately to the Secretary of State a certificate of the committal and a report upon the case.

After the expiration of a period from the committal of the prisoner, which shall never be less than fifteen days, the Secretary of State shall, by order under his hand and seal, order the fugitive criminal to be surrendered to such person as may be duly authorized to receive him on the part of the Government of His Majesty the King of Denmark.

II. In the case of a person convicted—

The course of proceeding shall be the same as in the preceding case of a person accused, except that the document to be produced by the Minister or other Diplomatic Agent of His Danish Majesty in support of his requisition, shall clearly set forth the crime of which the person claimed has been convicted, and state the fact, place, and date of his conviction. The evidence to be produced before the police magistrate shall be such as would, according to the law of England, prove that the prisoner was convicted of the crime charged.

After the police magistrate shall have committed the accused or convicted person to prison to await the order of a Secretary of State for his surrender, such person shall have the right to apply for a writ of *habeas corpus*. If he should so apply, his surrender must be deferred until after the decision of the Court upon the return to the writ, and even then can only take place if the decision is adverse to the applicant. In the latter case the Court may at once order his delivery to the person authorized to receive him, without the order of a Secretary of State for his surrender, or commit him to prison to await such order.

Article III.

In the dominions of His Majesty the King of Denmark other than

den, eller for en anden Politimyndighed i London. Dersom det Bevis, der föres for denne, er af saadan Beskaffenhed, at det efter Englands Love vilde berettige til at bringe den Anholdte for Domstolene, hvis den Forbrydelse, som han sigtes for, var bleven begaaet i England, skal Politimyndigheden sætte ham i Fængsel for der at afvente Statssecretairens Befaling om hans Udlevering. Attest om Fængslingsbefalingen samt en Beretning om Sagen skal ufortövet sendes til Statssecretairen.

Efter Udlöbet af en vis Tid efter Fængslingen, hvilken Tid aldrig maa være kortere end femten Dage, skal Statssecretairen ved en under sin Haand og sit Segl udfærdiget Befaling beordre den undvegne Forbryder udleveret til den Person, som af Hans Majestæt Kongen af Danmarks Regjering maatte være tilbörlig bemyndiget til at modtage ham.

II. I det Tilfælde at den Person, der fordres udleveret, er domfældt,

Skal Fremgangsmaaden være den samme som i det foregaaende Tilfælde, hvor den Paagjældende var anklaget, dog med Undtagelse af, at her det Dokument, som Hans Majestæt Kongen af Danmarks Minister eller diplomatiske Agent har at overlevere til Stötte for sin Begjæring, paa en tydelig Maade skal fremstille den Forbrydelse, for hvilken den Person, der fordres udleveret, er domfældt, og derhos angive den Handling, for hvilken, Stedet hvor og Tiden naar han er bleven dömt. De Bevisligheder, der skulle fremlægges for Politimyndigheden, skulle være af saadan Beskaffenhed, at de efter Englands Love vilde begrunde den Fængsledes Domfældelse for den Forbrydelse, som han er sigtet for.

Efter at Politimyndigheden har befalet, at den anklagede eller domfældte Person skal sættes i Fængsel for der at afvente Statssecretairens Befaling angaaende hans Udlevering, skal den Fængslede have Ret til at forlange "a writ of *habeas corpus.*" Hvis den Fængslede gjör Brug af denne Ret, skal Udleveringen opsættes, indtil Retten har afgivet sin Kjendelse, og ikkun finde Sted, hvis Kjendelsen gaaer den Fængslede imod. I sidste Tilfælde kan Retten enten strax beordre den Fængsledes Udlevering til den dertil bemyndigede Person, uden at afvente Statssecretairens Befaling om hans Udlevering, eller paany lade ham sætte i Fængsel for der at oppebie denne Befaling.

ARTIKEL III.

I Hans Majestæt Kongen af Danmarks Lande, med Undtagelse af

the Colonies or foreign Possessions of His said Majesty, the manner of proceeding shall be as follows:—

I. In the case of a person accused—

The requsition for the surrender shall be made to the Minister for Foreign Affairs of His Majesty the King of Denmark by the Minister or other Diplomatic Agent of Her Britannic Majesty at Copenhagen, accompanied by (1) a warrant for the arrest of the accused, issued by a Judge or Magistrate duly authorized to take cognizance of the acts charged against him in Great Britain; (2) duly authenticated depositions or statements taken on oath before such Judge or Magistrate, clearly setting forth the acts on account of which the fugitive is demanded; and (3) a description of the person claimed, and any other particulars which may serve to identify him.

The Minister for Foreign Affairs of His Majesty the King of Denmark shall transmit such requisition for surrender to the Minister of Justice of His Majesty the King of Denmark, who, after having ascertained that the crime therein specified is one of those enumerated in the present Treaty, and satisfied himself that the evidence produced is such as, according to Danish law, would justify the committal for trial of the individual demanded if the crime had been committed in Denmark, shall take the necessary measures for causing the fugitive to be delivered to the person charged to receive him by the Government of Her Britannic Majesty.

II. In the case of a person convicted—

The course of proceeding shall be the same as in the preceding case of a person accused, except that the warrant to be transmitted by the Minister or other Diplomatic Agent of Her Britannic Majesty in support of his requisition, shall clearly set forth the crime of which the person claimed has been convicted, and state the fact, place, and date of his conviction. The evidence to be produced shall be such as would, according to the laws of Denmark, prove that the prisoner was convicted of the crime charged.

Kolonierne og andre Bilande, skal fölgende Fremgangsmaade anvendes:—

I. I det Tilfælde at den Person, der fordres udleveret, er anklaget—

Skal Begjæringen om Udlevering skee til Hans Majestæt Kongen af Danmarks Udenrigsminister ved Hendes Britiske Majestæts Minister eller diplomatiske Agent i Kjöbenhavn, og denne Begjæring skal være ledsaget (1) af en Fængslingskjendelse, der er udstedt af en Dommer eller anden Retsembedsmand, som er behörig bemyndiget til at gjöre de Handlinger, der lægges ham til Last i Storbritannien, til Gjenstand for Undersögelse; (2) af behörig legaliserede Udsagn og Forklaringer, der ere edeligen afgivne for en saadan Dommer eller Retsembedsmand, og som give en tydelig Fremstilling af de Handlinger, paa Grund af hvilke Udleveringen er begjært; og (3) af en Beskrivelse af den Person, der fordres udleveret, og af en Meddelelse af andre Data, som kunne tjene til at godtgjöre hans Identitet.

Hans Majestæt Kongen af Danmarks Udenrigsminister fremsender den saaledes modtagne Udleveringsbegjæring til Hans Majestæt Kongen af Danmarks Justitsminister, der, naar han efter anstillet Undersögelse finder, at Udleveringsbegjæringen har Medhold i denne Tractat, og at det Bevis, der fremlægges er af saadan Beskaffenhed, at det efter Danmarks Love vilde berettige til at bringe den Person, hvis Udlevering begjæres, for Domstolene, saafremt den Forbrydelse, for hvilken han sigtes, var bleven begaaet i Danmark, træffer de fornödne Foranstaltninger til den Undvegnes Udlevering til den Person, som af Hendes Britiske Majestæts Regjering er tilbörligt bemyndiget til at modtage ham.

II. I det Tilfælde at den Person, der fordres udleveret, er domfældt,

Skal Fremgangsmaaden være den samme som i det foregaaende Tilfælde, hvor den Paagjældende var anklaget, dog med Undtagelse af, at her det Dokument, som Hendes Britiske Majestæts Minister eller diplomatiske Agent har at overlevere til Stötte for sin Begjæring, paa en tydelig Maade skal fremstille den Forbrydelse, for hvilken den Person, som fordres udleveret, er domfældt, og derhos angive den Handling, for hvilken, samt Stedet hvor og Tiden naar han er bleven dömt. De Bevisligheder, der skulle fremlæges skulle være af saadan Beskaffenhed, at de efter de danske Love vilde begrunde den Fængsledes Domfældelse for den Forbrydelse, for hvilken han sigtes.

Article IV.

A fugitive criminal may, however, be apprehended under a warrant issued by any police magistrate, justice of the peace, or other competent authority in either country, on such information or complaint, and such evidence, or after such proceedings as would, in the opinion of the person issuing the warrant, justify the issue of a warrant if the crime had been committed, or the prisoner convicted, in that part of the dominions of the two Contracting Parties in which he exercises jurisdiction: Provided, however, that in the United Kingdom the accused shall, in such case, be sent as speedily as possible before a police magistrate in London; and that in the dominions of His Majesty the King of Denmark the case shall be immediately submitted to the Minister of Justice of His Majesty the King of Denmark; and provided, also, that the individual arrested shall in either country be discharged, if within fifteen days a requisition shall not have been made for his surrender by the Diplomatic Agent of his country, in the manner directed by Articles II. and III. of this Treaty.

The same rule shall apply to the cases of persons accused or convicted of any of the crimes specified in this Treaty, committed on the high seas, on board a vessel of either country which may come into a port of the other.

Article V.

If the fugitive criminal who has been committed to prison be not surrendered and conveyed away within two months after such committal (or within two months after the decision of the Court, upon the return to a writ of *habeas corpus* in the United Kingdom), he shall be discharged from custody, unless sufficient cause be shown to the contrary.

Article VI.

When any person shall have been surrendered by either of the High Contracting Parties to the other, such person shall not, until he has been restored or had an opportunity of returning to the country from whence he was surrendered, be triable or tried for any offence committed in the other country prior to the surrender,

ARTIKEL IV.

En undvegen Forbryder kan imidlertid blive anholdt ifölge en Anholdelsesbefaling, der er bleven udstedt af en Politimyndighed, Fredsdommer eller anden kompetent Myndighed, i et af de to Lande ifölge saadan Anmeldelse eller Klage og saadanne Bevisligheder samt under Iagttagelse af den formlige Fremgangsmaade, som efter dens Mening, der udsteder Anholdelsesbefalingen, vilde retfærdiggjöre sammes Udstedelse, dersom Forbrydelsen var bleven begaaet eller Forbryderen domfældt i den Del af de kontraherende Parters Territorium, hvor vedkommende Myndighed er kompetent. Dette kan dog kun skee paa den Betingelse, at i saadant Tilfælde den Anklagede i det Forenede Kongerige saa hurtigt som muligt stilles for en Politimyndighed i London, og at Sagen i Hans Majestæt Kongen af Danmarks Lande uopholdelig forelægges for Hans Majestæts Justits-minister, samt at i begge Lande den anholdte Person skal löslades, dersom der ikke inden femten Dages Forlöb skeer en Begjæring om hans Udlevering ved hans Lands diplomatiske Agent paa den Maade, som er angiven i Artiklerne II og III i denne Traktat.

Den samme Regel skal komme til Anvendelse paa Personer, der ere anklagede eller domfældte for nogen af de i denne Traktat opregnede Forbrydelser, naar disse ere begaaede i rum Sö ombord paa et af de to Landes Skibe, og dette maatte være löbet ind i en Havn i det andet Land.

ARTIKEL V.

Dersom den undvegne Forbryder, som er bleven fængslet, ikke er bleven udleveret og bortfört inden to Maaneder efter Fængslingen (eller inden to Maaneder efter den Domstols Kjendelse, som i det Forenede Kongerige er afsagt ifölge "writ of *habeas corpus*,") skal han löslades af Fængslet, medmindre der kan paavises tilstrækkelig Grund til det Modsatte.

ARTIKEL VI.

Naar en Person er bleven udleveret af den ene af de kontraherende Parter til den anden, skal han, saalænge han ikke er bleven tilbageleveret eller har havt Leilighed til at vende tilbage til det Land, hvorfra han er bleven udleveret, ikke kunne drages til Ansvar eller dömmes for nogen anden Forbrydelse, som han

other than the particular offence on account of which he was surrendered.

ARTICLE VII.

No accused or convicted person shall be surrendered, if the offence in respect of which his surrender is demanded shall be deemed by the Government upon which it is made to be one of a political character, or if in the United Kingdom he prove to the satisfaction of the police magistrate, or of the Court before which he is brought on *habeas corpus*, or to the Secretary of State, or in Denmark, to the satisfaction of the Minister of Justice of His Majesty the King of Denmark, that the requisition for his surrender has, in fact, been made with a view to try or to punish him for an offence of a political character.

ARTICLE VIII.

Warrants, depositions, or statements on oath, issued or taken in the dominions of either of the two High Contracting Parties, and copies thereof, and certificates of or judicial documents stating the fact of conviction, shall be received in evidence in proceedings in the dominions of the other, if purporting to be signed or certified by a Judge, Magistrate, or officer of the country where they were issued or taken, and provided they are authenticated by the oath of some witness, or by being sealed with the official seal of the Minister of Justice or some other Minister of State.

ARTICLE IX.

The surrender shall not take place if, since the commission of the acts charged, the accusation, or the conviction, exemption from prosecution or punishment has been acquired by lapse of time, according to the laws of the country where the accused or convicted person shall have taken refuge.

ARTICLE X.

If the individual claimed should be under prosecution, or in custody, for a crime or offence committed in the country where he may have taken refuge, his surrender may be deferred until he shall have been set at liberty in due course of law.

forinden Udleveringen maatte have begaaet i det andet Land, end den, paa Grund af hvilken han blev udleveret.

ARTIKEL VII.

En anklaget eller domfældt Person skal ikke udleveres, naar den Part, til hvem Begjæringen om Udlevering er rettet, anseer den Forbrydelse, formedelst hvilken Udleveringen begjæres, som en Forbrydelse af en politisk Karakter, eiheller dersom han i det Forenede Kongerige paa en Maade, der er fyldestgjörende for den vedkommende Politimyndighed eller for den Domstol, for hvilken han er stillet ifölge "a writ of *habeas corpus*," eller for Statssecretairen og i Danmark for Hans Majestæt Kongens Justitsminister godtgjör, at Begjæringen om hans Udlevering i Virkeligheden skeer i den Hensigt at drage ham til Ansvar eller straffe ham for en Forbrydelse af en politisk Karakter.

ARTIKEL VIII.

Fænglings- og Anholdelsesbefalinger, Forklaringer og edelige Vidnesbyrd, der ere udstedte eller optagne i et af de to höie kontraherende Parters Lande, eller Afskrifter af saadanne og Attester og Retsdokumenter, som godtgjöre Domfældelsen, skulle tages for gyldige ved Retsforhandlingen i det andet Land, dersom de vise sig at være underskrevne eller bekræftede af en Dommer, Retsbetjent eller anden Embedsmand i det Land, hvor de ere udstedte eller optagne, under Forudsætning af at de ere bekræftede ved Vidners Ed eller ved at være forsynede med Justitsministerens eller anden Ministers officielle Segl.

ARTIKEL IX.

Udleveringen skal ikke finde Sted, dersom der, efter at Gjerningen er bleven begaaet, eller Anklagen er reist, eller Dommen er fældet, er forlöben saa lang Tid, at Retsforfölgningen eller Straffen er bleven forældet ifölge det Lands Love, hvor den Anklagede eller Domfældte har taget Tilflugt.

ARTIKEL X.

Dersom den Person, som fordres udleveret maatte være under Retsforfölgning eller i Fængsel for en Forbrydelse eller en Forseelse, som er bleven begaaet i det Land, hvor han har taget Tilflugt, kan hans Udlevering udsættes, indtil han atter lovligen er bleven lösladt.

In case he should be proceeded against or detained in such country on account of obligations contracted towards private individuals, his surrender shall nevertheless take place, the injured party retaining his right to prosecute his claims before the competent authority.

Article XI.

Every article found in the possession of the individual claimed at the time of his arrest, shall be seized, in order to be delivered up with his person at the time when the surrender shall be made. Such delivery shall not be limited to the property or articles obtained by stealing or by fraudulent bankruptcy, but shall extend to everything that may serve as proof of the crime. It shall take place even when the surrender, after having been ordered, shall be prevented from taking place by reason of the escape or death of the individual claimed.

Article XII.

Each of the two Contracting Parties shall defray the expenses occasioned by the arrest within its territories, the detention, and the conveyance to its frontier, of the persons whom it may consent to surrender in pursuance of the present Treaty.

Article XIII.

The stipulations of the present Treaty shall be applicable to the Colonies or foreign Possessions of the two High Contracting Parties, in the following manner:—

The requisition for the surrender of a fugitive criminal who has taken refuge in a Colony or foreign Possession of either of the two Contracting Parties, shall be made to the Governor or chief authority of such Colony or Possession by the chief Consular Officer of the other Party in such Colony or Possession; or, if the fugitive has escaped from a Colony or foreign Possession of the Party on whose behalf the requisition is made, by the Governor or chief authority of such Colony or Possession.

Such requisitions may be disposed of, subject always, as nearly

Dersom der maatte være anlagt Sag imod ham, eller dersom han maatte være arresteret i dette Land formedelst Forpligtelser, som han maatte have paadraget sig imod private Personer, skal hans Udlevering ikke destomindre finde Sted, men den formeentlig forurettede Part beholder Ret til at forfölge sin Sag for den kompetente Myndighed.

ARTIKEL XI.

Enhver Gjenstand, som findes i den Persons Besiddelse, der fordres udleveret, paa den Tid, han fængsles, skal tages i Forvaring, for derefter, samtidig med hans Udlevering, at blive afleveret. Denne Aflevering skal ikke indskrænke sig til den Eiendom og de Gjenstande, som ere erhvervede ved Tyveri eller svigagtig Fallit, men skal udstrække sig til enhver Ting, som kan tjene som Bevis for Forbrydelsen. Den skal fremdeles finde Sted, selv om Udleveringen, efterat der er bleven givet Befaling til samme, forhindres paa Grund af den Persons Undvigelse eller Död, som fordres udleveret.

ARTIKEL XII.

Enhver af de to kontraherende Parter skal indenfor sit Territorium betale de Omkostninger, som foranlediges ved Anholdelsen, Fængslingen og Transporten til dens Grændser af de Personer, til hvis Udlevering den ifölge nærværende Traktat maatte give sit Samtykke.

ARTIKEL XIII.

Bestemmelserne i nærværende Traktat skulle komme til Anvendelse paa de to höie kontraherende Parters Kolonier eller Bilande paa fölgende Maade:—

Begjäringen om Udlevering af en undvegen Forbryder, som har taget Tilflugt til en Koloni eller til et Biland, der tilhörer en af de to kontraherende Parter, skal skee til Gouverneuren eller den overordnede Myndighed paa saadan Koloni eller Biland ved den anden Parts överste konsulare Embedsmand i vedkommende Koloni eller Biland, eller, hvis Undvigelsen har fundet Sted fra en Koloni eller et Biland, der tilhörer den Part, i hvis Navn Udleveringen begjæres, ved Gouverneuren eller den överste Myndighed i den paagjældende Koloni eller Biland.

Saadanne Begjæringer om Udlevering kunne afgjöres, dog i saa

as may be, to the provisions of this Treaty, by the respective Governors or chief authorities, who, however, shall be at liberty either to grant the surrender or to refer the matter to their Government.

Her Britannic Majesty and His Majesty the King of Denmark shall, however, be at liberty to make special arrangements in their Colonies and foreign Possessions for the surrender of criminals who may take refuge therein, on the basis, as nearly as may be, of the provisions of the present Treaty.

Article XIV.

The present Treaty shall come into operation ten days after its publication, in conformity with the forms prescribed by the laws of the High Contracting Parties.

After the Treaty shall so have been brought into operation, the Convention concluded between the High Contracting Parties on the 15th of April, 1862, shall be considered as cancelled, except as to any proceeding that may have already been taken or commenced in virtue thereof.

Either Party may at any time terminate the Treaty on giving to the other six months' notice of its intention.

Article XV.

The present Treaty shall be ratified, and the ratification shall be exchanged at Copenhagen as soon as may be within four weeks from the date of signature.

In witness whereof the respective Plenipotentiaries have signed the same, and have affixed thereto the seals of their arms.

Done at Copenhagen, the thirty-first day of March, in the year of Our Lord one thousand eight hundred and seventy-three.

(L.S.) Charles Lennox Wyke.
(L.S.) O. D. Rosenörn-Lehn.

nöje Overeensstemmelse som muligt med Forskrifterne i denne Traktat, af de respektive Gouverneurer eller överste Myndigheder, men det skal dog staae dem frit for enten at samtykke i Udleveringen eller at henvise Sagen til deres Regjeringer.

Hans Majestæt Kongen af Danmark og Hendes Britiske Majestæt skulle dog ogsaa have Ret til at træffe særlige Bestemmelser for deres Koloniers og Bilandes Vedkommende angaaende Udleveringen af de Forbrydere, som maatte tage deres Tilflugt til disse, hvilke Bestemmelser dog skulle holdes saa nær som muligt til Forskrifterne i nærværende Traktat.

Artikel XIV.

Den nærværende Traktat skal træde i Kraft 10 Dage efter dens Offentliggjörelse i Overeensstemmelse med de Former, som ere foreskrevne ved Lovgivningen i hvert af de höie kontraherende Parters Lande.

Naar denne Traktat saaledes er traadt i Kraft, skal den imellem de höie kontraherende Parter under 15 April 1862 afsluttede Konvention ansees som ophævet, undtagen forsaavidt der maatte være bleven foretaget eller paabegyndt noget Skridt i Overeensstemmelse med samme.

Enhver af de to Parter kan til enhver Tid sætte Traktaten ud af Kraft, naar denne Hensigt er bleven meddelt den anden 6 Maaneder i Forveien.

Artikel XV.

Denne Traktat skal ratificeres, og Ratifikationerne skulle udvexles i Kjöbenhavn saasnart som muligt i Löbet af fire Uger fra Traktatens Undertegning.

Til Bekræftelse heraf have de respective Befuldmægtigede undertegnet denne Traktat og paatrykt samme deres Vaabensegl.

Givet i Kjöbenhavn den 31 Marts i Herrens Aar Atten Hundrede og Tre og Halvfjerdssindstyve.

(L.S.) Charles Lennox Wyke.
(L.S.) O. D. Rosenörn-Lehn.

BRAZIL.

TREATY BETWEEN HER MAJESTY AND THE EMPEROR OF BRAZIL, FOR THE MUTUAL SURRENDER OF FUGITIVE CRIMINALS.—*Signed at Rio de Janeiro, November 13,* 1872.

[Ratifications exchanged at Rio de Janeiro, August 28, 1873.]

HER Majesty the Queen of the United Kingdom of Great Britain and Ireland, and His Majesty the Emperor of Brazil, having judged it expedient, with a view to the better administration of justice, and to the prevention of crime within their respective territories and jurisdictions, that persons accused, or convicted, of the crimes hereinafter enumerated, being fugitives from justice, should under certain circumstances be reciprocally delivered up, have resolved to name their Plenipotentiaries for the celebration of a Treaty for this purpose, that is to say:

Her Majesty the Queen of the United Kingdom of Great Britain and Ireland, George Buckley Mathew, Esquire, Companion of the Most Honourable Order of the Bath, Her Envoy Extraordinary and Minister Plenipotentiary to His Majesty the Emperor of Brazil;

And His Majesty the Emperor of Brazil, the Marquis of S. Vicente, a Councillor of State, Dignitary of the Order of the Rose, Senator and Grandee of the Empire;

Who, having communicated to each other their respective full powers, found in good and due form, have agreed upon and concluded the following Articles:—

ARTICLE I.

The High Contracting Parties engage to deliver up, reciprocally, those persons who, being accused or convicted of having committed crime in the territory of the one Party, shall be found within the

Sua Magestade a Rainha do Reino Unido da Grã Bretanha e Irlanda, e Sua Magestade o Imperador do Brazil, julgando conveniente, com o fim de melhorar a administração da justiça e prevenir o crime dentro de seus respectivos territorios e jurisdicções, que as pessoas accusadas ou convictas dos crimes abaixo enumerados, refugiadas do alcance da justiça, sejão reciprocamente entregues, mediante certas circumstancias, resolverão nomear seus Plenipotenciarios para a celebração de um Tractado com esse objecto, a saber:—

Sua Magestade a Rainha do Reino Unido da Grã Bretanha e Irlanda, o Senhor George Buckley Mathew, Cavalleiro da muito honrada Ordem do Banho, Seu Enviado Extraordinario e Ministro Plenipotenciario junto de Sua Magestade o Imperador do Brazil;

E Sua Magestade o Imperador do Brazil, o Marquez de S. Vicente, Conselheiro d'Estado, Dignitario da Ordem da Rosa, Senador e Grande do Imperio;

Os quaes, depois de terem communicado seus respectivos plenos poderes, achados em bôa e devida fórma, ajustárão e accordárão nos seguintes Artigos:—

Artigo I.

As Altas Partes Contractantes se obrigão a entregar reciprocamente os individuos que sendo accusados ou convictos de ter commettido crime no territorio de uma dellas, forem encontrados

territory of the other, under the circumstances and conditions that are laid down in the present Treaty.

Article II.

The crimes for which the extradition shall be granted are the following:—

1. Murder, or attempt to murder.

2. Manslaughter.

3. Illegal fabrication, counterfeiting or falsification, uttering or bringing into circulation counterfeit or falsified money.

4. Forgery, or imitation, counterfeiting or falsification, of any document or paper (comprising the crimes designated in the criminal code of Brazil as imitation, counterfeiting, or falsification of paper money, notes of banks, or other securities public or private, as well as the intentional use or the bringing into circulation of any papers imitated, counterfeited or falsified.

5. The purloining, or embezzlement, of moneys or effects, public or private, by abuse of confidence.

6. Frauds, or false or fraudulent pretences, to obtain moneys or effects from another.

7. Bankruptcies subject to criminal prosecution, according to the laws applicable thereunto.

8. Malversation, or fraud, committed by a bailee, banker, agent, factor, trustee, or director, or member, or officer of any company, made criminal by any law in force.

9. Rape, by force or threats.

10. Abduction.

11. Child-stealing.

12. Housebreaking, with intent to steal, or to commit other crimes.

13. Crimes resulting from the acts of wilfully setting fire to a house, or to buildings connected therewith, to the prejudice of another.

14. Robbery with violence.

15. Piracy according to the law of nations.

16. Sinking or destroying a vessel on the high seas, or the attempt to perpetrate such acts.

no territorio da outra, mediante as circumstancias e condições que são estabelecidas no presente Tractado.

Artigo II.

Os crimes pelos quaes se deverá conceder a extradição são os seguintes :—

1. Homicidio sujeito á pena de morte ("murder"), e tentativa d'elle.

2. Homicidio ("manslaughter").

3. Fabricação illegal, contrafacção ou falsificação de moeda, emittir ou introduzir na circulação moeda contrafeita ou falsificada.

4. O crime de falsidade, ou imitação, contrafacção, ou falsificação de qualquer documento ou papel, comprehendendose os crimes designados na lei criminal do Brazil, de imitação, contrafacção, ou falsificação do papel moeda, notas dos bancos, ou outros titulos publicos ou particulares; assim como o uso premeditado ou introducção na circulação de quaesquer papeis imitados contrafeitos ou falsificados.

5. Subtracção, ou extravio, de dinheiros ou valores publicos ou particulares, com abuso da confiança.

6. Artificios, ou pretextos falsos ou fraudulentos, para acquisição de dinheiros ou valores de outrem.

7. Crimes de banca rota sujeitos ao processo criminal na forma das leis que lhes são applicaveis.

8. Malversação ou fraude commettida por depositario, banqueiro, agente, corrector, curador, director, membro, ou empregado de alguma companhia, considerada crime por lei em vigor.

9. Defloração ou violação ("rape") por violencia óu ameaças.

10. Rapto violento.

11. Subtracção de criança.

12. Arrombamento de caza com o fim de roubar ou para commetter outro crime.

13. Crimes resultantes do incendio voluntario de uma caza, ou de edificios connexos com ella, em prejuizo de outrem.

14. Roubo.

15. Pirataria segundo o direito das gentes.

16. Destruição de navio no alto mar, ou facto de mettel-o a pique, ou tentativa de taes actos.

17. Crimes arising from assault on board a ship on the high seas, with intent to cause death or grievous bodily injuries.

18. Crimes arising from the revolt of two or more persons on board a ship on the high seas against the authority of the captain.

19. Extradition will also take place for participation in any of the above-named crimes, provided that such participation shall be punishable by the laws of both the States of the High Contracting Powers.

Article III.

No British subject shall be delivered up by the Government or authorities of the United Kingdom to the Government or authorities of the Empire; and in like manner no Brazilian subject shall be delivered up by the Government or authorities of the Empire to the Government or authorities of the United Kingdom.

If, however, the person who has taken refuge in the territory of the other High Contracting Party shall have become naturalized there after the perpetration of the crime, such naturalization shall not be an obstacle to his extradition according to the stipulations of this Treaty.

Article IV.

The extradition shall not take place if the person claimed has already been tried and acquitted, or punished, or if he is under trial, for the same crime for which extradition is asked. If he should be under trial for any other crime, his extradition shall be deferred until the conclusion of the trial, and the fulfilment of the punishment, when such may have been awarded.

Article V.

The extradition shall also not take place if, after the perpetration of the crime, or the institution of the penal prosecution, or the conviction thereon, the refugee shall have acquired exemption from prosecution or punishment by lapse of time according to the laws of the State appealed to.

Article VI.

The person claimed shall not be delivered up for crimes of a political character, and when he shall have been delivered up on other grounds he shall not be punished for anterior political crimes.

17. Crimes resultantes de assalto a bordo de um navio no alto mar, com intenção de causar a morte, ou graves offensas physicas.

18. Crimes resultantes da revolta por duas ou mais pessoas de bordo de um navio em alto mar contra a auctoridade do capitão.

19. A extradição terá tambem logar por cumplicidade em algum dos crimes acima declarados, uma vez que tal cumplicidade seja punivel pelas leis de ambos os Estados das Altas Partes Contractantes.

Artigo III.

Nem um subdito Britannico será entregue pelo Governo ou auctoridades do Reino Unido ao Governo ou auctoridades do Imperio; e semelhantemente nem um subdito Brasileiro será entregue pelo Governo ou auctoridades do Imperio ao Governo ou auctoridades do Reino Unido.

Entretanto si o refugiado no territorio da outra Alta Parte Contractante ahi se tivesse naturalizado depois da perpetração do crime, tal naturalisação não servirá de obstaculo a extradição segundo as estipulações deste Tractado.

Artigo IV.

A extradição não terá logar si o individuo reclamado já tiver sido processado, e absolvido, ou punido, ou si estiver sendo processado, pelo mesmo crime pelo qual se pede e extradição. Si estiver sendo processado por outro qualquer crime, a sua extradição será demorada até a conclusão do processo, e cumprimento da pena, quando lhe tenha sido imposta.

Artigo V.

A extradição não terá tambem logar, si depois da perpetração do crime, ou da instauração do processo criminal, ou da sentença condemnatoria, tiver o refugiado adquirido, por meio da prescripção, segundo as leis do paiz ao qual se fez o pedido, a isenção da accusação ou da punição.

Artigo VI.

O reclamado não será entregue por crimes de caracter politico, e quando for entregue por outros fundamentos não poderá ser punido por crimes politicos anteriores. Não será tambem entregue si elle

He shall not, moreover, be delivered up if he can clearly prove that the requisition is made with the object of trying him, or of punishing him, for a political crime.

ARTICLE VII.

A person surrendered cannot be kept in prison, or brought to trial, in the State to which the surrender is made, for any other crime, or on account of any other matters than those for which the extradition has been granted. This statement is not applicable to crimes committed after the extradition.

ARTICLE VIII.

If the person whose extradition is demanded by one of the High Contracting Parties shall be also claimed by one or more other Governments, on account of crimes committed in their respective territories, the following rule shall be observed:

If he shall be a subject of the High Contracting Party who claims him, the surrender shall be made to it. If he be not so, the other High Contracting Party shall have the power of delivering him up to the reclaiming Government which in the case in question may appear to the former best entitled to the preference.

ARTICLE IX.

A requisition for extradition shall be made through the respective Diplomatic Agents of the High Contracting Powers.

When it relates to a person accused only, it must be accompanied by the warrant of arrest, issued by the competent authority of the State applying for it, and by such evidence as, according to the laws of the place where the accused is found, would justify the arrest if the crime was there committed.

If the extradition refers to a person already convicted, the application must be accompanied by a copy of the sentence of condemnation passed against him, given by a competent tribunal of the State making the requisition.

The requisition cannot, however, be founded on a sentence passed *in contumaciam*, that is to say, when the delinquent has not been personally cited to defend himself.

evidentemente provar que a requisição é feito com o fim de processal-õ ou punil-o por crime politico.

Artigo VII.

O individuo entregue não poderá ser conservado preso ou submettido a processo no Estado ao qual se fez a entrega por outro crime, ou em virtude de outras causas que não sejão aquellas pelas quaes se conceden a extradição. Esta estipulação não é applicavel aos crimes commettidos depois da extradição.

Artigo VIII.

Si o individuo cuja extradição uma das Altas Partes Contractantes pedir, for igualmente reclamado por outro ou outros Governos, em consequencia de crimes commettidos nos seus respectivos territorios, observar-se ha o seguinte:

Si for subdito da Alta Parte Contractante que o reclamar, a entrega será feita a ella. Si não for, a outra Alta Parte Contractante terá a faculdade de éntregal-o ao Governo reclamante que no caso dado lhe pareça que deve ter a preferencia.

Artigo IX.

A requisição para a extradição será feita por intermedio dos respectivos Agentes Diplomaticos das Altas Partes Contractantes.

Si ella referir-se a um individuo sómente accusado, devrá ser acompanhada do mandado de prisão expedido pela auctoridade competente do Estado que a solicitar, e de prouvas que segundo as leis do logar onde o accusado for encontrado justificassem a captura quando o crime fosse ahi commettido.

Si a extradição referir-se a um individuo já sentenciado, o pedido deverá ser acompanhado do traslado da sentença condemnatoria expedida contra elle pelo Tribunal competente do Estado que fizer a requisição.

A reclamação não pode porem ser fundada em sentença proferida *in contumaciam*, isto é, quando o reo não for pessoalmente citado para defender-se.

Article X.

If the requisition has been in conformity with the foregoing stipulations, the competent authorities of the State to which it has been addressed shall proceed to the capture of the refugee. The prisoner shall be brought before a competent authority, who is to examine him and conduct the preliminary investigations of the case just as if the apprehension had taken place for crime committed in the same country.

Article XI.

The extradition shall in no case take place before the expiration of fifteen days, counted from the apprehension, and after that delay it shall only be carried out when the evidence has been found sufficient according to the laws of the country applied to, either for subjecting the prisoner to trial if the crime had been there committed, or to prove the identity of the person convicted and condemned by the Tribunals of the State making the requisition.

Article XII.

In the examinations which are to be made in conformity with the foregoing stipulations, the authorities of the State to which application is made shall admit as valid evidence the sworn depositions or declarations of witnesses which were taken in the other State, or the respective copies thereof, as well as the judicial documents, warrants or sentences, transmitted therefrom, provided they are signed or certified by the hand of the Judge, Magistrate, or public officer of that State, and authenticated either by the oath of some witness or by the official seal of the Minister of Justice or some other Minister of State.

Article XIII.

If within two months, counting from the date of arrest, sufficient evidence for the extradition shall not have been presented, the person arrested shall be set at liberty. He shall likewise be set at liberty if, within two months of the day on which he was placed at the disposal of the Diplomatic Agent, he shall not have been sent off to the reclaiming country.

ARTIGO X.

Si a requisição estiver de conformidade com as anteriores estipulações, a auctoridade competente do Estado a que ella se tiver dirigido procederá á captura do refugiado. O preso será levado á presença da auctoridade competente, que terá de examinal-o, e de dirigir as investigações preliminares do cazo como si a captura fosse effeituada por crime commettido no mesmo paiz.

ARTIGO XI.

A extradição nunca terá logar antes da expiração de 15 dias contados da captura, e depois d'esse prazo só se effeituará quando as provas forem julgadas sufficientes segundo as leis do paiz á que for pedida, ou seja para sujeitar o preso á processo si o crime fosse ahi commettido, ou seja para justificar a identidade da pessoa convicta e condemnada pelos tribunaes do Estado que fez a requisição.

ARTIGO XII.

Nos exames á que se tiver de proceder de conformidade com as precedentes estipulações, as auctoridades do Estado, á que se fez o pedido, admittirão como provas os depoimentos sob juramento, ou as declarações, das testemunhas, que forão tomadas no outro Estado ou as respectivas copias, assim como os documentos judiciaes, mandados, ou sentenças, expedidos d'allí, com tanto que sejão assignados ou legalisados pela propria mão do juiz, magistrado ou empregado publico d'aquelle Estado, e authenticados ou por juramento de alguma testemunha ou com o sello official do Ministro da Justiça, ou de qualquer outro Ministro d'Estado,

ARTIGO XIII.

Si dentro de dous mezes contados da data da captura, não forem apresentadas provas sufficientes para que se realise a extradição, o preso será posto em liberdade. Tambem será posto em liberdade si, dentro de dous mezes contados do dia em que for declarado que está á disposição do Agente Diplomatico, este não o tiver remettido para o Estado reclamante.

Article XIV.

All the articles found in the possession of the person demanded, at the time of his apprehension, shall be seized in order to their delivery with him when his extradition shall take place.

This delivery shall not be limited to effects or articles robbed, stolen, or obtained by other crimes, but shall extend to all that might serve as evidence of the crime: it shall be made even when the extradition could not be made after orders to that effect, on account of the flight or death of the person claimed.

Article XV.

The High Contracting Parties renounce whatever claims they may have for the reimbursement of the expenses incurred for the apprehension and maintenance of the persons to be delivered up, and for their conveyance until they shall be placed on board ship; as they agree to defray these outgoings in their respective countries.

Article XVI.

The stipulations of the present Treaty shall apply to the Colonies and other Possessions of Her Britannic Majesty.

The requisition for the surrender shall be made to the Governor, or to the chief authority, in the Colony or Possession, by the highest Consular Agent of Brazil.

The surrender shall be made by the Governor or the chief authority, who shall however have the power either to make it or to refer the matter to his Government.

Both in the requisitions and in the surrender, the conditions established by the foregoing Articles of this Treaty shall be, as far as may be possible, adhered to.

As Her Britannic Majesty has the power to adopt special arrangements in the Colonies and Possessions respecting the delivering up of delinquents, Her Majesty will facilitate the reclamations of Brazil in this respect as far as may be possible, with due regard, however, to the provisions of this Treaty.

Article XVII.

The present Treaty shall come into force ten days after its

Artigo XIV.

Todos os objectos encontrados em poder do individuo reclamado, ao tempo de sua prisão, serão apprehendidos afim de serem entregues com o individuo quando se verifique sua extradição.

Essa entrega não se limitará ás propriedades ou artigos furtados, roubados, ou obtidos por outros crimes, mas se extenderá á tudo quanto possa servir para a prova do crime: ella terá logar ainda quando a extradição depois de ordenada não se possa verificar por fuga ou morte do individuo reclamado.

Artigo XV.

As Altas Partes Contractantes renuncião quaesquer reclamações que tenhão por fim o reembolso das despezas feitas com a prisão e manutenção dos individuos que tem de ser entregues, e com a sua conducção até serem postos á bordo, por isso que concordão fazer essas despezas em seus paizes reciprocamente.

Artigo XVI.

As estipulações do presente Tractado serão applicaveis ás colonias e outras possessões de Sua Magestade Britannica.

A requisição para a entrega será feita ao Governador, ou á auctoridade principal, da colonia ou possessão, pelo respectivo Agente Consular mais graduado do Imperio do Brazil.

A entrega será feita pelo Governador ou auctoridade principal, a qual todavia terá faculdade de realisal-a, ou de submetter o assumpto ao seu Governo.

Tanto na requisição como na entrega, observar-se ha, quanto possivel, as regras estabelecidas nos precedentes Artigos deste Tractado.

Como Sua Magestade Britannica tem a faculdade de adoptar disposições especiaes quanto ás colonias e possessões, em relação á entrega de delinquentes, Sua Magestade facilitará as reclamações do Brazil a semelhante respeito, quanto possivel, cingindose todavia as bases deste Tractado.

Artigo XVII.

O presente Tractado começará á vigorar dez dias depois de sua

publication, and in conformity with the forms prescribed by the laws of the countries of the High Contracting Parties. It will remain in force until one of these shall give notice for its termination, but it shall then remain in force for six months, counted from the day of this notification.

This Treaty shall be ratified and the ratifications exchanged in Rio de Janeiro within three months, or sooner if possible.

In witness whereof the respective Plenipotentiaries have signed the present Treaty, and have affixed thereto the seal of their arms.

Done at Rio de Janeiro, on the thirteenth day of the month of November, of the year of our Lord Jesus Christ one thousand eight hundred and seventy-two.

(L.S.) GEORGE BUCKLEY MATHEW.
(L.S.) MARQUEZ DE S. VICENTE.

The Undersigned, Plenipotentiaries of Her Majesty the Queen of the United Kingdom of Great Britain and Ireland, and of His Majesty the Emperor of Brazil, charged with making a Treaty for the extradition of criminals, upon which they have at this present agreed, having met in conference, took into their consideration the following subjects:—

They directed their attention to the fact that the criminal law of England punishes the crime of infanticide with the same penalty as that of murder, when accompanied by corresponding circumstances, and that it results therefrom that extradition should take place even for attempting to commit that crime.

On the other hand, they observed, that according to the Brazilian law, infanticide is not punished as murder, nor even as manslaughter, but as a crime distinct from both, and by a minor punishment, and that consequently extradition should not take place for the attempt.

They consequently resolved to declare that extradition shall solely take place for the crime of infanticide, and not for an attempt to commit that crime.

publicação, e de conformidade com as formulas prescriptas pelas leis dos Estados das Altas Partes Contractantes. Elle perdurará até que qualquer d'ellas denuncie a sua cessação, mas ainda então terá vigor por seis mezes contados do dia de tal notificação.

Este Tractado será ratificado, e as ratificações trocadas no Rio de Janeiro dentro de trez mezes, ou antes si for possivel.

Em testemunho do que os respectivos Plenipotenciarios assegnárão o presente Tractado, e lhe pozerão o sello de suas armas.

Feito no Rio de Janeiro aos treze dias do mez de Novembro do anno de Nosso Senhor Jesus Christo de mil oitocentos e setenta e dois.

(L.S.) GEORGE BUCKLEY MATHEW.
(L.S.) MARQUEZ DE S. VICENTE.

Reunidos em conferencia os Plenipotenciarios de Sua Magestade a Rainha do Reino Unido da Grã Bretanha e Irlanda, e de Sua Magestade o Imperador do Brazil, abaixo assignados, encarregados de ajustar um Tractado de extradição de delinquentes, em que nesta data accordarão, tomarão em consideração a seguinte materia:—

Ponderou-se que a lei criminal Ingleza pune o crime de infanticidio com a mesma pena do crime de *murder*, quando acompanhado das circumstancias deste, e que dahi resulta ter lugar a extradição mesmo por tentativa.

Por outro lado ponderou-se que segundo a lei Brasileira, o infanticidio não é punido como o homicidio sujeito á pena de morte, nem mesmo como homicidio, sim como crime distincto d'elles, e com pena menor, e que consequentemente não deve ter lugar a extradição por tentativa.

Resolverão pois declarar que a extradição só poderá verificar-se pelo crime de infanticidio, e não pela tentativa d'elle.

With this declaration they agreed to close this conference, from which the present Protocol emanates, which being found in conformity, was signed, each having a copy thereof.

Done in the city of Rio de Janeiro, the thirteenth day of November of 1872.

(L.S.) GEORGE BUCKLEY MATHEW.
(L.S.) MARQUEZ DE S. VICENTE.

Com esta declaração entenderão terminar esta conferencia, da qual se lavrou o presente Protocollo, que depois de achar-se conforme foi assignado, ficando cada um com o seu exemplar.

Feito na Corte do Rio de Janeiro aos treze dias de Novembro de 1872.

(L.S.) GEORGE BUCKLEY MATHEW.
(L.S.) MARQUEZ DE S. VICENTE.

SWEDEN AND NORWAY.

TREATY BETWEEN HER MAJESTY AND THE KING OF SWEDEN AND NORWAY, FOR THE MUTUAL SURRENDER OF FUGITIVE CRIMINALS.—*Signed at Stockholm, June* 26, 1873.

[Ratifications exchanged at Stockholm, August 28, 1873.]

HER Majesty the Queen of the United Kingdom of Great Britain and Ireland, and His Majesty the King of Sweden and Norway, having judged it expedient, with a view to the better administration of justice and to the more complete prevention of crime within the respective countries, that persons charged with or convicted of the crimes hereinafter enumerated, and being fugitives from justice, should, under certain circumstances, be reciprocally delivered up; Their said Majesties have named as their Plenipotentiaries to conclude a Treaty for this purpose, that is to say:

Her Majesty the Queen of the United Kingdom of Great Britain and Ireland, The Honourable Edward Morris Erskine, a Companion of the Most Honourable Order of the Bath, Her Majesty's Envoy Extraordinary and Minister Plenipotentiary to His Majesty the King of Sweden and Norway;

And His Majesty the King of Sweden and Norway, Henrick Wilhelm Bredberg, Grand Cross of the Order of the Polar Star, His Majesty's Councillor of State and Acting Minister for Foreign Affairs;

Who, after having communicated to each other their respective full powers, found in good and due form, have agreed upon and concluded the following Articles:—

ARTICLE I.

The High Contracting Parties engage to deliver up to each other those persons who, being accused or convicted of a crime committed in the territory of the one Party, shall be found within the territory of the other Party, under the circumstances and conditions stated in the present Treaty.

ARTICLE II.

The crimes for which the extradition is to be granted are the following:—

1. Murder (child murder and poisoning included) or attempt to murder.

2. Manslaughter.

3. Counterfeiting or altering money, uttering or bringing into circulation knowingly counterfeit or altered money.

4. Forgery, or counterfeiting, or altering, or uttering what is forged, or counterfeited, or altered, comprehending the crimes designated in the Swedish and Norwegian penal codes as counterfeiting or falsification of paper money, bank notes, or other securities, forgery or falsification of other public or private documents, likewise the uttering or bringing into circulation or wilfully using such counterfeited, forged, or falsified papers.

5. Embezzlement or larceny.

6. Obtaining money or goods by false pretences, except as regards Norway, cases in which the crime is not accompanied by aggravating circumstances according to the law of that country.

7. Crimes by bankrupts against bankruptcy law.

8. Fraud by a bailee, banker, agent, factor, trustee, or director, or member or public officer of any company, made criminal by any law for the time being in force.

9. Rape.

10. Abduction.

11. Child stealing.

12. Burglary or housebreaking.

13. Arson.

14. Robbery with violence.

15. Threats by letter or otherwise with intent to extort, except as regards Norway, cases in which this crime is not punishable by the laws of that country.

16. Sinking or destroying a vessel at sea, or attempting to do so.

17. Assaults on board a ship on the high seas with intent to destroy life or to do grievous bodily harm.

18. Revolt, or conspiracy to revolt, by two or more persons on board a ship on the high seas against the authority of the master; except, as regards Norway, conspiracy to revolt.

The extradition is also to take place for participation in any of the aforesaid crimes, provided such participation be punishable by the laws of both the Contracting Parties.

ARTICLE III.

No Swedish or Norwegian subject shall be delivered up to the Government of the United Kingdom; and no subject of the United Kingdom shall be delivered up to the Swedish or Norwegian Government.

ARTICLE IV.

The extradition shall not take place if the person claimed has already been tried and discharged or punished, or is still under trial in the country where he has taken refuge, for the crime for which his extradition is demanded.

If the person claimed should be under examination for any other crime in the country where he has taken refuge, his extradition shall be deferred until the conclusion of the trial, and the full execution of any punishment awarded to him.

ARTICLE V.

The extradition shall not take place if, subsequently to the commission of the crime, or the institution of the penal prosecution, or the conviction thereon, exemption from prosecution or punishment has been acquired by lapse of time, according to the laws of the country where the criminal has taken refuge.

ARTICLE VI.

A fugitive criminal shall not be surrendered if the offence in respect of which his surrender is demanded is one of a political character, or if he prove that the requisition for his surrender has in fact been made with a view to try or punish him for an offence of a political character.

ARTICLE VII.

A person surrendered by either of the High Contracting Parties to the other, cannot, until he has been restored or had an opportunity of returning to the country from whence he was surrendered, be triable or tried for any crime committed in the other country other than that on account of which the extradition shall have taken place.

This stipulation does not apply to crimes committed after the extradition.

ARTICLE VIII.

The requisitions for extradition shall be made through the Diplomatic Agents of the High Contracting Parties respectively.

The requisition for the extradition of an accused person must be accompanied by a warrant of arrest issued by the competent authority of the State requiring the extradition, and by such evidence as, according to the laws of the place where the accused is found, would justify his arrest if the crime had been committed there.

If the requisition relates to a person already convicted, it must be accompanied by the sentence of condemnation passed against the convicted person by the competent Court of the State that makes the requisition for extradition.

The requisition ought, as far as possible, to be accompanied by a description of the person accused or convicted, in order to identify him.

A requisition for extradition cannot be founded on sentences passed *in contumaciam*.

ARTICLE IX.

If the requisition for extradition be in accordance with the foregoing stipulations, the competent authorities of the State applied to shall proceed to the arrest of the fugitive.

The prisoner is then to be brought before a competent magistrate, who is to examine him and to conduct the preliminary investigation of the case, just as if the apprehension had taken place for a crime committed in the same country.

The extradition shall not take place before the expiration of fifteen days from the apprehension, and then only if the evidence be found sufficient, according to the laws of the State applied to, either to justify the committal of the prisoner for trial, or to prove that the prisoner is the identical person convicted by the Courts of the State which makes the requisition.

ARTICLE X.

In the examinations which they have to make, in accordance with the foregoing stipulations, the authorities of the State applied to shall admit as entirely valid evidence the sworn depositions or statements of witnesses taken in the other State, or copies thereof, and likewise the warrants and sentences issued therein, provided such documents are signed or certified by a Judge, Magistrate, or officer of such State, and are authenticated by the oath of some witness, or by being sealed with the official seal of the Minister of Justice or some other Minister of State.

Article XI.

If sufficient evidence for the extradition be not produced within two months from the date of the apprehension of the fugitive, he shall be set at liberty.

Article XII.

All articles seized, which were in the possession of the person to be surrendered at the time of his apprehension, shall, if the competent authority of the State applied to for the extradition has ordered the delivery thereof, be given up when the extradition takes place; and the said delivery shall extend not merely to the stolen articles, but to everything that may serve as a proof of the crime.

Article XIII.

Each of the High Contracting Parties shall defray and bear expenses incurred by it in the arrest, maintenance and conveyance of the individual to be surrendered till placed on board ship, as well as in keeping and conveying the articles which are to be delivered up in conformity with the stipulations of the preceding Article.

The individual to be surrendered shall be conveyed to the port specified by the applying Government, at whose expense he shall be taken on board the ship to convey him away.

If it be necessary to convey the individual claimed through the territories of another State, the expenses incurred thereby shall be defrayed by the applying State.

Article XIV.

The stipulations of the present Treaty shall be applicable to the Colonies and foreign Possessions of the two High Contracting Parties.

The requisition for the surrender of a fugitive criminal who has taken refuge in a Colony or foreign Possession of either Party, shall be made to the Governor or chief authority of such Colony or Possession by the chief Consular Officer of the other in such Colony or Possession; or, if the fugitive has escaped from a Colony or foreign Possession of the Party on whose behalf the requisition is made, by the Governor or chief authority of such Colony or Possession.

Such requisitions may be disposed of, subject always, as nearly as may be, to the provisions of this Treaty, by the respective Governors or chief authorities, who, however, shall be at liberty either to grant the surrender or to refer the matter to their Government.

Her Britannic Majesty shall, however, be at liberty to make special arrangements in the British Colonies and foreign Possessions for the surrender of Swedish and Norwegian criminals who may there take refuge, on the basis, as nearly as may be, of the provisions of the present Treaty.

Article XV.

The present Treaty shall come into force ten days after its publication, in conformity with the forms prescribed by the laws of the High Contracting Parties. It may be terminated by either of the High Contracting Parties, but shall remain in force for six months after notice has been given for its termination.

Article XVI.

The present Treaty shall be ratified, and the ratifications shall be exchanged at Stockholm, as soon as may be possible.

In witness whereof the respective Plenipotentiaries have signed the same, and have affixed thereto their seals.

Done at Stockholm, the 26th day of June, in the year of our Lord one thousand eight hundred and seventy-three.

(L.S.) E. M. Erskine.
(L.S.) H. W. Bredberg.

AUSTRIA.

ORDER IN COUNCIL, DATED 17TH MARCH, 1874.

WHEREAS by an Act of Parliament made and passed in the Session of Parliament holden in the thirty-third and thirty-fourth years of the reign of Her present Majesty, intituled "An Act for Amending the Law relating to the Extradition of Criminals," it was amongst other things enacted, that where an arrangement has been made with any foreign State with respect to the surrender to such State of any fugitive criminals, Her Majesty may, by Order in Council, direct that the said Act shall apply in the case of such foreign State; and that Her Majesty may, by the same or any subsequent Order, limit the operation of the Order, and restrict the same to fugitive criminals who are in or suspected of being in the part of Her Majesty's dominions specified in the Order, and render the operation thereof subject to such conditions, exceptions, and qualifications as may be deemed expedient:

And whereas a Treaty was concluded on the third day of December last between Her Majesty and the Emperor of Austria, King of Bohemia, &c., &c., and Apostolic King of Hungary, for the Mutual Extradition of Fugitive Criminals, which Treaty is in the terms following:—

Her Majesty the Queen of the United Kingdom of Great Britain and Ireland, and His Majesty the Emperor of Austria, King of Bohemia, &c., &c., &c., and Apostolic King of Hungary, having judged it expedient, with a view to the better administration of justice and to the prevention of crime within the two countries and their jurisdictions, that persons charged with or convicted of the crimes hereinafter enumerated, and being fugitives from justice, should, under certain circumstances, be reciprocally delivered up; Their said Majesties have named as their Plenipotentiaries to conclude a Treaty for this purpose, that is to say:

Her Majesty the Queen of the United Kingdom of Great Britain and Ireland, the Right Honourable Sir Andrew Buchanan, a Member of Her Majesty's Most Honourable Privy Council, Knight Grand Cross of the Most Honourable Order of the Bath, Her Majesty's Ambassador Extraordinary and Plenipotentiary to His Imperial and Royal Apostolic Majesty;

And His Imperial and Royal Apostolic Majesty, the Count Julius Andrassy of Csik-Szent-Király and Kraszna Horka, His Imperial and Royal Majesty's Privy Councillor, Minister of the Imperial House and of Foreign Affairs, Grand Cross of the Order of St. Stephen, &c.;

Who, after having communicated to each other their respective full powers, found in good and due form, have agreed upon and concluded the following Articles:—

Article I.

The High Contracting Parties engage to deliver up to each other those persons who, being accused or convicted of a crime committed in the territory of the one Party, shall be found within the territory of the other Party, under the circumstances and conditions stated in the present Treaty.

Article II.

The crimes for which the extradition is to be granted are the following:—

1. Murder, or attempt to murder.

NACHDEM Ihre Majestät die Königin des Vereinigten Königreiches von Grossbritannien und Irland, und Seine Majestät der Kaiser von Oesterreich König von Böhmen U. S. W. und Apostolischer König von Ungarn behufs besserer Verwaltung der Rechtspflege und zur Verhütung von Verbrechen innerhalb der beiden Reiche und deren Gerichtsbarkeiten es für zweckmässig befunden haben, dass Personen, welche der in diesem Vertrage aufgeführten strafbaren Handlungen beschuldigt oder wegen solcher Handlungen verurtheilt und vor der Justiz flüchtig geworden sind, unter bestimmten Umständen gegenseitig ausgeliefert werden sollen; so haben Ihre eben gedachten Majestäten behufs Abschliessung eines solchen Vertrages zu Ihren Bevollmächtigten ernannt, nämlich:

Ihre Majestät die Königin des Vereinigten Königreichs von Grossbritannien und Irland den Sehr Ehrenwerthen Sir Andrew Buchanan, Mitglied Ihrer Majestät Höchstehrenwerthen Geheimen Rathes, Grosskreuz des Höchstehrenwerthen Bath-Ordens, Allerhöchstehren ausserordentlichen und bevollmächtigten Botschafter bei Seiner Kaiserlichen und Königlich Apostolischen Majestät;

Und Seine Kaiserliche und Königlich Apostolische Majestät, den Herrn Julius Grafen Andrássy von Csik-Szent-Király und Kraszna Horka, Allerhöchstehren wirklichen geheimen Rath, Minister des Kaiserlichen Hauses und des Aeussern, Grosskreuz des St. Stefan-Ordens, etc.;

Welche, nachdem sie sich gegenseitig ihre Vollmachten mitgetheilt und dieselben in guter und gehöriger Form befunden, die folgenden Artikel vereinbart und abgeschlossen haben:—

ARTIKEL I.

Die hohen vertragschliessenden Theile verpflichten sich einander diejenigen Personen auszuliefern, welche wegen einen, auf dem Gebiete des einen Theiles begangenen strafbaren Handlung beschuldig oder verurtheilt sind und in dem Gebiete des anderen Theiles aufgefunden werden, soferne die in dem gegenwärtigen Vertrage angegebenen Fälle und Voraussetzungen vorhanden sind.

ARTIKEL II.

Die strafbaren Handlungen, wegen deren die Auslieferung zu gewähren ist, sind folgende:—

1. Mord, Mordversuch.

2. Manslaughter.

3. Counterfeiting or altering money, uttering or bringing into circulation counterfeit or altered money.

4. Forgery or counterfeiting or altering, or uttering what is forged or counterfeited or altered; comprehending the crimes designated in the Austrian Penal Laws or in the Hungarian Penal Laws and Customs as counterfeiting or falsification of paper money, bank notes, or other securities, forgery or falsification of other public or private documents, likewise the uttering or bringing into circulation, or wilfully using such counterfeited, forged, or falsified papers.

The definition is to be determined accordingly with the Austrian Penal Laws if the extradition shall take place from Austria, and accordingly with the Hungarian Penal Laws and Customs if the extradition shall take place from Hungary.

5. Embezzlement or larceny.

6. Obtaining money or goods by false pretences.

7. Crimes against bankruptcy law: comprehending the crimes considered as frauds committed by the bankrupt in connection with the bankruptcy, according with the Austrian Penal Laws if the extradition shall take place from Austria, and with the Hungarian Penal Laws if the extradition shall take place from Hungary.

8. Fraud by a bailee, banker, agent, factor, trustee, or director or member or public officer of any company, made criminal by any law for the time being in force.

9. Rape.

10. Abduction.

11. Child stealing, kidnapping, and false imprisonment.

12. Burglary or housebreaking.

13. Arson.

2. Todtschlag.

3. Nachmachen oder Verfälschen von Metallgeld, Verausgabung oder Inverkehrbringen nachgemachten oder verfälschten Metallgeldes.

4. Fälschen oder nachmachen oder Verändern, oder Inverkehrbringen von Gefälschtem oder Nachgemachtem, oder Verändertem umfassend alle Verbrechen, welche nach den oesterreichischen Strafgesetzen oder nach den ungarischen Strafgesetzen und Gewohnheiten als Nachmachen oder Verfälschen von Papiergeld, Banknoten oder anderen Werthpapieren, Nachmachung oder Verfälschung anderer öffentlichen oder Privat-Urkunden, imgleichen Verausgabung oder Inverkehrbringen oder wissentliches Gebrauchen solcher nachgemachten oder gefälschten Papiere bezeichnet sind. Der Begriff ist nach den oesterreichischen Strafgesetzen festzustellen, wenn die Auslieferung aus Oesterreich erfolgen soll, und nach ungarischen Strafgesetzen und Gewohnheiten wenn die Auslieferung aus Oesterreich erfolgen soll, und nach ungarischen Strafgesetzen und Gewohnheiten wenn die Auslieferung aus Ungarn erfolgen soll.

5. Diebstahl und Unterschlagung (Veruntreuung.)

6. Erlangung von Geld oder andern Sachen durch falsche Vorspiegelungen (Betrug).

7. Betrügerischer Bankerott, umfassend die Verbrechen, welche, wenn die Auslieferung aus Oesterreich Platz greifen soll, nach den oesterreichischen Strafgesetzen, und wenn die Auslieferung aus Ungarn Platz greifen soll, nach den ungarischen Strafgesetzen als ein, von dem Gemeinschuldner in Zusammenhange mit dem Bankerott verübter Betrug anzusehen sind.

8. Untreue Seitens eines Verwalters und Beauftragten, Banquiers, Agenten, Prokuristen, Vormundes oder Curators, Vorstandes, Mitgliedes oder Beamten irgend einen Gesellschaft, soweit diese Untreue nach den bestehenden Gesetzen mit Strafe bedroht ist.

9. Nothzucht.

10. Entführung.

11. Kinderraub, Menschenraub, unbefugte Einschränkung der persönlichen Freiheit eines Menschen.

12. Einbrechen und Eindringen in ein Wohnhaus oder dazu gehöriges Nebengebäude mit der Absicht, ein Verbrechen zu begehen, zur Tageszeit (housebreaking) oder Nachtzeit (burglary).

13. Vorsätzliche Brandstiftung (Brandlegung).

14. Robbery with violence or with menaces.

15. Threats by letter or otherwise with intent to extort.

16. Sinking or destroying a vessel at sea, or attempting to do so.

17. Assaults on board a ship on the high seas with intent to destroy life or to do grievous bodily harm.

18. Revolt, or conspiracy to revolt, by two or more persons on board a ship on the high seas, against the authority of the master.

19. Perjury or subornation of perjury.

20. Malicious injury to property, if the offence be indictable.

The extradition is also to take place for participation in any of the aforesaid crimes, as accessory either before or after the fact, provided such participation be punishable by the laws of both the Contracting Parties.

In all these cases the extradition will only take place from the Austro-Hungarian States when the crimes, if committed in Austria, would, according to Austrian law, constitute a "verbrechen," or, if committed in Hungary, would, according to the laws and customs being in force in Hungary, constitute a crime ("buntett"); the extradition from Great Britain only when the crimes, if committed in England, or within English jurisdiction, would constitute an extradition crime, as described in the Extradition Acts of 1870 and 1873.

Article III.

In no case and on no grounds whatever shall the High Contracting Parties be held to concede the extradition of their own subjects.

Article IV.

The extradition shall not take place if the person claimed on the part of the Government of the United Kingdom, or the person

14. Raub mit Anwendung von Gewaltthätigkeiten oder Drossungen.

15. Erpressungen.

16. Vorsätzliche Versenkung oder Zerstörung eines Schiffes zur See, oder Versuch dieses Verbrechens.

17. Angriffe auf Personen an Bord eines Schiffes auf hoher See in der Absicht zu tödten oder eine schwere Körperverletzung zu verüben.

18. Widerstand mit Thätlichkeiten (*revolt*) gegen den Schiffsführer an Bord eines Schiffes auf hoher See, wenn dieser von zwei oder mehreren Personen verübt wird, oder Verschwörung zu einem solchen Widerstande.

19. Falsche eidliche Aussage, Verleitung zu derselben.

20. Boshafte Beschädigung fremden Eigenthums, insoferne sie nicht blos als Uebertretung strafbar ist.

Die Auslieferung findet auch wegen Betheiligung an einer der vorbezeichneten strafbaren Handlungen statt, ohne Unterschied, ob die Betheiligung vor oder nach der That erfolgte, jedoch nur unter der Voraussetzung, dass sie nach den Gesetzen beider vertragschliessenden Theile als Verbrechen strafbar sei.

In allen diesen Fällen findet die Auslieferung aus den oesterreichisch-ungarischen Staaten nur dann Statt wenn die strafbaren Handlungen, falls sie in Oesterreich begangen worden wären, nach dem oesterreichischen Gesetze ein Verbrechen begründen, oder falls sie in Ungarn begangen worden wären, nach den in Ungarn in Geltung stehenden Gesetzen und Gewohnheiten ein Verbrechen (büntett) begründen, die Auslieferung aus Grossbritannien aber nur dann, wenn die strafbare Handlung, falls sie in England oder innerhalb der Englischen Jurisdiktion begangen worden wäre, ein Auslieferungsverbrechen in Sinne der Extraditions Akte von 1870 und 1873 begründen würde.

Artikel III.

In keinem Falle und aus keinem Grunde sollen die hohen vertragsschliessenden Theile gehalten sein, die Auslieferung der eigenen Unterthanen zuzugestehen.

Artikel IV.

Die Auslieferung soll nicht stattfinden wenn die Person, deren Auslieferung aus Oesterreich-Ungarn verlangt wird, in einem der

claimed on the part of the Government of Austria-Hungary, has already been tried and discharged or punished, or is still under trial, in the Austro-Hungarian dominions, or in the United Kingdom respectively, for the crime for which his extradition is demanded.

If the person claimed on the part of the Government of the United Kingdom, or if the person claimed on the part of the Government of Austria-Hungary, should be under examination for any other crime in the Austro-Hungarian dominions, or in the United Kingdom respectively, his extradition shall be deferred until the conclusion of the trial, and the full execution of any punishment awarded to him.

Should an individual whose extradition is demanded be at litigation, or be detained in the country on account of private obligations, his surrender shall nevertheless be made, the injured party retaining the right to prosecute his claims before the competent authority.

ARTICLE V.

The extradition shall not take place if, with respect to the crime for which it is demanded, and according to the laws of the country applied to, criminal prosecution and punishment has lapsed.

ARTICLE VI.

A fugitive criminal shall not be surrendered if the offence in respect of which his surrender is demanded is one of a political character, or if he prove that the requisition for his surrender has in fact been made with a view to try or punish him for an offence of a political character.

ARTICLE VII.

If an individual whose extradition is demanded by either of the High Contracting Parties in accordance with the terms of this Treaty, be also claimed by one of several other Powers on account of other crimes committed on their territory, he shall be surrendered

Länder der Oesterreichisch-ungarischen Monarchie, oder die Person, deren Auslieferung aus Grossbritannien verlangt wird, im vereinigten Königreiche, wegen derselben strafbaren Handlung, wegen deren die Auslieferung beantragt wird, in Untersuchung gewesen und ausser Verfolgung gesetzt worden, oder sich noch in Untersuchung befindet, oder bereits bestraft worden ist.

Wenn die Person deren Auslieferung begehrt wird, in dem Staatsgebiete, wo sie sich befindet, wegen einer anderen strafbaren Handlung in Untersuchung oder Strafe ist, so soll ihre Auslieferung bis zur Beendigung dieser Untersuchung und vollendeter Vollstreckung der etwa gegen sie erkannten Strafe aufgeschoben werden.

Sollte ein Individuum dessen Auslieferung begehrt wird, wegen privatrechtlicher Verpflichtungen in Prozess stehen oder zurückgehalten werden, so soll dessen Auslieferung nichts-destowenger stattfinden; die verletze Person behält jedoch das Recht ihre Ansprüche vor der zuständigen Behörde zu verfolgen.

Artikel V.

Die Auslieferung soll nicht stattfinden, wenn in Betreff des Verbrechens, wegen dessen die Auslieferung begehrt wird, nach den Gesetzen des um die Auslieferung angegangenen Staates, die Strafverfolgung oder die Strafvollstreckung durch Verjährung erloschen ist.

Artikel VI.

Ein flüchtiger Verbrecher soll nicht ausgeliefert werden, wenn die strafbare Handlung, wegen deren seine Auslieferung begehrt wird, einen politischen Character an sich trägt, oder wenn er darthut, dass der Antrag auf seine Auslieferung in Wirklichkeit mit der Absicht gestellt worden ist, ihn wegen eines Verbrechens oder Vergehens politischer Natur zu verfolgen oder zu bestrafen.

Artikel VII.

Wenn ein Individuum dessen Auslieferung in Gemässheit dieses Vertrages von einer der beiden Vertragsmächte begehrt wird, noch von einer oder mehreren anderen Mächten wegen anderer Verbrechen, die in deren Gebiete begangen wurden, reklamirt wird, so ist das-

to the Government in whose territory his gravest crime was committed; and if his crimes are all of the same gravity, or a doubt exists as to which is the gravest, to the Government which first made application for his surrender.

Article VIII.

A surrendered person shall in no case be kept in arrest or subjected to examination in the State to which he has been surrendered on account of another previous crime, or any other grounds than those of his surrender, unless such person has, after his surrender, had an opportunity of returning to the country whence he was surrendered, and has not made use of this opportunity, or unless he, after having returned there, reappears in the country to which he has already been surrendered.

This stipulation does not refer to crimes committed after surrender.

Article IX.

Requisitions for surrender shall be made by the Diplomatic Agents of the High Contracting Parties.

To the requisition for the surrender of an accused person there must be attached a warrant issued by the competent authorities of the State which demands extradition, and such proofs as would, according to the laws of the place where the accused was found, justify his arrest if the crime had been committed there.

If the requisition refers to a person already convicted, the sentence passed by the competent Tribunal of State demanding his surrender must be produced.

No requisition for surrender can be based on a conviction *in contumaciam.*

selbe der Regierung, in deren Gebiete die schwerere Gesetzes-Uebertretung begangen wurde, und wenn die von ihm verübten strafbaren Handlungen gleich schwer wären, oder wenn es zweifelhaft bleibe, welche die schwerere sei, derjenigen Regierung auszuliefern, welche zuerst das Ersuchen um die Auslieferung gestellt hat.

Artikel VIII.

Die ausgelieferte Person darf in dem Staate an welchen die Auslieferung erfolgt ist, keinenfalls wegen einer anderen früher begangenen strafbaren Handlung oder auf Grund anderer Thatsachen als derjenigen, wegen deren die Auslieferung erfolgt ist, in Haft gehalten oder zur Untersuchung gezogen werden, es wäre denn, dass sie nach der Auslieferung Gelegenheit gehabt hätte, in das Land zurückzukehren, aus welchem sie ausgeliefert wurde, und diese Gelegenheit nicht benützt hätte, oder dass sie, nachdem sie dahin zurückzukehrt war, freiwillig in dem Land wieder erschienen wäre, an das sie schon einmal ausgeliefert wurde.

Auf strafbare Handlungen, welche nach erfolgter Auslieferung verübt sind, findet diese Bestimmung keine Anwendung.

Artikel IX.

Die Anträge auf Auslieferung sollen durch die diplomatischen Agenten der hohen vertragenden Theile gestellt werden.

Mit dem Antrage auf Auslieferung eines Beschuldigten müssen ein Haftbefehl, welcher von der zuständigen Behörde des die Auslieferung begehrenden Staates erlassen ist, und solche Beweise beigebracht werden, welche nach den Gesetzen des Ortes, wo der Beschuldigte aufgefunden wird, dessen Verhaftung rechtfertigen würden, wen die strafbare Handlung dort begangen wäre.

Betrifft der Antrag eine bereits verurtheilte Person, so muss das Straf-urtheil beigebracht werden, welches von dem zuständigen Gericht des die Auslieferung begehrenden Staates gegen den Verurtheilten erlassen ist.

Auf Straf-urtheile welche auf Ausbleiben des Beschuldigten (*in contumaciam*) erlassen sind, kann der Auslieferungsantrag nicht gegründet werden.

Article X.

If the requisition for extradition be in accordance with the foregoing stipulations, the competent authorities of the State applied to shall proceed to the arrest of the fugitive.

The prisoner is then to be brought before a competent magistrate, who is to examine him and to conduct the preliminary investigation of the case, just as if the apprehension had taken place for a crime committed in the same country.

Article XI.

A fugitive criminal may, however, in urgent cases be arrested under a warrant of a police magistrate, judge of the peace, or of any other competent authority in either country, on such information or complaint, or such evidence as would, in the opinion of the person issuing the warrant, justify the issue of a warrant if the crime had been committed or the prisoner convicted in the district in which the authority happens to be; provided, however, that he shall be discharged if, within the shortest time possible, and at the utmost within fourteen days, a requisition for his surrender in accordance with the terms of Article IX of this Treaty is not made by the Diplomatic Agent of the State which demands his extradition.

Article XII.

The extradition shall not take place before the expiration of fifteen days from the apprehension, and then only if the evidence be found sufficient, according to the laws of the State applied to, either to justify the committal of the prisoner for trial, in case the crime had been committed in the territory of the said State, or to prove that the prisoner is the identical person convicted by the Courts of the State which makes the requisition.

Artikel X.

Wenn das Auslieferungs-Begehren nach den vorstehenden Bestimmungen begründet ist, so sollen die zuständigen Behörden des ersuchten Staates zur Festnahme des Flüchtlings schreiten.

Der Ergriffene wird sodann vor den dazu gesetzlich berufenen richterlichen Beamten gebracht, welcher ihn ebenso zu verhören und den Straffall verläufig zu untersuchen hat, als wenn die Ergreifung wegen einer im Inlande begangenen strafbaren Handlung erfolgt wäre.

Artikel XI.

Ein flüchtiger Verbrecher kann ausserdem in dringenden Fällen in folge eines Verhaftsbefehles eines Polizeirichters, eines Friedensrichters, oder einer anderen in jedem der beiden Staaten hiezu berufenen Behörde, auf Grund solcher Anzeigen oder Beschwerden und solcher Nachweisungen oder nach solchen Erhebungen verhaftet werden, welche nach dem Dafürhalten der Person, welche den Verhaftsbefehl ausstellt, die Ausfertigung eines Verhaftsbefehles rechtfertigen wurden wenn die Verübung der That oder die Verurtheilung des Gefangenen in dem Gebiete, in welchem sich diese Obrigkeit befindet, erfolgt wäre.

Vorausgesetzt wird übrigens, dass in der kurzesten Frist und zwar längstens binnen 14 Tagen bei sonstiger Entlassung des Verhafteten, durch den diplomatischen Vertreter des um die Auslieferung ersuchenden Staates, eine Requisition wegen der Auslieferung in der dem Artikel IX dieses Vertrages entsprechenden Weise erhoben wird.

Artikel XII.

Die Auslieferung erfolgt nicht vor Ablauf von fünfzehn Tagen seit der Ergreifung und nur dann, wenn die Beweise für genügend befunden worden sind, um nach den Gesetzen des ersuchten Staates entweder die Verweisung des Ergriffenen zur Hauptuntersuchung zu rechtfertigen, falls die strafbare Handlung im Gebiete dieses Staates begangen wäre, oder darzuthun, dass der Ergriffene mit der von den Gerichten des ersuchenden Staates verurtheilten Person identische ist.

Article XIII.

In the examinations which they have to make in accordance with the foregoing stipulations, the authorities of the State applied to shall admit as entirely valid evidence the sworn depositions or statements of witnesses taken in the other State, or copies thereof, and likewise the warrants and sentences issued therein, provided such documents are signed or certified by a Judge, Magistrate, or officer of such State, and are authenticated by the oath of some witness, or by being sealed with the official seal of the Minister of Justice or some other Minister of State.

Article XIV.

If sufficient evidence for the extradition be not produced within two months from the date of the apprehension of the fugitive, he shall be set at liberty.

Article XV.

All articles seized, which were in the possession of the person to be surrendered at the time of his apprehension, shall, if the competent authority of the State applied to for extradition has ordered the delivery thereof, be given up when the extradition takes place; and this delivery shall extend not only to property of the accused, and to the stolen articles, but also to everything which may serve as a proof of the crime. If the extradition cannot be carried out in consequence of the flight or death of the individual who is claimed, the delivery of the above-mentioned objects shall take place nevertheless.

Article XVI.

Each of the Contracting Parties shall defray the expenses occasioned by the arrest within its territories, the detention, and the conveyance to its frontier, of the persons to be surrendered in pursuance of this Treaty.

ARTIKEL XIII.

Die Behörden des ersuchten Staates haben bei der Prüfung, welche ihnen nach den vorstehenden Bestimmungen obliegt, den beeideten Zeugenaussagen, welche in dem anderen Staate zu Protokol genommen sind, imgleichen den Abschriften solcher Original-Zeugenaussagen, und ebenso den Haftbefehlen und Strafurtheilen volle Beweiskraft beizulegen, vorausgesetzt dass diese Schriftstücke durch einen Richter, eine obrigkeitliche Person oder einen anderen Beamten dieses Staates unterzeichnet oder bescheinigt und durch einen beeidigten Zeugen oder durch Beidrückung des Amtssiegels des Justiz- oder eines anderen Staatsministers beglaubigt sind.

ARTIKEL XIV.

Wenn zur Auslieferung genügende Beweise nicht binnen zwei Monaten von dem Tage der Ergreifung des Flüchtigen an beigebracht werden, so ist der Ergriffene auf freien Fuss zu setzen.

ARTIKEL XV.

Alle in Beschlag genommenen Gegenstände, welche sich zur Zeit der Ergreifung im Besitze des Auszuliefernden befinden, sollen, wenn die zuständige Behörde des um die Auslieferung ersuchten Staates die Ausantwortung derselben angeordnet hat, bei Vollziehung der Auslieferung mit übergeben werden, und es soll sich diese Ueberlieferung nicht blos auf die Habe des Verfolgten und auf die entfremdeten Gegenstände, sondern auf Alles erstrecken, was zum Beweise der strafbaren Handlung dienen kann.

Wenn die Auslieferung, nachdem sie angeordnet worden ist, wegen Flucht oder Tod der reklamirten Individuums nicht mehr vollzogen werden kann, soll dennoch die Uebergabe der oberwähnten Gegenstände stattfinden.

ARTIKEL XVI.

Jeder der vertragenden Theile wird die Kosten tragen, welche durch die Festnahme und Anhaltung der auf Grund dieses Vertrages auszuliefernden Personen innerhalb seiner Staatsgebiete und deren Transport bis an seine Grenzen verursacht werden.

Article XVII.

The stipulations of the present Treaty shall be applicable to the Colonies and foreign Possessions of Her Britannic Majesty.

The requisition for the surrender of a fugitive criminal who has taken refuge in any of such Colonies or foreign Possessions shall be made to the Governor or chief authority of such Colony or Possession by the chief Consular Officer of Austria-Hungary in such Colony or Possession.

Such requisitions may be disposed of, subject always, as nearly as may be, to the provisions of this Treaty, by the said Governor or chief authority, who, however, shall be at liberty either to grant the surrender or to refer the matter to his Government.

Her Britannic Majesty shall, however, be at liberty to make special arrangements in the British Colonies and foreign Possessions for the surrender of Austro-Hungarian criminals who may take refuge within such Colonies and foreign Possessions, on the basis, as nearly as may be, of the provisions of the present Treaty.

The requisition for the surrender of a fugitive criminal from any Colony or foreign Possession of Her Britannic Majesty shall be governed by the rules laid down in the preceding Articles of the present Treaty.

Article XVIII.

The present Treaty shall come into force ten days after its publication in conformity with the forms prescribed by the laws of the High Contracting Parties. It may be terminated by either of the High Contracting Parties, but shall remain in force for six months after notice has been given for its termination.

The Treaty shall be ratified, and the ratifications shall be exchanged at Vienna as soon as possible.

In witness whereof, the respective Plenipotentiaries have signed the same, and have affixed thereto the seal of their arms.

ARTIKEL XVII.

Die Bestimmungen des gegenwärtigen Vertrages sollen auf die Colonien und auswärtigen Besitzungen Ihrer Grossbritannischen Majestät Anwendung finden.

Der Antrag auf Auslieferung eines flüchtigen Verbrechers, welcher in einer dieser Colonien oder auswärtigen Besitzungen Zuflucht gefunden hat, soll an den Statthalter oder die oberste Behörde dieser Colonie oder Besitzungen durch den obersten Consular Beamten der oesterreichisch-ungarischen Monarchie in dieser Colonie oder Besitzung gerichtet werden.

Ueber solche Anträge soll der gedachte Statthalter oder die gedachte oberste Behörde so viel als möglich nach den Bestimmungen des gegenwärtigen Vertrages vorgehen, jedoch soll denselben freistehen, entweder die Auslieferung zu bewilligen oder über den Fall an ihre Regierung zu berichten.

Ihre Grossbritannischen Majestät soll es jedoch freistehen, in den Brittischen Colonien und auswärtigen Besitzungen über die Auslieferung von Staatsangehörigen der oesterreichisch-ungarischen Monarchie, welche innerhalb dieser Colonien und auswärtigen Besitzungen Zuflucht gefunden haben, auf möglichst gleicher Grundlage mit den Bestimmungen des gegenwärtigen Vertrages besondere Anordnungen zu treffen.

Anträge betreffend die Auslieferung von Verbrechern, welche aus einer Colonie oder auswärtigen Besitzung Ihrer Grossbritannischen Majestät geflüchtet sind, sollen nach den Bestimmungen der vorstehenden Artikel des gegenwärtigen Vertrages behandelt werden.

ARTIKEL XVIII.

Der gegenwärtige Vertrag soll zehn Tage nach seiner, in Gemässheit der durch die Gesetzgebung der hohen Vertragenden Theile vorgeschriebenen Formen erfolgten Veröffentlichung in Kraft treten. Der Vertrag kann von jedem der beiden hohen vertragenden Theile aufgekündigt werden, bleibt jedoch nach erfolgter Aufkündigung noch sechs Monate in Kraft.

Der Vertrag wird ratifizirt und die Ratifikationen werden so bald wie möglich, in Wien ausgewechselt werden.

Zu Urkund dessen haben die beiderseitigen Bevollmächtigten die gegenwärtige Uebereinkunft unterzeichnet und mit ihren Wappen untersiegelt.

Done at Vienna, the 3rd day of December, in the year of Our Lord one thousand eight hundred and seventy-three.

(L.S.) ANDREW BUCHANAN.
(L.S.) ANDRASSY.

And whereas the ratifications of the said Treaty were exchanged at Vienna on the tenth instant:

Now, therefore, Her Majesty, by and with the advice of Her Privy Council, and in virtue of the authority committed to Her by the said recited Act, doth order, and it is hereby ordered, that from and after the thirtieth day of March, one thousand eight hundred and seventy-four, the said Act shall apply in the case of the said Treaty with the Emperor of Austria.

ARTHUR HELPS.

So geschehen zu Wien, am 3tem December, im Jahre des Heils Ein tausend achthundert siebenzig und drei.

(L.S.) ANDREW BUCHANAN.
(L.S.) ANDRASSY.

INDEX.

LONDON. PRINTED BY WILLIAM CLOWES AND SONS, STAMFORD STREET, AND CHARING CROSS.

Made in the USA
Monee, IL
04 November 2026

67391579R00213